WHAT DO YOU CALL THAT NOISE?

AN XTC DISCOVERY BOOK

WHAT DO YOU CALL THAT NOISE?

AN XTC DISCOVERY BOOK

Edited by Mark Fisher | www.XTCLimelight.com | Published by Mark Fisher Ltd, Edinburgh 2019

CREDITS

Editor: Mark Fisher
Designer: Lucy Munro
Production: The List Ltd
Cover: Mark Thomas
www.markthomasillustration.co.uk

Contributors: Imogen Bebb, Allison Burke, Camille English, Mark Fisher, Quinn Fox, Leslie Gooch, John Irvine, Kyrsten Leland, Michael John McCarthy, Kevin Mathews, Peter Mills, Kev Moore, John Morrish, Christopher Nadeau, Hugh Nankivell, Kevin Nixon, Mia Rankin, Robert G Rawson, James Reimer, Rob Roberts, Marco Rossi, Robert G Rowson, Michio Sakurai, Erich Sellheim, Jim Spencer, Garry Stuart, Cormac Thomas, Mark Thomas, Steve Warren, David White, Eric Winick, Yvonne Wootton, Lou Dommett Young and David Yurkovich.

First published in 2019
© 2019 Mark Fisher Ltd
Editorial address: 9a Annandale Street, Edinburgh EH7 4AW
Great Britain

www.XTCLimelight.com

Mark Fisher and the contributors named above have asserted their right under the Copyright, Designs and Patents Act, 1988, to be identified as authors of this work.

All rights reserved. No part of this publication may be reproduced or transmitted in any form or by any means, electronic or mechanical, including photocopying, recording, or any information storage or retrieval system, without prior permission in writing from the publisher.

British Library Cataloguing-in-Publication Data
A catalogue record for this book is available from the British Library

ISBN: PB: 978-1-9997461-1-7

Printed by Bell & Bain Ltd, 303 Burnfield Road, Thornliebank, Glasgow G46 7UQ

Thanks to:
Barry Andrews
Terry Arnett
Paul Badger
Louis Barfe
Gaz Barrett
Todd Bernhardt
Rick Buckler
Terry Chambers
Mark Cobb
Jane Ellis
Mikey Erg
Lotte Fisher
Shigemasa Fujimoto
Dave Gregory
Ian Gregory
Robin Hodge
John Irvine
Laurie Langan
Michael John McCarthy
Shauna McLarnon
Colin Moulding
Hugh Nankivell
Rohan Onraet
Pat Mastelotto
Dave Mattacks
Sarah Palmer
Andy Partridge
Debbi Peterson
Pete Phipps
Prairie Prince
Andy Rankin
Stu Rowe
Sebastian Rüger
Chuck Sabo
Mark Thomas
Steve Warren
Maurice "mOe" Watson
David White
All the fabulous musicians who contributed to *A Chain to Hold All Battleships in Check* and *Now These Shoes Fit All Too Well* – and the generous Neon Shufflers who bought their copies of *What Do You Call That Noise?* in advance.

CONTENTS

8 A DANCE FOR THE HUMAN RACE
A big list of the Neon Shufflers who were good enough to stock up on this book in advance

11 WE PLAY THE SONGS MUCH TOO LOUD
A word from the editor

12 THE EVERYDAY STORY OF SMALLTOWN
Formative Swindon landmarks in the XTC story

22 THINGS WE DID IN CLASS
A music student draws nourishment from an earlier era's pop

24 CHALKHILLS' CHILDREN
A new generation is discovering XTC: a 14-year-old Australian, a 19-year-old American and a 19-year-old Brit swap notes

32 PLEASE DON'T PULL ME OUT
Going younger still, a ten-year-old Beatles fan listens to three classic XTC albums for the first time

36 A CHAIN TO HOLD ALL BATTLESHIPS IN CHECK
An interlinked line-up of musicians spin their favourite XTC tracks and explain why they love them

78 EMOTION AT THE DROP OF A HAT
In periods of crisis and times of joy, how does XTC's music articulate our feelings?

94 AND ALL THE WORLD IS KEYBOARD SHAPED
Would Andy Partridge's songs have sounded the same without the shape of the instruments they were written on?

98 THE RHYTHM IN HIS HEAD
Why Terry Chambers was the best drummer of his generation

100 ALL ROADS LEAD TO BEATOWN
Terry was a force of nature on stage, say Andy Partridge, Dave Gregory and Barry Andrews

102 BEAT SURRENDER
Rick Buckler of the Jam remembers a post-punk career that ran in parallel to that of XTC

112 DO YOU KNOW WHAT NOISE AWAKES YOU?
A song-by-song breakdown of the inspirational Chambers technique

126 WHO'S PULSING?
Pete Phipps, Ian Gregory, Prairie Prince, Pat Mastelotto, Dave Mattacks and Chuck Sabo look back on their stints with the band

136 WHERE DID THE ORDINARY PEOPLE GO?
In his love of observational detail, Colin Moulding has a surprising amount in common with one of the great poet laureates

143 NOW THESE SHOES FIT ALL TOO WELL
Tribute acts share the secrets of bringing a rich and varied catalogue to the stage

154 A DISCO TROT FROM GERMANY
One man's epic quest to record translated covers of the entire XTC catalogue

156 ME AND MY MATE CAN SING
Barry Andrews on songs, Swindon and sympathy for Andy

166 INSIDE THE HAUNTED BOX OF SWITCHES
The man who defined the sound of *White Music* and *Go 2* reflects on his relationship with the piano

170 TUNES OF GOOD
Dave Gregory talks about guitar solos, string arrangements and piano parts in his most in-depth interview ever

198 A CHORD IN MY HAND
Musical theory and songwriting instinct with Andy Partridge

206 JUST FOR ME TO MIX IN SPACE
Andy's home-studio secrets

208 LIFE BEGINS AT THE HOP
The novel-like story of Colin and Terry's long-awaited return to the stage as TC&I

220 INDEX

A DANCE FOR THE HUMAN RACE

Many thanks to these groovy pace-setters for the early purchase of What Do You Call That Noise? In return for getting ahead of the beat, each is hereby inducted into the Venerable League of Neon Shufflers. It is to them we must turn for our electricky weather. All hail!

A... Kouichiro Abe, Robert Abramowicz, John Addison, David H Adler, William Allen, Ross Allister, Sergio Amadori, Eric Anderson, Mats Andersson, Mark Andrews, Mark Anthony, West Anthony, Julian Armstrong, Terry Arnett, Per Aronsson, Theo Arp, David Ash, Stephen Ash, Simon Ashberry, Andy Ashfield, John Auker, Rick Avard, Philippe Aveline

B... Elizabeth Babish, Chris Bainbridge, Allyson Baker, David Baker, Kevin Baker, Tim Baker, David "Deep Dream Steam" Bandler, Steve Banister, Andrew Barker, Vince Barnard, Michael Paul Barnes, Danny Barnhoorn, Baz Barrell, Nick Barrett, Yumi Bartholomew, Stuart Batsford, Greg Batten, Mike Bear, Pam Bearce-Lopez, Keith Beck, hal9000 Beers, Joel Bell, Matt Bell, Eduardo Benatar, Wendy Bennett, Robert Bennison, Robert P Benoit, John Bent, David Beresford, Mike Berg, Gordon Berg, Morten Berger Karlsen, John Berman, Todd Bernhardt, Asier Berrondo Arbelaiz, John Bertrand, Mark Best, Jean Berwick, David Biasotti, Jon Birkett, Paul Bishop, Michael Björn, Paul Blackmore, Jonn Blackwell, Mark Blake, Belinda Blanchard, Chris Blanden, Troy Blosser, Michael Bloys, Tanya T Boerhave, Richard Boneham, Martin Boorman, John Bormanis, Andy Bowen, Kieron David Bowker, Martin Bowie, Anthony Boyle, Dom Bradshaw, Ask Brantenberg Cold, Caroline Breen, David Bregande, Paul Brennan, Mitchell Brenner, David Brereton, Philip Briddon, Tony Bridgeman, Jonathan Bridgland, Eddie Brill, Adrian Britton, Glen Brooks, Chris Brown, David Brown, Kay Brown, Kenny Brown, Margaret Brown, Shuggy Brown, David Browne, Jim Browne, Chris Browning, Hal Bryan, Tim Bryan, Steve Buckley, Darryl Bullock, Tony Bullock, Chris Burch, Michael Burdett, Mike Burgess, John Burt, Tony Burzio, Christopher Butler, Warren Butson, Kieran Byrne

C... Timothy Neil Cadman, Colleen Cahill, Nigel Cain, Alister Caldwell, Ian Caldwell, Bill Campbell, X Tessier Campbell, Andrew Campbell-Howes, Louis Cannizzaro, Gregory A Canu, Ian Capstick, Mr Scott Carrick, Tim Carlson, Thomas Carnell Fout, Nigel Cates, Franco Paolo Castiglioni, Andrew Celauro, Van Ceunebroecke, Mark Chadderton, Kristoff Chadowski, John Chadwick, John Paul Chadwick, Jonathan Chadwick, Barron Chandler, Tim Chaplin, Chris Chard, Diane Chard, Michael Chominski, Andrew Chorlton, Chris Christopher, Keith Chuck, Simon Clare, Peter Clarke, Keith Clarkson, J David Clifton, Stewart Clough, Amy Clum, Nick Coard, Michael Coffey, Mark Coleman, Tim Coles, Stevyn Colgan, Mark Colton, Margaret Comino, Steve Conte, Andrew Cook, Mark Cook, Paul Cook, Cathy Cooper, Gaylan Cooper, Jeff Cooper, Martin Corbishley, Sam Corless, Steve Cox, Bob Crain, Paul Crane, Ian Cranna, Jake Keziah Crawford, Thomas Crawford, Corinne Creek, Giuseppe Cristiano, Matt Crivelli, Sean Crockett, Ian Crutchley, Dallas Cupps, Paul Curd, Brian Curtis

D... Anthony Dagnall, Stefano Dallera, Mick Daniels, Brian Danks, Lynn Darling, Brian Dart, Peter Dasent, Alan Davies, Neal Davies, Hays Davis, Peter Davis, Keith Dawson, Mark Dawson, André de Koning, Andre de Zwart, Kevin DeBolt, Marcus Deininger, Thomas Demi, John Denley, Kevin Denley, Adam Denton, Jerome Deupree, John Devaney, Pascal Devillers, Domenico Di Giorgio, Paolo Di Modica, Ernesto Di Fenza, Broose Dickinson, Becki diGregorio, Mike Dixon, David Dodge, Carl Doherty, Jim Doherty, John Dore, John James Dougal, Neil Dowden, Kevin Downey, Simon Doyle, Edward Drake, Stuart Draper, Joe Duffin, Robert B Duffy, Liam Duggan, Martin Dumont, Jamie Dunn, Ronald Dunn, Mary Dunster, Adrian Durham

E... Mark C Easter, Darryl Ebbatson, Mitchell Edmond, Ian Edmundson, Bo Edström, Mr Edward Dalton, Hannah Edwards, Stanley Edwards, Håkan Einarsson, Brian Ekberg, Peter Eldridge, Eric Eliasson, Carl Ellis, Richard Ellis, George Ellison, Michelle Elsbury, Ian Stuart Emery, Brian Emrich, Remco Engels, Camille English, Millie English, Alun Evans, Greg Evans, Peter Evans, Ron Evans, Dale Everett, Jacques Eversdijk, Ludger Exo Rößner

F... Guillaume Facon, Dale Fairbrass, James Falvey, Dennis Fano, Steven Fant, Chris Farnell, Jeff Farris, Helen Fay, Ken Fegan, Mike Fennell, Paul Ferguson, Peter Fermoy, Martin Finch, Martin Fioretti, Frank Fischer, Simon Fisher, Jon Fitt, Stephen Flaherty, Gary Fleming, Colin Fletcher, Richard Flood, Guy Flower, Jon Flynn, Terrence Follmer, Marty Fopp, Tim Foran, Steve Forrest, Andy Fossett, Darren Fox, David Fox, Quinn Fox, Robert Frandsen, Robert Frazza, Paul Freethy, Orit Friedland, Mitch Friedman, Paul Friend, Stefan Fritz

G... Marc Gadd, Paul Gaff, Stephen Gale, Matthew Gallagher, Thomas Gallo, Jesper Gammelgaard Nielsen, R Kevin Garcia Doyle, Andy Gardner, Brent Gardner, Alan Gasmer, Steven Geoffrey Rose, Douglas Gerlach, Robyn Gibson, Jeff Gilchrist, Alison Giles, Barry Giles, Thomas Gilles, Goran Gimsoy, Todd Gitzlaff, Stephen Goldsack, Luis Miguel Gonzalez Martinez, Leslie Gooch, Richard Goodall, Ross Goodall, Miles Goodman, Phil Gorman, Pál Gorondi, Kevin Gover, Douglas Gowan, Richard Gower, Thomas Graf, Scott Granoff, Sarah Grant Duff, Simon Grant, Kenneth Gray, Michael Grayson, Brian Grealy, Andrew Green, Dan Green, Glen Green, Jimmy Dusty Gregory, Andrew Griffin, Thomas Griffin, Tim Grossklaus, Calum Gunn, Molly Gunn, Ronnie Gurr, Dean Gustafson, Ralph Gutierrez, Barbara M Guzdial

H... Gilles Hachey, Scott Haines, Ray Hales, Chris Hallam, Andy Hallbery, Michael Halsted, Edwin Albert Hambley, Fiona Hammond, HL Hampson, Roger Hanson, Andrew Hapeman, Mark Harbottle, Paul Harbour, Graham Harley, Justin Harman, Nick Harper, Tony Harris, Mike Harrison, Shawn Harrison, Christopher Hart, Jari Hartikainen, Andrew Hartley, Neil Harvey, David Hathaway, Rob Haughton, Melinda Hautala, Gary Hawkins, Jude Hayden, Ian Hayward, Jonathan Hayward, Jason Hazeley, Jason Headrick, Robin Heald, Lois Heath, Reinhard zur Heiden, Rob Henderson, Paul Henly, Paul Henri, David Henriksen, Camille Henry, Martin Herles, Allan Heron, Joseph T Herring, Malcolm Herrstein, Andreas Herzo, Joe Hetz, Brian Hewetson, John Hickey, Richard Higgins, Bryan Hill, Raymond Hill, Jennifer Hjorthaug, Chris Hobbs, Frank Hockney, Alan Hoff, William Hoffman, Dave Hogan, David Hohman, Peter Holden, Robin Holden, Joni Holdsworth, Raymond R Holloway, Chris Holt, Stephen Hope, Jeffrey D Hoppa, James Horan, Shaleem Hosein, Takashige Hosoya, Robert Howard, Vincent Howells, Michael Howlett, Doug Huggins, Neil Hughes, Shane Hunter, Rob Hurst

I... David Iacini, Jordi Ibañez Llaurado, Joseph Ierano, Kent Ihrén, Jørn Inge Frostad, Nick Irwin, Yasushi Ishino, Ilsa Izkovits

J... Martin Jackson, Stephen Jackson, Peter Jacobs, Jack Jacovides, Michelle Jacques, Jonathan Jago, Thomas Jakob, Gary James, Theo Jansen, Simon Jeffery, Derek Jeffrey, Dan Jennings, Lennart Johansson, Christopher Johnson, Christopher Johnson, David Johnston-Smith, Chris Jones, Gareth Jones, Gary J Jones, Jeffrey M Jones, Stephen Jones, Todd Jones, Brian Jones, Michael Jopling, Vincent Jupe

K... Akiyoshi Kaji, Jonathan Kaley-Isley, Don Kamps, Scott Kanengeiser, Robert Kass,

Yamato Kawada, Stephen Kearley, Michael Keeley, Karl Keeling, Paul Kelly, Chris Kemp, Graham Kemp, Timothy Kendrick, Tony Kerkhove, Eamonn Keyes, Margaret Keyse, Prem Khanna, Steve Kidwell, Michael Kijser, Vincent Kilken, Mike King, Herbert Kirchhoff, Jane Kirk, Greig Kirker, Keith Kirkhope, Peter Kitney, Murray Knox, Akiko Kogure, Michael Kolpien, Arno Kolster, Todd Kopp, Michael Korzenok, David Kovacs, Jeffrey Kovarsky, Marek Kraus, Wayne E Krempach, Stephen Krupa

L... Brian Lacey, David Lake, Roy Lane, Vince Lang, Mark Langdell, Brian Last, Robert Laversuch, Ashleigh Lawrence, Major Tom Lawrence, Chris Lawrenson, Ewan Lawrenson, Jean-Francois Le Douarin, Iain Lee, Lorraine Lee, Randy LeMasters, Guido Lengwiler, Julie Lenten, Dominic Lesnar, Andrew Leszczynski, Jerry Lewis, Gary Lichtenberg, Ira Lieman, Tor Lier, Sean Lindsey-Clark, Local Studies (Swindon Libraries), Dennis Locorriere, Simone Lodovigi, Lee Lodyga, Paul Loft, David Logan, Dirk Lohmann, Christopher Loin, Rob Long, Jerry Longhi, Bernie Lopez, Gino Lorenzelli, Philip Lort, Rick Lovering, Steven J Luc, Anders Lundquist, André Luth, Peter G Lymer, Christine Lymer-Dennis, Jonathan Lynas, Elizabeth Lynch, Gerald Lynn, Mr P Lynn-Smith

M... Paul McAtamney, Liam McCann, Desmond McCarron, Trevor McCarthy, Gerard Mc Cavana, Kevin Mcclements, Cary McDonald, Ian McFarlane, George McGowan, Robert John McGowan, George McKeeve, Sean McLaughlin, Andrew MacMillan, James McMurtry, Kevin McNally, Mark McNeill, Mr M Machin-Cowen, Isabel Macho, Werner Mack, Gordon Mackie, Steven Madge, Brian Magee, Kenneth Maiuri, Rob Mallows, Stephen Manley, Steve Chris Manning, Douglas Marklein, Vincent Marné, Brian T Martin, Keith Martin, Steve Martin, Trevor Martin, Geoff Mason, Yannick Massenot, Michael Massey, Kevin Mathews, Peter Mathias, Julie Matthews, Peter Mattinson, John Mavroudis, Josh Mayer, Guy Mayman, Evan Mays, Nathaniel Mead, Randolph W Meeder, Dermot Meehan, Murray Meikle, Benjamin Mellonie, Alan Melvin, Guy Meredith, Mark Meredith, Robert Meyer, John Miller, Charles Miller, James Milne, Derek Miner, Matthew Mirapaul, Chuck Miserendino, Mark Moerman, Alistair Moffat, Thomas Mohr, Thomas Monaghan, Thomas Monroe, Mikel Montoya, Chris J Mooar, Tracey Moon, Bill Moore, Kev Moore, Scott Moore, Michael Moran, David Morgan, Leigh Morgan, Edward Morneau, Keith Morris, Matt Moser, Youssef Mourra, Gereon Mueller, James D Mumford 3rd, John Munton, Akira Murakami, Dave Murphy, John Murray, Peter Murray, Matt Musso, Paul Musson, Ian Muttoo, Per Myklebust, John Myles

N... Christopher Nadeau, Keith Nainby, Terry Naraine, Karen Neill, Robbie Nelson, Håvard Ness, James Newall, Nik Newark, Tipper Newton, Michael Noble, David Nolan, Simon Nolan, Jim Nordstrom, Eigil Nordstrøm, Jeffrey J Norman, Nigel Norman, David Norris, Deborah Norton, Will Norton, Mikhail Noskov, Derek Notman, Andisheh Nouraee, Tony Nowikowski, Göran Nyström

O... Rob O'Connor, Tim O'Regan, Thomas O'Shea, John O'Sullivan, Christian Odor, Joe Odukoya, Claus Oexle, Jefferson Ogata, Patrick Ogelvie, Yuji Okuda, Yoshifumi Okuyama, Paul Oldman, Cousin Olivier, Atsushi Ono, José Rubén Orantes García, Carlos Ortanez, Tony Osborne, Jonas Österlöf, Karl Øvre

P... Gray Packham, Marc Padovani, John Paige, Christopher Painter, John Palagyi, Michael Palmer, Dave Parker, Ami Parkerson, Greg Parr, Simon Parrish, Simon Patrick, Steven Patrick, Darren Peace, Mick Pelc, Robert Pelletier, Ingolf Pencz, Jon Pender, Scott Penn, Scott Pennicott, Alan Percival, Ed Percival, Ian Percival, Sunisa Petchpoo, David Peters, Larry Peterson, Chris Phillips, Martin Phillips, Suzanne Phillips-Wooten, Yorick Phoenix, Stephen Pieper, David Piper-Balston, Glenn Platt, Wallace Polsom, John L Ponder, Noel Ponting, Timothy Porterfield, Andrew Poulton, Anil Prasad, Gregory Press, Paul Price, Kevin Price, John Pullen, Ian Purser, Paul Putner, Jason Pytka

Q... Shane Quentin, Andy Quinn

R... James Radley, Leslie Randall, Jennifer Randles, Gordon Rankin, Les Rankin, Mia Rankin, Timo Rauhaniemi, Glen Rebyak, Mark Reed, Chris Rees, David Rees, Joanna Rees, Taff Rees, James Reimer, James Reimer, Jostein Reistad, John Relph, Steve Rempis, Alberto Repetti, Steven Reule, Linda Reynolds, Christopher Reynolds, Ginny Rhind, Peter Rickard, David Rickinson, Thomas Riha, Giorgio Rimini, Andrew Rimmer, David Ristrim, Nick Ritchie, Susanne Rittsel, Michael Rivard, Ed Roberts, Glynn Roberts, John Roberts, Rob Roberts, Keith Roberts, Paul Robinson, Stephen Robinson, Colin Rolfe, Clive Roper, Eva Rose, Sara Roseman, Dean Rothwell, Richard Rowley, Daniel André Roy, Greg Rubins, Justin Ruddock, Paul Rudge, Sebastian Rüger, Paul Rush, Peter Rustin, Ian Rutherford

S... Egidio Sabbadini, Mark Sach, Gunnar Sæbø, Sam Samson, Thierry Samzun, Russ Sanders, Gregory Sandoval, Michael Sansano, Jr, MD, Bård Sarheim, Larry Savage, Todd Savelle, Sten Sawicz, Neil Sayer, Scott Sbrana, Liam Scanlon, Christian Scanniello, Richard Scarr, Mike Scharff, Damon Scharlatt, Evelyn A Schmidt, Wolfgang Schmitz, Andrew Schtirbu, Greg Schultz, Stefan Schwarz, Joseph J Sciortino, Damian Scott, Michael Scott, Paul Scott, William H Sederholm, Drew Sentivan, Mike Serafino, Ivan Serra, Keiko Setowaki, Tim Shap, Gary Sharpless, Gavin Shelley, Pierre Shepard, Steve Shephard, Robert Shepherd, Neil Sheppard, Ivan Shiel, Yuriko Shimizugawa, Karl Shoffler, Henri Siebens, Christina A Silbermann, Mike Silver, Charles Silverman, Dean Simmonds, Dave Simms, Nick Simon, Ian Simpson, Todd Sitrin, Andreas Sjögren, Matt Skelland, Gordon Skinner, Derk Jan Slagter, Jodie Sleed, Simon Smart, Alec Smight, Anthony Smith, David Smith, Howard Smith, Ian Smith, Mark Smith, Mike Smith, Peter Smith, Philip Smith, Reece Smith, Richard Smith, Paul E Sousa, Graham Spackman, Steve Spangler, Jim Spencer, Christian Spoo, Jon Sprague, Mark Stalker, Rock Stamberg, Johan Stapel, Daniel StCharles, Peter Steckel, Zoe Stevens, Sandra Stevenson Leffew, Andrew Stewardson, Rae Stewart, Ian Stoik, Glynn Stokes, John Stokes, Adrian Stones, Kevin Stout, Michael Stout, John Stow, Alan Strickland, Garry Stuart, Robert Styles, Yoshikazu Sugaya, Detlef Sult, Hans-Peter Sutter, Andrew Swainson, Ade Swatridge, Steve Swift, Michael Sykes

T... Kevin Tanswell, Malcolm Tarbuck, Sean Taylor, Christine Terbijhe, Troy Thiel, Wim Thijssen, David Thomas, Jeff Thomas, Mark Thomas, Adam S Thomason, Gary Thompson, Mark and Karyne Thompson, Neil Thomson, William Thomson, Jonathan Thorpe, Simon Tickle, Ray Tierney, Craig Tigwell, Kevan Tiley, Steve Tilling, Todd Tilton, Ryan Tippins, Martin Tolcher, Paul Tornbohm, Raymond Totilo, George Tresidder, Simon Trott, Dimitris Tsiantis, Masanobu Tsuruki, Robert Tunick, Gavin Turnbull, Stephen Turner, Steve Turner, Paul Tuxworth, Simon Tyler

U... James Unwin, Evan Urkofsky, Dominic Van Abbe, Rob van der Valk, Ron van Uum

V... Jim Vander Putten, Ann VanderMeer, Mark Vaughan, Georges Vedeau, John Venzon, Ewald Verkerk, Bruce Vernon, Diane Vidler, Trevor Vigors-Evans, Paul Vincent, John Viney, Tim Virgo, Martijn Voorvelt, Marc Vormawah

W... Neil Wade, Nick Waite, Martin Walker, Eian Wall, Karen Wallace, Nigel Waller, Gerry Walter, Michael Ward, Andrew Warder, Neil Warren, Stephen Warren, Daniel A Wasser, Duncan Watson, Neil Watson, Robert Watson, Stephen Watt, Steve Wattz, Alec Way, Barry Webb, John Wedemeyer, Chris Weeks, Robert Wegmann, ArtÐrs B Weible, Alexander Weis, Lars Wenker, Patrick Wensor, Franz Adrian Wenzl, Sascha Werner, Mike Wheeler, Simon Whit, Dave Whitbread, David White, Paul White, Paul Whiteman, Thomas Wiegert, Bill Wikstrom, Paul Wild, Joerg Wilke, Steve Wilkes, Mike Williams, Trevor M Williams, Andrew Willis, Keith Wilshere, Derek Wilson, Jeff Wilson, Eric Winick, Per Winqvist, Geoffrey Winterowd, Hank Wirtz, Richard Wolff, Craig Wolfgram, Benjamin Woll, Steve Wood, Simon D Wood, Nick Woolley, Buddah Worthmore, Robert Wratten, Alan Wright, Duncan Wyatt

Y... Koji Yokota, David Yurkovich

Z... Dean B Zemel, David Zimelis, Mike and Gaye Zimmerman, Guido Zimmermann, Patty Zubov, Nicolas Zufferey, Stefano Zuppet

THE XTC BUMPER BOOK of FUN for BOYS and GIRLS

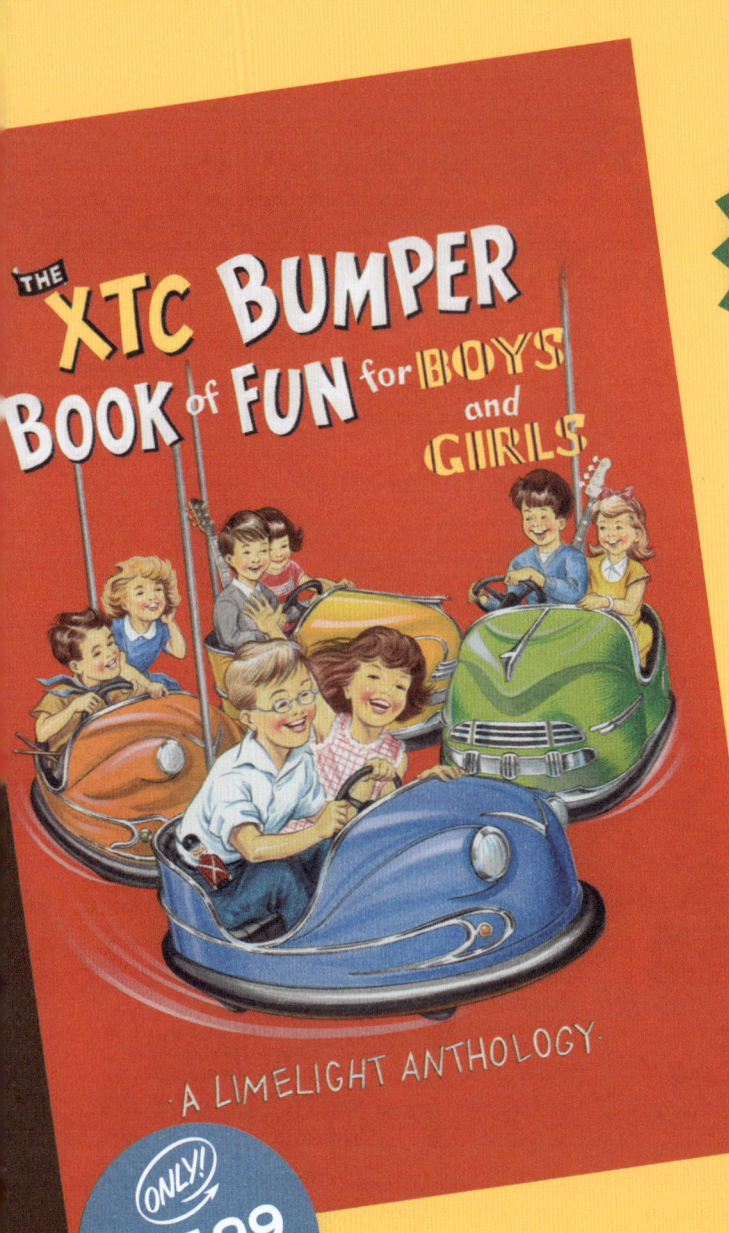

A LIMELIGHT ANTHOLOGY

ON SALE NOW!

ONLY! **£17.99** + FREE UK P&P (£5 INTERNATIONAL P&P)

"The most comprehensive and incisive book about XTC yet published"
DOM LAWSON, PROG MAGAZINE

"A delicious thing to dive in and out of"
IAIN LEE, TALK RADIO

"An outstanding record of a superb band"
DAVE JENNINGS, LOUDER THAN WAR

"Fans new and old will pore over this"
JAMIE ATKINS, RECORD COLLECTOR

"Varied, surprising and fun"
SAMANTHA BURKE, CENT MAGAZINE

www.XTCLimelight.com

A WORD FROM THE EDITOR

WE PLAY THE SONGS MUCH TOO LOUD

The article I enjoyed writing the most in *The XTC Bumper Book of Fun for Boys and Girls* was the one in which comedians talked about each other's favourite XTC songs. Despite their jobs, Kevin Eldon, Phill Jupitus, Stewart Lee, Joanna Neary and Paul Putner were not trying to be funny; they just spoke with passion and insight about the music they loved. It was a joy to hear.

I wondered if I could take the idea further. If comedians could be as interesting as this, I reasoned, how much more fascinating would musicians be? What fresh perspectives could we get from people who knew their way around a fret board and could tell their ride cymbal from their hi-hat? XTC fans are unusually blessed in having a front man as articulate as Andy Partridge, who shared his insights so revealingly with Todd Bernhardt in *Complicated Game* (Jawbone Press). That's fantastic, but I wanted to know what the music sounded like on the receiving end.

That idea is at the heart of *What Do You Call That Noise?* It was, for example, an indulgent privilege to talk to the 40 professional musicians who chose their favourite moments from the XTC catalogue (see page 36). Even better that they seemed to enjoy the conversations as much as I did. An equal honour was to pick apart the beats that make Terry Chambers such a formidable rhythm machine in the company of drummers including Rick Buckler from the Jam and Debbi Peterson from the Bangles. Great too to read the trials, tribulations and triumphs of tribute acts in David White's chapter about fans reproducing the band's material live.

Then, of course, is the input of XTC themselves, not least Dave Gregory who generously gave up a day to give his most in-depth interview ever. Quizzed by musician Hugh Nankivell, he speaks lucidly about guitar solos, keyboard parts and orchestral arrangements. Elsewhere, Andy shares his home-recording tips and talks about his happy ignorance of musical theory. As well as the post-Chambers drummers recalling their time with XTC, Barry Andrews writes about his changing relationship with the piano and explains why he has "a lot more sympathy with Partridge".

And if it's music you're after, there was plenty going down at Swindon Arts Centre where Colin and Terry played live for the first – and, sadly, last – time in 36 years as TC&I. There's a full report of the first four gigs.

Keeping the fanzine spirit of *Limelight* alive, there are also chapters about exploring the sights of Swindon, discovering XTC for the first time, turning to XTC in periods of heightened emotion, understanding the physicality of Andy's songwriting and finding illuminating parallels between the songs of Colin Moulding and the poems of John Betjeman. I'm hugely grateful to everyone who contributed – it couldn't have happened without you.

Now, how many references can you spot hidden by designer Mark Thomas in his fabulous cover?

www.XTCLimelight.com

Do XTC strike a chord? Have you noted how they scale heights, raise the bar and stave off fear when you're feeling flat? Don't be downbeat – look sharp and sing the praises of a major ensemble

BY MARK FISHER

WHAT DO YOU CALL THAT NOISE?

THE EVERYDAY STORY OF SMALLTOWN

One two three four five boys who changed the world, and a little town that grew and grew

WORDS BY JOHN MORRISH

PHOTOGRAPHS BY YVONNE WOOTTON

It's a little scary, like a song in 5/4. Five traffic circles, arranged in a circle around a circle. We're heading south, from Dave's house; go with us, up the stem of the tarmac flower. To our left, at eight o'clock, there's the football ground: T for Terry, who had a trial but was released. At eleven o'clock, there's the road from the east, where Colin made his rural stand. Barry, a London Swindonian, went thataway, and early. At two o'clock we have the road to Old Town, where Andy lives, but the sign keeps his secret. Andy can go anywhere; if only he could drive. But now it's four o'clock; tea and biscuits for the wage slaves. Ah, the song. *English Roundabout* is in 5/4, which is odd, coming from Colin. Dave can count in 5/4. He can count in 13/16. But you can do what I do: count it in two (only having two legs) and plough on. The same goes for the roundabout. Fear not. It's safe, smooth and rather beautiful, if you co-operate. Know where you want to go – and arrive in one piece.

THE EVERYDAY STORY OF SMALLTOWN

WHAT DO YOU CALL THAT NOISE?

TOP: Penhill, pronounced Pen'ill if youA're a local, was called Pen Hill in pre-1939 maps. It was a geographical feature. No one lived there. Then the gigantic council estate was thrown up. Some municipal romantic commissioned this sign, with a sun-god motif and a vaguely uncial font. It was duly vandalised. **BOTTOM:** Purton is the leafy antithesis to Penhill. Dave and his two brothers were brought up here. They had a happy family and music lessons. Andy and Colin had neither.

TOP: Latton Close. Andy, born in Malta, arrived in the Valley in 1957, when it was new. Here he had a vision of God on a throne with angels. Just to the north were open fields.
BOTTOM: Tilshead Walk. The Moulding family's second house in Penhill. Colin lived here before his dad got a job as caretaker at Headlands School. He would walk to Andy's house in Leigh Road, where Andy's Mum would send him away, saying Andy wasn't at home.

WHAT DO YOU CALL THAT NOISE?

ABOVE: Andy, Colin and Terry played their first gig as the Helium Kidz at Swindon Arts Centre, Old Town. When Terry left XTC, Andy created the Self-Indulgent Parakeet Ensemble; they improvised while a friend ate a Chinese takeaway downstage. **RIGHT TOP:** St Peter's Church and Hall, Penhill. In 1969, Andy saw Dave playing his red Hofner Verithin in Pink Warmth and was gobsmacked. **RIGHT MIDDLE:** Four years later, Dave stumbled on a Helium Kidz rehearsal in Hook Village Hall. He subsequently auditioned for Andy and was rejected. **RIGHT BOTTOM:** this was Ian Reid's Affair. After XTC played here in September 1976, Reid secured them a deal with Virgin. To celebrate, they played four songs on ukulele, stylophone, fuzz bass and bucket. The Mayor and Mayoress of Thamesdown attended. Dave played here with Gogmagog.

THE EVERYDAY STORY OF SMALLTOWN

ABOVE: In the 1970s, Kempster's sold records. All the members of XTC frequented the shop. Andy and Dave met there sometimes on Saturday mornings. An assistant called Rose would play requests, while Andy "melted in her presence". Guitars were upstairs; much noodling and ernieing took place when Jeff Kempster wasn't watching. Andy bought his Ibanez Artist here: he thought it was Spanish.

THE EVERYDAY STORY OF SMALLTOWN

TOP: The crumbling Mechanics Institution, the community centre created by the railway workers in 1855. Andy's and Colin's mums danced here, hence *Meccanik Dancing*. In 1983, while rehearsing for *Mummer*, Terry split for Australia. He stayed for 35 years. **BOTTOM:** the old Town Hall. Dave's Alehouse gigged here. Colin and Barry made demos together before *Drums and Wires*. Andy made demos for *Black Sea*.

WHAT DO YOU CALL THAT NOISE?

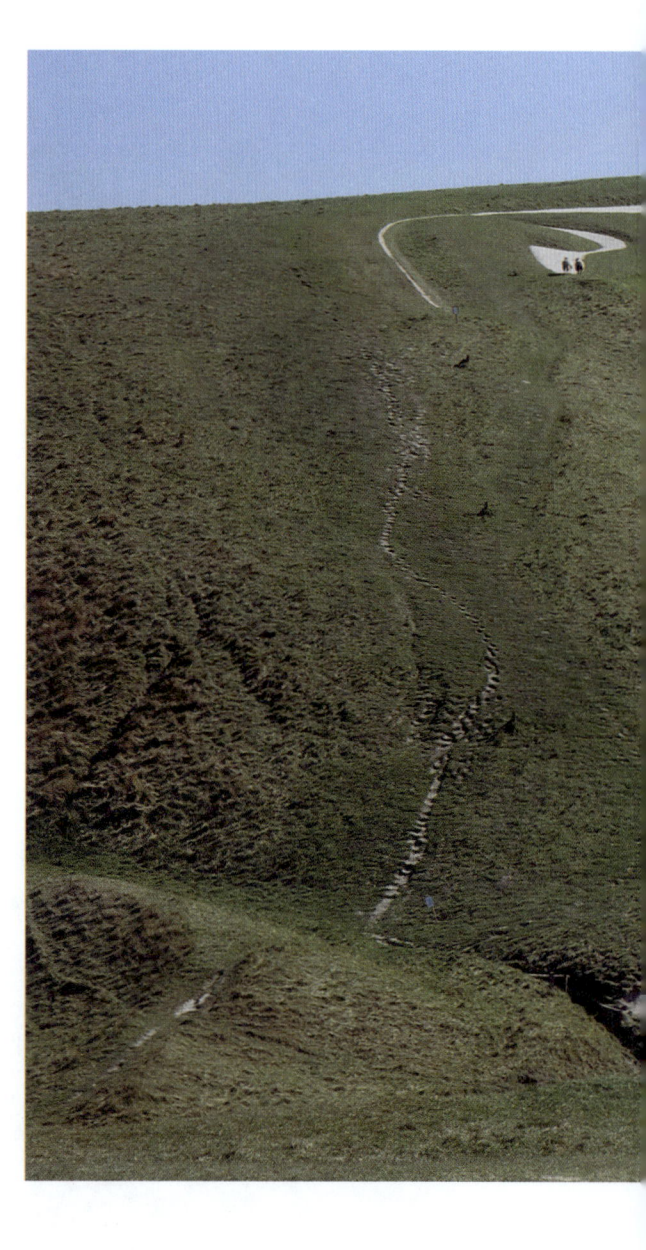

THE EVERYDAY STORY OF SMALLTOWN

ABOVE: the Uffington White Horse, which Andy calls "Dobbin". It is at least 3,000 years old. You can only see it properly from the sky. In *Chalkhills and Children*, Andy is flying, having taken off from nearby Ermin Street, the Roman (and most likely pre-Roman) road that skirts Swindon. Here Be Dragons.
LEFT TOP: Swindon Bowl, which has hosted the Helium Kidz, XTC with Jon Perkins and, for the 1984 Channel 4 documentary *XTC Play at Home*, Andy and Dave playing an early acoustic version of *Train Running Low on Soul Coal*. **LEFT MIDDLE:** Bowood Road, the real *Respectable Street*. The caravans have moved from their front gardens. **LEFT BOTTOM:** one of 243 model cottages built by the Great Western Railway in New Swindon for its workers. In *Play At Home*, the cottage is where Farmboy Andy writes to his darling and prepares for marriage.

THINGS WE DID IN CLASS

Why would a student musician take inspiration from a band that formed more than two decades before she was born? When the band is XTC, the answer is simple

BY IMOGEN BEBB

In my experience, every musician, no matter to what level or standard they play, has a few artists they aspire to be like and that motivate them to try and get better at what they do. For me, the most recent (and perhaps the most efficacious) addition to my own list of these artists is XTC.

It's their songs that are, of course, the most important thing. *Love on a Farmboy's Wages* was the first song by the band I listened to. I was fascinated by the way the single sleeve was made to look like a wallet, so bought it on a whim from a local record shop. It was unlike any pop song I'd ever heard. It made me want to pick up an acoustic guitar and learn how to play. It made me want to find out more about the characters in this narrative that was slowly unravelling out of the speakers of my record player.

It was XTC's unique style of songwriting, as well as the range of genres they tackled (often within one song) that really drew me to them to start with.

Take *Mayor of Simpleton*. Very rarely do you hear a song like that – one that isn't just a song, but a glorious wall of sound that never once falters in pace or effortlessness. Intertwining guitar melodies, luscious bass lines, sugar-sweet backing vocals... it's got everything! And all that is simply setting the scene for some of the most conceptually brilliant and hopelessly charming lyrics ever written.

And then there's the performance side of the band. You think all there is to XTC is good songwriting? Think again. Even though the band stopped touring in 1982, from any of the live footage available (particularly from the early days), you can tell their gigs were something special. To me the energy just seems to pummel its way out of the screen like a chained animal desperately fighting to escape its shackles, and the band's playing is just as tight as on the original records.

I once read a review of a Clash gig from the late 70s where the reviewer commented that

"Joe Strummer sang and played every note as if it was a matter of life or death." Surely that must have been true of Andy Partridge's performances as well; whether it was his natural stage persona, the prescription drugs he was on or a combination of both, I don't know, but I watch his almost violent dedication to any song he played and it is just completely infectious.

It's not like I'm saying this from the point of view of someone who was there at the time either (no matter how hard I wish, that time machine never appears!) XTC formed more than two decades before I was born, but that doesn't make it any more difficult for me to appreciate them. Their output, particularly from 1979 onwards, has a timelessness that a lot of music from that era does not; it seems that whatever mood I'm in, I can put any of their albums on and it will always be enjoyable to listen to.

And while playing the records, I also often find myself not only enjoying them as a fan, but also listening in utter awe as a musician. One day, I tell myself, I will write a song with as much joie de vivre as *Life Begins at the Hop*. I'll write words as deliciously melancholy as the lyrics of *Didn't Hurt a Bit*. Something as thunderously quirky as *No Thugs in Our House*, as blunderingly honest as *When You're Near Me I Have Difficulty*, as terrifyingly gorgeous as *Easter Theatre* or *Vanishing Girl* or *Wrapped In Grey* or even *Love on a Farmboy's Wages*. The list goes on.

And I know that as a music student in my second year of college, I still have a way to go before music, in whatever form, becomes something I can make a career out of. I may lose interest in it completely and pursue something else. But the day I stop wanting to be a musician is also the day I stop listening to and appreciating the unique creativity, ability and, at times, unquenchable insanity of bands like XTC.

And that certainly isn't going to be happening any time soon.

Imogen Bebb: in awe as a musician.

CHALKHILLS' CHILDREN

As a new generation of listeners are discovering XTC for themselves, two young fans in Australia and the USA share their passion for the band, one letter at a time. Meanwhile a third from the UK reports back on the TC&I gigs she saw in Swindon

BY MIA RANKIN, KYRSTEN LELAND AND IMOGEN BEBB

Mia Rankin (top) and Kyrsten Leland: put it in a letter (what could be better?)

Hi!

My name's Mia, I'm 14 and I'm from Australia. At school I've always been known as that person who likes "old music" or music everyone's mum and dad likes. It's all my dad's fault really. He's from England, and since I was born he raised me on a steady diet of music from the 70s (mainly prog) and whatever else took his fancy.

XTC were one of those bands that were actually part of my childhood, but I didn't realise it until years later. The songs I remember vividly from that time are *Making Plans for Nigel*, *Senses Working Overtime* and *Helicopter*. *Helicopter*, in particular, is one I have fond memories of. I can recall dad and I singing "oh heli!" together at the top of our lungs. At that age (probably five or six), I thought the lyrics were really funny more than anything else.

Then, several years later, I was watching an Australian music quiz show called *Spicks and Specks*. One of the rounds involved analysing a music video. That episode featured Richard Branson as a panellist and so the producers chose *Generals and Majors*. I remembered hearing the name XTC somewhere. I looked them up, realised I'd listened to them all those years ago, and decided to give them a go again, properly this time.

Eventually it got to the point where I was listening to *Drums and Wires* and *Black Sea* obsessively, probably to the point where I could recite the lyrics backwards in my sleep. Before long, I fell in love with the rest of their work, especially *Skylarking*. The rest is history!

So, Kyrsten, how did you get into XTC?

Mia

Hi Mia!
My name is Kyrsten, I'm 19, and I live in the US. Like you, I've always had a taste for older music. Gotta have something to talk to your friends' parents about, right? Coincidentally, my dad is also the one to blame - I cut my musical teeth on bands like Black Sabbath and Metallica. Aside from the occasional Duran Duran or the Police, he never strayed too far from hard rock and metal, so I wasn't exposed to XTC from an early age like you were - I'm quite jealous! I wish I had been introduced to them when I was young, how cool that must have been. As far as I know, XTC weren't even on my dad's radar.

Admittedly, I'm a fairly new fan of XTC. I tripped and fell head first into the XTC rabbit hole while driving around listening to the English Beat's *Special Beat Service* only a few months ago. Spotify has this cool little feature that queues songs to play after the album you're listening to that they've deemed related in sound or era. So, *Special Beat Service* ended and Spotify's queue began to play various related songs, eventually playing *Summer's Cauldron*, much to my confusion.

I wish I could accurately describe the look on my face as the chirps began. Had I somehow left all my windows down? Had a family of crickets taken up residence under my driver's seat? Whose dog is that? Then Andy began singing and I was instantly hooked - who was this band?

From that point on I frantically made my way through their catalogue and consumed all the content I could get my hands on.

What initially drew you to them? What was it about their music that made you want to hear more?

Kyrsten

Hey Kyrsten!
Honestly at the time of rediscovering XTC, I was a sucker for any band from the late 70s and early 80s. This usually meant anything and everything new wave or post punk (though I wouldn't classify XTC as either genre - would you?) The likes of Split Enz, the Cars, and Echo and the Bunnymen made up my daily listening. In some ways, I think it was a necessary release from the 20-minute keyboard solos and concept albums about aliens and witches that I'd encountered in all my years listening to prog. So musically, XTC fit into what I was craving at the time.

But in a way, XTC had more depth than the other bands I listened to. They approached their music in an interesting and creative style. I mean, what band bangs on a pipe to get an anvil noise for their song? What band needs an anvil noise in the first place? (*Towers of London*, I'm looking at you.) There's so much variety to their music, which I love. *Go 2* and *Nonsuch*, for instance, are such vastly different albums. I love how they've eluded being thrown into any one specific genre. There's an XTC album for every mood. Want odd, jerky keyboard driven stuff? I'll point you to *White Music*. Want a 60s sounding album but with actual decent production? *Skylarking*'s for you.

The thing I love about XTC the most, though, is the lyrics. It's not necessarily how many topics they cover or how they address them (though they do that brilliantly) but how they're written.

Andy in particular has such a way with words I've never heard before. He is one of my favourite - if not my all-time favourite - songwriters. Who else writes songs about pumpkins decaying in their front garden or skeletons having a night out, really? I've yet to see anyone else write in a way like Andy does.

At the core of it all, XTC are such wonderfully talented musicians. And so, so underrated. The solo on *Real by Reel*! The bass on *Toys*! The jangly Rickenbackers of *Mayor of Simpleton*! The drums on *Black Sea*! My Dad, who's a drummer, could gush about Terry Chambers' skills for days.

I did try to refrain from raving about XTC too much here and sounding like a blinded fanatic (didn't really succeed though). What did it for you? What set them apart from the rest?

Do you have any favourite XTC songs?

Mia

PS That Spotify feature is so good for finding new bands (*Special Beat Service* is a great album)!

....

Hello again!
You've lost me on whether XTC is new wave/post punk, but based on what I do know, I suppose their earlier albums are new wave? I'm really showing my lack of musical knowledge here, aren't I? I was never really a "music person" before I discovered XTC. I never found a band with more than a handful of songs that I genuinely liked. That's why I was so delighted when I found them. I kept anticipating the let-down, but it never came.

I absolutely agree with your comment on the depth of their music. I hear something new in their songs with every listen, which can't be said for most bands. I remember listening to *River of Orchids* through headphones for the first time. I couldn't believe all the tiny details that fell through the cracks of my car speaker. That unique quality to their music makes you want to keep listening and I think that's a huge part of what draws people to XTC and keeps them so enthralled.

I'm so glad that you brought up the fact that there's an XTC album for every mood because I couldn't agree more. For me, each album represents a specific mind-set. If I've had a difficult day and want an excuse to yell or make ridiculous noises, I'll put on *White Music*.

If I just want to drown (cue *Summer's Cauldron*) in beautiful sounds, I'll put on *Skylarking*. It's all very hard to explain because it's entirely subjective, but I think every album evokes a very specific feeling or mind-set for the listener. (Surely I can't be the only one that reaches for an invisible cowboy hat when *Shake You Donkey Up* is playing?)

Ah, the lyrics, yes! I'm a huge fan of wordplay in general, so Andy's songwriting is right up my alley, and so fantastic. He is easily my favourite songwriter. I love his refusal to shy away from certain topics and the subtle, yet intricate, storytelling. He can say in a few lines what some can't seem to express in a full song. It's a truly wonderful thing to sit back and admire. Half of the time I'm marvelling at the lyricism and the other half I'm asking myself, "How on earth did he come up with that?"

Oh, favourite song, my least favourite question! It depends on my mood, really. I love all their more popular songs, of course (the day I don't count during *Senses Working Overtime* is the day I've lost both my hands). I love *Summer's Cauldron* and *Grass*, no two songs flow together quite like those two. A few others that come to mind are *Scarecrow People*, *Real by Reel*, *Toys*, *Another Satellite*, *In Loving Memory of a Name*, *Neon Shuffle*, *Church of Women* and on and on. Try to keep me still during *Living Through Another Cuba*, I dare you.

Don't worry, I had to check myself for fanatic rambling a few times. What're some of your favourite songs? Do you have any favourite lyrics of Andy or Colin's, or some that have really stuck with you?

Kyrsten

(I'm so sorry for the delayed response! Last week was the first week of classes so it's been hectic)

....

Hi there Kyrsten!
Don't worry about the late reply – I've just returned to school myself. Only two weeks in and it's already crazy! Gosh, how to pick favourite XTC songs without

basically going into an all-out list? *Wrapped in Grey* is not only one of my favourite XTC songs, but one of my all-time favourite songs in general.

In terms of favourite XTC lyrics, I'd pick any line out of that song. "Your heart is the big box of paints, and others, the canvas we're dealt," is a line that has stuck with me for ages. *One of the Millions* resonates with me too: "And every time I get the urge to strike out on my own, insecurity wraps me up, it's cold outside the fold."

You'll find I'm a sucker for the darker stuff – *This World Over, Another Satellite, Cynical Days, All of a Sudden (It's Too Late)* and what have you. In contrast, though, *The Mayor of Simpleton* is my go-to cheer-up song. Other assorted favourites include *Living Through Another Cuba, Train Running Low on Soul Coal, That Is the Way, Complicated Game, Season Cycle, Fly on the Wall, Stupidly Happy, Wonderland, I'd Like That, Toys* and *Don't Lose Your Temper*. Looks like I didn't really succeed in holding back a list!

At the risk of sounding like my dad, or anyone over the age of 40 really, pop music has evolved so much from the 80s, and I really don't know how we got over here from there. Obviously, nothing really sounds like XTC at all on the radio today. (That's not to say all music today is rubbish, though; people just need to dig a little deeper.) It's a shame. I've genuinely tried to like mainstream music, but I can't. Perhaps I've been corrupted by my parents' record collection already.

That being said, I've tried to find music akin to XTC from the 70s and 80s. There isn't anything quite like them in that time period either. The closest thing I can find is the work of Robyn Hitchcock, who also has an unusual, but interesting, approach to music. I was pleased, though slightly unsurprised, to see he had worked with Andy. *'Cause it's Love (Saint Parallelogram)* is a great song too!

Even if there's a very minimal trace, if any, of XTC in pop music today, there's certainly no doubt in my mind they've influenced artists regardless. There's Steven Wilson, who's talked about them several times. Marty Willson-Piper of the Church has enthused about how much he loves *Skylarking*. Being a huge Crowded House fan, I was delighted to find out Neil Finn covered *Making Plans for Nigel*, and Mark Hart had cited *Drums and Wires* as one of his favourite albums. I can really hear XTC in a lot of Blur's work too. In the Blur community I'm that person that's always plugging them – "I'm begging you, check out XTC! Did you like *Modern Life Is Rubbish*? Let me introduce you to the masterpiece that is *English Settlement*..."

So, what about you? Are there any artists today (or even from the 80s) that remind you of XTC? What are your thoughts on mainstream music today? Does listening to older music ever make talking about music difficult with your friends? (I know it does for me – many jokes have been made at my expense because of it!)

Mia

Hey Mia!

It looks like we both like their darker stuff! I really had to struggle to only choose a few (and I use the term "few" loosely) favourite songs but I also really love many, OK all, of the songs you mentioned. Even now I'm kicking myself for omitting a few songs from my list!

I'm a huge believer that they "just don't make music like they used to any more". I say that at the risk of sounding like my dad, but I stand by it. I've found some alternative and lesser-known artists from the past few years that I can enjoy (if you haven't listened to Pugwash yet, give him a go. Found him thanks to Andy), but overall, mainstream music doesn't do much for me at all. I couldn't tell you the last time I voluntarily listened to the top 40 or anything of the sort. I think there's an authenticity to music like XTC's and other bands from the 80s that is seriously lacking in mainstream music. My dad always talks about how painstaking it was to create a good, solid album back then, but now a kid with a Mac, a pair of headphones, and some samples can create an album in his mom's basement. Whether said album is good or not is debatable, but my point still stands.

Thankfully, most of my friends share my love of older music. My best friend and I spent most of the summer listening to the Doors, the Beatles, David Bowie, the Beach Boys and XTC (she wasn't really given a choice on that one), so I'm not entirely alone. I introduced her to *Summer's Cauldron* and *Grass* and she's officially an XTC fan, thank God, or we might have had a serious discussion about music taste. I'm all too familiar with the jokes, though. Don't give up hope on finding friends who love older music and will gush about it with you! They're out there. Try walking around blasting *Making Plans for Nigel*, maybe you'll catch some fish.

I have yet to find any band or artist that sounds even remotely like XTC. Maybe I'm just not looking hard enough, but I have trouble believing there is one. There's something so individual about every lyric, every riff, every song, that can't be matched. I just don't hear in any other band what I hear in XTC's music. I think it has a lot to do with the authenticity that I mentioned before. You can hear the work they put into each and every song, lyrically and musically, and that, for me, really elevates them miles above any mainstream band or artist you could find today.

I'll have to give those songs/bands you mentioned a listen! I've heard a little bit of newer Blur but everything else you mentioned is new to me. Thank you for the suggestions! Do you think that XTC's music feels old or from a different time? What do you think sets them apart from mainstream music? You seem to know a little bit more about music in general than I do, so I'm very curious to get your opinion!

Kyrsten

....

Hi Kyrsten!
First of all, thanks for the compliment! I do geek out about music a lot and pour through old copies of music magazines a lot (it's all to win those music pub quizzes, really). I'll give Pugwash a go by the way - thanks for the recommendation!

To me, XTC don't sound new, but they don't sound dated either. I think it's something to do with the production of these songs, and how music production has gradually improved over time. For example, a lot of early Pink Floyd songs sound very old because they were produced in the 60s, using technology of the time. Even comparing Blur's older stuff to their new album really shows a leap in production.

But then, what makes XTC less dated than their contemporaries? Personally, I don't think they sound very 80s at all - probably the one exception being when they dabbled a lot with synths in *Wonderland*. I think what kept XTC from sounding old was their choice of producers (and engineers). Steve Lillywhite and Hugh Padgham are brilliant producers in their own right, and, besides XTC, they've worked on some of my other favourite albums. I love that video of XTC recording *Black Sea* at the Manor, and seeing how they went through the recording process. (I'm going all music nerdy and analytical on you here, sorry!)

What really sets XTC apart from mainstream music for me, primarily, is their lyrics. You and I both share a love for Andy's knack for wordplay, puns and the like! While XTC's lyrics were truly unique then and now, I think a lot of the difference between mainstream music today and mainstream music of the past is the approach to lyrics. Most pop music lyrics today deal with some form of relationship or having a good time or partying or, well, you get the idea. XTC wrote many love songs, but they took it from such a different and creative angle. And like I mentioned earlier, they wrote about so many different things too.

I totally agree with you about the authenticity and the effort you can hear in their music - I especially love listening to XTC through headphones, because sometimes you can pick up tiny little details that weren't noticeable before. Often I'll listen to them, hear bits of songs and go, "How did they come up with that?" which is typically followed by "How did they know it would fit perfectly with that song?"

With the risk of adding "snob" to my traits,

mainstream music today lacks a certain personality. It all feels the same. It sounds so black and white, whereas XTC feel like a big burst of colour. They've got their own sound, approach, a sense of Englishness (I don't know how bands sound like a country exactly, but XTC sounds English in the way that the Hoodoo Gurus sound Australian or REM sound American. It's probably that Wiltshire "burrr"), and a way of being able to come across as quick witted and whimsical yet so sincere at the same time. We could probably speculate for ages about what makes XTC tick, but will we ever really know what truly sets them apart from the others? Who knows?

Do you agree? Do you think XTC sound like they're dated? What do you think has made mainstream music nowadays pale in comparison to bands such as XTC? I'm interested to hear your thoughts!

Mia

....

Hey Mia!

XTC don't quite sound old or new to me, either. The first time I heard *Summer's Cauldron*, I spent a good few minutes trying to determine what era it was from. Initially I thought this mysterious new band were a lesser-known indie band from the last ten years. Then I was certain they were from the 80s. Then I was baffled because I started to question even that conclusion. I'm so drawn to them for that reason; you simply can't pin down their sound. It's all just beautifully crafted music. Not to say they completely skirted 80s territory. Songs like *Wonderland* and *In Loving Memory of a Name* push me slightly towards the contrary, but they managed to create music with such a timeless quality album after album.

I can absolutely agree with your comment on the lyrics setting XTC far apart from the mainstream. I'm glad you've also noticed the decline in lyricism in today's popular music. Simplicity and repetition have proven to sell music, and lyricism seemed to go by the wayside when that realisation was made.

Aside from the occasional repetitive, albeit catchy, song, anyone who has heard more than one XTC song can assure you they're quite possibly the exact opposite.

Top-notch wordplay aside, the content and topics of their songs set XTC apart from any mainstream artist. Like you said, most popular music today is about relationships or partying. But, XTC's songs range from the stupid happiness of a new love to the stoking of human coals and everything in between, with a few phallic metaphors thrown in here and there for good measure. When top lyricism and intriguing topics collide, there you find ecstasy (and XTC).

When it comes down to it, we live in an era when so many artists aren't even involved in the writing of the songs they perform. To hear a band like XTC that not only has the lyrics and the subject matter, but the musicianship to back it up, is a privilege. It's not often these days that you find a band with such mastery of all three of those things. You either find great musicians with mediocre lyrics or soaring poets with mediocre instrumentation. Don't even get me started on the subject matter.

I agree with you about XTC's music bursting with colour and personality. My friends that listen to mainstream music will play me a few songs by different artists and ask which is my favourite and I always must resist the urge to reply, "Wait, that wasn't just one really long song?" They all sound the same! I'm having trouble coming up with two XTC songs that have just about anything in common. I also agree they do sound very English, although I'm not quite sure how that works out, either.

Do you have any idea what might make them seem so English to you? I've always thought they were extremely English but never really considered what makes me think that, so I'm glad you brought it up! I'm also really curious to see how the fact we're from different countries might impact how we see their "Englishness".

Kyrsten

Hey Kyrsten!

Sorry for the really late reply. School has been absolute hell!

I've been thinking about what makes XTC so English, and truth is, I think there's no distinct answer. Influences are one thing for sure. Groups like the Beatles and the Kinks, as well as more prog bands like Pink Floyd are undeniably English and have been frequently referred to in XTC interviews as influences. (That's not to say they were only influenced by English acts – there's all those psychedelic acts like the Electric Prunes, and Andy's esoteric jazz tastes too). There has to be some correlation between influences and the band, right? Take other groups for example, like REM. While they had some overseas influences, they all listened to primarily American artists such as Patti Smith, the Ramones and Neil Young. Split Enz may have all been influenced by the 60s groups on top 40 radio in New Zealand, but they also listened to a lot of local groups.

I think the influence not only comes from groups, but from what's around them as well. The subject matter of many an XTC song is very English too (though I'm pretty sure *Red Brick Dream* is the only song to actually name-check Swindon). Songs like In *Loving Memory of a Name* and *Respectable Street* come to mind in particular. The stories these songs tell and the characters in them are so English to me. The soldier fighting for England, those rows of identical houses and the people that live in them, etc. It's things like that which, for me, make XTC a little more English than other bands.

In my opinion, it's also the references in their lyrics that make XTC such an English band. The Oxo and Sally Army in *The Everyday Story of Smalltown* or the tea cosy in *Dying* really paint pictures. There's often mentions of trains and the like (basically the whole *Big Express* album, right?) which add to it as well.

I don't know exactly if I've hit the nail on the head there – you can't really put a finger on why a band sounds like a country. But maybe you can? Do you agree with what I've said or have you got other ideas? Having lots of English relatives and family, I can understand some of the references in their songs, but others just go right over my head!

As an American, do you have a different view? I'd love to know.

Mia

Hey Mia!

I'm inclined to agree with you, I'm sure there's a myriad of reasons XTC's music feels and sounds so English; from the music they heard growing up to simply living in the little English town of Swindon. Whatever it is I can't pinpoint it either (this seems to be a recurring theme in our conversation, how difficult they are to pin down in every aspect).

I strongly agree with you on that one, that the subject matter of their songs is often unapologetically English, thus making the "English" tag unavoidable. From *Red Brick Dream*, which I also think might be the only song to name-check Swindon, to *The Everyday Story of Smalltown* and *English Roundabout* to only name the songs that are purposefully English.

I also agree that references play a huge role in their music being perceived as especially English. Peckham Rose in *River of Orchids*, British Steel in *Making Plans for Nigel* (an obvious one) and *Meccanik Dancing* referencing the Mechanics' Institute dance hall, the big stick and Aunt Sally's head in *The Wheel and the Maypole*, just to add a few to your list. I've had to Google a few references and terms, like Oxo and even ladybird (I've only ever heard them called ladybugs), in their songs simply because as an American I'm not exposed to those seemingly very English things. Thankfully the expansive *Chalkhills* website has lyric sheets complete with footnotes for those kinds of things!

I wish I could pinpoint the origin of their English essence and sound but, as I said before, they aren't an easy animal to pin down. As I've heard time and again in interviews and such, I think part of their allure to fans outside of England is their Englishness. Beyond the obvious alluring talent and musicianship, I think that people from other countries are drawn to them because they are "quintessentially English" as Steven Wilson put it.

Kyrsten

Hi Kyrsten and Mia,

My name is Imogen and I'm from Shropshire in the UK. I'm 19 years old and have liked XTC for a few years now, as well as a number of other 70s and 80s artists like OMD, Duran Duran, David Bowie and 10cc.

It's been fascinating reading your letters about XTC, particularly hearing your thoughts on their albums and how you found out about the band. My own discovery of them was quite similar to yours Kyrsten, in that it was accidental; I found the 7" single of *Love on a Farmboy's Wages* in a local record shop and bought it purely on the strength of the artwork. After that it was like opening the floodgates to the rest of their back catalogue, which is still probably the most varied (and underrated!) of any artist I have ever come across.

For this reason I find it very difficult to name an XTC album that I would cite as my favourite, although I always find myself going back to *Black Sea*. My favourite track, however, has to be *Standing in for Joe* from *Wasp Star*, which I could (and often do!) listen to over and over again and not get bored.

Last year I was also lucky enough, not only to interview Colin Moulding for my music blog, but also to hear *Standing in for Joe* played live twice at the TC&I gigs in Swindon, which I have to admit was incredibly surreal!

The two gigs I attended were definitely two of the best I have ever been to. As well as the remarkable range of the 25-song setlist (made even more remarkable when you consider all the tracks played were written by Colin, with the exception of one) which covered everything from *White Music* to *Skylarking* to TC&I's EP *Great Aspirations*.

What also really surprised me was how great Colin's voice still is, and of course Terry Chambers' drum playing was top notch and really held everything together. The band put a bit of a different spin on certain XTC tracks too; *Wonderland* in particular was quite different to the version on *Mummer* but it worked really well.

The venue (Swindon Arts Centre) was really intimate and cosy which made for such a wonderful atmosphere, particularly towards the end when the band started playing the big hits (*Generals and Majors, Making Plans for Nigel, Life Begins at the Hop* etc) and the audience were encouraged to stand up and dance!

Anyway, once again it was really interesting reading about your own thoughts on the band and their music. It's great that there are other younger fans out there to fly the XTC flag too!

Imogen

Imogen Bebb with Terry and Colin: overwhelming greatness

PLEASE DON'T PULL ME OUT

A ten-year-old Beatles fan listens to Skylarking, Wasp Star and Nonsuch for the first time and finds himself drowning in summer's cauldron

BY HUGH NANKIVELL

There is a young musician I know and work with who is ten years old. His name is Cormac Thomas, he lives in the Scottish Borders and he plays drums, piano, guitar and trombone. He listens to loads of music and loves the Beatles. I recently discovered he had never listened to XTC. In fact, he had never heard of them (not so surprising given the year), but considering I have known him all his life, I felt rather ashamed I hadn't brought the joy of XTC to his attention earlier.

Anyhow, this has given me an opportunity to feed Cormac the entire works of the Swindon band gradually and also to garner his reviews. After much debating in the CD store over a limited range, I bought him *Skylarking* - with Andy Partridge's originally preferred cover. I posted it to Cormac and then spoke to him about a couple of months later.

Our conversation was punctuated with Cormac tapping like a woodpecker on the table or the phone, and moving around his home finding different things and going in and out of signal. A restlessly energetic person.

INTERVIEW ONE: SKYLARKING

Hugh: What do you think of it?
Cormac: I think it's great - I've attempted to rank them from best to worst:

> *Summer's Cauldron*
> *Grass*
> *Earn Enough for Us*
> *Season Cycle*
> *Ballet for a Rainy Day*
> *The Man Who Sailed Around His Soul*
> *That's Really Super Supergirl*
> *The Meeting Place*
> *Sacrificial Bonfire*
> *Mermaid Smiled*
> *Dying*
> *Dear God*
> *1000 Umbrellas*

I don't not like any of them, but if I had to choose a worst it would be *1000 Umbrellas*.
Hugh: How many times have you listened to it?
Cormac: Well, the thing is, the problem about it - which is a good problem - is when you listen to the first, like, three or four songs, you like them so much that you have to keep listening to them again and again and again and it stops you listening to the rest of them.
Hugh: What bands do you think they sound like?
Cormac: Well, it depends what song you're talking about. If you're talking about *Earn Enough for Us*, it's more like the Beatles' early days, but then with stuff like *Ballet for a Rainy Day*, it's quite different.
Hugh: And who do you think *Ballet for a Rainy Day* is like? Is there anything you'd compare it to?
Cormac: I'm not sure actually.
Hugh: When you listen to them, do you listen to the words or music or both?
Cormac: I try to listen to both, but the music sometimes does take over the words. But I have ranked these mostly on the music.
Hugh: If they played live would you like to see them?
Cormac: I would, yes.

Cormac Thomas: "You have to keep listening to them again."

Hugh: What is it about *Summer's Cauldron* that you like enough to put it at the top of the list?
Cormac: Well, first of all, I like the beginning with the birds and then the sudden-but-gradual [sic] change to the more rocky feel from the whatever-it-is, and I think the chorus is very good.
Hugh: And have they stuck in your head?
Cormac: They have.
Hugh: When you have your next album from me, would you rather have an earlier or later one?

Cormac then asks me where this came in the chronology and I say about album seven, without clearly thinking about it. I am wrong; it was the eighth, not including reissues and compilations, and in the middle of their career (although in fact there were only four more afterwards!)

Cormac: OK - so it's like the *Revolver* of the group or the *Rubber Soul*.
Hugh: That's an interesting way of putting it.
Cormac: So they've still got some of their old classics, but they've started to experiment?

We then have a brief chat about similarities to the Beatles in the way that after they stopped playing live their recordings developed and changed.

Cormac: Hang on - I'll toss a coin.

Long pause while Cormac tosses a coin.

Cormac: I've tossed it and it's tails which means something after.
Hugh: OK, I'll send you something. Do you know anyone of your age that likes XTC?
Cormac: I don't actually. Most of the people in school are into the horrible modern pop kinds of things.
Hugh: And do you not like that?
Cormac: No - stuff like Little Mix I don't like.
Hugh: And what do you think it is about XTC that makes you interested in a way that Little Mix doesn't?
Cormac: Basically it's just the type of music. It's not all screamy/shouty/horrible boring-tune kind of thing. It's different, you know? But it's also nice and similar (!!!) Another thing I did like was the transitions between the songs, like from *Summer's Cauldron* to *Grass* and *1000 Umbrellas* and *Ballet for a Rainy Day*.

INTERVIEW TWO: WASP STAR

I sent Cormac the CD of Wasp Star, *he copied it and then made a hand-crafted CD case for it. A month later we had a chat on the phone about it*

Hugh: So *Wasp Star*?
Cormac: I definitely know which is my least favourite song on the album. It's *Wounded Horse*. It sort of drags on a little bit. You always seem to be checking the CD player to see when it will end. I'm not saying it's too long, I'm just saying it's the one to skip.

We then have a chat about my least favourite being Standing in for Joe *and how they are next to each other on the album.*

Cormac: My favourite one is *I'm the Man Who Murdered Love*. It's the one I always seem to like - it's the music, I don't know about the words though. It would probably be at the bottom if it was just for the words! Another one I liked a lot was *Playground*. *Stupidly Happy* was pretty good. I found *Stupidly Happy* pretty catchy. I tried working it out on the piano for about five minutes, but it was too hard.

We then talk about the opening two songs and the ending three being really strong and the weaker ones in the middle.

Cormac: The funny thing is that *Boarded Up* would seem to me to be like a track that would be last on the album. I wasn't saying *Boarded Up* was bad, just saying I'd put it at the end.
Hugh: Why?
Cormac: It's just the kind of vibe of it - more "settled down".
Hugh: What do you think of *Wasp Star* compared with *Skylarking*?
Cormac: I have to say I do prefer the album cover a lot on this one. [He has the updated one of Andy's "mangina" with flowers.]
Hugh: That wasn't the original one - the original was a picture of a line drawing of a couple playing flutes.
Cormac: Oh good. I think I probably prefer *Skylarking*, but they were both very good.
Hugh: Why did you prefer *Skylarking*?
Cormac: The feel has changed a bit. When I first listened to this [*Wasp Star*] and I heard *Boarded Up*, I thought this is completely different. On *Skylarking* you have *The Man Who Sailed Around His Soul* which is jazzy.

I ask about The Wheel and the Maypole *and about it being two songs together and Cormac talks about how he likes the segueing in* Skylarking.

Hugh: *Wasp Star* was the last album they made and there were only two of them left.
Cormac: So this one is the *Abbey Road* of the group? But I mean it's a bit more of *Let it Be* as well. When Paul McCartney was recording *McCartney* at the same time.

INTERVIEW THREE: NONSUCH

I sent Cormac *Nonsuch* and then two weeks later we had a phone chat. Nice to chat with him again - and great to hear the pauses as he thought about the questions. I sometimes have to remember he is only ten years old. Throughout the conversation I could hear him drumming his fingers on the table. He musically fiddles all the time. Wonderful to hear it. I'm sure I did the same and recall playing the piano on any surface (I still do today).

For me, what comes across from this little chat is the way that

    A. he has made Beatles connections and is still pursuing that parallel.
    B. he can identify an XTC song, but not define what one is.
    C. he is able to respond to the "simpler" lyrical songs - for example, *The Smartest Monkeys* - because they can be clearly understood by a bright ten year old.
    D. you can be put off a song by the title - for example, *Books Are Burning*.
    E. he likes time-signature changes. Interesting to think about whether Andy Partridge is ever conscious of that when composing his songs.

Hugh: Tell me some of your favourite songs from *Nonsuch*.
Cormac: Favourite? Well, the thing is they are all very good tracks and I wouldn't classify any as bad. *Peter Pumpkinhead*, I like. I like *Rook* and *War Dance*, I like.
Hugh: Do you? Why do you like *War Dance*?
Cormac: I like the little wind bit.

Then a little chat about whether it was a real clarinet or a keyboard and whether it was the tune he liked or the sound.

Cormac: I just like the wind tune, which is a very small part.

Hugh: Do you like *Bungalow*?
Cormac: The thing is, I like the chords a lot, but the verse, I'm not sure of.
Hugh: Mmm – and what do you like about *Peter Pumpkinhead*?
Cormac: Well, I like the instrumental little bit *[he sings a bit]*, you know... I like the sort of repetitive bit, you know. For a normal song, it might be a tad too long, but for that song, it's just the right length: four minutes. Another one I like was *Dear Madam Barnum*.
Hugh: What do you like about that one?
Cormac: I thought it was very XTC.
Hugh: Very interesting after only hearing two albums. What makes a song "very XTC"? What do you think makes XTC XTC?
Cormac: It's like the Beatles, you can't really pick a genre for them. It has its own genre. If I was describing XTC and I had to put a certain genre in there I would never make up my mind, because it would seem to have the best-of-all-worlds in genres.
Hugh: Is that the same for the Beatles?
Cormac: Well, early Beatles, I'd give them rock'n'roll, but when they were getting all experimental I'd give them "Beatles genre". *[Laughs]*
Hugh: With XTC, what is it that makes their own genre? Is it to do with vocals?
Cormac: Well yeah – I get to recognise them, but I can't yet tell the two singers apart!

I try to push Cormac on this...

Hugh: When you say *Madam Barnum* is very XTC what do you mean – is it the vocals, the chords, the melody, the arrangement?
Cormac: Um – I'd probably need to listen to it a thousand times more to work that out! I just think of it as a very XTC song.
Hugh: What do you like about *Rook*?
Cormac: I like that it changes time signature... Yeah, I like any song that changes time signature. It's always a must when I'm writing my own songs.

Hugh: It's a must, is it?
Cormac: Well, not a must, but I should get to changing time signature at some point in my own song.
Hugh: Do you like the strings in *Rook*?
Cormac: Yes – the thing I like about this album is there isn't all the same things (which is the problem I had with *Wasp Star*); there's a bit more variety.
Hugh: But *Wasp Star* has variety, doesn't it?
Cormac: Yes, but not as much.
Hugh: Ah, OK. Are there some songs you don't notice so much?
Cormac: Well, I think *The Smartest Monkeys* – I notice the lyrics a lot, but not so much the tune... I found that XTC are good with their lyrics. The only problem I had with early Beatles is that they get all the way to *Nowhere Man* before having a song that wasn't about "I love, you love," you know?

Then a brief chat about how Cormac has never heard early XTC, and yet they never really have an obvious "I love, you love" song, to use his definition.

Cormac: You know the song *Dear God*? At first, I wasn't too sure if that was a song about religion or about atheism?
Hugh: And what do you think now?
Cormac: Well, now I think it's definitely an atheist one, but that might be just because I read on Wikipedia about that song.
Hugh: Sometimes it helps to research and find things out, doesn't it?
Cormac: Yeah.
Hugh: Cormac, do you like *Books Are Burning*? It's the last one.
Cormac: To be honest, the thing I didn't like about it is the title. I never like books being burned. But it is a good song. I liked it.
Hugh: If you were saying this was like a Beatles album which would this be?
Cormac: Well, *Skylarking* was like *Rubber Soul* or *Revolver* and *Wasp Star* was like *The White Album* and this one is like *Help!*.

WHAT DO YOU CALL THAT NOISE?

A CHAIN TO HOLD ALL BATTLESHIPS IN CHECK

What do professional musicians hear when they play their favourite XTC songs? Leading players talk about their jukebox selection before passing musical recommendations down the chain of command

BY MARK FISHER

Who but Andy Partridge would have the wit to coin the phrase "Future Dogs Die in Kaiser Ferdinand's Hot Hot Car Party"? This was 2005 and Andy was describing a wave of guitar bands who bore the influence of XTC. In their drums-and-wires angularity, those early 21st-century groups seemed to echo XTC's new-wave spirit pioneered 25 years earlier. To add to Andy's list, which in full would read Futureheads, Dogs Die in Hot Cars, Kaiser Chiefs, Franz Ferdinand, Hot Hot Heat and Bloc Party, you could add Everything Everything, Dutch Uncles and, from the previous decade, Blur.

The influence, however, is not always certain. Consider the case of Field Music, a band much admired by XTC fans and assumed to be inheritors of the tradition, but who say they have "hardly heard any of their records". The Field Music sound is more likely a result of those musicians listening to many of the same records XTC listened to. It's possible the same is true of Super Furry Animals.

Spotting the influence, in other words, can be a tricky business. What is more certain is the esteem in which XTC are held by musicians. The characteristic quality of conversations I had for this chapter was one of adulation and awe. Forget record sales and chart success, XTC are musicians' musicians, admired by their contemporaries and discovered afresh by subsequent generations of songwriters and players.

One person who would know is Chris Difford, whose debut album with Squeeze was released in 1978, just two months after *White Music*. "I remember seeing them play at the Nashville Rooms in London," says the lyricist. "I thought they were lively, lippy and the thing I recall the most is the songs. They stood out from other shows I had seen at the time. Andy looked liked he loved the chaos of the moment and came across amazingly well."

Although they never toured together, Squeeze and XTC were part of a generation of literate pop makers, such as Elvis Costello and the Specials, who took the energy of punk and fashioned something more artful. It's worth noting that

Costello said he modelled the arrangement of *White Knuckles* on a couple of XTC songs and that Terry Hall of the Specials went on to write songs with Andy Partridge. "Seeing them on TV was like being in a tribe," says Difford. "Together I thought we might rule the world, with our interesting songs and attitude, which was seldom that clear. I think we would have made good bedfellows on tour."

Did XTC influence him? "Yes all the time," he says. "The lyrics and the songs themselves were a constant on my CD player. I was always looking for a new record from them and when one came out I played it all the time. Yes, I stole from them. I'm sure I was not the only one. The wit did woo me. I fell head over heels for the clever word play, the charge of the story and the sentimental Britishness of it all. I liked the words, and then I liked the music."

We won't dwell on the unfortunate fortnight XTC spent in Difford's studio as work commenced on *Apple Venus*, something the songwriter himself regrets. "I will always rue the day that the studio was not working at its fullest," he says. "Sadly the studio manager confiscated the tapes without me knowing." More fruitful, however, was the day Difford spent writing with Andy. He doubts the songs will be released but it sounds as if they deserve to be.

"I showed Andy some words on my laptop, he pulled out a guitar and made his way through seven songs like a plough across a field. I love them, from memory, eccentric and very much parts of us both in equal measures."

Difford's enthusiasm is typical of the conversations that follow in this chapter. The brief was to talk about an XTC song (or a moment within a song) that fascinated the musicians in some way. Having talked about their choice, each contributor then suggested a song for another musician to talk about, linking them in a chain of XTC fandom. We start in San Francisco with bass player and songwriter Becki diGregorio and a highlight from *Oranges and Lemons*.

Becki diGregorio
THE LIQUID SCENE, SOLO

CHOSEN TRACK
Poor Skeleton Steps Out

I love how XTC's music supports the lyrics in a most descriptive and ingenious way. Here, Andy offers us his take on how the skeleton is a slave to the body and sings how one day every skeleton will be free:

Poor skeleton steps out
Dressed up in bad blood,
Bad brains, bad thoughts and others' deeds

At the same time, the music offers us an aural image of what dancing skeletons might sound like.

A lone buzzy guitar starts us off with the promise of something foreboding and exciting – thanks, Dave! – before drummer Pat Mastelotto digs in with a thumping kick drum and the sound of a xylophone gives us that quintessential "dancing bones" sound. Colin's staccato bass lines during the verses are short choppy punches that hint at a tribal solidness. The xylophone doubles Andy's vocals, accentuating the light, delicate bone sound. Colin then switches up in the pre-chorus section and plays an off-beat bass line that adds an element of unsteady playfulness. It puts you in mind of cartoon skeletons dancing in unison in a delicately swaying movement. I see them wearing top hats, but maybe that's just me.

To build up the song sonically, they gradually add instruments without fanfare but whose elimination we'd surely miss. They raise the chorus energy with an edgy, scratchy, scrape-y sandpaper percussive sound that you feel as well as hear. Then right after the first chorus there appears this single guitar note (Dave again?) on the up-beat that continues into the following verses and pre-chorus, perfectly dropped in to add to the pulsating dance of sounds. Harmonies on the last verses elevate the mood once again, and added guest voices, like a reverb-filled mad-boned chorus, raise the dancing-skeleton bar.

And the dropped drumstick at the very end of the track: stick = bone!

BEQUEATHED TRACK

Collideascope

I am bequeathing *Collideascope* to the next musician. As a lover of all things psychedelic, I'm a huge fan of music from the late 60s. Discovering the Dukes of Stratosphear albums only fuelled my desire to produce such an album myself. Andy Partridge was kind enough to let me cover his song *Susan Revolving* for my second album (he also wrote another verse for it, and told me to listen to Pink Floyd's first album *The Piper at the Gates of Dawn* for a week straight before heading into the studio!) Three years ago I released a full-length psychedelic album under the band name of the Liquid Scene with nine original songs. I'm grateful to Andy for his support, and of course to Dave Gregory for adding guitar and keyboards on my first two albums. The music of XTC is unequalled, and being a fan of theirs for many years has truly changed my life...

Craig Northey
ODDS

INHERITED TRACK

Collideascope

I fell on the floor laughing so hard when I heard the opening of this tune because it encapsulated everything they were doing with that record. "Collideascope/Careful, don't look down the wrong end." Musically, of course, it was a total psychedelic pastiche, but with those words on top of it, it meant: "Get ready for the fun. The fun begins now. We are having a riot with this." Those lyrics combined with that opening were just stellar. Their embracing of everything that was dumb and everything that was great is exactly what people love about them. What was intelligent? What was dumb? What was intelligent because it was dumb?

CHOSEN TRACK

No Language in Our Lungs

You said you could pick a moment in a song that slayed you musically. I started picking apart everything about *No Language in Our Lungs* that I loved and tried to figure out what that one moment was. When he gets to the end of the first chorus and he sings the word "lungs", it's like being punched in the gut. Everything musically leads to this F sharp minor with an 11 in it, a point when there is nothing left in his lungs and he's letting it all out. The whole song is structured like the feeling of this prehistoric man - that person inside all of us - trying to get his feelings out. It's a plodding, half-time feel and the low guitar melody is the unison melody with the vocal for a lot of the verse. It's heavy and it has that feeling of sinking under water, trying to get your ideas out. Then all of a sudden, the music, the feeling and the lyric all come together in such a cool way.

Andy Partridge asks, "How can I create that feeling with these chords?" He puts his hand on his guitar and moves it in little increments to find that feeling rather than using musical theory to determine what he should do next. He's always trying to break patterns to find where that emotion is. All the things I stole from XTC (which are myriad) are in their jazz approach to the Beatles. Everything's bending and twisting, everything's close together and chromatic. You can find those chords by moving your hands just a little bit. It's never crazy, it's just a sense that this tightness will create more angst. *No Language in Our Lungs* has all that in one song.

In all the solos I play I find that weird little intro that disappears and is gone, like in *Towers of London*, bending a note against an open string that creates beautiful *Revolver*-type riffs. I was influenced by *And Your Bird Can Sing* and *Nowhere Man* as much as XTC were. It's that thing that resonates with your soul. Somehow, it works its way even into my improvisations.

The line, "I would have made this instrumental but the words got in the way," is the brilliant part of dumb. It's funny. I laugh a lot. People miss the humour when they take these things too seriously. In Odds, when we started in the late 80s, the two bands that all of us liked were the Beatles and XTC. I guess we liked musicians with a gallows humour and a self-consciousness about being too serious about themselves. When you listen to those kind of jokes in songs, it endears you to them. They understand there's nothing precious.

BEQUEATHED TRACK

Earn Enough for Us

That leads me to Steven Page and Barenaked Ladies because I saw in them that unwillingness to be pretentious or to give in to the seriousness of rock. I know Steven will find something in *Earn Enough for Us* because I can recognise some of him in that tune.

Steven Page
BARENAKED LADIES AND SOLO

INHERITED TRACK

Earn Enough for Us

Although I'd been a fan and probably had all the XTC records, *Skylarking* for me was an amazing gift. It was all the things I liked about XTC tied up in this sweet little package. There's nothing difficult about *Earn Enough for Us*, it's very McCartney-like, but in a way that's what you want McCartney's songs to be like. It has the right sections of a perfect pop song. It's complete. There aren't a lot of left turns, but I know when I write a song that's straightforward, it runs the risk of being boring and this isn't that. It's exciting and uplifting. It was part of my musical education into how to construct a pop song: where to take things lyrically, how to build a story. It's not an A to B to C plotline; there's a sense of understanding the character over the course of the verses.

From the first record onwards, XTC's music has always been there in my consciousness. I think about it a lot when I'm making records. I made my first solo record after I left Barenaked Ladies with producer John Fields who's a huge XTC fan as well. Lots of times we were referencing individual songs and saying, "OK, let's go with a bass line that sounds like a Colin Moulding bass line," and, "What did the Dukes of Stratosphear do here?"

XTC was our common ground so it made it a lot of fun. It was an opportunity to make the kind of pop record I'd always wanted to.

By *Skylarking*, Andy started to write stuff that was more political or world-focused. That had an influence on how I would write songs with a focus outside of myself without being fist-pumpingly self-important. There's a sense of outrage or observation but it's all from my perspective, and that's what Andy does. I also love that so much of their stuff is about everyday life. They come across as an everyday group of people and that's very much what Barenaked Ladies were about too – living as ordinary a life as you can in a bizarre lifestyle like rock'n'roll.

The other exciting thing about XTC is their sense of both harmony and rhythm and how to fuck those things up. Whether it's the guitar pattern at the beginning of *Wake Up* or the way drum beats turn around. Even on Andy's home demos, his drum-programming instincts are not ordinary. Things get swapped around and should be disorientating but they fit inside the song. That was a big influence on me. But the cleverness doesn't come at the expense of the musicality. The song comes first.

CHOSEN TRACK

Terrorism

I had it as the B-side of *The Meeting Place* which had a few home demos. At that point in my life, I was just getting into recording at home. I would have been about 17 and had started writing songs. Other kids when their parents went away for the weekend would have a big party, drink a lot of beer and trash the house, but my friend and I would rent a four-track cassette recorder and record songs. I'd hear these things and think, "This is just Andy at home with a really clangy sounding acoustic guitar, loud bass and this drum programming which is so propulsive." His skill as a drum programmer is second to none and he doesn't get enough credit for it.

Terrorism is such an exciting track. A home-recorded song can lose energy really quickly (I know because I've done this when recording by myself), but the energy in *Terrorism* is there right from the beginning. As a demo, it's ragged and abrasive, which makes you sit up. A band version with fully realised arrangements would have had a place on any of the albums of that era. He's got all this major-key-over-minor-key stuff that creates a musical tension that sounds Middle Eastern, but a lot of the harmonic choices are the same as he would make in a traditional XTC song. It's a great encapsulation of what Andy can do and it gave me inspiration to make music in my basement like he would do in his shed.

It's a political song in the spirit of *Dear God* in that he's making a proclamation and there is a sense of outrage, but it is clever enough not to feel like didacticism, it feels like music. As a writer, you question direct songs the most: "Do I want to put that out there? Is it as valid as a more universal or more nuanced song?" But Andy does a good job at saying there's terrorism on every continent from every walk of life. He's not pinning it down to one group, which makes it close to home for him in the England of the 1980s. As a younger person, good songs like this helped me form my own points of view, value system and understanding of the world. By listening to songwriters I respected, I found my way around politics. I always appreciate that in a writer as long as they can do it with the same sense of art as they do everything else.

BEQUEATHED TRACK
Brainiac's Daughter
This has such an infectious melody, funny and perfect lyrics, and I'm such a sucker for that kind of piano feel. How perfect those records were in their pastiche without being totally mocking; alongside the Rutles, it's as good as it gets. I'm a huge Beatles fan, but honestly, I think I know the Rutles songs as well and in some ways I think they're just as good. The Dukes are so much more than a joke. If it was a joke it would be a fun listen once, but it's as good as the music it's paying tribute to. *Brainiac's Daughter* has classic XTC vocal harmonies, where one part goes up and the other goes down, which in this setting is even more perfect.

Jim Moray
SOLO, FALSE LIGHTS

INHERITED TRACK
Brainiac's Daughter
Andy spent the first few albums trying to be a snarly, angry Lennon fan and then, at some point, he gave in to the urge to write McCartney-style Tin Pan Alley songs with interesting chords that were gentle and clever. *Brainiac's Daughter* scratches loads of itches for me because it's Partridge and McCartney all at once. The thing that Neil Innes and the Rutles have got in common with the Dukes is they're not pastiching a single song. We can all agree it's Beatles-y, but it's so finely chopped that you have to be meticulous to spot where all the bits have come from. The drums in the middle eight are from the middle of *A Day in the Life*, but over chords and a melody that are unlike *A Day in the Life*. Then there's that swanee whistle that's from *I'm the Urban Spaceman* by the Bonzo Dog Doo-Dah Band, which McCartney produced [with Gus Dudgeon]. The bass line is very McCartney and very Colin Moulding as well. "Three bags full, sir" is like when John and George sing *Frère Jacques* as the backing vocals over the third verse of *Paperback Writer*. Nursery rhymes are also like 1967 psychedelia, which was very Lewis Carroll-based.

The melody is an interesting example of doing repeats where you pull the phrase out to last an extra bar or so. Lyrically, the rhythm is repeated with an extra tail on it. In the "yes sir, yes sir, three bags full sir" section, it pulls it for an extra couple of syllables to play with the meter and the expectation of where the next bit is going to land. Someone once said everything McCartney writes seems inevitable after you've heard it, which is the same as this: it seems like that's the only place the melody could resolve, but only the moment after you've heard it. Your brain is going, "Oh, yes, of course it goes there." But everything sounds natural and flowing; it's not deliberately wrong-footing you in the way that some XTC does. It doesn't seem predictable but it seems like it's naturally gone to every place. *Brainiac's Daughter* is an amazing flexing of pop muscles.

CHOSEN TRACK
All You Pretty Girls

I don't know Andy Partridge very well, but I had quite a lot of interaction with him for a short period of time, which was before I recorded my cover of *All You Pretty Girls*. It was the compromise: instead of writing something new with him, I ended up covering one of his old ones. I had signed a publishing deal with Warner/Chappell and they were pushing me into co-writing. Steve Young, who did the distribution deal for my first album, was managing XTC at the time. I got a phone call from Andy and we discussed it. He said, "Just put something down on a tape, send me the tape in the post and I'll overdub something, then when we've got something, we can meet up to record it properly." For a period afterwards, I would get calls at random times of the day when he was thinking of something. The writing didn't come to anything. I didn't work very well like that because I want to get things better before I send them to people. I don't think I ever sent him a tape.

It's not that *All You Pretty Girls* is my favourite, it's just that straight away I could see how it fitted into a folk framework. It has the sea-shanty element but also in 2008, Bellowhead were getting big. Their thing was slightly tongue-in-cheek silliness, but playing to bigger audiences. I could see how I could marry this well-constructed song with a thing audiences liked at that moment. I love the song and I love performing it, but I knew I'd hit a goldmine that nobody else had thought of. I knew it would go down really well.

Andy won Best Original Song for *All You Pretty Girls* at the tenth BBC Radio 2 Folk Awards in 2009. There was a run of songs that were 20 years old; for a while, it was also an award for the most significant reworking, so cover versions won a lot. I did well because the song is really good. In the folk scene, there is a tradition of writing new songs vaguely in that style, but Andy is more of a pro at it than some writers. There are lots of influential people in folk who really like XTC and I think it's because of the genre-blind way of constructing songs.

Playing *All You Pretty Girls* live, you have to do a bit of front-manning to do the it justice. It's not Freddie Mercury, but you've got to conduct the crowd and have a singalong. It always came at the encore and I'd divide them in half like a pantomime – proper cheesy front-manning. But it worked and it worked for me, because I didn't have any material that was like that.

My version is quite dumbed down. Listening to it again just now, I remembered how complicated the chords are. I didn't play anything like that complicated. A melodeon has certain chords in certain directions of the bellows and, by definition, you can't put that diminished chord in the verse and you can't make that chord sequence quite so spiky. The instrument won't do it, so between the three of us, we made an approximation. With Andy, his thing is trying to make the accordion do things it doesn't do. He goes against the ergonomics. That's where a very high level of skill comes in. Striving to do something that's almost impossible on your instrument is the thing that keeps him going.

Andy understands harmonies by stacking notes. "If you do this shape, but you move this bass note, it makes a new chord." Instead of thinking holistically, he's constructing out of fragments stacked on top of each other. Instinctively, I think of harmony like that as well, maybe because my harmonic knowledge was on the piano first: "If you do this with your right hand, but change the shape on your left hand, it'll make a new chord." It feels like his development of chords when he was learning was based on this sort of mechanical picture. *Dear God*, for example, uses a conventional A minor shape on the guitar, but with your spare finger doing things on a different string to make this bonkers chord sequence. Dave Gregory is a conventionally talented guitar player and is therefore having to modify the modes and the scales to fit what Andy's doing. You get this push and pull as Dave filters what he does through somebody else's lens to create a layered painting.

All You Pretty Girls is one of those songs where at certain points you have to do Andy's inflection or the song doesn't work. In the verses, you have to do the yelpy thing at the end of "The more that I have to drink, the more that I can think to say." Finding my way of doing that was tricky. Musically, there's a note I changed. Not many people noticed, but those that did were outraged. I "corrected" the second note of the chorus into being a far more conventional folky note, dropping down to the fifth, whereas it actually drops down to the sixth with parallel fourths as the harmony. It has a more plainchanty thing about it than I did. It's an example of how Andy instinctively does things that are more jazzy and that someone who was more formally trained would have to deliberately do rather than relying on their instincts. The mitigating circumstance for changing the note was playing it on the melodeon, but if I was doing it again I would probably not change it because the nuance is more important to me now.

It's one that people still request and one I haven't played for a while. I did a tour with Eliza Carthy five years ago, and after the last gig I thought it should be the last time I played lots of my repertoire. In that era I had to borrow songs to fill those gaps. I got more confident in finding my own material. In this case, that itch is scratched by this band False Lights that I do with Sam Carter. We've got some songs where the structure comes from that version of *All You Pretty Girls*, it's just we've generated them from scratch instead of stealing them off Andy!

BEQUEATHED TRACK
All of a Sudden
The starting point is how un-dated Hugh Padgham's production sounds. The drum sound is mighty. It's the same gated reverb as *In the Air Tonight*, but it doesn't sound dated, so maybe he'd perfected the technique by the time he did *English Settlement*. Those toms are incredibly big, the chiming 12-string is pretty characteristic of Dave Gregory and the bass is full and consistent; there's no chance of it getting lost. Then you've got that interesting parallel harmony of the bass line and the vocal in the chorus. It's a very 3D mix with lots of front-to-back depth, which is a credit to Hugh Padgham. When you look at *English Settlement* on Spotify, it leaps out how long a lot of the tracks are - 15 songs of which a fair chunk go over six minutes - but it doesn't feel like that when you listen to it. Maybe that's something about the space.

David McGuinness
CONCERTO CALEDONIA

INHERITED TRACK
All of a Sudden
There is so much space in it. Like *Snowman*, it has an infectious groove but lots of places where nothing happens and it doesn't matter. It's such a simple arrangement with hardly anything going on, just lots of great big holes and it doesn't feel empty, except where it's supposed to. To have the nerve to do that... it's one of those apocalyptic songs like *This World Over* that's unremittingly depressing. There's a bit of *Train Running Low* in there about getting old and not having done things, and it has that same melancholic harmonic tinge to it, suggesting missed opportunities. There's a burst of optimism in the middle - that beautiful line about "it's more a way you have to give" - but it is surrounded by real darkness.

If you look at the intro to *All of a Sudden*, it's just a scale with an F sharp major chord on the end. That in itself is not very interesting, but he's chosen it for its colour, meaning and mood, which is so specific and so beautifully chosen. Andy's attention to mood is acute. The song is the end of side two and leaves you hanging when the opening riff is played again. To get out of that mood, you have to get the other LP out and put side three on, which takes you in a different direction. Then at the end of side four, you've got *Snowman* - another simple song where nothing much happens. The words about being cut off by someone are similarly dismal, but this time, the music works entirely against it. It is upbeat and uplifting with an irresistible groove.

CHOSEN TRACK
Heatwave
Normally, I don't buy the "vinyl sounds better" argument, but on *Beeswax*, this sounds staggering.

If you look at the label closely enough, Tony Cousins gets a credit for cutting the record – and he's since become a legendary mastering engineer, still working at Metropolis. It's a fantastic-sounding record with shed-loads of honest tape hiss which I've always really liked.

Heatwave is a strange one to pick because in traditional terms, the song is almost non-existent. Colin didn't do it in the TC&I gigs and I'm sure he's slightly embarrassed about it now. There's nothing there, just a string of silliness. As a piece of songwriting craftsmanship there isn't much to recommend it, but what they build on top is stunning. It gives the band free rein to do something that's as much like them musically as it could be.

It feels like a precursor to the sound we were talking about on *All of a Sudden*, partly because they had Mutt Lange producing. There's a huge sound with a rock-solid pumping groove. The earlier version, *Heatwave Mark 2 Deluxe*, that's on *Coat of Many Cupboards* is just not happening at all and I'm guessing Mutt Lange worked them really hard. On something like *Meccanik Dancing* you've got the interplay between Barry and Andy; that happens a bit on the early version of *Heatwave*, but on this one, it's like Lange has noticed the action is all happening on the guitar. There are big chunks where Barry is not playing anything.

You've got this solid rhythm that, like with any other XTC record, is never quite the obvious thing. Everything's just a little bit off from what a normal person would do. That's used as a platform for Andy to let rip with all his favourite guitar tricks. There's that stunning intro from Barry with the clavinet bass and the organ that skitters away. Then you think, "Hang on, is this a joke?" as Partridge plays this brilliantly dissonant guitar solo that's so insistent about how dissonant it is. "No, I'm going to keep playing what you think of as the wrong notes. I'm just awkward – deal with it."

On the video for *Heatwave*, you see Andy play some of the guitar solos and it looks perfectly relaxed because it all sits under the fingers. It's just the fingers aren't where they would usually be. Everything is more interesting than it needs to be. If Andy is playing a repetitive riff, he won't play it the same all the time; it'll have little sparks where it's a different length or it moves around. It's always restless and buzzing. XTC records manage to resist the obvious. Going into the second guitar solo, you get the line, "In the conservatory," but it goes, "In the con–" and the guitar solo comes in mid-word. Both guitar solos sign off with silly noises. I can't even work out where he plays the first one; he just flies off the top of the neck. The second one has a silly harmonic; he takes an artificial harmonic and bends it so you get a high squeaky noise.

The musical craftsmanship is stunning and the thing somehow keeps going despite its punk decoration – every possible crazy thing stuck on it that would normally stop it from functioning. It doesn't because the underlying structure is so strong. On *Take Away/The Lure of Salvage* it became *The Day They Pulled the North Pole Down*. *Heatwave* sounds sticky, oppressive and hot, but they managed to make the dub mix as cold as possible. They slowed it down, took the activity out and made a chilling atmosphere. It comes back to that idea of deciding very specifically what the mood is.

BEQUEATHED TRACK
Then She Appeared
Listening to it again, I realised going into the bridge first time round the bass has a bit of *Taxman* (sort of) at 1:44 and nearly the end of *Paperback Writer* at 1:59. It's a bit like *19th Nervous Breakdown* at the end of *My Love Explodes* – and this could have been a Dukes song. The whole song is a delight, from the beautiful chiming guitar onwards. What they all pull off – and it's a difficult thing to do – is the mixture of humour, which comes from self-consciously taking bits of psychedelia and plugging them in, and being entirely sincere. The song piles up the backwards cymbals, the psychedelic gags and this imagery (throwing in "the first photograph on Fox Talbot's gel" right at the beginning) and then it gets to the

last line – "Now shines from her blue eyes" – which seems so naive and innocent in comparison.

Musically, the masterstroke for me is the diminished seventh chord before "little frightened" and "a little dazzled" – the way he uses that pivot chord to turn the whole thing around. It is perfectly expressing what the words are saying at that point and performing a really useful musical function between the relatively conventional parts on either side of it. And I love the way he makes the word "weird" sound weird – it's the sort of thing you'd expect to hear in the *White Music/Go 2* days, but he's refined it.

Mark Vidler
GO HOME PRODUCTIONS

INHERITED TRACK

Then She Appeared

A chiming cavalcade of Byrdsian Rickenbacker guitars on a wave of reverse cymbals announce XTC in full-on psych-pop mode. There are phased vocals, Monkee Tork organ stylings and a bankful of "ooooooooh" backing vocals alongside a subtle doffing of the cap to McCartney's bass line from *Rain*. The day-glo pop tones of *Oranges and Lemons* had matured by the time XTC arrived at *Nonsuch* and I remember feeling it was more of an adult-sounding album, both in terms of music and lyrics. *Then She Appeared* had a touch of the Dukes about it too.

CHOSEN TRACK

Paper and Iron (Notes and Coins)

This brilliant track has everything that was classic 1980 XTC: strident and purposeful drums, itchy-and-scratchy guitars on high-skank alert, both Andy and Colin on vocal duty – and whistling.

Rising Echoplex guitars introduce the track via the chorus melody, which is joined by a tension-building high synth note. All of a sudden, Terry and Colin barge their way in with a rhythm of threatening toms, double snare-strike and bass thump that knocks you for six as Andy deadpans the "Paper, iron, won't buy, Eden" refrain.

After Andy draws us in on solo vocal for the first chorus we are propelled into the verse via a beautifully repetitious descending interplay of drums, bass and guitars over which Partridge pines: "I pray the kids aren't starving, no chicken for the Sunday carving, I'll stay for one more farthing!"

And just as you think things can't get any better, we fall headfirst into a glorious outbreak of skanky guitars and rubbery bass over Terry's whack-'em-hard-and-hearty drums as Andy tells us of "taking home his notes and coins, every week". Dave answers Andy with his best guttural Keef licks in one channel, as Partridge himself plays full-on choppy skank in the other. Another deadpan refrain follows and then Colin joins Andy on the "Working for paper and for iron" hook, raising things a notch or five.

An equally punchy second verse and "take home my notes and coins" moves things on until we reach a goosebumps-inducing, middle-eight nirvana via the "I'm still a proud man" lyric that is bursting through Partridge's vocal delivery.

It's as if you can feel his pride and then resignation to it being a golden cage he's heading for and not necessarily a golden age.

Have I mentioned the tea-tray solo yet?

Black Sea was my first experience of XTC in the album format, when I bought it in 1980. The green bag, the lyric sheet, the discovery of the letters XTC in the front-cover backdrop. It's still my favourite XTC long player and I guess it always will be.

BEQUEATHED TRACK

Knuckle Down

Andy Partridge is one of a very select handful of songwriters that can make me grin from ear to ear. No, I take that back. He's the *only* songwriter that makes me grin like a Cheshire. *Knuckle Down* is a prime example of that smile factor. It's a beautiful rolling melody of open arms reaching out after putting the fists away. The key shifts fill you with optimism while the majestic, acoustic guitars are flighty and rustic, swelling at several imperious moments. Colin pulls out his best dub-style bass line to complement

Terry's equally reggae-infused thumping and Dave sounds like he's having fun twisting out that insistent bluesy riff before conjuring up a great distorted lead that fades out waaaay too soon! Apparently this solo was an outtake tacked onto the end but I'll forgive myself for wanting to believe it was otherwise. And let's not forget Andy's frog impersonations. I had the personal pleasure of getting this track some airplay on BBC Radio 6 Music several years ago, while being interviewed by Phill Jupitus on his breakfast show. We share a common love of all things XTC.

Steven Clark
BATTERIES, BIS

INHERITED TRACK
Knuckle Down

This never resonated as much as the other songs on *English Settlement* but taken out of context it's quite clearly another easy Partridge classic. I just used it as a guide to tell me the astonishing *Fly on the Wall* was coming next, but now my youth has been subsumed I can appreciate its place in the canon. Could quite easily have been a better follow-up single to *Senses* than *Ball and Chain* but we'll leave the politics out of that one. It's funny how the favourites change.

CHOSEN TRACK
Meccanik Dancing (Oh We Go!)

My first real introduction to XTC as a six year old is on some terrible *Hits 82*-style compilation, with *Senses Working Overtime* among the 20 songs strangled onto a single record. I play it over and over but am still wholly committed to Adam Ant so don't investigate further.

Thirteen years later, bis start playing shows outwith our hometown of Glasgow and each of us make mix tapes for the gruelling car journeys down to London. As the driver, I get first priority but at some point I relent and let John put his tape on. The first thing I hear is what sounds like an atonal guitar made of knives slicing through the speakers, then a groove kicks in that's like a 2 Tone record falling down

ARRANGEMENTS WORKING OVERTIME

MICHAEL JOHN MCCARTHY

XTC were one of the first bands that made me think about arrangements and the way instruments could be deployed in little details. With *Senses Working Overtime*, in particular, I became aware of what you could do with a drum fill.

DAVID WHITE

After the middle eight of *Senses* has shot off into orbit, it comes back down and then there's silence for a beat: "One, two, three, four, five, [silence], senses working overtime." Marillion's version, with Dave Gregory on guitar, is great but doesn't have that pause – shame as I was listening out for it! That absence is key to the song.

HUGH NANKIVELL

Terry Chambers has a Keith Moon element to him, which is unlike a lot of other drummers, but at the same time, Keith Moon wouldn't have left a gap. He'd have filled it up.

MICHAEL JOHN MCCARTHY

The drum part feels composed. Vampire Weekend's *Modern Vampires of the City* is one of my favourite albums. Similarly to XTC, there's a complexity of arrangement that has developed album by album. Apparently, part of their thinking was, "How can every instrument be playing a catchy part – even the drums?"

the stairs with someone soundchecking an organ a-rhythmically on top. I'm hooked. It settles down into a lop-sided disco: playground melodies, wee funny bits, whistling, those ska chanks. Then the happy/sad, major/minors kick in and a chorus of keening joyous melancholy. The disconnections hit my synapses and my only urge is to *make music like this*. And I'm still trying to. My mix tapes full of Britpop rubbish were thrown out of the car window and John's homemade XTC compilation was on rotation for the rest of 1995. We've been writing songs about social mores and discos ever since. I had 13 years to catch up on from *Hits 82**, but what a catalogue to absorb.

(*Found it on discogs: *Action Trax 1*. Also featured *Cambodia* by Kim Wilde – my other favourite.)

BEQUEATHED TRACK
Life Begins at the Hop
Another song about social mores and discos. Moulding nails the mixture of nostalgia and unknowable future, the 50s foam of the doo-wop bridge into a coming-of-age chorus that tugs all those heartstrings. Partridge gets to be the entertaining sideshow, undermining the misty-eyed whimsy with some brutal guitar clanks and chops in the gaps. There's never been a pizzicato solo like this one either, beautifully opening up into the chorus. For a simple song, it's so utterly complex. It's my kids' second favourite car song, beaten only by Madness's *House of Fun*.

Anne McCue
SOLO, RADIOS IN MOTION

INHERITED TRACK
Life Begins at the Hop
We were lucky – we had a great radio station called Double J in Australia that played all the newest English stuff. The first XTC song I remember hearing was *Radios in Motion*. I feel like *Life Begins at the Hop* was the next one and I loved it.

XTC's arrangements are exceptionally good. People probably didn't understand how good they were at the time. It's like a painting by Van Gogh; it's lasting, it's getting brighter and more illuminated as time goes on. It's so innovative and musically unexpected, in terms of the arrangements and the notes they chose. And these three Colin Moulding songs I'm talking about, *Life Begins at the Hop*, *Ten Feet Tall* and *Generals and Majors*, are all so very catchy.

CHOSEN TRACK
Ten Feet Tall
Usually, listening to music is like looking at a painting: you're not looking at the brush strokes, the technique and the journey the artist went on. But when you start listening to something to record it, you get to hear what they're doing and how interesting the chord progressions are. When I recorded a version of *Ten Feet Tall*, I didn't change the arrangement because it would have defeated the purpose. It's not like a blues song: "I'm just going to sing it the way I feel." The beauty of it is the arrangement. For me the fun was discovering what they were doing on the song – the guitars especially. *Ten Feet Tall* is so beautiful and actually very classical. When you work out the lead parts, you realise it's the same three chords but played all the way up the neck. It's a very good guitar lesson in itself. But just the chords themselves and the way he chooses them – Andy and Colin both do it – all of a sudden they'll go to an F major 7. It's something out of the blue and it works. That is not easy to do. They must hear those chord changes.

Dave Gregory plays the stuff I love – like on *Yacht Dance*, which is the song I would have chosen had I not covered *Ten Feet Tall*. Together, he and Andy Partridge are an amazing team. That's what a real band is, where they're all on the same page – and it's a very interesting page. Andy's ear is unusual and brilliant at the same time (you can be unusual and it can suck). I watched a video of him talking about playing guitar and he said, "Play an A scale over a G." He's like a revolutionary. You know how they say, "If they give you paper with lines, turn it sideways." He's like that.

I would love to hear some of these songs as string quartets. If you dive into those chord progressions and the arrangements and played them with a string section you would say it was contemporary classical music. The way it all comes together with XTC is perfect pop, so you don't take that aspect into consideration. That's the genius. XTC are one of the best bands ever and they're still rising to the top.

BEQUEATHED TRACK
Generals and Majors
I bought *Drums and Wires* and *English Settlement*, which are still my two favourites, and my sister had *Black Sea*, so I love that as well. *Generals and Majors* is another great song and it'll be an interesting conversation with Joseph Lekkas because he has broad knowledge and knows all the XTC albums. Joseph and I have a band called Radios in Motion and are just writing and recording our first song. We have talked about doing an XTC covers band too, but it would take a long time to do well. Here in Nashville we could do bluegrass covers – that would be really interesting! *[See page 143 for more on cover bands.]*

Joseph Lekkas
PALMGHOSTS, RADIOS IN MOTION

INHERITED TRACK
Generals and Majors
This song is classic XTC in so many ways. An energetic and syncopated drumbeat – colourful textures and melodies come at every turn. Like most XTC songs, the first time you hear it, you can't begin to process all the sonic layers coming at you. There are literally ten different melodic hooks in this song alone that weave together and somehow stay out of each other's trajectory. Never a boring moment.

CHOSEN TRACK
Heaven Is Paved with Broken Glass
I love the relatively simple melody, the tribal drums and the lyrics ("you made a fool of me and physics"... come on, Andy Partridge is the only person who could get away with a lyric like that!) I also love the strange synth sound that lurks in the background throughout the song, oddly shadowing the vocal melody. The staccato guitar work keeps the energy of the song constant.

Although I love it, I can understand why it was a B-side. It's got a great melody, like all XTC songs, but it doesn't change enough to be considered a single. It's also pretty long and the weird synth textures and tribal drums that I love could also turn off the casual listener to pop radio. A bit too wonderfully weird.

As a musician, I'm attracted to the avant-garde nature of it. XTC are masters of making high art into pop music. At their best, they are almost alien in their approach to writing and recording music. Even as a musician, it always takes me several listens to comprehend what is going on. Layers and layers of textures. Hooks for days. Honestly, everything by XTC has influenced me in some way. When I write songs, even if they only have a couple of chord changes, there has to be a steady flow of melodies and layers. XTC never allow boredom to set in, and I try to reflect that in my own compositions.

BEQUEATHED TRACK
Knights in Shining Karma
This song is very Beatle-esque in its mood, a bit like *Dear Prudence*, but almost jazzier and a bit more psychedelic. The lush layers of harmonies are also very beautiful. This song has a very wintry feel to me. Grey skies and deep introspection.

Rosie Vela
SOLO

INHERITED TRACK
Knights in Shining Karma
A wistful melody of lilting lacy guitars opens a beautifully hypnotic song. This song I love to hear before I go to sleep. It feels like home. The heart is home. I think of the joys of childhood. Jumping on the bed laughing. Hope, love, dreams and fairytales. Swings. Video of Andy splashing around in the pool with his children is a moment in paradise. Love and innocence. Sunshine of soul. Forever free. Beautiful.

CHOSEN TRACK
Across This Antheap

The beginning of *Antheap* reminds me of Miles Davis. It turns into a kool rock groove with a melody that makes me feel like a Middle Eastern belly dancer. We are like the antheap here: nurses, queens and drones. The main guitar riff feels like a King Tut groove. It's powerfully sung – "hey hey" – with kool jazzy rhythmic phrasing. This track burns.

The layer of sounds is an XTC spider web with intricate rhythms. The bass and drums drive it. The bass doesn't play on the downbeat. Beat "one" is empty. The main drums hit on beat "three". Everything in the background ploughs right on through like a rollercoaster.

Andy's vocal is passionate. Beautiful harmonies weave in and out like butterflies – "On and on and on and" – interlacing harmony with the melody in the tag grooves. The words are art. Incredible. "The fur is genuine but the orgasm's faked… hey, hey…The stars are laughing at us… On and on and on…"

BEQUEATHED TRACK
Prince of Orange

I have no idea what this song's about but when I hear it I think of Charlemagne and the futility of war. Lives lost in the battles for titles, crowns, lands and riches in a self-defeating waste of time. I love the sound of man crying softly as death approaches. It's so vulnerable. It says everything. Trophies are fleeting and fragile. So much for bravado. It always touches my soul. I *love* the tuneage of XTC.

James Hayward
FASSINE

INHERITED TRACK
Prince of Orange

This track really is a strange one: the fanfare organ that disintegrates into playful, tongue-in-cheek twinkles and flashes; the bedroom four-track production sound; the random crying fit at the end! I get the sense this was an experiment of throwing together disparate elements and seeing what appeared. Perhaps, it was an opportunity for Andy to give people a bare-bones look at what makes him tick with songwriting. A lot of Andy's trademark songwriting flourishes are present and accounted for. For me, the music represents a different type of protagonist like some form of rodent (named Louis XIV?), rather than rays of light. Then again, isn't context life's biggest casualty?

CHOSEN TRACK
Complicated Game

I like how the track sits alone in the first three albums as a black sheep, full of ideas above its station, but serving as the harbinger for a musical approach that XTC would explore in more depth later on. The gradual escalation of intensity; the collection of solid ideas that pass the baton across the track; that quirky noise solo that sounds like a polygon with a contorted breathing pattern floating through space… They all form something that sounds so much more ambitious and aspiring to transcendence to me than anything else from the first three albums. With this track, I like to picture tense, angsty, time-starved scenes unfolding in a 70s, rainy metropolis.

BEQUEATHED TRACK
Towers of London

Because those lyrics could've so easily been a trainwreck instead of a solid song. Fearless behaviour!

Guy Sigsworth
SONGWRITER

INHERITED TRACK
Towers of London

The XTC song where the four musicians most clearly merge their individual sounds to form one giant musical instrument. Even the Einstürzende Neubauten metal-bashing feels like a shading, a tint to the backbeat, rather than a wacky "I'm so weird" overdub or Art of Noise style sound grab. I hear subtle influences from the Beatles and the Kinks, and I also hear how this period of XTC influenced a whole set of US bands who probably all made far more money...

CHOSEN TRACK
This Is Pop

I especially connect with XTC's earliest and latest music. The two albums I know best are *White Music* and *Apple Venus Volume 1*. *White Music* is a wonderfully nutty debut. Short, fast songs with plenty of personality; plus, you have the distinctive keyboard playing of Barry Andrews. *This Is Pop* is a personal favourite. In the verses it's the way Andy stretches out every sibilant in the lyric, the way he plays this strange funk-gone-wrong chord progression, the way Colin plays exactly the right wrong notes against it, the way Terry plays that cool tom tom beat (it presages his wonderful beat for *Making Plans for Nigel*). Then you have a chorus which is so-pop-it's-not; with the deliberately dumb lyric "This is pop, yeah yeah" endlessly repeated.

It's nothing like anything I'd ever write, but it has this wonderful off-axis quality I utterly love. It's the sound of a band who always speak pop with a strange inflection. People notice that musically askew quality in Krautrock bands like Can and Neu. But to me, XTC has it too. Pretty much every great XTC song has some quirk in the harmony somewhere, some tic in the guitar voicing, some risqué note in the bass. It's not a matter of using sophisticated jazz chords or something, more a matter of not streamlining, not self-censoring bold ideas out of the songwriting.

BEQUEATHED TRACK
Easter Theatre

On *Apple Venus* I love the *Wicker Man* pagan imagery, especially on *Easter Theatre*. You'd have to be deaf not to hear the *Magical Mystery Tour*-era Beatles influence, complete with *Penny Lane*-style trumpet. But the result, for once, isn't pastiche. It feels more like Partridge and Moulding have taken that most ambitious period of the Beatles as their point of departure, specifically as a way to challenge themselves. The chord structure of the song is amazingly brave – it's much closer to, I don't know, Prokofiev or Benjamin Britten than to World Party or Oasis. It's even got a melodic guitar solo – but one accompanied by bassoon and woodwind, rather than hard-riffing barre chords. The song has this perfect counterpoint between spiky dissonances in the verses and smooth, sweeter chords in the choruses.

Sarah Palmer
FASSINE

INHERITED TRACK
Easter Theatre

This is among many wonderful songs on *Apple Venus*, especially my favourite, *I Can't Own Her*. XTC's break from the studio for many years really did help the creativity and experimentation on their work here. They're not confined by anything at all.

The eruption of strings and horns elevate me into elation, and I love how Andy often sings right on the edge of his range. This song for me, feels like it could accompany a sequel to *The Tale of Peter Rabbit*, where it follows lots of mischievous little rabbits setting out for a big adventure!

CHOSEN TRACK
I Can't Own Her

Apple Venus Volume 1 and this song in particular illustrates just how much the band experimented and expanded as composers, arrangers and musicians in the studio. The orchestration is glorious, the classical elements giving new light to the music. I love the string arrangements that erupt into a Disney-like euphoria with the tremolo and string-run embellishments that then cascade back down into gloom. Lyrically, I love the vulnerability and honesty of this track and the longing tone in Andy's voice.

BEQUEATHED TRACK
Books Are Burning

What did we learn from covering *That Wave*? Complexity! And never to cover XTC again! Though, I think we did a pretty good job. The original has a wave-like feel and we wanted to see if we could do that too but in a much more chaotic and stormy fashion. The song I've chosen to bequeath is *Books Are Burning*, also from *Nonsuch*. The brilliant simplicity of this track is, again, another reason why XTC are so revered; the space in the song, the parts they choose to not put in, are what makes it so perfect.

Sean McGhee
SINGER, SONGWRITER, PRODUCER AND PROGRAMMER

INHERITED TRACK
Books Are Burning
This is an interesting song in so many ways. The arrangement is quite minimal. It would have been easy to go down the Jeff-Lynne-doing-the-Beatles/ELO production route because you've got this hint of a *Hey Jude* singalong at the end with the backing vocals, but that's obscured by those marvellous guitar solos. I'm not normally first off the block to say, "Oh that guitar solo was great," because I like solos to be melodically driven. Dave has this flashier, studied rock approach that's very effective, then when Andy takes his turn it's much more freewheeling, improvisatory and unusual, and hits on things you wouldn't expect. You forget what a good guitar player he is because he doesn't get much opportunity to put that flash right at the front of things. It's a beautiful way to end the record and it's one of their best songs as well: in form and in concept. I love the lyric, the melody and the way it's put together.

When you get to mid-80s XTC, the Dukes and specifically *Pale and Precious*, it's like a switch goes on and they say, "OK, we're not afraid of doing pastiche now." That can be dangerous. The interesting things in art often happen because people try to recreate something and fail, but the failure is in itself interesting. XTC could easily have gone, "Oh, we can rip that stuff off exactly," but they found a way to weave it into the work in an appealing way. Another song on *Nonsuch* is *Wrapped in Grey*, where it would have been easy to go 100% *Pet Sounds* on it, but it maintains enough of its own character because they're being thoughtful about how they approach the material. *Books Are Burning* is the same. It's also a tremendous closing track.

CHOSEN TRACK
Love on a Farmboy's Wages
Mummer is my favourite XTC record. Part of it goes back to the length. It's perfectly constructed. Every track pulls its weight and it's over before it's become too long. *Love on a Farmboy's Wages* has such an unusual sound; those odd sounding dead toms. Steve Nye's production leads out of *Tin Drum*; if you listen to *Talking Drum* by Japan and then to *Love on a Farmboy's Wages*, there's a thread connecting them. Steve Nye is an extremely good engineer and in an era when everybody was getting into bigger sounding artificial reverbs, he made it all very close and dry – quite 70s really. You've got that beautiful contained drum sound and this minimal bass line – and the choices Colin makes musically are some of his best. Quite often it's one note for quite a long time and then when it stops being one note at the end of the chorus and it's in harmony with the vocal, it's such a simple choice but it's a beautiful one.

My favourite bit – and it's one of my favourite moments in any XTC song – is the four bars at the end of the middle eight, after he sings the words "And it's breaking my back." Andy is the king of discord and really knows how to use discordant harmony in a pop context. He's never one to go for the obvious chords. For most of *Love on a Farmboy's Wages*, the chord choices are slightly more standard that you might expect from him as a writer. But when you get to that strange moment of suspension at the end of the middle eight, it feels like Steely Dan have been beamed in for four bars. It's a really unusual chord; it's not major, it's not minor, it's lacking both of the things that would make it that. It has this uncertainty that perfectly expresses what's going on around it lyrically. Then it resolves back into the sunshine of the major chord when the pre-chorus comes in straight afterwards. It's wonderful.

It's such an unusual and lovely song, it's amazing it did so badly commercially. It landed right at the end of new pop. You start to think about Trevor Horn, Dollar, ABC and these exquisite pop mini-symphonies – and if that's the kind of thing that's exciting at that moment, then this couldn't be further removed. This was the point when XTC stopped being a live band and started to explore what it means to use the studio as an instrument, what you can do with arrangements and what you can do with sound that is outside what you can do with four people playing in a room. *Love on a Farmboy's Wages* is a perfect summation of that approach because every sound and every colour is in the right place. Every song on *Mummer* has got something new going on in it.

BEQUEATHED TRACK
Wounded Horse
I want to see if someone can find some goodness in an XTC song I don't like. *Wounded Horse* is a boring bluesy trudge. It's everything I don't expect from XTC. "OK, you got divorced, I get it. I got it on *Apple Venus Volume 1*, thanks, so I don't need to get it again." Once you've written *Your Dictionary*, what else is there to say? I'd love to hear if somebody can find some joy in *Wounded Horse*.

Anton Barbeau
SOLO

INHERITED TRACK
Wounded Horse
It's admittedly not one of my favourite tracks, but it's on one of my favourite albums. I adore *Wasp Star*. I've never spent any time listening to *Wounded Horse* away from the context of the record itself and it fits the record really well. It's a gorgeous recording, as everything on *Wasp Star* is. I'm a little less brutal about it than Sean McGhee. I'm such an album guy that I'm pretty forgiving. I listen to something from start to finish; I don't pick out a track and fixate on it. So *Wounded Horse* has always been just part of that record.

There are all the bits and pieces; that guitar that sounds like it's a cranked-up amp over in that corner of the room, I've never really noticed the bass before and, of course, Colin's doing his thing. And the solo section is great, that noisy guitar with the keyboard behind it. It's a gorgeous pop construction, even though, over all, it's a straight track. It's interesting in its own way for XTC to play it straight. It serves the sentiment.

One of the things we love Andy for so much is his blatant honesty. His personal life is something he shares openly. Knowing the story of the song, it's a little bit raw, but the track itself, however bluesy, is very polished. It's a fine piece of pop music absolutely expressing betrayal. Andy does that really well. *Your Dictionary* is actually a much more uncomfortable thing for me to listen to. I don't think I like that song and it's partly because of the sentiment. It's Andy expressing something that is so raw and personal (and more power to him) that it makes for an uncomfortable listen, whereas this one is a softer, sweetened version. It's interesting that on the same record, *You and the Clouds Will Still Be Beautiful* was also written for his wife. It's nice to see that balance among the songs because that's a real truth, that life is messy and complex, and we're inconsistent and contradictory creatures. If Andy were to have made only a divorce album, that would be a painfully unlistenable experience, but *Wasp Star* is full of so much joy as well.

CHOSEN TRACK
Senses Working Overtime
I can't believe I got to talk about this one. For me, it's a life-changing song. I was in a band with a guy who was the one who said, "You don't know the Clash? You don't know Joe Jackson? You don't know Elvis Costello? Here, you've got to listen to this record." After rehearsal, this guy would play us everything we needed to know. He played XTC and I remember *Making Plans for Nigel* and thinking, "This is brilliant. What a great track." I'd mixed up XTC with Gang of Four and thought Sara Lee was the bass player for

LONG OR SHORT?

JOHN IRVINE

My favourite XTC songs are usually the more lengthy ones: *Complicated Game, Melt the Guns, Train Running Low on Soul Coal, Snowman* et al. My favourite album, *English Settlement*, has an average track length of 4:50. No other album of theirs comes near this average, and I'm sure it's not a fluke that I like it the most – it's progressive, with a small "p". Furthermore, it could tell us that XTC is best over a larger-scale piece.

....

MICHAEL JOHN MCCARTHY

I'm not sure. I don't think of length as being one of the defining characteristics of XTC at all.

....

HUGH NANKIVELL

XTC are utterly not revolutionary. They're completely and fantastically evolutionary. They've taken the past couple of hundred years of songwriting form and distilled it. The craft of songwriting is what they're brilliant at. *Travels in Nihilon* is an exception because it is not so like songwriting. When you think of bands that do extended jams, they lose the form and structure of the song. XTC work within that structure. They give themselves three minutes to make a perfect song.

XTC, so when I saw the video for *Senses Working Overtime* I was surprised they didn't have a woman playing bass. But that song changed my life in an instant.

I knew I liked XTC from having heard *Drums and Wires*, but *Senses Working Overtime* set me on a different musical and emotional course. I had been listening to so much synth pop – Gary Numan and Ultravox, which I still love – but hearing the construction of *Senses Working Overtime* as a piece of music, the craft that goes into it, but also the genius inspiration made me think, "I want to be a real songwriter." I was probably 15 when I first heard it and this is the one that made me think, "This is how songs are supposed to go."

I grew up listening to the Beatles, of course, but XTC was part of this new thing. *Senses Working Overtime* stood out like nothing I'd ever heard. Every single time I listen to it, I get that same feeling. That's what I want out of so much pop music. Somehow, the song evolves; I hear it differently every time, but its magic is timeless. It just sits there like a perfect chair. With that four-piece line-up, everybody's right there, everybody's performance is perfectly matched. The verses are strange, with that medieval quality and the deep backing vocals – I still don't know what that sound is and it's perfect. What a gorgeous track.

The lyrics of *Senses* are as detailed and evocative as anything Andy writes. He's always imagery-rich in his writing, but this one stands out; the lyrics don't serve the song in the same way that almost everything else he writes does. He is describing things of the senses and yet there's something ephemeral about it. He keeps giving you nouns, details, colours and tastes and yet there is this magic that's happening. It takes you somewhere else; it's not about the details. *Wounded Horse* is about the image of biting your tongue out, for example, and so many of Andy's songs take the music to spin around the images. But *Senses* takes me somewhere other. You're only barely there for kicking the football into space or the lemons and limes; the song comes from somewhere other and takes you somewhere other.

I wouldn't dream of going near *Senses Working Overtime* to cover it because it's a perfect piece of music. It's untouchably beautiful. I've tried to rewrite it many, many times in my own songwriting, it's one of my templates, but I would never try to cover it.

BEQUEATHED TRACK
Great Fire

I've chosen *Great Fire* because, like *Senses Working Overtime*, it's not just the song itself, it's the experience of hearing it. I was obsessed with *English Settlement* and on a small community radio station I heard *Great Fire*. I knew it was XTC, but I couldn't track down the song title. I knew it had fire in the title and I knew I had to have it. I went out to Tower Records and looked through all the XTC records I didn't own yet. I bought *Black Sea* because it had *Burning with Optimism's Flames* and I thought maybe that was the one. Of course, I loved it, but it wasn't it. I went back and bought *White Music* with *I'll Set Myself on Fire*. None of them had the song, but I'd become a lifetime committed XTC fan. It wasn't for another six months before the album was released in the US because it was delayed, so when it came out with that song on it I was overjoyed. That one song cost me a lot of money!

Henning Ohlenbusch
SOLO, GENTLE HEN

INHERITED TRACK
Great Fire

I like to imagine Andy Partridge teaching this song to the rest of the band. "OK, it starts like this. Then it goes into this other bit, then it all changes to this thing, hold on, now it's a different part, OK, wait, wait, now there's a new section, OK, back to that other bit, now the second thing, do an instrumental thing here but let's do it all different, OK, you get it? Cool. Key change! OK now this new thing…" The structure of the song is like a peek into a squirrel's brain. "I'm in a tree! I'm on a rock! Look up! Run over here! Dig! Look, a nut!"

But, like so many XTC songs, once you know it, it all makes sense. The aggressive machine-like intro complete with fire bell (ride cymbal), the regal British choruses, the muted staccato guitar solo (which plays in a round; left speaker first, right speaker follows). The comical brass animal noises. The cellos whinnying. This is XTC on fire. Bring water. Bring *waaaaaater*!

CHOSEN TRACK
Scarecrow People

February and March in Western Massachusetts have a tendency to stretch on forever. Outside of the frosted college dorm window, the campus trees were a tangle of bare branches, the ground if not covered in snow, was frozen and hard. Sand and dirt that had splashed up from the roads coated everything. Further off in the distance, cornless stalks leaned on each other in rows like soldier skeletons marching towards the frozen Connecticut River.

And here was this new XTC album. Its modern digital sounding production as cold and sleek as the weather. Though the warmth of *Skylarking* and *English Settlement* was not present, I found myself happily sifting through the gangly dense production. There was so much going on in my Walkman headphones. Sounds coming at me from the left, right, close, far, up, down, this album was going to take hundreds of listens to fully understand. But that's what we did back then. You only had so much music to chose from so what you chose became part of your family.

When I look back at that album and those aimless times, one microscopic half second always stands out as the flashing beacon atop it all. At the three minute mark of the eighth song on the album, a lone woodblock takes a one hit solo and to me, it's the highpoint of the year.

Scarecrow People is seemingly designed to be hated by any person who is not already a seasoned fan of XTC. You'd have to have allowed your cells to be infected over the years by the snotty, in-your-face, singing of Andy Partridge. You need to be already versed in the dissonant and disagreeable quest to never sing the expected note, to be at all times open to that aggressively contrarian shove in an unfamiliar direction.

The melody makes no sense. Until it does. The bass and the guitar usually are moving in different directions from each other. The percussion is relentless and it comes at you from all directions like you fell down a staircase covered in bones and broken xylophones. None of it is comprehensible. Until it is.

This incessant barrage of notes and rhythms sticks into you like pins and needles and as the song ploughs on, it starts to connect. It sounds like the music scarecrows would make, if their A&R guys and producers just left them alone. When even the crows are nowhere to be seen, the music starts to sound ancient and earthy and crunchy like brittle frozen corn stalks.

A little more than halfway through the song, there's a tension build like no other. Andy's voice strains to hold a single high note as the guitar rises and rises and the bass falls and falls and the percussion unrelentingly increases its intensity. It's a volcano about to erupt, a balloon blown up too far, a piano string wound too tight, a spring stretched too far and then, at its zenith, when it finally reaches its limit, a single woodblock "clop" comically relieves all the tension and the music crashes back in with laughing fiddles and musical applause.

That little clop is musical perfection. It's a character in itself. It's humorous but powerful, tiny but crucial. Who's idea was it? Did someone else fight against it in the studio? Was it spontaneous or was it intentionally sought out? I don't want to know the answers.

BEQUEATHED TRACK
Scissor Man
I knew the German story, *Der Struwwelpeter*, before the song. Flipping through a picture book as a child, I stumbled upon this terrifying threat of a tale. Now whenever I hear the song that gangly drawing appears in my head. I love the energy of the song

as it is on *Drums and Wires*, but then I heard the live version, which was a million times faster and more manic. Woah. Andy has this way of singing words as sound effects. It's all automatic onomatopoeia with him and nowhere is it apparent than here. "Snipping snipping snipping."

Dennis Locorriere
DR HOOK

INHERITED TRACK
Scissor Man
XTC's unconventional but perfect arrangements make them a top contender for the most original band in the world. *Scissor Man* is an exciting example of how they played with the rhythm to drive the story. And, then comes the moment when Mr Partridge, once again, reveals his affection for a fetching echo to vocally bounce around on: "Snipping, snipping…"

CHOSEN TRACK
Making Plans for Nigel
The first track on *Drums and Wires* was a "shut up and pay attention" moment for me. I'd been aware of the band for a while but, as I listened to the beginning of that song, an extraordinary leap forward was immediately evident to my ears. It was like a whole new kind of music!

The vocals were confident, placing the cool lyrics right in your face. The guitars and bass weaved urgently in, out and around each other. The song was interesting, challenging and catchy as hell. And, then, you had the drums! Oh, those drums! XTC has always known something about working with rhythm that most bands never even consider. On *Nigel*, Terry Chambers' exciting, inventive style drives the track forward while laying down a foundation so solid that playing against it must have been irresistible to explore. Just listen to the fantastic guitar solo!

As *D&W* played on, one song after another pulled me further in. The addition of Dave Gregory at that time could only be classed as a genius move. I played the album several more times over the next couple of days. I knew I'd found something I was gonna love and return to for a long time to come. The whole XTC catalogue has since fallen into that category. Early releases, *Go 2* and *White Music*, had gone into my record collection and were enjoyed, but, after hearing *Making Plans for Nigel*, XTC went straight into my brain and has never left.

BEQUEATHED TRACK
Melt the Guns
I've chosen this one because it has, unfortunately, been relevant for far too long.

François Ribac and Eva Schwabe
COMPAGNIE RIBAC-SCHWABE

INHERITED TRACK
Melt the Guns
François: This is clearly the old XTC when the singing was hysterical and intense. Andy was a singer like David Byrne where you don't know if he is psychotic or playing the role of someone who is crazy. It was the same with Pere Ubu. They are not in the Beatles tradition where you sing as yourself. For *Melt the Guns*, it was the early XTC when Andy was always super excited. I wonder who is crazy – is it the singer or the figure created by the singer? This is part of the charm and pleasure of this band, this LP and this song. When you ask what a star is, what makes a popular actor or singer, I would say it is somebody who creates a tension between what is supposed to be the private, authentic, real person and the performance on the record or the stage.

When we hear this song we understand that those people were listening to many types of music. It's very particular to this band. It starts with a lot of neo-Brazilian sounds, you have the arpeggio of Dave's 12-string, which borrows from the Kinks and the Beatles, and at the end you have this rim-shot, tack-tack-tack-tack. Then there are all the echoed voices with their onomatopoeia. It's no longer new wave.

The last point is what we love about XTC: their incredible fantasy. Andy was always reading books about history, soldiers and battles. All this comes into the songs and every song is a complete world. Because I am French, I can listen to English songs without paying any attention to the words. It's a big advantage because you can invent your own fantasy. So, OK, the topic of the song is about the guns, but it's not obligatory for me to be connected with that. If you compare *Melt the Guns* with *Books Are Burning*, both have a political meaning, but the earlier song is so crazy, at the limit of irony, you don't know exactly if it's true or not, so for me, the political meaning is slightly different. It's more Tim Burton than Jean-Paul Sartre. By the time of *Books Are Burning*, the singer became Andy Partridge.

CHOSEN TRACK
Jason and the Argonauts
François: In 2003, we came to a very rainy and grey city in England called Swindon and visited Andy. I asked him about this song because I was intrigued by the Greek mythological background and how he would collect a story like *Jason and the Argonauts*. He told me something very important for me as a composer and it helped me understand how he works. He said for him everything was pictorial. Paintings were important to him, not only because he was himself making paintings but also because it was a specific way to have ideas and translate his ideas into music.

He thought of *Jason and the Argonauts* as a ship sailing on the ocean and he thought about the waves. The waves are the da-da-de-da-da-da-da-de pattern, which would normally be something you would play on guitar, piano or voice as a training exercise [*sings scales*]. It's very banal, but if you take that and make a lot of variations, modulations, strange and interesting chromaticisms of the theme (G A B C# D C# B A – if I'm not wrong), while at the same time singing about somebody sailing on the sea, you have a different meaning. The compositional process is very interesting. It's not somebody who says, "Let's take a riff," or, "Let's take the sound of this record."

To make the song, it seems Andy connected his first idea about this mythological story to his music using pictures. Pictorial ideas are the translation between the Greek story, the band and the song. It's fascinating. What I like on *Jason* is Andy not only plays the waves with the theme but also he is able to entangle music, images and lyrics. He told me when he composes he puts together lyrics and chords from the beginning. That's not so common for songwriters who often find chords and add lyrics afterwards.

Also important for me – and Andy has spoken about this – is Judee Sill. I adore her music and her voice and when you listen attentively to how Andy sings some end notes in *Jason and the Argonauts* it is coming from her. It's an inflection at the end of notes. The last thing is Dave Gregory. You can find on the web a few live versions of this song, including one at the Rockpalast in 1982, when Dave at 2:36 has an excellent, strange and hyper-modern solo on 12-string guitar. You see how he framed the sound of the band. On stage and probably when they were jamming and recording, they were able to pass the borders of the songs. With this incredible, contemporary 12-string solo, where you don't really have a pitch or a tune – it goes in a non-tonal way – you see how free they were. They could go in a direction you wouldn't expect by only listening to the song on the record. It gives an important focus on the place of Dave.

BEQUEATHED TRACK
Bungalow

Eva: I listened to *Bungalow* driving around the south of France, so to me *Bungalow* is connected to the forests and the high Scots pines. When you hear that song, you always think that around the next turn the bungalow will come. It's a very nice word to sing: "Bungalow." I am German and for me it's a 60s house, very modern. They built a bungalow for Chancellor Erhard in 1963 and the chancellors of Germany had to live in this bungalow because this was modern! The word comes from Hindi. It's a word for a house with one floor and a thatched roof: bangla. So it comes directly from the colonial work of the British!

For me, it's very melancholic. You see the dream of the bungalow and the end of the song is – clack! – there's no end. This is astonishing for me and a kind of impression of the 60s. Colin uses very few words, but it's enough because he repeats the word "bungalow" so much that everybody can dream about it.

François: The meaning is not the meaning of the song itself, but the listener's meaning. The musicians can say how it is made, but *Bungalow*, for us, is being on the road in 1999 in the south of France. Something very interesting is the phrase "luxury accommodation traps the sun". It could be, like many songwriters, that he took it from some newspaper advert. It's typically British; the half-obscurity of the lyrics. You have to ask the songwriters what the meaning was, like a Dylan song. The obscurity makes it possible to remember the song as connected to travelling with the car in the forest because the meaning is very open. The song's production adds to this obscurity because there's a filter on the voice in the beginning. The song's structure is unconventional and there's something typical of the Beatles when you have something very flat – "bungalow" – and suddenly the chorus and bridge are so open, and you have interesting chords. Everything is obscure, not only the meaning of the words.

Colin Moulding has a talent that means when you hear a song you feel you already know it. It's so clear, it's like it already existed. He has an incredible talent to put chords and melody together and they sound like you always knew them, but at the same time, the sound, the arrangement and the structures are always a bit strange. He is the more eccentric composer of the band, whereas Andy is always understood as the most eccentric because of his singing and he's an eccentric guy. Andy has an incredible catalogue of songs, but Colin is someone who is very classic and completely strange.

He's also an extraordinary singer. He has a control of his voice which is, in French, *formidable*. From the beginning it was more controlled than Andy's. I always loved Andy's voice, but he became a very round singer, really controlled and personal, only in the mid 80s. Colin always had a controlled, deep voice. It's an important aspect of their music: it's a band with two voices, not one. People love them so much because of that.

Mike Keneally
FRANK ZAPPA, ANDY PARTRIDGE, SOLO

INHERITED TRACK
Bungalow

Colin's purest embrace of corn, and so committed that it becomes a thing of hugely wistful beauty. The chord progressions evoke broken seaside nostalgia with aplomb – who else in a rock band in the 90s made music that felt like this? And the melody/harmonic structure is highlighted by one particularly unexpected heart-tug – the pyramiding melody "we can fly a---" on the E flat minor 7, resolving on a completely left-field half-step-up E minor 7 on "---WAY"... so beautiful. The second time it happens it's additionally punctuated afterward by a magical bell-tree swoosh – terribly cinematic in an unashamedly romantic way (for me this moment echoes, certainly unintentionally, the similar gentle "swoosh" that accompanies Chance the Gardener dipping his umbrella into the water in the final scene of *Being There*, and it's just as eye-moistening for me). If *Bungalow* was meant to be the least bit sardonic in a Ray Davies *Shangri-La* sort of fashion, that doesn't in any way detract from its profound emotion – if anything, the layers of complexity enhance its depth of feeling.

CHOSEN TRACK
Roads Girdle the Globe

I was pretty late getting around to XTC – I didn't give any of their music a serious listen until I saw the then-current *Senses Working Overtime* video on MTV and fell powerfully in love with them, at which point I had the blessed privilege to explore their already rich back-catalogue of albums, EPs and singles. *Drums and Wires* was a particular joy because I found within its grooves, unexpectedly, a strong adherence to avant-garde rock sonorities and rhythms. Even the fact the US pressing I had was mastered quietly – just like *The Henry Cow Legend*! – was wonderful to me, as it made me feel I had to lean way into it to decode its mystery. I was ensnared by *Senses* because I thought on the aural evidence that Andy had to be a Beatle fan like me; what a delight to listen to *Roads Girdle the Globe* and suss out that he was evidently also a Beefheart fan like me, with the clangorous, seemingly at-odds dual guitars meshing into an ugly-beautiful machine that runs smooth and takes no prisoners. Un-transcribable for usage in the *Eleven Different Animals* songbook because of the complexity of its overlapping guitar voicings, this song is joy from start to finish – the rubber-band bass intro leading into an ever-widening roadway of clashing chordal delights, its lyrics a *Trout Mask*-procession of automotive haiku, its forward propulsion unyielding. The guitars are clean-with-an-edge, again *Trout Mask*-style, so that while the effect is satisfyingly nasty and clashy, each compound chord rings out with complete compositional clarity, every note audible and expertly chosen.

BEQUEATHED TRACK
Ladybird

And then, practically at the moment I became a hardcore XTC fan, collecting their music and magazine articles as though I were just discovering the Beatles once again, it seemed the whole thing was in danger of crashing down – from what I could glean from the early-80s alternative rock press, the group was quite possibly a done deal after the *English Settlement* non-tour. All of a sudden it seemed this Partridge fellow, about whom I found myself caring very deeply, was a goner on a Syd-like scale. So what blessed relief to come across the *Great Fire* import single at my local Off the Record store, and what glory to eventually buy *Mummer* and find, not a songwriter, singer and musician bloodied and cowering as a result of his trials, but one with an increasing writerly ambition that paid off continually, and a seeming positivity that radiated from the grooves, from the first beat of *Beating of Hearts* to the final joyous piss-off of *Funk Pop a Roll*. And how validating to my sensibilities, as someone who'd taken to extolling Andy's harmonic sophistication to some disbelievers who'd written him off because he "sang like that," to find he'd expanded his chordal palette with *Ladybird*, which adds a jazzy sensitivity theretofore a bit buried in the band's discography. There's mastery in the way the opening chords twist around the same repeating two-note clarion call, and beautiful usage of the sort of clusters only a piano can provide on the verses' resolution chord, which I *think* is the notes A#, B, C# and D# over an E bass (what to call it?) - not the sort of chord you'll find in your Mel Bay guitar book with accompanying graph. And there's gratifying structural complexity in the way the song has a seemingly unending supply of bridges: surely "All through the wintertime" starts the bridge, but wait, what should we call the part that starts "And as you're walking past"? Then why not have another variation on the first bridge with "All through the iron season" for good measure? This is pure generosity on the part of the composer. Beautifully sensitive performances from every one of the lads on this also - Pete's brushwork, Colin's fretless, Dave's piano, Andy's acoustic, all deft and perfect. And a lyric and vocal performance just custom-built for a romance in its budding, wide-eyed early stages. *Ladybird* is utterly heart-warming.

Andrew Falkous
FUTURE OF THE LEFT, MCLUSKY

INHERITED TRACK
Ladybird
Somebody described *Ladybird* to me as middle of the road. That's misleading because when you listen to what's actually going on, like the bizarre melody and the weird chords, there's something strange about it. There's just a weird lurch to it. The definition of middle of the road to me is you know exactly what's coming next. That's the whole purpose of a Foo Fighters song. There are bands who are successful because they sound instantly familiar because they're not doing anything new.

The first time I listened to *Ladybird*, I thought it was almost the exact mid-point of *Pet Sounds* and the Beatles with loads of messing to make it more interesting to the person writing it. The style is jazz but the voice is still distinctive.

The melody sounds as if it's going to give you something you expect and then twists. There is a similarity between *Complicated Game* and *Ladybird* in that if we were looking at it classically, the last note in the sequence is "wrong". When he sings "complicated ga-a-a-me", the last note, both vocally and in terms of the chord, isn't what you expect it to be. It's the same with "if I woke you with my thinking/Ladybird," which introduces a bass note at the end that is totally unexpected. It's unsettling because you're listening to this thing that should all be familiar but it's touching you inappropriately - not in a way that is actionable in a law-and-order sense, but something that makes you look around and go, "Did the cat just walk past?"

Mummer was the first album after they stopped touring and even with good live monitoring there are some lyrics that are difficult to pitch. When he sings "are" at the end of "No weeping willow was ever as beautiful, sad as you are", it sounds like even he's not sure how he's pitching it. You can also hear it in the line before in "wish" about 1:43 in. It sounds like he's got a melody, but this one word, he kind of just half says. It's as if it's part of the melody, but just a bridge to get from the first half to the second.

Having listened to *Mummer* a couple of times, I'm very grateful Mike Keneally has chosen one of my favourite songs off it. My note says, "And Andy wrote a song about a fucking ladybird." I'm sure on some level it could be concerned with the human condition, but I suspect it's just about a ladybird.

CHOSEN TRACK
Complicated Game
Drums and Wires could have been made last week (apart from *Making Plans for Nigel* which is very

much of its time, as great a song as it is). It's so brilliant to have the last two songs on the album being the best two songs. The first time I heard *Drums and Wires* I liked it a lot, but to have it topped off at the end is an incredible feeling. The vocal performance on *Complicated Game* is demented. It is either somebody with a throat infection (and I mean that in a good way) or who doesn't give the merest fuck about sounding cool. At times, he sings the wrong notes and sounds like a cartoon character. The thing that always attracts me to music is somebody being themselves, the idea of a personality being fully revealed to you. In *Scissor Man* you get the more playful part of it, but *Complicated Game* sounds like a man having a breakdown.

The vocal performance is so ridiculous: some of the lower notes on it are just wonderful. And the guitar solo is fantastic. It's got nothing to do with the song - in fact, Andy recorded it without his headphones on. I did it once myself, but only because the headphones fell off. That's what guitar solos are meant to be, not expressions of time spent learning scales in a bedroom. It's meant to be rock'n'roll.

We have a rule in our band that if somebody comes up with a part or a riff, nobody's allowed to find out what key it's in. You've just got to play, to get it wrong. In music when you get something wrong, you create something unique. Whereas, if somebody says, "Well, this is on the third fret," then everybody goes there and starts playing there and you end up with something you'd expect. There is an adventure in just putting your hand on the guitar and saying, "We're going to write a song around the first farty noise I make."

The Pixies were my big band and when Andy is being expansive, I hear Black Francis. The other comparison for me is between Talking Heads and XTC because they were around roughly at the same time. Talking Heads had a sense of the ridiculous - you only have to see the *Stop Making Sense* suits to know that - but a lot of the people involved were cool, using the accepted parameters of the word, or deliberately silly: "We are being silly now, but we're still cool."

With XTC, there's no pretence of cool. They're from Swindon. That for me is where the difference is. The things that are wrong in *Complicated Game* seem instinctively wrong as opposed to designed wrong. I'm not saying one is better or worse, but I would prefer an instinctive wrong (and I love Talking Heads).

I get the impression Andy just turned up and coughed his way through the song and went, "What do you reckon?" They listened to it later and they went, "Yeah, that can go on the record. Even your weird, slightly-out-of-time guitar-tapping at the start." That makes it for me. If Talking Heads were doing that, the guitar at the start would have been regimented to a click or whatever, whereas with XTC it's more human.

When it comes to the dynamics, if you think about a modern pop record, I always use the example of a Butch Vig production where everything is exactly as loud as you'd expect it should be. That's partly because if it's going to be played on the radio, it needs to be a constant loudness to keep people engaged. The start of *Complicated Game* sounds like an accident. It sounds like you've just wandered in to this person whispering.

At the end of *Complicated Game* you've got the vocals echoing over each other. That can at times make it sound like some kind of industrial record from five or six years later, but one thing those records don't have is that song. Even after very limited exposure in the last year and half, *Complicated Game* is definitely in my top ten/twenty songs.

BEQUEATHED TRACK

Helicopter

I've chosen this one because when I first listened to *Drums and Wires* it was the song that grabbed me least. It just seemed insubstantial the first time I listened to it, but I've changed my mind on that now. All it took was listening to it more than once. As a musician you can come to conclusions very quickly, but you know you wouldn't want people to come to those conclusions about your art.

Tracey Bryn
VOICE OF THE BEEHIVE

INHERITED TRACK
Helicopter

The early XTC stuff was a huge reason that I moved to London in 1985. Then, I became obsessed with everything from *Skylarking* on. I also love *Nonsuch* and nearly chose *Then She Appeared* as one of my songs. Going back to *Helicopter* reminds me of the energy and excitement of the new-wave music that was coming out of the UK in the late 1970s when I was a teenager. Growing up in California, everything seemed so homogenised in comparison and London was where I wanted to be.

CHOSEN TRACK
Holly Up On Poppy

I can never believe it when I say or write this, but I got to write a few songs with Andy Partridge. I was so incredibly nervous on the train to his home in Swindon for the songwriting session that I thought I was going to be sick. I drank two mini-bottles of brandy on the way there and it didn't touch the nerves. (I was hardcore then.) I finally got to his home and he opened the door and... he was an actual human being! Then, he spoke and the voice was so familiar that it caught me off guard. I tried to be cool and appear somewhat gathered but I was scared. He asked me in and I noticed all of these homemade toys in his living room. It turned out that Andy had made them for his children. I was standing there, even more enchanted with him. But, still nervous. My hands were at my side and I felt the tiniest little hand slide into mine. It was his little boy, Harry, and he gave me his dinosaur and told me that I could have it. He looked exactly like Andy must have at four years old. He both melted and stole my heart. They both did. So, when I hear the song, I remember the toy horse with the little hand-painted poppy on its cheek in their living room.

Besides the personal meaning of the song, I love the way it musically unfolds. That steady even guitar strum at the intro and then the instruments almost answering back to each other and it assumes this kind of wobbly merry-go-round innocence (with a hint of sinister lurking in the background). Then, his gentle vocals come in with these beautiful and gentle lyrics (that the critics took as a drug reference). As usual with Andy's writing, I adore the way he changes the meaning while keeping the same sounding word: "Where they make beautiful girls/ Where they bake beautiful girls." Classic Andy. Innocent then dark.

The line "She talks and banners unfurl/Their secrets crayoned in swirls" – forget it. It doesn't get better than that. It means even more when you realise that he's singing about his daughter. Beautiful.

BEQUEATHED TRACK
Shake You Donkey Up

I know this is a song that divides fans because of its off-beat rhythms and country-and-western stylings, so I thought it would be fun to see what another musician made of it.

Chris Butler
THE WAITRESSES, TIN HUEY, SOLO

INHERITED TRACK
Shake You Donkey Up

My first reaction was, "Oh, that's such a goofy song. Why did I agree to this?" But the more I listen to it, the more it is classic XTC. I liked it back when I was listening to everything, but I was taken aback when I was asked to talk about it. You have a loopy lyric which is written in some kind of ethnic slang, but then you have this incredible chorus where the bass line is steady and the lyrics slide off the time. I tried to figure it out on my bass. There are two approaches: the bass on the demo is more rhythmic and the one on the recorded version has more space, but they each have a set pattern. The counting is remarkable because if you zero in on the bass line, it is keeping to the 4/4 rhythm, but the lyric slides out and winds up back on the "one". It's math rock before it was invented.

And then it jumps to the key of C – there's a bridge

in there that's psychotic. This is a song that Ralph Carney, my bandmate from Tin Huey, could have written because Ralph was the master of loopiness, time shifting and strange chord progressions. Once again, I'm knocked out by XTC. If you drill in to their arrangements, they just floor you. It's so smart and interesting.

I love the message that if you dump on somebody there's going to be payback. It's a little strange and maybe English eccentric to use that whole phrase, "shake you donkey up". It's Andy at his most lyrically playful. It recalls the Beatles line, "Me hiding me head in the sand," like someone speaking English when English is not their first language. And it works! With a corkscrew lead guitar part and a great riff, it's top-to-bottom stunning.

Something I love about XTC is they break the number one "rule" of songwriting which is you're supposed to be able to play this song on an acoustic guitar with just one singer. The thing about XTC is their arrangements are always definitive. You can't imagine it being any other way. They are masters of putting something in like an acoustic guitar just at the bridge or a little synth noodle in the third verse, just a little part that comes in that is perfect, says what it has to say and then goes away and is never heard again. The criticism of XTC is they have too many ideas - I love too many ideas. I love hearing smart people make records and they are the gold standard for me.

CHOSEN TRACK
Mayor of Simpleton
This is a very simple song by XTC's standards. I hear one guitar, I hear bass, I hear drums. They didn't have something that comes in just on the bridge or whatever. It's stripped down for XTC. I'm resisting using the word "cluttered" because they don't clutter - everything is precise and everything works - but they did resist filling it up with those ear tickles because the song has enough strength on just its melodies and its forward propulsion. The bass pretty much covers any of the extra noodly bits that they would customarily add to an arrangement. It's just perfect.

Andy says in *Complicated Game* that some of the drums were done live and some, particularly the kick drum, with looping. I'm knocked out because matching sounds from a live studio to a loop is really difficult. I'm not sure how they did it but there's a consistency in the sonics of the bass drum all the way through, which is an engineering feat.

At the end of *Simpleton*, they hold that note. That's artificially done. There's a freeze function on this unit called a Quantec Room Simulator that was a relatively new technology at the time. It would capture whatever you fed into it and sustain it. I think they used something like that to extend that harmony, because nobody's going to have that much air. Again, the backing vocals slide out of time and it just works. It's so artful.

The song is filled with forward motion - it just grinds away. It doesn't come in square on the "one", it comes in on the "and" of "one", which instantly gives it a forward motion. It sounds like an edit. I wish there would be a tape somewhere of them trying to count it off to get that up feeling, that jump beginning. Somebody thought that up, because on the demo it's on the "one". Everything is on-and-on-and-on-and-on and it just drives. It works because of the *(Don't Fear) The Reaper* guitar line and, of course, that incredible bass part, written by Andy himself. It's the most intelligent and musical bass line. I swear I'm going to sit down and learn it because it just fits everything perfectly.

Then you've got these golden harmonies and we haven't even reached the point about how witty the lyrics are. It's kind of a piss-take on their own intelligence, Andy saying that depth of feeling is all that matters, which is almost humorous coming from people who were so erudite in their approach to recording. The title is not the most intellectual of puns, but putting the music aside, I am in awe of the lyrical content of these songs and how deep they go. There's a lot of fun in these songs too. They maintained a sense of playfulness, even on the most dire, depressing songs. Harry Shearer, who appeared in the *This Is Pop* documentary, is the kind of person who is an XTC fan: lateral, funny, intellectually curious. The writing is deliciously intellectually stimulating – and it doesn't hurt. You don't have to strain. You just think, "Ah! How nifty." It's the well-turned phrase, the Oscar Wilde quip, a scene out of *The Avengers*, it's delicious in its Englishness but also transcending that. There's a delight in word play and note play. It's life-affirming that people can create something so rich, smart and lovely.

BEQUEATHED TRACK
Ella Guru
What an incredible cover! I read some criticism, somebody saying, "Well, they just did the song straight..." Yes, they did the song straight, but do you know how hard that is? As well as getting the voice right to capture Beefheart's incredible vocal range and tonal quality, this is another example of their Dukes of Stratosphear-style perfection in capturing period sounds. It's a demonstration of how good they are to replicate an incredibly difficult, idiosyncratic song and get it right.

David Yazbek
SOLO, SONGWRITER

INHERITED TRACK
Ella Guru
When I first met Andy Partridge we connected because he and I were both obsessed by two bars in Frank Loesser's *Standing on the Corner (Watching All the Girls Go By)*. There's this one moment after they've sung the title line where there's this countermelody – it's completely angular and very goofy and we both agreed it was the crux of the whole song. From there, we had a lot of stuff in common in terms of what we both really liked.

Then he would do that influencer thing: "Have you heard this?" He was the person who turned me on to Captain Beefheart. Even though I write musical theatre, Beefheart is a giant influence on everything I do. Andy Partridge said, "Do you know Beefheart?" and I said, "Well, I know who he is and I know the stuff he did with Zappa, but I never plunged into it because *Trout Mask Replica* sounds shitty." He said, "Just listen to it more than two times."

Ella Guru was a great example of Andy probably thinking what everybody thinks when they first hear that album which is, "Jesus, what kind of mics were they using? Why couldn't Frank Zappa make this sound good?" On that whole album, there's stuff going on that is mind-blowing. It's deconstructing the history of American blues. I said to Andy that Beefheart was the unsung genius of American blues and Partridge said to me, "Yes, none of us has gone further." With *Ella Guru*, my guess is Andy said, "I want to hear that the way it's supposed to sound." The first time I met him, I asked him to show me *Respectable Street* on guitar. He said, "This is the shape." He never said, "This is the chord." For his brain, he was probably the best person to do *Ella Guru*.

It makes me feel like I'm part of a continuum because Partridge worshipped at Beefheart's feet and I worship at the feet of XTC. I feel like I'm connected not just to Beefheart but a certain type of artistic sensibility through that. It makes me feel a little more legitimate. It's one of the best things about music; it's a language that passes down. One of the things Partridge believes – and it's something I try to teach – is to keep yourself open to the widest frame of reference, don't pooh-pooh a type of music because of what it's called or because someone says it isn't cool. If you don't get it the first time, try to listen to it again, because the biggest tool you can have in your toolbox as a composer is a true, energetic curiosity and enthusiasm about all kinds of music. Andy said, "This is pop," he meant it and he really represents it.

CHOSEN TRACK
Burning with Optimism's Flames
This wasn't the first XTC song I heard, which was probably *Nigel* or *Generals and Majors* on the radio, but I didn't know yet who the band was. I was in college with Chris Smylie, who eventually ended up

being the bass player in my band for a long time. I was in his dorm room and he said, "I need to play you something." The first thing he played me was *Burning with Optimism's Flames* - and then everything else that he had. We were there for two hours listening.

With *Burning with Optimism's Flames*, the thing that got me - and it's as a clear in my mind as the first time I ate Indian food because it was a mind-fucker - was the lyric near the beginning of the song:

> Never seen her glowing
> All that bright she's throwing like some aurora
> From her head, it's growing
> Reaching to the ground
> And all around like a Navajo blanket

Here was this sung melody literally doing what the lyric was saying. Back then, I knew what a Navajo blanket looked like because my girlfriend was from New Mexico, but also the melody is literally going down, it's reaching to the ground and then it goes on a little too long, a little longer than you expect and, because it does that, part of the Navajo blanket is on the ground. That was a majorly influential two bars of music and lyrics for me.

That combination should be the holy grail for songwriters. Every interview I ever do around my theatre stuff, people ask me, "Lyrics first or music first?" The point is you start with the emotion. Sometimes you're playing the guitar or the piano and it inspires an emotion that then triggers an image or a lyric - or vice versa. I've written with Andy and I happened to be with him in his shed and I was just playing the keyboard and he started singing. Somewhere I have a recording of this, we never finished the song, but based on the music, he started singing these lyrics about Igor and Dr Frankenstein. They also had a double meaning: an assistant helping someone in an evil act. He's singing them off the cuff and he's rhyming them - they're not perfect but they're pretty good. They have all these layers and for him, it all came out of the feeling of what I was playing. He'll find something on the guitar, start singing to it, so a melody will come up and eventually a lyric will come up. I would be amazed if the words came first on *Optimism's Flames*, at least for that moment I'm talking about.

If you listen to a great guitar player then what you hear is music that is delightful, satisfying or harrowing. But if you listen to a near-genius level musician like Partridge play a guitar solo (and I've been there when he's putting down guitar solos), you're listening to someone who is doing that synaesthesia of emotion. On *Love at First Sight*, he plays a chord faster and faster - to me, that's among the guitar solos in the Song Book, not just of XTC, of everybody. It's one of the great solos. He gets away with it because a) no one had ever done it and b) it's emotionally perfect for what's going on musically. He's a brilliant musician. Andy gave me as much if not more than any other composer or musician dead or alive, not in terms of sitting there and showing me stuff, just in terms of the music he wrote.

BEQUEATHED TRACK
Day In Day Out
This is my favourite song of Colin's after *Bungalow*. It's so catchy. The lyrics are very simple, but really just paint a picture - boom! That circle of fifths chorus is both delightful and mind-numbing. It's going round and around and you really feel it; the meaning is locked into the music. It's something that Colin did a lot: *Grass* paints this vivid picture and *Dying* - this guy saw this stuff and he felt it.

Working in musical theatre, I often have to explain to a book writer that, just as subtext is the most important thing in the script, if I hit stuff right on the nose in a song, I'll feel embarrassed every time I hear it. *Bungalow* is the pinnacle of this melding of emotion and music. It's all the hopes, dreams, desires and hunger of a working-class couple and it's so sad, yet you feel it - if we can only have this bungalow. It's bleak but it's also understandable because that's what everyone does; everybody funnels their hopes for the future into something that eventually you're going to lose because you're going to die.

ASCENDING MELODIES

HUGH NANKIVELL

The melody of *Travels in Nihilon* is almost the same as *Omnibus* but a lot slower and it goes from low to high. Most melodies start high and come down. They're called tumbling strains. This is a bold and stupid thing to say, but all African music starts high and comes low.

DAVID WHITE

I think that's often noticeable in highlife, for instance.

HUGH NANKIVELL

Lots of Andy's tunes do that, but at times, he thinks, "What can I do to counter that?" *Travels in Nihilon* goes up – it ends on the second top note – and there's a very different feeling. On *Nonsuch*, for example, *Omnibus* goes up and *Dear Madam Barnum* comes down. Is it because the clown is falling down? Whenever I hear *Omnibus*, I always imagine he's going up the stairs on a London double-decker bus because that's what he's singing.

JOHN IRVINE

The opening melody of *Travels in Nihilon* is a fantastic example of Andy's use of chromaticism. He will usually begin by setting up the dissonances by first giving us something conventionally melodic (here, it is an E major triad) before setting off to touch on some "outside" notes at the end of the phrase. On the word "lessons" he adds the flattened 5th and on "that" the b9. Typically, the chromaticism appears over bitter lyrics – "time so cheaply spent".

Jason Falkner
JELLYFISH, SOLO

INHERITED TRACK
Day In Day Out

Drums and Wires was the first record of theirs I heard and it made such a huge impact on me. My top three things that hit me at just the right time in my early teens are XTC, Costello and Bowie, with XTC probably being the most important of the three. I love the juxtaposition of what appear to be straightforward, well-crafted songs with this element of atonal, discordant playing over it, mainly in the guitar department. That's what made it sound so new to me. It was this weird experimental thing overlaid on songs which, if you played them on an acoustic guitar, don't possess any of that in the structure. *Day In Day Out* is a classic example. My favourite moment comes out of the first chorus when this saturated reverb guitar slides out for the second verse. It's just that juxtaposition between very tuneful songwriting and weird middle-finger playing that runs through a lot of the record.

With Colin's lyrics, there are a lot of dots you have to connect, which is something I inherited. I like it when you don't tell an entire story. I wish I was Bob Dylan but I'm not, so I like to keep it abstract, leaving it up to the listener to fill it in. I also love the dub influence, the spastic 16th-note guitar stuff and the dual guitar attack on *Drums and Wires*. *Real by Reel* was the first song on that record where I was, like, "What the hell is happening here?" and then that freakin' solo kicks in... I didn't know these guys were complete shredders as well. And that's Dave, right? In that era, guitar solos had become a little "raised eyebrow". New wave and punk bands didn't do guitar solos because the late 70s rock bands had ruined it for everybody by doing such shitty solos. This clean guitar solo was a revelation to me. Usually a solo is distorted, but this was like a jazz solo. He's not just shredding; the notes are fantastic and it completely fits. That was a revelation to me: "Yes, you can still be proficient on your instrument." I loved the Damned and Buzzcocks, but there were all of these other bands, with XTC at the forefront, that were really sophisticated and intelligent. The golden era – *Drums and Wires, Black Sea, English Settlement, Big Express* and *Mummer* – is just heaven.

CHOSEN TRACK
The Everyday Story of Smalltown
I could listen to the outro of this song on a loop and be lowered into the earth for my final sleep. That's the sound that's just constantly in my head as I'm walking down the street every single day – even before I heard that song. The chord structure and the melody over it is so musically satisfying. My favourite moment in the song is in that ascending part after the bridge when he sneaks in the major third over the line "as singles and weds". You're not expecting him to go to that major third even though it's in the chord. The chord shifts right there and makes it the perfect thing to do. It's just genius. It sets up perfectly for the last chorus and then that outro.

Nobody writes like Andy. I can't tell whether the song is a triumphal celebration or a critical analysis of the whole small-town scenario. It's critical but very loving. The Kinks and Blur might have taken on the same subject matter, but the Kinks would have been way more simple and Blur would have been way too clever. I always think of Andy in *Smalltown* being like a bed-and-breakfast talking about the tenants. I went to England when I was 16 because of my dad's job and we lived in Highgate village in London. *Smalltown* reminds me of this quaint feeling of travelling through the UK and staying in these little bed-and-breakfast places. The glorious celebratory tone reminds me of that, but it's also acknowledging the stuffy smallness of the experience.

The Big Express is more cacophonous than anything they'd done before, but I liked a challenge. If something doesn't hit you right away, it probably means it's more interesting. That's the antithesis of the pop mentality. *The Big Express* is crazy and ambitious but it's not laborious – it's got way more depth because of this overreaching ambition that I hear. There's something challenging about it and that's something I inherited, willingly or not, in my own music.

BEQUEATHED TRACK
What in the World??...
I heard this at a party when I was 16 or 17. The local weirdo hippy guy with super-long hair, Coca-Cola bottle glasses and acne put it on. Normally he would be playing psychedelic records from the 60s. He was just looking at me like, "You don't know what this is?" Just imagine Neil from *The Young Ones*. "This is XTC, man. And they don't even put their names on it. They all have fake names." I remember listening to *25 O'Clock* on my dad's headphones, falling asleep then having to rip the headphones off because it was scaring the crap out of me.

Many years later, I took the old 'shrooms with that record and it's the most incredible record for that experience ever made. It's like the songs were recorded, then they applied crazy, weird arpeggiated Mellotrons, backwards tracks and vari-sped things that are really fast or really slow so there's this crazy stereo bed of mania going on in every song. That's the stuff that really hits you when you're out of your mind – but also not out of your mind because I listened to that record many times prior to ever doing that. I love both records, but the first one is the most psychedelic record ever made. It's tougher than any other XTC thing and has a bad-ass quality I love. It's a weird masterpiece.

Iain Sloan
THE WYNNTOWN MARSHALS,
ABEL GANZ AND BLUE ROSE CODE

INHERITED TRACK
What in the World??...
First of all, what a privilege to have a song bequeathed to me by Jason Falkner! I've been a big fan of JF's since those early Jellyfish days and have bought all his releases ever since. So this is pretty cool for me. Anyway, on to this amazing tune…

My good friend and fellow Edinburgh musician

friend Al Denholm regularly regaled me with tales of how good the Dukes were when I used to record down at his Merchant House Studio in Leith which, incidentally, had a Dukes of Stratosphear T-shirt hanging on the wall "overseeing" every note we played and sung in there! That was my first introduction to this amazing project.

On this tune, the early Floyd influence is obvious, but that fantastic McCartney-esque bass line from the Red Curtain is sublime and really drives this along with ElEl Owen clearly having an absolute ball on the drums. Every time I hear this, I also wonder just how much fun Gregory and Partridge had putting down all those backwards guitar tracks with John Leckie. So much fun. This has a really great lyric from Moulding too, brilliantly delivered. And I just love how those deadpan vocal harmonies weave in and around all those brass parts and swirling sound effects and samples. Just genius. The Dukes of Stratosphear didn't simply replicate and pay homage to the psychedelic era. I think they probably bettered it!

CHOSEN TRACK
The Ballad of Peter Pumpkinhead
Clearly, everyone reading this knows Andy and Colin are both incredibly gifted lyricists, musicians, and songwriters. However, what is often overlooked is how adept they both are at subversively welding socially aware or more political themes onto songs with wonderfully commercial melodies and arrangements. Their assaults on the singles charts are littered with great examples of this (*Making Plans for Nigel, Towers of London* and so on). However, to these ears, there is no better example than *The Ballad of Peter Pumpkinhead* from 1992's *Nonsuch*.

The first time I heard this track, I was hooked right from the moment Gregory plugged in his guitar and Partridge kicked in with that fantastic guitar intro. And the drum sound on those tom fills from Dave Mattacks! Crikey! Partridge was quoted somewhere regaling the amazing drum sound captured by studio engineer Barry Hammond and saying, "Aren't they the best-recorded tom-toms that you've heard?"

Yes, Andy. They truly are! Massive sound. This song was absolutely built for commercial radio. So, why on earth did it only ever peak at number 71 on the UK singles chart? Utterly baffling, isn't it?

One of XTC's strengths is in the complexity and intricacy of their arrangements – especially the manner in which Dave and Andy are capable of creating beautifully intricate guitar lines that intertwine, with layer-upon-layer of different tracks creating those sumptuous aural masterpieces. However, the arrangement of *Peter Pumpkinhead* is unexpectedly and deceptively simple for such a massive-sounding production. There are really only those two main guitar parts throughout and neither is overly complex or as angular as many of the guitar arrangements across their incredible back catalogue. Two big chiming guitars and Partridge's brilliant harmonica hook sit atop Mattacks' fantastic groove and Moulding's trademark dynamic and really musical bass line. As the song progresses, a few extra little features creep in and out pretty unobtrusively, as the guitars, bass, drums, and Andy's uplifting lead vocal are complimented only by occasional touches of lovely Hammond playing and little winding guitar arpeggios from Gregory, an occasional backing vocal, and some church bells.

Gus Dudgeon and mix engineer Nick Davis created a big, anthemic sound for one of Partridge's best lyrics. Although I am also a huge fan of some of their more obtuse and spiky tunes, there's something liberating and just joyous in how the band go about their business here – embracing a big wall of relatively straightforward, radio-friendly jangle – to great effect. I love the instant sugar high of Andy's glorious melody aligned to those massive guitar chords and huge drum sound, but it was only after repeated listens that the majesty of Andy's lyrics really started to unpeel and reveal their beauty to me.

Now, over 25 years after its release, in this world of so-called fake news and with social media permitting greater numbers of us to have our eyes opened to the corruption and manipulation of the media and big government, we can see how a lyric like "But he made too many enemies of the people who would keep us on our knees" has even greater relevance than ever. People with good hearts are frequently pushed down – their motives questioned and attempts made by the media or those in power to sully their reputations. Forget this being one of my favourite XTC tunes. This is one of my favourite songs by *anyone* ever.

BEQUEATHED TRACK
Are You Receiving Me?
I got into XTC a bit later – around the time the likes of *Making Plans for Nigel*, *Sgt Rock* and *Generals and Majors* were hitting the singles chart. So when I got a copy of *The Compact XTC* I was blissfully unaware of their spikier, keys-enhanced line-up and this song caught my ear instantly. I love its energy and spikiness.

Daniel Wylie
COSMIC ROUGH RIDERS

INHERITED TRACK
Are You Receiving Me?
This was released as a single, just before *Go 2* but not included on the original album release (super fans and collectors love non-album releases), and it seemed Virgin Records were pushing XTC for a hit single. That kind of pressure can sometimes force great results but, alas, didn't work for XTC on this occasion. Despite being a super-catchy, jaggy, melodic slice of pop, the UK public didn't buy into *Are You Receiving Me?*, although fans loved it. Heaps of critical acclaim but still missing that big hit single that would catapult the band from cult to mainstream... it wouldn't be long though... and despite Andy's genius, Colin would score the band's first hit.

CHOSEN TRACK
Battery Brides (Andy Paints Brian)
I've been an XTC fan since buying the *3D EP* when I was a teenager. To choose just one song is a mighty task... so many works of genius to choose from. I felt right away that *Go 2* was a natural progression from *White Music*. The band were definitely stretching out musically... developing. A song like *Battery Brides*, the way it arrives, speeding up and fading in, leaving you hanging (like a new-wave version of David Bowie's *Sound and Vision*) for Andy's vocal to arrive... and when it does, he sings a melody beautiful enough to melt you.

Although produced by the amazing John Leckie, in my head, this song could have been on an early Roxy Music album or one of Eno's early solo pop records. It had that kind of Roxy Music thing of creating exotic music but never at the expense of a good tune or an intriguing lyric. It was slightly at odds with the jerky pop they were known for at the time and hinted that future XTC music could be an even more interesting prospect.

The experimental mini album that came free with early copies of *Go 2* was further proof that XTC was a band that wouldn't and couldn't stand still and as we all know, right till the end, XTC was driving down new roads, exploring new musical destinations. Now... if only they'd make even just one more album... please... pretty please...

BEQUEATHED TRACK
Travels In Nihilon
That song has always made me think of the New Zealand traditional warrior ritual, the haka. I wonder if I'm out on my own there... but even if I am, music should give you something personal to you.

Daniel Steinhardt
TIN SPIRITS

INHERITED TRACK
Travels in Nihilon
This is an example of why Andy Partridge is going to go down in history as one of the great songwriters of the 20th century and beyond. His songwriting very rarely goes to the place you think it's going to go, therefore listening to XTC is never a passive experience. Of course the music is emotional and beautiful, but as a musician, I also get involved with

it on a cerebral level. For example, in *Senses Working Overtime* after that acoustic riff, the chords go to a C sharp minor. The obvious chord to go to next is E major, because that's in G, but he goes to an E minor. You'd think that wouldn't work, but the melody he sings over it works perfectly. As someone who knows music and the function of chords, I find it amazing to hear someone who can effortlessly break the rules, not for the sake of breaking the rules, but because that's where he's artistically led. He creates these beautiful melodies that become so much part of the song that you can no longer think of any other possible melody over those changes.

But *Travels in Nihilon* is the opposite. There are no changes. Instead, the melody becomes the changes. He sings modally over this drone with almost an altered scale, but it doesn't sound like laboured experimental jazz. It is emotional and meaningful. It's not about amazing chord changes – he can do the same thing with one note. For me, that song cements Andy as one of the greatest song writers who has ever lived.

The extraordinary thing about the melody of *Travels in Nihilon* is he'll go to a minor second, which is the first note away from the tonic. It's common in Eastern music. Then he breaks away before coming back to it. In a jazz sense, that's hard to do. You have to be confident and comfortable with your instrument to make those sorts of statements. Andy just opens his mouth and this amazing, poignant, dark, powerful melody falls out.

Where on Earth could that come from?

In tunes like this and *Complicated Game* where he uses his voice texturally as well as melodically, there's no notion of Andy trying to sing like a pop star to be successful and famous. When these songs came out, the only way you were going to have any material success was by making songs that were so accessible, but Andy's attitude was, "Well, no, my songs are accessible because they're honest and that's what people are going to connect to." People aren't going to just connect to a pretty melody, they're going to connect to the emotion.

Travels in Nihilon is frightening and I love that Andy is not afraid to go there and didn't try and lighten it up. I often think about whether there was anything going on socially that would have sent him that way, but no, Andy can just feel something and he is so capable of expressing it in music, more so than anyone I can think of. He doesn't hold anything back when he writes. It all comes out. If you listen to the stuff he did on *Monstrance*, it gives you an understanding that it just pours out of him. Dave says it often all came out piped together: lyrics, melody, everything.

CHOSEN TRACK
Real by Reel

This was the first guitar solo of Dave's that I learned off by heart. The song is Andy having fun – it's got that amazing energy – but then Dave comes in with that solo and it sums up perfectly what he can do in eight bars. A lot of times in that era, a solo was heavily distorted and was meant to be this glory moment. This solo isn't that at all. The tone is clean, Dave is whipping around the outline of these chords and what he does better than anyone is contribute to the song. I don't think there's any song where Dave goes, "Well this is what I'm capable of doing," and just shows off his skill. He is truly subservient to what the song's about, even when the song affords him the opportunity to just go. He always supports the song.

One of the great joys of my life was our first gig as Tin Spirits at Riffs Bar in Swindon. We were doing prog covers but in the middle of it we'd go into this freeform XTC jam. We started playing *Scissor Man* and in the middle of that we both broke out into the *Real by Reel* solo at the same time. Having been so affected by it and being on stage with the man himself, I'll never forget it. Dave Gregory is my favourite guitar player in the world and *Real by Reel* is a perfect example of how he is subservient to the tune. Being subservient is not just about playing simply; with this tune and the energy of the song, it couldn't be any other guitar solo.

BEQUEATHED TRACK
Millions
This song holds a lot of memories for me personally. I was on tour with Australian artist Max Sharam in the mid 90s and the drummer in the band Paul Wheeler, who also is the drummer from Ice House, happened to be a huge XTC fan. This was one of the first songs we bonded over and we've been close friends ever since. The trance-type drum groove (coincidently a great example of how versatile Terry was - a hugely underrated drummer) and feel from the chorus-heavy bass sits in such contrast with the choppy rhythm guitar parts. Andy's melody sitting over some pretty hairy chords makes me think, "Is there anything the guy can't sing over?" It's a great moment on a stellar album.

Gregory Spawton
BIG BIG TRAIN

INHERITED TRACK
Millions
Despite having a brother called Nigel and, of course, being very aware of the *Making Plans* song, I started getting into XTC as their music moved into their more pastoral phase with *Skylarking*. So *Millions* was new to me and I approached with cautious interest. After a few listens, I have to say this isn't my cup of tea (thanks Dan!) as there is too little in the way of melody for my tastes. And yet, there is still something beguiling about it; the guitar interplay over Colin's ostinato bass is lovely, and it feels like the band are reaching for something beyond the ordinary.

CHOSEN TRACK
Wrapped in Grey
This song means a lot to me. For many years I was stuck behind a desk in an office job and the words to *Wrapped in Grey* acted as a sort of calling for me to move on and try to make a go of it as a songwriter and musician. Eventually, I was able to take my "big box of paints" and leave the office behind and I sang this song as I left the building for the last time. Alongside the lyrical content, *Wrapped in Grey* also delivers a beautiful tune, with a lovely Burt Bacharach influence. I asked my friend and bandmate Dave Gregory what he thought of the song and he described it as "one of the posher tunes on the album". When pushed for a definition of "posh" in this context, he said: "Well, sort of prog really."

BEQUEATHED TRACK
Chalkhills and Children
If XTC were reaching for greater heights in their early years, with this song they scaled Olympus. *Chalkhills and Children* is five minutes of extraordinary beauty, masterful in concept and execution. Great title, great lyric idea; verses, choruses and middle eight, all perfect; music that seems to float above the ground. Dave Gregory got the shivers when he was recording the keyboard parts and it does the same to me every time I hear it. And hats off to Andy for letting Pat Mastelotto let rip in the play-out.

Danny Manners
BIG BIG TRAIN

INHERITED TRACK
Chalkhills and Children
XTC had something of a tradition of striking or unusual album closers - *Complicated Game, Travels In Nihilon, Train Running Low* - and *Oranges and Lemons* didn't disappoint with this beautifully dreamlike and very personal number. The Beach Boys influence is obvious, of course, adding a touch of California to the slightly hallucinatory Wiltshire vibe. The way the melody and chord sequence drift up and down is a good example of Andy's skill at marrying music and lyrics. The only real moment of harmonic resolution is to the warm, homely F major underscoring "back to earth eternally and ever Ermine Street".

But it was two other details that tickled me on early listens. The strange organ registration, with everything doubled at a fifth above, casts an unworldly harmonic sheen. And Pat Mastelotto's drum excursion in the outro is one of those "Huh?"

moments I love - something in a track that seems completely out of place or random at first listen, but just works. Why the drum pyrotechnics in such a song? I don't know whether they were one of those happy studio accidents or something that Andy planned. Perhaps they suggest the clatter and hurly burly of the music biz that's been left behind. But anyway, they just work - any incongruity smoothed over by dream logic.

CHOSEN TRACK
Rook

One of the delights of XTC for a musician is that, although the song always takes precedence (instrumental solos are rare and concise, and track length is usually under four or five minutes), the band were always skilfully inventive in deploying instrumentation, arrangement and production to create an appropriate atmosphere and illustrate the lyrics for each song. *Summer's Cauldron*, with its musical heat haze, is a good example; *Train Running Low* is about the furthest they went with literal tone painting.

Rook is a masterpiece of economy in this respect. In terms of forces used, it's essentially vocal and piano, with string quartet and trumpet adding colours, and just a touch of synth and percussion. Verse and chorus are compressed into one - a four-chord sequence with one more at the end - and there's a bridge that, again, is just four chords. (The song even has - almost - the shortest title in the XTC canon.)

With these modest materials, the song creates a unique atmosphere: a mixture of yearning and hopefulness with existential disquiet that's perfectly matched to the lyrics. It has always conjured up a very definite scene for me: a bleak and hilly heathland. And very particular weather: one of those changeable, windy days with a lot of scudding clouds, when the light can shift suddenly from optimistically sunny to forebodingly overcast.

Those four verse/chorus chords always fascinated me. If you analyse them, the roots are B flat, C, D, E, but they all have the fifth of each chord at the bottom. They're second inversions, to use the technical term, and traditional music pedagogy will tell you a second inversion is inherently unstable and needs careful handling. Four in a row is just plain wrong. Of course, they work perfectly here, and the harmonic instability just enhances the uncertain, questioning mood of the piece. The chord sequence always looked to me like the sort of thing a non-pianist (albeit an inquisitive one) would find at the piano: the note combinations are unusual but fall fairly easily under the fingers. I've since discovered that Andy came up with the sequence on guitar, which might explain the second inversions with their interval of a fourth at the bottom.

There's a couple more things to say about this sequence. The chords use quartal harmony, based on stacking up intervals of a fourth (albeit in inversion), rather than the usual intervals of a third: it makes them more ambiguous and less grounded. And there's a dislocation between the B flat in the first chord and the B natural in the second which further unsettles things. The sequence resolves onto a D chord at the end of the verse/chorus. Only it doesn't completely resolve - it's another second inversion and there's a suspended fourth in there - just as the lyrics never resolve the protagonist's questions.

The vocal line very much has the feel of a nursery rhyme: the questions the lyrics ask are childlike in their basicness. The melody has entirely stepwise motion apart from that heartfelt octave leap up in the middle. Further suggestive of a children's song is that it could be sung as a "round", with several singers starting one after the other so the tune overlaps itself. Andy chose not to do that vocally - multiple vocal parts would have detracted from the sense of a lonely individual that the lyrics convey - but the strings do it.

The bridge section, with Dave Gregory doing sterling work on the piano, conjures up more of a feeling of soaring, both of the bird and the emotions. I've always loved Dave's final two chords: perhaps a distant bell, suggested by the lyrics, but they've also always sounded to me like a little sigh.

I'm sure none of those technical details were in Andy's mind when he wrote *Rook*, but arose out of sheer intuition. As a musician, when I hear magic I like to put on my analyst's hat to work out how the conjuring trick was done. As a listener, I just enjoy the magic of this unique and wonderful song, which I think is among Andy's best.

BEQUEATHED TRACK
River of Orchids
It knocked me out when I first heard it: an unexpected new direction for Andy, drawing on minimalism/systems music but entirely Partridgesque.

Andy Cutting
BLOWZABELLA, LEVERET, MARTIN SIMPSON

INHERITED TRACK
River of Orchids
I played *River of Orchids* on *Late Junction* when I was doing a live session the other year and got a Twitter message from Andy Partridge thanking me! They asked me to pick a track to play and I tried to think what would be a good "in" to XTC for BBC Radio 3 listeners. There was no doubt I was going to play an XTC track - I couldn't play *Dear God*, really, or *Your Dictionary*, which I was thinking of doing, but *River of Orchids* is just a great song. It's a finely edited bit of work. It sounds like an orchestra but it's not quite; there's something slightly odd about it. It doesn't have that natural orchestra sound, but it works perfectly. I think a lot of editing has gone on to get it rhythmically right. That's a positive: it just sounds like it is.

Andy is so incredibly uncompromising which, musically, is very unlike me. I'm very much about the people I work with. They do the things they do. Sometimes I would rather they did things in a certain way, but I would never say that so they can just be themselves. That's massively important to me, but in the other side of my head, I love this absolute controlling thing. *River of Orchids* has several grids and when they interlock it becomes another thing. Every time I listen to it, I'm sure the horns come in at a different place. It's not cold or mathematical because the song humanises it. It's someone's plea to get rid of the roads, plant something that's beautiful and natural - slightly idealistic! Andy doesn't drive, so it's, "Let's write a song about not driving."

CHOSEN TRACK
The Loving
The first XTC I knowingly heard was *Oranges and Lemons*, on tour around England just after it came out in 1989 - a cassette. I thought it was amazing. I love *The Loving* for one reason which is its guitar solo. The shape and set-up of the song is great. It's such a simple tune with a simple musical and lyrical story, and it's beautifully produced: the dynamics, the way the drums in the chorus are so driving, the artificial crowds clapping, you're kind of unaware it's happening - and then that fantastic guitar solo. It's not very long but the solo does the job perfectly. "Here we are on an album, trying to make the sound of a big stadium rock gig and now it's the sound of a guitar solo!" It's very Dave Gregory: a beautiful melody and then it's done. I always think it's longer than it actually is because it leads you beautifully on.

It's common for people writing songs influenced by other things to start the wrong way round, so when they hear XTC they pick up on all the bits and pieces they think the band uses, rather than remembering you've got to have a good tune and really good lyrics. With XTC, there is always a good tune. The melody is always strong - and it's not always mental. The melody of *The Loving* is so simple and that's a hard thing to carry off.

BEQUEATHED TRACK
Train Running Low on Soul Coal
The Big Express was the second XTC album I got. I love the whole album, the way they try to make the LinnDrum human. Andy did a very good job at that. He could have got a drummer to do it, but it would have been a bit rubbish. It's just a great sound. They

managed to make an electronic drum feel soulful, not by programming it to be soulful but by being so mechanical, so unforgiving that somehow, with their writing and everything else, it became really soulful.

They were big fans of all that constructed stuff going off and at the start of *Train Running Low* you don't quite know where you are until the guitar comes in. It's not dissimilar to *River of Orchids*. It's rhythmically glorious and it's another intense piece of work that you can't ignore. There's something hugely admirable in writing a piece of music that grabs you immediately.

John Wedemeyer
GUITARIST, RIGHTEOUS BROTHERS

INHERITED TRACK
Train Running Low on Soul Coal
The Big Express is probably their most overlooked album, but some of their greatest songs are on it. It's also the album where Andy fell in love with the open-E tuning. It's in *Liarbird, Blue Overall* and I think it might be in *Reign of Blows*, but *Train Running Low* is the prime example. I remember the first time trying to play *Train Running Low* and it wasn't until much later that I figured out it was an open tuning and it was so much easier than what I was doing.

It's one of their best album closers and a great example of how, through the music and production, they're able to paint the picture that the lyrics suggest. Everything about the track – the way it ends with the guitars and even the LinnDrum – sounds like a train grinding to a halt. At the time, I thought it was a bit like *Ra Ra for Red Rocking Horse*, talking about XTC's career and how they were being overshadowed by younger, prettier, more successful bands with big hit songs. But now I read it as a song about getting older. I haven't had a breakdown like Andy had, but as I get older, watching the world pass me by, I can relate to it more. He sounds like a much older guy singing those words, even though we know he was only 30.

Andy Cutting makes a good point about *River of Orchids*, the way it starts with a random sound, then another random sound and the next thing you know, all the random sounds turn into a groove and the song starts. I thought the same thing the first time I heard *River of Orchids*, the way all the ingredients fall together and turn into a groove. Andy does that a lot in demos as well; *Rocket from a Bottle* is one where the groove comes in and I have no idea where the "one" is until he starts singing. *Train Running Low* is one of those and so is *Millions* – I hear the "one" in a totally different place until the vocal comes in.

It appeals to me because it isn't cerebral. I'm generally not impressed by people who set out to do that. Andy is just being himself and it comes out left of what we think of as normal. It's not him trying to impress us or show off his chops, it's how he hears it. I get hired to play guitar and I'm around musicians all the time. You run into so many musicians who are trying to impress you: "I went to the Musicians Institute," or, "I went to Berklee College of Music, check out this polyrhythm." My eyes glaze over. But with people like Andy, that's just how they breathe, it's how it comes out of them. It just feels good. With Andy, it's his default setting. That's why I love his music so much. There are plenty of bands I can listen to if I want to be impressed with sheer virtuosity, but I'd much rather listen to *The Big Express* than Toto.

CHOSEN TRACK
Rocket from a Bottle
This encapsulates everything I love about XTC in one track. It's the band with Terry on drums, Colin with his moaning bass, the guitar interplay between Andy and Dave, and, of course, a brilliant song. If an alien landed and wanted to know what XTC sounded like, it would be *Rocket from a Bottle*.

It's a perfect pop song that evokes the euphoric feeling of falling in love. The whole track is happy, upbeat and positive, but I want to focus on the middle eight and the guitar solo into that incredible modulation. Dave comes up with these solos that are note-for-note what the song requires, no more, no less. There are so many examples – *Real by Reel, Pink Thing* – but *Rocket from a Bottle* is my favourite.

It's a little composition within the song. It sounds like it was worked out but is still spontaneous and a little rough around the edges. It has a lot of attitude. I love the way it snakes around the chords and the way it sounds like a rocket shooting into the sky and spinning around with smoke behind it. To paint a picture that stays with the theme of the song is hard to do. I've been in that situation in sessions and when somebody asks me to come up with a solo that fits with the vibe of the song, *Rocket from a Bottle* is my go-to solo. Dave's got a real gift for that. For me, it's George Harrison and Dave when it comes to evoking the mood of the song and not a note wasted.

Meanwhile, the chords beneath the solo almost give way. You're so busy listening to Dave you don't realise it's happening until Andy comes in singing and the song has gone down a half-step. The song is in the key of F, but it modulates down to E, which is the coolest modulation I've ever heard. It's a subliminal thing. Until you sit down and analyse it, you know something cool is happening but you don't know what it is. The guitar stays with the melody in the last two bars when the chords start heading south. The moment Andy starts singing, the song opens up and becomes enormous. I've heard other people do it and I've tried to do it myself when writing, but I've never heard anybody pull off a downward modulation like *Rocket from a Bottle*. Those eight bars are the best. The hair stands up on my arms every time I hear it.

BEQUEATHED TRACK

Take This Town

This was always one of my favourite XTC deep-cuts. I first heard it on the *Wake Up* single. It's the perfect bridge between *Drums and Wires* and *Black Sea*; it has that punk energy but you can hear the pop thing and the Beatles influence shining through. Once again, the energy and the groove perfectly match the lyrics and the sentiment. It sounds like *Punch and Judy*'s close cousin and that was always one of my favourite *English Settlement*-era tracks. It's almost the same tempo and groove.

I dig the hook and love the sound of the guitars. It was 1980, so this was when the Police were taking over the world with *Zenyatta Mondatta*. The clean chorus-y ascending chord progression Dave plays on *Take This Town* sounds very similar to Andy Summers. I don't know which one influenced the other, but in 1980 that was the sound. My favourite part is the outro which is when Dave gets his Billy Gibbons on. The pinch harmonic lick that repeats over and over is one of my favourite XTC moments. I wouldn't be surprised if Dave was listening to *La Grange* by ZZ Top at that time.

Steve Conte
NEW YORK DOLLS, STEVE CONTE NYC

INHERITED TRACK

Take This Town

Once again XTC surprises me with a song that when I first hear it I think, "Nah, this is too weird. I'm not into it," and then after a few listens I'm a true believer, amazed by its creative genius. I first heard XTC in the early 80s when some of the guys in my college dorm would play *Black Sea* and *Drums and Wires* in their rooms. I remember thinking they sounded too "noisy" and avant garde (back then I was into the Police and old bebop jazz...) but one day I heard *Melt the Guns* on my college radio station and everything clicked! I went out and got *English Settlement*, fell in love and then went back to *Black Sea* and *Drums and Wires* and fell for them as well... and nearly every album after.

Apparently, I've had *Take This Town* in my CD collection for years, not realising it. It's on the XTC compilation *Rag and Bone Buffet* that contained some of my faves like *Blame the Weather*, *Tissue Tigers* and *Punch and Judy*, and while I loved those almost instantly I ignored *TTT* until I was asked to listen to it for this project. I wasn't aware of the film *Times Square* that it was on the soundtrack of either, but I've watched the trailer and now knowing what the film is about and knowing the lyrics, I can see that Andy Partridge wrote it especially for this film.

Musically, it's a crazy song and I hear many of the

same things John Wedermeyer heard. In particular, the Andy Summers guitar sound (the clean chorus-effect coupled with those fancy jazz 11th chords) and the uncharacteristic (for Dave Gregory) pinch harmonics on the outro solo... but my favourite Dave moment on this is his entrance into guitar solo/bridge. It starts with a line that is a bit weird for the key that it's already in but where it lands, that last note – it resolves into a different key – totally genius.

CHOSEN TRACK
No Thugs in Our House

The intro of *No Thugs in Our House* has one of my favourite beats from Motown. It's right from Stevie Wonder's *Uptight*, which the Stones stole for *Satisfaction* and a million other bands stole after that. It's that four-on-the-snare with the kick drum accenting and Terry Chambers' amazing drum sound. Not only is it a cool beat, but the acoustic guitar is playing one of my favourite chord movements – an open E major to a D with a ninth in it (with an open E string at the top and no F sharp). Then when the band comes in – that guitar riff and Colin's chromatic bass line which is just slightly out, which is why I love it, and then Andy screaming over the top of it: "Aagh!" It's one of my favourite moments ever recorded. It's up there with the Beatles.

When I first heard it, I had no idea what he was singing – this one-note melody that goes into a long-held note that's very melodic – but Andy's lyrics are genius. It's like a queen bee in her nest with "insect headed" and "waspies" which is a corset, so you've got Andy's wordplay already. Then you've got "polypaste breath" which is a reference to toothpaste.

He's painting such a picture of a typical English home: wallpaper, pipe and slippers, newspaper, sitting in his chair...

Then you've got a boy in blue, which is the policeman trying to get in. And Graham is such an English name! It makes me think of *A Clockwork Orange* when Malcolm McDowell comes back and his parents are sitting there with Joe the lodger. I picture that wallpapery, very proper, stodgy scene and the kid is dreaming of doing whatever he wants to do – Andy was writing in the early 80s when there was a rise of right-wing racist violence.

I love the double chorus when Andy sings a melodic line ("Oh-oh oh-oh-oh-oh oh") right along with Terry's drum fill ("Ga-ga ga-ga-ga-ga ga"), just before the middle eight with the innocent and delicate organ. It's like the part Dave Gregory does in the middle of *Real by Reel* where he plays *Rock-a-bye Baby*; Andy is talking about sleep, so he plays a lullaby.

Then the delicate melody Andy sings at the beginning of *No Thugs* becomes raw and stretched out – "Hang her waspies on the li-i-i-ine" – to make it more intense because now you've got the whole story. It's a little movie. Right at the end, the "our house" is so dissonant and the guitar goes "gank-gank-gank" playing triplets against the straight beat – everything is rubbing, there's all this friction going along with the story.

Andy's always self-deprecating about his voice: "It sounds like a seal." I always tried to be a "good" singer myself; I love Stevie Wonder, Sly Stone and all these soul singers. But I notice I pick up on some of Andy's mannerisms in my own songs and I can see how influenced I was by this track. He's also got the kind of voice that can pull those lyrics off. You couldn't hear Marvin Gaye going, "Brother, brother, what's up with your polypaste?" This is definitely not lovey and sexy. It's angry and angular. His playing is angular, his point of view is angular, his singing and his note choices are all angular.

I hung out with Andy when I was in Swindon a few years back... what an amazing day. He's such a lovely bloke. He told me of how he wanted to be in the New York Dolls, which is one of the ways we got to talking online although he was into the band long before I was a member. We also both know Steve Lillywhite which is what really sealed the deal for our meeting. We had another connection in our mutual friend, Dennis Fano, who built guitars for him and played Andy one of my records years before. And then Andy actually liked my music! When he heard the lyrics to my song *Dark in the Spotlight*, he said, "Rhyming 'distortion' with 'fame and misfortune' is a stroke of genius." We played guitars, showed each other riffs and songs, told jokes, watched YouTube videos, listened to new recordings of his in the "shed" at his engineer Stu Rowe's house. He showed me how to play *Scarecrow People*. It was a pinch-me situation for a fan and musician like me.

BEQUEATHED TRACK
It's Nearly Africa
It's very cinematic with its tribal drum beat and the marimba sample on the Prophet-5, which always sounded like bones to me – hence the line "shake your bag of bones", a trick I believe Andy pulled off again on *Poor Skeleton Steps Out*. In my mind, I see the African plains with camouflage safari-gear wearing folks riding in Land Rovers with wildlife roaming around... especially rhino, for some reason.

Laurie Langan
FASSINE

INHERITED TRACK
It's Nearly Africa
"That's not traffic roar/That's a leopard in your heart" hidden among the jungle of lyrics is one of my favourite lines. A hypnotic, rhythmic and almost tuneless song that leans back on the drums and bass and allows the vocals to journey where they wish with a strong stream of consciousness. Joyful horn exclamations break you from the daydream before you're plunged back into the rhythm and reminded that "We're dancing with disaster".

CHOSEN TRACK
Another Satellite
This is lyrically bruising, with a melody that bends, melts and creaks like scorching metal. A deceptive bossa nova type beat and the relaxed drag of the guitar lull you into the other-worldly feel of this space trip. Achingly heartfelt the song is a beautiful letter of denial and letting go. Wonderful.

BEQUEATHED TRACK
Wake Up
This is an incredible Colin track from a very, very underrated album. *The Big Express* has grown to be a favourite of mine the more I listen to it.

Simon Barber and Brian O'Connor
SODAJERKER

INHERITED TRACK
Wake Up
The Big Express was one of two XTC albums recommended to us when we were about 16 by our GCSE music teacher, who was a huge fan of the band (*Mummer* was his other top tip). We actually found it a difficult record to like at first, not as immediately accessible as others, and quite of its time in terms of the drum sounds and so on, but now we think it might well be their most underappreciated record.

Colin's *Wake Up* kicks things off in striking fashion with its syncopated stereo guitar assault (said by its author to represent the relentless, repetitive grind of the working day). It's fairly untypical of Colin's tunes in that the vocals have a more aggressive, rapid-fire delivery in the verse than you might expect from him, with a lot of words packed into a line, and some pleasingly abrasive harmonies. In fact, you could be forgiven for thinking it's actually Andy singing when the vocal first comes in; the melody sounds not unlike something Andy would write and, for us, seems to foreshadow his own *The Ugly Underneath* from *Nonsuch*. The song is based on a few simple chords, but in the capable hands of producer David Lord and the band becomes something truly atmospheric.

The lyrics are much more in keeping with a lot of Colin's writing – a keenly observed, everyday slice of life in the Ray Davies vein, the mundanity of the subject matter contrasting nicely with the relative bombast of Lord's production. We particularly love the dramatic outro with its upper register piano flourishes and ethereal choir. As a song it's admittedly pretty slight, but it works perfectly as an album opener and demonstrates how even the most straightforward of songs can be transformed into an compelling listening experience with an inventive arrangement and a dash of studio ingenuity.

CHOSEN TRACK
1000 Umbrellas

Having one's heart broken has been grist to the songwriter's mill since time immemorial, but only a writer like Andy Partridge can turn the agony of rejection into such a deliciously cathartic three-and-a-half minutes of chamber pop. One thing that strikes us about this song is how, melodically, Andy deviates from his normal approach in that his tune closely follows the nagging, hopeless descent of the chords in the verses; not what you expect from an almost habitually inventive melodist, but it fits the song's despairing mood perfectly. The clouds lift a little as the song moves into its B section, shifting to the major, but it's only a fleeting moment of respite, as Andy's narrator then proceeds to scoff at the mindless optimists who attempt to lift his spirits: "How can you smile and forecast weather's getting better, when you've never let a girl rain all over you?"

Lyrically, this is Andy at the top of his game (as he is throughout much of *Skylarking*). As any XTC fan well knows, the man has a gift for evocative imagery and fiendish wordplay to make any songwriter gnash their teeth with envy, and it's evident in abundance in *1000 Umbrellas*, with its tear-filled teacups, roadmaps to misery, vistas "golden in hue", jesters striking down monarchs and "salt seas recalled from school atlas".

Damn his eyes, he's good.

Amazingly, producer Todd Rundgren was less than keen on this track in its stripped-down demo form. It took Dave Gregory's masterful string arrangement to convince him to spare it from being dumped as unceremoniously as the song's protagonist. By all accounts, Gregory spent a considerable amount of time on it, and the results speak for themselves - it's an arrangement of which the late George Martin would've been proud and elevates a great piece of songwriting into a baroque masterpiece.

BEQUEATHED TRACK
Dear God

We're bequeathing *Dear God* because we'd love to know what the next person makes of Andy's commentary on the idea of a divine creator ("Did you make mankind after we made you?"), and any thoughts on the way in which the song was realised with the use of young voices.

Chris Braide
DOWNES BRAIDE ASSOCIATION, SONGWRITER

INHERITED TRACK
Dear God

This is a song I've heard 300,000 times. It's part of the DNA of why I love pop music. It's a great example of something that is incredibly catchy, but incredibly complicated as well. What I loved about it when I first heard it was this note in the opening chords - the F# on the E string that comes after the A, F and G. You don't expect it to go there. A more natural place for the chord progression to go would be A, F, G, E minor, which is what the Pet Shop Boys do in the verse of their song *Rent*.

Andy always writes in images - I can picture things when I listen to his songs - so, for me, there's a sense of unease: "Dear God, hope you got the letter..." this is really serious. Then he goes to the C, which is totally weird and is like sarcasm: "I don't need a big reduction in the price of beer." He's kind of saying "fuck you" with these bass notes. Then it goes to the D, which is the sense of seriousness again - "Let's get back to the point." It's so clever. Words and music are in a perfect marriage.

Andy and I worked on *Skyscraper Souls* with Geoff Downes. He made *Glacier Girl* sound ice cold because of the way he arranged it and the way he sees images. It's the same in *Dear God*; I can hear the unease, the sarcasm and the seriousness.

The bass notes are centre stage. Even when he's playing the chords at the beginning, there's an emphasis on the bass notes, which give you that sense of unease or seriousness. It's not just a few chords to accompany the vocal, it's integral. I love Colin's bass in the middle eight. Suddenly, the bass aesthetic changes to a beautiful chorus with a delay effect that's Chris Squire-esque or Beatle-esque.

I love the arpeggio guitar throughout the second verse and then, of course, the lyric is brilliant. I love the folklore around it, the fact that it wasn't going to be included on *Skylarking*, that it was the B-side to *Grass*. Typical XTC, to make life difficult for themselves. It's this absolute gem, as good as a Beatles song, and they stick it on a B-side.

They're never straightforward, which is what we love about them.

I also love the instrumental. The high violin plays that beautiful melody and the cello is basically following the bass line. Then they converge and the instrumental melody plays under the final verse. It's an exercise in brilliant arranging. Just the sound of it: the toms at the end over "don't believe in heaven and hell" and the fact that the strings are playing fours initially and then they start playing eights, going up and up until you get to that last chord. There's a real drama, a sense that this guy really means what he's singing about.

Simon Barber and Brian O'Connor said they wanted to know my thoughts on the idea of a divine creator. I don't believe in a supernatural sky wizard and I see evidence of his/her absence and even downright cruelty every day (teenage cancer, for one example). But I do look at the sky, the trees, my two children, the oceans, music and feel in awe of all its wonder and the beauty of life and feel I can't explain it. God, for need of a better word, is every rock, blade of grass or hair on my kids' heads, but I don't believe it's a man with a beard looking down on my family, keeping us safe. We're on our own down here.

I hate and detest religion, that's a different beast altogether. The way in which religion punishes children, indoctrinates, instils fear in young, beautiful minds and breeds guilt is deeply abhorrent to me, so the use of the child's voice in the opening verse is particularly poignant. The idea of the Catholic church punishing children for thought crimes, where the child's every thought must be monitored and then judged accordingly is the real sin. And God forbid they have any thoughts about sex and sexuality.

Pity that the sky wizard wasn't more closely monitoring the many, many child sex abusers in the Catholic church. That is the very definition of evil. So, "did you make mankind after we made you?" Yes, probably, but I still can't explain why I'm here and why I love the wonder that is my children so deeply. Call it God if you like, but don't wait up for divine intervention or use it to absolve personal responsibility. Just be kind, don't hurt another soul and accept that you're going to die one day. What a miracle it all is!

CHOSEN TRACK
The Disappointed

I love the feel of it, the Beach Boys intro, the chuggy guitar and the fact that it sounds very economical. The previous album, *Oranges and Lemons*, was "let's pile as many things onto the multi-track as possible" and *The Disappointed* was the first single from the follow-up album, *Nonsuch*, and it was almost back to the punk aesthetic. It sounds like four people in a room but it's arranged so beautifully. I know what it's like when I'm producing my own stuff or for other people, there's a tendency to want to fill every harmonic hole. They don't do that on this track and I think that was a conscious decision after the previous album being so Technicolor.

The lyric is mournful but there's also something uplifting about it because of the surf thing. I love the cellos throughout, especially the way they develop over the last verse, playing this mournful part.

I just love every XTC song ever written!

Additional commentary

John Irvine (www.johnirvine.co.uk), **Michael John McCarthy** (www.michaeljohnmccarthy.com), **Hugh Nankivell** (www.soundcloud.com/hugh-nankivell) and **David White** (www.soundcloud.com/boy-48)

EMOTION AT THE DROP OF A HAT

From bereavement to bullying, from break-up to breakdown, these true-life tales by XTC fans explore what the music makes us feel in the best of times – and the worst

THE BELT'S ALREADY TIGHT
Late-night soul coal for an over-worked employee

For ten years, I was a copywriter in the marketing department of a large regional US department store. While the things I wrote about were rather frivolous – trendy clothes and housewares, cosmetics and shoes – the work and the workplace were anything but. It was a surprisingly political atmosphere, full of outsized egos and more than a few leaders whose concern was not nurturing a capable team but simply remaining in positions of power.

It didn't start this way. In the first five years, working overtime was a relatively rare occurrence, happening only before our most challenging retail seasons. After that, the workload crept up and up to the point that I stayed late most nights. As my responsibilities grew, it was common for me to be there 12 or more hours nearly every weekday. It seems ridiculous now, but at the time, I thought that was the price of being in my senior role and earning the money I did. To do excellent work, it simply required that level of commitment. Or sacrifice.

To get me through the late nights, I would choose an album or two to listen to all the way through. One night, I chose an old favourite – XTC's *The Big Express*, an album generally never regarded as their best but one I had always related to in a visceral way. The edginess of Andy's growls, the clanging guitars and the pounding beat of many of the songs had always resonated, especially if I needed to power through a challenge or navigate through complicated emotions.

Focused on my work that night, I half-listened until *Train Running Low on Soul Coal* came on – a song, I confess, I used to skip many times in my youth because I couldn't get past the discordant opening and had never given full attention to the words.

> *Me train running low on soul coal*
> *They push-pull tactics are driving me loco*
> *And they shouldn't do that*
> *No no no they shouldn't do that*

I stopped working and listened.

They pull me whistle too hard me bound to scream

I let the song play, then played it over and over

I'm a thirty year old puppy doing what I'm told

Suddenly, I got it in a way I never had – the slow start; the build to clashing and clanging; the relentless, hammering beat; the deep despair of the lyrics.

Can't find the wound from where I'm bleeding
He's just a nut and he's cracking

Hearing this song for the 50th time but also the first time, alone in a darkened corporate office, late at night when I should have been home – I began to understand what I had refused to see: that this job was wrecking my health and my mental clarity. That my company, as much as I had once loved it, was more than content to use me up.

I knew this and – not seeing any ready alternatives, too tired to contemplate a big change – I stayed two more years. I went back to *The Big Express* to get me through so many days (and nights) I didn't want to be there but felt I couldn't leave. The insistent chord that opens the album. The thundering drums and whipcracks. Lyrics about seeing people and places for what they are, not what you want them to be.

How she carry you
Over thick and thin ice
You still dug you spurs in

That's this world over, over over and out

Blue overall
Overall my anvil gives no further sparks
Blue overall
Overall my fears swim hammer headed sharks

I give emotion at the drop of a hat

In my last year there, it did become about the wall on which they dash the older engines. The company was sold to a private equity firm, which suddenly regarded legacy employees as overpaid and inherently disloyal (not true). Almost everyone in my department was eliminated or pressured to leave, and those of us who hung on, believing things would eventually settle down, were not only pushed into isolated roles but even physically moved away from the new leadership, who wanted as little to do with us as possible.

Reign of blows cascading down upon your shoulders

You didn't notice that the record's over

He who hesitates is lost

I was still working long days, now for people who demanded the moon but refused to value the efforts made to bring it to them. I told myself every day, this is temporary. One day, this will be over. And suddenly it was. My first outside interview led to an offer for the job I hold today. I love my new team, I hear words of appreciation, I make more money, I can see the sky from my desk for the first time in ten years, and I go home on time.

Little did I know that on a rainy day
All the little wishes that I put away
Would bring you

Things are good now, really good. I'm still reflecting on everything that happened over the last few years, especially that I allowed it to happen, but one thing I know is how much music of all kinds helped get me through. In particular, I am profoundly grateful for *The Big Express*, an album that still fires me up, reminds me to see clearly and not to wait, gets angry and noisy and weeps and wishes with me, and keeps me rolling strong down the track ahead.

Camille English

HURT LIKE KRYPTONITE
Reeling from the loss of a Supergirl

Skylarking helped me through the great difficulty of divorce with two young children. The details of the breakup are both tawdry and ultimately irrelevant, but let's just say my heart was broken, deeply. We had brokered an arrangement wherein we shared the kids (then six and two). This situation, while not ideal for the kids, did provide the opportunity to spend half the week as super-parent, the other half as free, if not-so-easy.

Skylarking had just come out when I moved into my modest bachelor joint. I had been following them avidly since discovering *Drums and Wires*. XTC was a huge favourite among the members of the music scene I was part of and one of my friends, a drummer who has since played with Alanis Morrisette, Susanna Hoffs and other theatre-fillers, played *The Man Who Sailed Around His Soul* while his band was setting up for a gig we were both playing. I was blown away. There was the familiar croon of Andy P, but with the amazing drumming of Prairie Prince (who I admire more than Terry Chambers, sorry) and a cool-ass 7/4 riff that sounded like a theme song to a 60s James Bond movie.

I went out and immediately purchased it. I immersed myself so heavily in it I was afraid my turntable would wear out. Side one, meditative with headphones, flip to side two, repeat ad nauseum. I felt like the record was talking to me in a way no other record by any band had.

My now ex-wife was Supergirl – so charismatic and powerful, yet unwilling to fulfill the promises once made. Its blend of exaltation and cynicism fitted my wounded state perfectly. I cried with *1000 Umbrellas*, cherished a chance to one day again "flatten the clover" on *Grass* and of course *Earn Enough for whoever "Us" might be*. *Big Day* and its sentiment laden with cynicism was perfect at the time, but *The Meeting Place* brought back ugly memories of my spouse's behaviour that led to the dissolution of our family. I even played it incessantly when my kids were around the house and they too became infected by its beauty.

Skylarking is still my favourite XTC record for its accessibility, its poppy jangle, its delicious drum sounds and its joyful stretching away from the gravity of the familiar tropes of pop music. It still summons those feelings from late 1986 and in the ensuing months/years, but in a cathartic way that feels good to this day.

Todd J, North Carolina

EVERYTHING IS BUZZ BUZZ
White Music beats the bullies

I'd discovered XTC in 1995, during my year out and during peak Britpop and was slowly getting through the back catalogue (I think I'd had *The Compact XTC* with the clown on, *Skylarking* and *Nonsuch* by the time I started uni) but not a huge fan yet. But when I arrived at university a horrible combination of things happened:

1. I found it very hard to mix and be sociable with people. Later this led to my diagnosis with Asperger's syndrome.
2. I was at the wrong university: Loughborough, full of sports and engineering students and I was neither.
3. I was doing the wrong course: library studies, having been cajoled into doing it by my parents.
4. I had had an old-fashioned church-going traditional upbringing which involved no alcohol or even any telly on Sunday. I was basically doomed from the start.

I was one of the few unlucky people to be bullied at university during my first night there because they didn't know why I didn't want to go out and drink and go clubbing. They banged on my door at three in the morning, laughing and jeering and destroying the drawing I did for my door to make me feel a bit happier.

Later on I realised they had completely forgotten having done this because of the amount they'd been drinking and wondered why I went from scared of them to actively hating them.

I was desperately lonely, sad and depressed. Most students at Loughborough were into Oasis and dance music and nothing else. So I had the pickings of a very good record shop in the town and was one of the few students to regularly take advantage of the record sellers in the students' union. Because I never went out and had saved up money from my year out, I had quite a lot to spend and most vinyl and tapes were only a quid. Thusly *White Music* came into my life.

In my first term, my music tastes were basically this: Syd Barrett, Nick Drake and Scott Walker during the day; the Boo Radleys' *Giant Steps* for when I was most distressed; *White Music* for when I had to get myself out of the rut I was in and face the world outside.

There was something about it, this weirdly energetic and giddy and awkward music that resonated. I could not be depressed with it. I could feel angry and somehow draw energy from it and use that to be able to leave my room. It was the only thing I had in my Walkman to get me around campus. I found a copy on vinyl, also for a quid and weirdly with the insert to *Go 2* on it (which I stuck on my wall), and would blast it out in my room when I needed to.

The other records were soothing or insular or somehow spoke to the chaos and deep, desperate depression I was going through. *White Music* was different. It buoyed me up for when I needed to go out. It was a suit of armour for the outside world. Until *Apple Venus* it was my favourite XTC album for that very reason.

Anonymous

THE GUTTER SHINES LIKE THE SWIRLING SKY
A bitter pill between relationships

When *Apple Venus* came out I was going through a period where one relationship was ending and another one was not quite beginning. The songs on it resonated with me, particularly the line "I may as well wish for the moon as her.... as there's more chance of that coming true..." Both relationships fizzed out ultimately and it was my own fault, but fortunately the album brought me comfort. It reminded me there were still beautiful things in the world (that album for example) and that my fortune would cycle around again eventually.

Anonymous

HURTFUL COMMENTS FROM THE BOSS
Stress, depression... and Skylarking

Back in 1986, I was in my first post-university corporate job. I was living on my own, dealing with a ton of stress on every level; my apartment had been robbed, work was overwhelming and I was dating a narcissist. I had a terrifying dream one night that left me in what seemed to be a never-ending anxiety attack. This led to depression, which I have been battling ever since. My mental restlessness left me unable to interact socially with people, to read or watch television. However, music was one of the few things I could focus on without it overloading my mind.

I had always considered myself to be on the cutting edge of music. I was involved in high school and university radio for years, and even had a job at a small AM Station, post college. I could route MTV (which at that time was very cutting edge) through my stereo without having to stare at the videos. This was when I became acquainted with

Skylarking. I was also an ardent Todd Rundgren fan, which further piqued my interest.

Over the course of the next year, this album became my salvation. *Earn Enough for Us* held particular significance since I was feeling so much pressure from my first real "boss". 1986 was not an easy time to find yourself in the throes of a mental illness. My struggles became common knowledge in my workplace, and I was openly ridiculed by everyone around me. Looking back, I am certain I was genetically programmed to develop anxiety/depression disorder, and the circumstances of my life just presented the "perfect storm" of triggers.

After having watched Andy in *XTC: This Is Pop* describe his struggles, I am amazed at how familiar they are to me. Panic attacks, brain melt, things in your life seeming out of control, a sense that bad things were just happening to me – "stop the world, I want to get off" – that was me as well. All of it was beyond my control. It was a long slow road to getting back to a new sense of normalcy.

But eventually I could listen to *Skylarking* without crying – major milestone! I remember feeling this was a step in the right direction. I could once again just enjoy the music, deep as it was. I continued to improve, and continued to follow XTC.

This past summer, was very hard. While at work one day, I stumbled across a disturbing find; while briefly stepping into the office of one of our corporate officers, I observed a pornographic DVD was loaded onto their laptop computer. The movie was not playing, but the title page/scene selection was disturbing enough. To make matters worse, based on the title I observed, it appeared to be children.

I was beyond shocked. I was sure I was going to be sick. I reported it to our management, but I still felt I should contact law enforcement, even though management had told me not to, they would investigate.

I called my elderly father after work. We had originally made plans to get together that evening, but he said he had had a tiring day in his assisted-living facility and I could tell he was tired. I was devastated by what I had discovered at work, but did not share with my dad. We ended our conversation saying we would try to get together the next day.

The next morning, I received a call at approximately 10.30am that my dad had passed. He was 85. It was a shock, but at the same time, it wasn't. Things went steadily downhill from there. Planning a memorial, cremation, we are Episcopalian (Anglican C of E) and so very fond of non-messy cremations and proper polite, stone-faced memorial services!

You know, no emotions here!

During the same time I was asked to meet with corporate attorneys concerning the situation at work. I told the truth from start to finish and was assured I would be kept in the informational loop. Did I mention that my husband had been living and working in a foreign country for the past two years? My son was at college and although his company has generous home visits allowed, I was essentially alone.

Long, long story short. Nothing ever really came of the "big, internal, investigation". By October, I was still working, with the perpetrator, no less, and just couldn't take it any more. My employment ended there in early November (on my terms) and I found myself having to deal with the delayed grief of my father's passing, still alone.

I floundered. I now had no reason to leave the house. I didn't get dressed, I barely interacted with anyone. The holidays (the first without my father) might as well have been any other day of the week. Getting through the day was my only priority. One day I was standing in my kitchen and I couldn't remember what day it was; I was in a serious depression and I needed serious help.

My brother and I were casually talking in January when he said, "Do you have Showtime? There is a great documentary on XTC that you *have* to see."

I had seen it on our programme guide and set it to record. I promised my brother I would watch and we would talk again to discuss. Once again, XTC entered my life at a critical time. I watched *This Is Pop* over and over (big crush on AP), dug out all our old CDs and started once again listening to music, when my mind could handle little else.

I am struggling with how to put this into words. I am 57 years old and once again dancing around the house to *The Mayor of Simpleton* by myself. Their music hasn't miraculously healed me, but it has definitely helped. I would even love to be involved in the music industry once again, even if it's only in an administrative role. I suppose you can take the girl out of rock'n'roll, but you can never take the rock'n'roll out of the girl.

So now I am a fully born-again rabid XTC fan and follower. I have joined three Facebook fan pages, and created a Twitter account solely for the purpose of following Andy. Yesterday he actually tweeted me back *and* used my name! I am starting to see there may be a way out of this. Yesterday another fan tweeted: "Rewatching *This Is Pop* brings me to tears each time. Why? It's impactful having those songs, that have been a big part of my life, presented so well and in such great context."

This is exactly how I feel. Maybe, if I can make it through *This Is Pop* without crying... it will be my next big step towards healing.

Anonymous

THE FLY THAT CLIMBED THE SUGAR HILL
A career break with Nonsuch

My young family and I had just moved to a lovely English country-style house which once sat on a suburban Chicago golf course. As the years passed the golf course became a subdivision but the beautiful home remained. And we loved it.

What my wife and I didn't love was commuting to the Chicago Loop every day. The costs of commuting and paying for childcare were a strain on our budget. My wife, a personal assistant to a well-known architect, was the breadwinner and so I decided to change jobs to be closer to home. I calculated that if I could get laid-off, collect unemployment and become a house-husband we'd come out ahead... child care and commuting expenses being what they are.

And so, in the spring of 1992 I bid farewell to the rat race. It was daunting because while I possessed the skills needed to be a good house-husband, I had to put my career on hold and decide what to do next. While I relished my time with my young sons I knew at some point I'd have to consider my career future. I was at a crossroads. Luckily for me, *Nonsuch* was released shortly thereafter and I found my summer talisman.

I absorbed *Nonsuch* from the very beginning. Summer mornings spent on the patio playing along to the songs on guitar. I still fondly recall our older son, who was five years old at the time, singing along to *Holly Up on Poppy*, *Dear Madam Barnum* and *Peter Pumpkinhead* as the summer slowly drifted by, relaxed in the undertow - sorry, wrong album.

Each day at 6pm my beautiful wife would return from work and I'd coyishly sing the first two lines of *Then She Appeared* to her as she stepped through the door. In those moments when I felt confused about my future, when it seemed my career path was obscured, there was always *Omnibus*, *The Ugly Underneath* and *Wrapped in Grey* to remind me that all was not lost.

I finally went back to work after a year. I thank Andy and the boys for seeing me through muddled times. *Nonsuch*, more than any album in my collection, harks backs to a particular time and place for me and as such will always remain very close to my heart and psyche.

Rob Roberts

TALK AND LET YOUR MIND LOOSE
Life lessons from a billion Arabian nights

I was a 14-year-old boy in Texas, who had realised very suddenly I was in a difficult situation; I was trapped living with a right-wing religious ideology I wanted nothing to do with, with no real path of escape. My parents were in deep with this ideology, as were the rest of my family. I was clearly different, and in their eyes, the black sheep.

Fortunately, I also entered high school at around the same time and being involved in the music programme meant I was in classes with kids older than me. Looking for any kind of escape, I found it in their music tastes. I soon learned of a radio station that was hard to pick up (nestled between the bad Christian rock station and the bad R&B station on the dial). Often, I could only get it at night, but they were playing new and strange sounds. One day a fresh track caught my attention; it sounded old yet new; pop yet so against the grain. It had choruses and verses and bridges, and the notes and harmonies were perfect. In fact, every piece of it fitted together perfectly. It was an updated Beach Boys or Beatles and it was marvellous. It was the perfect pop song. I learned from the DJ (who might be reading this... hi Jeff K!) it was by the band XTC and the song was *The Mayor of Simpleton*. That went down on the list. At the top.

I'm pretty sure I bought it near the time it came out, as they had some posters up of it in the Sound Warehouse where I tended to buy my cassettes. I was excited to get to my room to play it on my cassette-player boom box. By then I had heard *Mayor of Simpleton* quite a few times and was giddy to be able to play it continuously. It was the second track, so I just had to get through the first one...

I pressed "play" and sat back to hear the music come in, with what seemed like leftover tracks from George Harrison circa 1967. The crescendo gets to the point and stops.

"Kid..." was so loud in my ears... the next few lines were a blur but the next one that made any sense to me was "Can't all think like Chekhov, but you'll be OK." I jumped up and rushed to the tape deck and stopped it. Rewind. Start over. What... the... hell? Scramble for the cassette case; are the lyrics in there? They are! Start again, listen closely. Now what was all this he was saying?

"Kid, stay and snip your cord off, talk and let your mind loose, can't all think like Chekhov, but you'll be OK." I didn't even know who Chekhov was, nor how to make sense of this lyric. Yet those lines that were initially a blur felt like a direct conversation with me. It felt like something out of *Alice in Wonderland*. Of all the music I had picked up, this was a three-dimensional colouring book of sounds... with colours. It was a hand coming out and smacking me across the face as if to say: "Pay attention!"

"Kid, is this your first time here? Some can't stand the beauty, so they cut off one ear, but you'll be OK." A Van Gogh reference! I knew him, the ear, but couldn't make sense of it, but needed to. For someone trapped in the bland situation I was in, this was a new voice with a new opinion, talking about things I wanted to know about. It was a far cry from the voices trying to tell me how to be; it was a voice enticing me to come find out things. This was the moment the doors of perception opened for me, this was the rabbit hole and I was sliding down freely.

"Welcome to the Garden of Earthly Delights..." comes blaring out, and the visual I had was the scene in *The Wizard of Oz* where it suddenly goes to Technicolor from black and white. It still sounds like that to me.

"Welcome to a billion Arabian Nights..." OK, I understood this, having read the book previously, so I could get some of what he was saying. It was at this point I realised whoever wrote this was a lot smarter than me and I wanted some of whatever this guy had.

"This is your life and you do what you want to do, this is your life and you spend it all..." this is the philosophical knowledge my brain had been seeking without the blinders being put on me at every angle by the adults in my life. This was profound.

"This is your life and you do what you want to do, just don't hurt nobody, and the big reward's here in the Garden of Earthly Delights". I could even live with the double negative because even that was so profound. How did they come up with the idea to do that scale run-up to the note on "- lights"? My heart beats a bit quicker at this point in the song. It has every time since...

Truth be told, I felt like I had a direct lecture from an adult finally being totally honest with me, without trying to control my thinking, saying, "Hey, it's going to be OK, it's your life, get out there and live it!" All wrapped in this incredible musical package of eastern beats, quirky bass-runs, catchy backing vocals, off-kilter guitar licks... oh, and then a segue straight in to the track I bought the album to hear. And everything in Technicolor, so much of it. The next day I went to the school library and looked up Chekhov. I clearly had a lot to learn, and my time would be best spent doing that sort of learning.

Fast-forward to now: it did get me through, and the emotions of a 14 year old subside to realise a lot of those blinders from adults were simply good intentions to keep me out of harm's way, and adults doing the best they could. But at the time, all I could see was being held down and here's one guy (well, three guys) showing me I'm not entirely wrong in my thinking. It lit a fire for knowledge, for pop, for critical thinking and for foreign dialects. But mostly, it lit a fire for XTC.

James Reimer

MY PENICILLIN DOES ITS BEST
The XTC road to recovery

In 1992, I was at home with full-blown bronchitis - high fever, clogged lungs, the works - after my GP had misdiagnosed my stomach flu as food poisoning. It was miserable. I was confined to bed and delirious for most of the time. What kept me sane was, in a lucid moment, I got the missus to pick up the new XTC CD - *Nonsuch*. I listened to the album non-stop to recovery in the next couple of days. I felt calm and comforted in a state of aural ecstasy (pun intended!) that I do believe aided my return to health. *Nonsuch* remains one of my favourite albums and listening to the music now recalls a dark cloud with a definite silver lining.

Kevin Mathews

SO CIRCLING WE'LL ORBIT ANOTHER YEAR
That Is the Way... to survive a tough time apart

I've been an insatiable fan of XTC since I was about nine years old. It started in 1986. My brother had initially turned me on to XTC about a year earlier with *Waxworks*, and I loved it. I was still quite young, and wasn't really sure what I was listening to, but I knew I liked it. *Nigel* was one of my favourites, and I listened to it *All. The. Time.* I was eventually given *Skylarking*, and it blew my mind. So lush, turquoise and insistent. I've been listening to it for over 30 years, and it's still my favourite album ever made. From there, things progressed - *Oranges and Lemons, Nonsuch*... you know the rest - but for some reason, I avoided the earlier XTC efforts.

Enter 2003. I'd finally earned the proper money, and gained the courage (!) to explore my nebulous history of XTC. Rather than go into *White Music* or *Go 2*, I went straight for *Transistor Blast*. This was my first sober taste of early XTC, and also of the SEGA-like, cosmic energy of their live shows. I was absolutely astonished.

Heh, in love. Just like I was with my girl. Wife, actually. And that very same year she left me. She ran into some hotshot with a Lexus, lots of money and just as many good looks, and she had a crush on him. (High School reunions are iodine on clean slacks.) Me? Aw hell, that is a different story. I was just a kid who loved XTC. Loved to sing the entirety of *Harvest Festival*, alone in the car. What could my chivalrous, stalwart heart offer anyone?

Well, that would be a multitude of efforts to explain, but we eventually got back together, stronger than ever. And that strength has a lot to do with XTC. You see, during the nearly-a-year we spent apart, I lived with a good friend of mine, and we constantly listened to album after album; *Transistor Blast* was one of them. When my wife left me, I was at the bottom of a bottomless heart. There was no consolation available from anyone. Family, friends, no one. I knew of no individuals that could help me. I truly felt completely isolated and marked for refuse. True, I had effortlessly supportive mentors, but I still felt like an iceman living in an iceman town...

But a group of people that I admired? That seemed to speak my same quirky language? Yeah, XTC. Partridge and company illustrated exactly what I was *always* feeling. Musically or lyrically, and often both. And bumping the corners of every musical pinball machine I popped a token into... the pictures of those familiar mates in the album notes... I wished I was them. *I am them.*

They guided me through the sharpest of thorns, thickest of thickets, and grizzliest of grasses. It's all about one tune, really. *That Is the Way*.

This is the tune that practically saved my life – and my marriage.

Picture and imagine: the landscape of the rural Indiana horizon in November with endless, flat-earth corn and soy-bean fields. Purple, distant barns hidden by condensation. Microscopic drizzle, wafts of dying weeds. The sky is a soft silver and the windshield is dirty. It's actually Thanksgiving Day and it's been a long drive to see her family. A short three-hour drive becomes a six-hour conversation, and while we shine our amateur-philosophy windows, we leave little left for the wipers. Gracious, she looked so beautiful. *So beautiful.* Tilting her head, giving me that longing look, smiling with the perfect addition of a smirk. Luminous, gracious and feeding the fields with her light... A goddess, indeed, poured from a vial of sunset. And that perfect, cosmic moment occurred while listening to this song.

And that is all I can think about when I hear that flugelhorn in *That Is the Way*, lamenting the curve of the Earth with its lilt. With those travelling guitars and reverb from miles away, I felt like freedom had finally reached my bubble. I can do whatever I want, go wherever I want, with a seemingly perfect and willing girl to take along for the ride. The clarity and focus of the memory is laughably clear. Hence, the song became etched in the walking stones of my brain, and played infinitely during that terrible year we spent apart.

But while we were separated, I managed to learn some XTC riffs, and best of all, listen to live recordings, demos and all kinds of various XTC albums available, and discovered that hearing them in their youth made *me* feel young again! This wasn't just some band that made some of the finest pop noises, they were rock'n'roll! When I finally gave serious listens to things like *Drums and Wires* and *English Settlement*, they transformed me *and* my tastes in rock history. These were songs I'd never heard before, a style I wasn't used to, and I was instantly smitten.

So yes, on the drive from Indianapolis to Valparaiso (and back), I brought along *Transistor Blast*, as I wanted to turn my lady on to it. She was receptive, thankfully. And how did that collection save my life? Simply put, it reminded me that life is still happening, and that there have been others in the world who have felt the same pains. It was just easier to listen to the music than it was the speech. For a time, I was as unhappy as the upturned snail, but hearing songs from XTC that reminded me of the beauty of living was what helped make me smile. And I have a good one.

That is the Way, indeed.

Quinn Fox

WORKING FOR PAPER AND FOR IRON
Never been a summer hot as this before

It was the summer of 1988 and my mother, who ran a small employment agency out of our home, had an interesting idea. "His name's Joe," she said. "He runs a stationery supply company and he needs someone to drive him around. It pays *[some sum I can't recall, but which at the time seemed princely]* a week and you'd be paid under the table. Tomorrow he needs you to pick him up in Ipswich (Massachusetts) and drive him to an appointment in New Haven, Connecticut."

Not having any job prospects for the summer, I agreed to the assignment, and set out the next morning for Joe's neatly appointed home in Ipswich, 45 minutes north of Boston. As soon as I pulled into the driveway, I saw what would become my chariot that summer: a brown Lincoln Town Car.

Joe himself was inside, getting ready with his wife and two small kids. That day, as we drove down Route 128, then Route 95 to New Haven, he explained he'd lost his license "for driving too fast," which made him sound like a daredevil, a guy who lived life to the fullest.

I came to like Joe, and enjoyed his description of mundane items like staplers. "The Bates 9000," he'd say. "Look at those curves."

"It doesn't look like your average stapler," was my uninspired response.

"That's because it's sleek," Joe said. "It's sexy."

We drove all over New England that summer. Every time we'd pick someone up, Joe would introduce me as "Eric, my driver," and the associate would chuckle as Joe told them the story he'd told me, about having his license stripped away because of too many tickets. Men being men, they accepted this response with the same sense of approval I had. If you're gonna lose the license, might as well go out in a ball of fire. Better to flame out than...

The only problem was the boredom. Because my job entailed shuttling Joe from his home to his office to appointments around New England, when I wasn't driving, I was waiting, mostly in parking lots. Joe let me keep the AC on, which was fortunate, as that summer was a scorcher (or as we called it in NE, "a scorcha".)

My other saviour was XTC. Besides being the first (and last) summer I spent as a chauffeur, it was also the first summer I spent as a fan of the boys from Swindon. The album that indoctrinated me was, of course, *Skylarking*, the one that got XTC a whole new raft of friends, mainly on the strength of *Dear God* and its superb video. But the friend who turned me on to XTC knew me well, so he'd slipped me the Dukes of Stratosphear's *Psonic Psunspot* at the same time. I was blown away at how, while one was pure psychedelic goofiness, *Skylarking* had enough Beatlesque whimsy to qualify as a bit of a throwback itself. Plus Todd Rundgren was producing, and if anyone knew how pop culture had evolved over the years, it was Todd.

Sitting in that Town Car, AC blasting while *Summer's Cauldron* blared alongside it, I experienced the kind of epiphany only music can provide.

It was my salvation the summer I worked a shitty job for a guy who turned out to be equally shitty. Months later, I learned he'd lost his license not for drag racing but for several instances of driving while intoxicated.

Before that summer, I'd have said that putting *me* behind the wheel of a Lincoln Town Car would have been equally foolish. But unlike Joe, I had a secret weapon: *Season Cycle, Earn Enough for Us, Vanishing Girl* and so many more. Andy Partridge was my patron saint, cooler than a Bates 9000 could ever be.

Eric Winick
[Some names and places have been changed.]

BRING YOUR HORN OF PLENTY
A release from religion and a mind set free

I think it all began with *Dear God*. I was raised in a Presbyterian family and attended an Episcopalian school from kindergarten through eighth grade. I was active in my church's youth group. As a child I won prizes for memorising Bible verses. I was pretty immersed in religion - not the fervent kind of religion we see so often today, it was pretty mild and calm, but still it was a huge part of my life.

Around the age of 13 or 14 I really started to doubt. I engaged in heated discussions in my church youth group. It crushed my optimistic heart so full of love to think of a God who would condemn most of the world's population just because they did not have the luck to be born into a Christian family. This made no sense to me.

I finally declared that if all the things my church was saying were true then I didn't want anything to do with that God. I recall even saying that I felt like I was a better person than the God they described. And I felt very alone… of course I knew there are millions of people who do not believe in God but I was convinced I did not know any.

It's a scary thing to let go of the faith you have been brought up with. So scary that I was not really prepared to admit that I do not believe in God until much, much later in life. I maintained for years that I just didn't believe in *that* God - my God was a really good guy, with nothing but love to give. Somewhere along the way I dropped that as well. At age 50 I still do not openly discuss the fact that I am an atheist.

I'm really not sure when I first heard *Dear God*, but I do remember feeling it completely captured my thoughts and feelings from the period of mentally wrestling with whether to hold on or let go…

True they are fairly common thoughts (if God is so good, why do such horrible things happen to good and innocent people?) but when you hear a song that completely mirrors your internal dialogue, it has an impact.

I think this is at the core of why people are so intensely affected by XTC songs and especially the breathtaking lyrics of Andy Partridge - he has an amazing ability to capture our thoughts and hearts in words we would never think to use but completely *feel*. And he invites us into his personal struggles. He shares his love, his disappointment, his vulnerability, his pain. We connect with all of these and it somehow builds an intimate relationship between people who have never met. Connected through our humanity.

There's a line in the 1985 movie *The Breakfast Club* that had a big impact on me: "When you grow up, your heart dies." I kind of vowed I would never let that happen to me and I definitely still have a pretty adolescent view. I think I have maintained that openness and am always attracted to people who seem to have a similar openness, who say how they feel despite the fact that some people may think that's not "cool". I guess I feel like Andy has this open quality - he writes beautiful songs that are *not* guarded, not constructed to be cool, just hangs it out there for all to see and enjoy and love… or not love. I think XTC fans also pick up on that openness, that complete sharing of private feelings. Of course - so many lyrics are like little miracles of wordsmithery, but it's the honestly that catches me.

Leslie Gooch

I RESIGN AS CLOWN
Life imitates art for a heart torn and broken

There are two incidents in my life where Andy wasn't just writing songs for me, he was writing about me…

The first was around the time of *Skylarking*, when I got involved with a young lady who was a few short months away from getting married to someone else. All of a sudden, *Earn Enough for Us* and *Big Day* attained even greater meaning and depth. At the time when I wanted to be making future plans with this wonderful woman, she was in the throes of planning for a wedding to someone else.

And yes, she went through with it.

We met again a few years later, and the spark was still there. But now she was living in domestic bliss with husband and daughter. I haven't seen her since, but I think of her often, and whenever I hear them, those two songs take me back and remind me exactly how I felt at that moment in time.

The second time an XTC song was a direct comment on my own experience was when *Nonsuch* came out. And there it was - track three - my hell exposed in two minutes, forty-nine seconds of musical genius.

Dear Madam Barnum was such an appropriate commentary on what was going on in my life that, once again, I wondered how Andy had managed to climb inside my head.

I was seeing a girl who (I probably should have realised) was a bit out of my league. But I made her laugh, and she seemed to enjoy my company. All seemed to be going well. But after about six months, she suddenly seemed to have a little bit less time for me. Just an evening here or there at first, but then this unavailability became the norm, and I couldn't help wondering whether someone else was providing even more compelling entertainment than I was.

Unfortunately, it turned out my instincts were right. She was seeing someone else on the side, and this warm and bubbly individual became an ice queen in a matter of weeks. I most definitely wasn't the sole fool who was pulling his trousers down any more, so I reluctantly (but for the best) resigned as clown.

There are other XTC songs that elicit memories so powerful that they're literally little time portals: I can never hear *Grass* without being transported back to a green field and a blissful romantic encounter in a field on a rare English summer's day; *Green Man* conjured up the sounds and smells of the British countryside when I was living thousands of miles away in Singapore; And I'll always remember a time when I was flying off on a holiday somewhere and choked up as I looked down from 30,000 feet on the people and towns that make up this small planet – with *This World Over* playing in my ears on my Walkman.

But those three tunes - *Earn Enough for Us, Big Day* and *Dear Madam Barnum* will always have a special place in my heart. I can't thank XTC enough for being such an important part of my life.

I never did find the gap in the fence that let them into my brain.

Jim Spencer

IN A MILK BAR AND FEELING LOST
A lifetime of musical nourishment

I was just turning 20 when I first heard "it". I'd already been in bands for 12 years, since I was a kid, growing up in Derby. Thinking back, my hometown probably shared a few things with Swindon. Provincial and a centre for the railways. For me though, it was also somewhere I needed to escape from, literally and figuratively. Music was my salvation in this regard... just a year from now, my life would be transformed, and I would be living in Copenhagen, playing in a full-time band, having gone pro.

"It" was *This Is Pop*. What the hell were they playing? What are those chords? *Are* they chords? They're so nasty. But, there was something else, rising like Olympus above this jagged cacophony: pure, perfect *pop*.

I grew up in the golden age of the single - T Rex, Slade, Sweet, etc - acts that were, unbelievably, to become friends and colleagues, acts that knew how to distill the magic into three beautiful minutes. This band, this new bunch of lunatics, were in on the secret. I bought *White Music* and told anyone who would listen that XTC were fucking amazing.

Then, they released *Go 2*. I didn't like it at all. It utterly passed me by. The difficult second album. I still don't have it. So it's all the more amazing that I jumped back on the bus later on.

I was living in Denmark, but visiting the UK for a month when *Making Plans for Nigel* came out. I was making a good living in a band, but bored to tears with the music I had to play. Seriously, I was climbing the walls. All in all, I spent pretty much two years of my life removed from the UK, at a time when there was no MTV, let alone internet. The bread-and-butter music I was playing became even further removed from what was happening at the cutting edge of pop. When I finally heard *Nigel* it was against a backdrop of incessant Eurotrash and mindless disco – it was musical manna from heaven. I cannot overstate the spur it gave me to kick this cushy gig to the kerb and strike out for something on my own. Their inventiveness was inspiring.

Drums and Wires made it clear to me that XTC were no mere flash in the pan, and it was from then onwards that they really had me. They became one of those bands where I would buy the albums sight unseen. I knew they would be of a certain standard, and they never let me down. Still purveyors of off-kilter riffs (*Sgt Rock*), they blazed a stunning trail with *Black Sea* – the lyrics, the imagery, the musicianship – pure delight. In an era that was lousy with mindless, soul-less synth pop, these boys had guitars and weren't afraid to use them.

By late 1981, I was back in the UK, unable to take the gig in Scandinavia any longer. I didn't want to play covers in Scandinavian clubs, I wanted to make *Drums and Wires Mk2*! I had helped form a band in Yorkshire on my return, meeting for the first time Trevor Midgley who had been signed to Polydor with his band the News. He and his brother-in-law Al Quinn were also heavily influenced by XTC. Al had previously played with Be Bop Deluxe's Bill Nelson, and went on to be part of his touring band Practical Dreamers. To be forming a band with like-minded musicians was wonderful, and our first single, *Telephone*, I had written under the influence of XTC. I paid homage to the quirky atonal riff, the irresistible chorus (I hoped). Trev gave it a solo Dave Gregory would have been proud of – beautifully constructed and off the wall. It didn't make any waves, but it fetches a tidy sum in Japan these days...

By 1982, I was struggling a bit, living in a bedsit in Leeds. A low point was being broken into, my meter raided, but a stack of our singles in picture sleeves left untouched, deemed not even worth nicking, never mind paying for. I had very little, just one room to live in, and the separate kitchen (which had been broken into through the cellar). That was probably the lowest point of my musical life. I was full of self-doubt. Had I done the right thing, chucking away an easy gig abroad? These were dark days, travelling hundreds of miles for little reward, sending demos off to record companies with scant hope of a reply, living my life in that one room. I had a bed, a TV and I had my stereo. The Falklands war had the country under a 24/7 pall of gloom, the BBC's Brian Hanrahan "counting them all out, counting them all back," the strange bald man from the Foreign Office reading out the daily losses like the football results on the evening news.

Into that atmosphere, on the humble music cassette, came *English Settlement*. I needed it more than I probably knew. I devoured this album. Chameleon-like, they had changed yet again, acoustic guitars to the fore, tales of English Roundabouts, Snowmen, Jason and his Argonauts on far flung seas and Nazis in suburbia. It was glorious. You didn't really need the pop video with XTC. You read the lyrics and you listened. You escaped. I left that room and wandered through the mindscapes of Partridge and Moulding. They took me out of myself, away from my troubles. My bedsit was nearly Africa. The pleasure it gave me, by extension, restored my pride in being a musician.

Mummer continued the theme… there was something stupidly happy about the music of XTC, full of unbridled joy somehow – I often break into a grin listening to it. It is strange to think all these years later, that Pete Phipps, drummer on this and *Big Express,* became my bandmate. XTC have formed the greater part of the soundtrack of my life, filled me with joy, and, when my train was running low on soul coal, helped me keep faith with my career as a musician, and I am forever in their debt.

Kev Moore

I'D LIKE THAT
Emotional truth and sonic surprises

The early 90s was a time of some turmoil for me. My father died in 1991. My mother's childhood diabetes started advancing to the point where the once-independent psychologist was wheelchair bound and dependent upon her only child for things she'd once taken for granted. Both of them were in their 40s. As if that wasn't enough, I was also dealing with unrequited love for someone I can only diplomatically refer to as intensely religious, and the loss of a 15-year friendship with a so-called friend who decided to steal money that I would have gladly given him anyway. In the midst of so much chaos and heartache, XTC showed me how pain and anguish could be funneled into something truly great.

That acquired knowledge turned out to be rather useful when my father died of lung cancer. Suddenly *Dying* from the *Skylarking* album meant a whole lot more. Colin Moulding's refrain "I don't want to die like you" felt like a battle cry to avoid self-destruction. *Across This Antheap* from *Oranges and Lemons*, with its gleefully nihilistic attack on all aspects of so-called civilisation, was a key to the freedom that comes with loss and suddenly realising all the day-to-day trappings of existence are crap.

And if that particular song (my favourite, by the way) didn't fully delve into nihilism, there was always *Complicated Game* to remind me how pointlessly absurd nearly everything was.

To say my worldview was shaped by XTC is probably an exaggeration. However, it's not one to say their music, Andy Partridge's in particular, helped shape it and hone it for better or worse.

Within a year I had obtained every major XTC release available at the time. I knew nothing of the backstage brawling between the band and its record company, so when *Nonsuch* was released in 1992, it barely registered that there had been a three-year gap between it and *Oranges and Lemons*. *Nonsuch* would turn out to be XTC's last studio album for seven years. It was also the first one I ever bought when it was released. In a sense, it became "my" XTC album, and I played it over and over for months.

By the time *Apple Venus Volume 1* was released in 1999, my mother had been deceased for a year and a half. I'd fallen out of XTC a bit over the years, the post-grunge mid-90s alternative scene having broadened my musical horizons even more. My then girlfriend mentioned the new album to me and I ran out and bought it. The decision to go entirely in an orchestral direction did not appeal to me. They'd already done similar on *Skylarking*, everybody's favourite XTC album except mine, and it was done better there. I felt dejected. It wasn't as if I'd waited for another XTC recording. I'd purchased all sorts of imports and collections over the years, content in my assumption that there would be no more new stuff from my favourite Brits. I'd moved on to newer artists, still returning to the boys from Swindon from time to time. Why had they returned, only to serve up an offering I could not get into?

I'm all in favour of pushing the creative envelope, but this felt too safe, too cautious in light of what XTC had done before. It felt like a betrayal. Then it dawned on me. That was the point. What was XTC if not a band that defied expectations?

By inverting the most traditional formula in western music, XTC did something new with something very old. It was an approach that would come to inform my fiction writing in ways both strange and fulfilling. And while it is still my least favourite of their albums and the one I listen to the least, it holds a special place among the superior works.

Apple Venus Volume 2 was more of a return to form minus Dave Gregory's impressive guitar work. There is a sense of struggle there as Andy attempts to hold the act together. He mostly succeeds but even when I heard the album for the first time, there was a swan-song feeling to it. Somehow I knew I was saying goodbye to my favourite band.

I've recently discovered a rather sizable online fanbase for XTC, which has revitalised my love for their underrated, innovative music. The majority of their work has stood the test of time and the emotions they once conjured in me occasionally return when I'm in my car, blasting their music. I can't even imagine life without Andy and Colin.

I don't want to either.

Christopher Nadeau

HEARTS ARE BUILT LIKE RUBBER
XTC: lost and found

> "This is a song Charles Manson stole from the Beatles. We're stealing it back..." - Bono's opening comment on *Helter Skelter* on *Rattle and Hum*

I was introduced to the music of XTC by a friend in 1982. From then on, there was no question about it. I'd found a new favourite band. Their music helped me through college. XTC was there when I celebrated triumphs and it consoled me through tragedies. I ordered hard-to-find recordings through music magazines and I subscribed to *The Little Express*. Life was good.

But for a long period I'd stopped listening to XTC. It wasn't that I'd burned out on the music (how could you burn out on *Black Sea*, *English Settlement* or any of the band's studio records?) No, this was personal. I was knee-deep in the mire of divorce and, unfortunately and without their knowledge, Andy and the boys were being pulled along for the ride. Understand that this wasn't a dispute about physical property. It wasn't that my soon-to-be ex was claiming rights to my vinyl collection. It's that during our years of sharing bands, as couples often do, I'd come to associate XTC, emotionally and mentally, with The Ex. I'd introduced The Ex to the boys from Swindon way back in 1987, and we'd spent many long car rides singing along to their catalogue in the years that followed. Probably would have been easier if she'd said, "This music sucks," back when I played it for her, to which I could have replied, "I think we should see other people." Sadly, it didn't shake out that way. The Ex and I separated in 1996 following a tumultuous marriage that spanned five or six years. It was odd, but in the months, and yes, years, that followed the collapse of our former union, I felt a wave of emotional pain whenever I tried to listen to any XTC song. Their music conjured up remembrances of The Ex, and I despised The Ex. In divorce, we often hear about the loss of property, the division of families, etc. In 1996, I lost something more.

The Ex had stolen my band.

Life went on, albeit differently. Other bands filled the void, but the thing is, I didn't want other bands to fill the void. There seemed to be no way out of the dilemma. Thus, in 2003, I decided to part with my vinyl, my fan club material and my CDs. I all but forgot about XTC.

The End, right?

Thankfully, not quite, for I was soon to experience an XTC emotional rebirth.

Two factors lead to me reclaiming XTC as my own. First, I'm blessed (or cursed, depending on your point of view) with a terribly poor memory. Over time, The Ex became a distant memory that was growing more distant by the day. Second, I missed hearing their goddam music. Still, I was reluctant to jump back onto the XTC big express. A part of me was still convinced that it would bring pain rather than enjoyment. I started repurchasing the XTC catalogue on CD. Before long, I'd amassed everything from *White Music* forward. I just didn't play them. A touch of reservation continued to dog me.

One rainy spring morning in 2004 I plunged back in. I figured it would be best to start with material that was new to me, reasoning that the songs would carry no emotional baggage since I'd never before listened to them. This was my introduction to *Apple Venus* and *Wasp Star*. Not surprising, XTC's 21st-century efforts are as inventive and enthusiastic as their recordings from the previous three decades. I was thrilled by the acoustic drive of *Apple Venus*, it took me right back to *Settlement* but, again, without any associations to The Ex. With *Wasp Star* I found new electric rock. It also occurred to me at that moment that XTC is both my favourite electric and acoustic artist. I can't think of any other band that could single-handedly fill that card. I played *Apple* and *Wasp* countless times throughout 2004. After becoming intimately familiar with these recordings, I began reabsorbing other material, from the main catalogue releases to compilations like *Coat of Many Cupboards*, *Transistor Blast* and Andy Partridge's brilliant and underappreciated *Fuzzy Warbles* series. Clearly, the band had been quite busy during the time I'd stopped listening to them.

While living in LA, I had a weird Amoeba moment. For those outside of LA, I'm referring to Amoeba Music, a colossal Sunset Boulevard warehouse stacked floor to ceiling with new and old vinyl, compact discs, VHS, DVDs and other esoterica. Amoeba is the Disneyland of record shops. Its hugeness is dwarfed only by its immeasurable store stock. In a word, it's impressive. I'd gone to Amoeba to trade in a few CDs and, naturally, shop. Upon entering the store, I was quite pleased and surprised to hear *Senses Working Overtime* playing on the overhead audio system. This was followed by *Jason and the Argonauts* and *No Thugs in Our House*. Suffice to say, I felt at home.

About five minutes into my shopping excursion I noticed a gal wearing a green shirt with white screen-printed graphics. It was, of course, a *Settlement* shirt. She was smiling and chatting on her mobile. I walked over to her and, without speaking a word, pointed at her shirt and then pointed to the ceiling speakers. She smiled and told her caller, "Another XTC fan just pointed out my shirt!" It was one of those weird moments of synchronicity, usually reserved for film, that make you realise you're awake. *Settlement* remained stuck in my head for days.

And that's the "downside" to XTC's music. It's addictive. It's like brainwashing. Once one of their tracks gets into your mind, there's a good chance it's going to sign a long-term lease and order a truckload of furniture. Your tenants may vary, though I literally had *Young Cleopatra* stuck in my head for three consecutive days. I'm half-convinced that Andy should place labels on the records stating, "*Warning*: Addictive Tracks Ahead."

Like the pop sounds of Cake or Fountains of Wayne, XTC's quirky, up-tempo music grabs hold of the mind and refuses to let go. It can be quite maddening but mostly it's refreshing.

Following the double-coincidence at Amoeba, I decided to discover *English Settlement* all over again. I won't waste your time or mine by trying to pen a capsule review of the album. It's been done before by writers whose trade is music criticism. If I were to tell you there's one or two bad songs on the album I'd be lying to you. As I became reacquainted with this album once again, I found myself taken back to memories of Pennsylvania winters, my freshman year at the University of Pittsburgh, Howard Chaykin's *American Flagg* series, and Bill Sienkiewicz's work on *Moon Knight*. To my delight, The Ex was not among my memories.

Losing XTC for a period of my life was painful. Having them back has been not only enjoyable, but has also provided me with new perspectives and a greater appreciation for their work. About two weeks ago, I played *Stupidly Happy* to my nine-year-old daughter as we were driving home from a craft store one weekend afternoon. When the song ended she said, without hesitation, "Play that again!"

Yeah, I think I will.

David Yurkovich
[David Yurkovich is the author of the novels Banana Seat Summer *and* Glass Onion, *and the author/illustrator of the graphic novels* Less Than Heroes, Death by Chocolate: Redux *and* Altercations. *He is the editor and graphic designer for Devil's Party Press. David and his family reside in Milton, Delaware, a town with fewer than 3,000 residents that's so small it makes* Smalltown *seem large by comparison.]*

WHAT DO YOU CALL THAT NOISE?

AND ALL THE WORLD IS KEYBOARD SHAPED

What comes first: a songwriting idea in a composer's head or an instrument's sound and shape? A professor of musicology argues that, with XTC, songs are often a product of the process. Without physicality and gesture, the music just wouldn't sound the same

BY ROBERT G RAWSON

Andy Partridge's description of composing *Seagulls Screaming Kiss Her, Kiss Her* must rank among the most unusual in rock music. He says it was the first song he composed at the keyboard – a Mellotron, in this case. Unlike the guitar, on which he was accustomed to writing, he had no clear frames of reference on the keyboard to relate the notes and chords to where to put his hands. His solution was to hold his hands carefully in the shape of the chords he found through experimentation and then trace them onto card from which he made cut-outs of his hand shapes. It's an example of the prominent role of physicality and gesture as songwriting devices in the music of XTC. I would like to look briefly at two indicative examples and the different results they can produce. One of them is *Seagulls Screaming*, the other is *Senses Working Overtime*.

Two recent, high-profile accounts of XTC have helped shed some light on the otherwise generally hidden practice of songwriting: Todd Bernhardt's book *Complicated Game* (2016) and the documentary *XTC: This Is Pop* (2018). In the latter, Partridge recalls that from an early age he took to writing his own songs because he felt he had little choice after struggling to learn by ear the songs of others. The irony will not be lost on any musician who has since tried to learn by ear some of the more complicated songs of XTC. Partridge himself has revealed some telling clues that bring us to the subject of physical gesture; but first via some background theories.

Philosophers have long been fascinated by the way in which a work of art is realised. How does it go from the initial stages of a mental concept to its final form as a physical one? In philosophical terms, this is the origin of phantasia – the idea that precedes the object, the image that comes before the externalisation. In musical terms, this process gets increasingly complicated. If, for example, a musician knows how a D major chord in a particular octave sounds (for example, their brain has memorised the sound through repetition), they only need to imagine "D major triad" and they can also imagine the sound. The next steps could include any manner of notation or aide-memoire; for example, the words "D major" or even "D" on a sheet of paper; or it could be written down in standard music notation.

There is a presumption being made here that the composer imagines those sounds and then externalises them in some way. Historically, some people have composed that way – and still do today: they "hear" something in their head, if you will, and then they externalise it, either by notating it or playing and recording it. This classical concept of having a mental model that you then realise in physical terms was challenged in the first half of the 20th century. The painter Jackson Pollock (1912-56), for one, turned the very act of externalisation (his movement toward creating) into an artwork in its own right. In other words, his gestures were sometimes of similar interest to the paintings those gestures produced. The photographs of Pollock in the act of splashing a canvas took on a value of their own, in part because they captured aspects of the creative gestures in a way not necessarily captured on the canvases themselves. There is a creative process and then an object – and both are interesting works of art.

To return to Andy's technique of writing *Seagulls Screaming* with cut-out hands, the closest practice I can think of is the "grip notation" used by some of the more experimental composers for violin and viol in the 17th century. Grip notation looks like ordinary staff notation, however in order to make musical sense, it requires a "key" to decipher it. First you must tune your instrument to a non-standard tuning

> '*Seagulls* preserves some Partridgeisms: the non-chord tones that don't resolve as expected and the melodic shapes that avoid clichéd riffs'

and then the notation, rather than telling you the names of notes, simply tells you where to put your fingers: in short, it may say in the notation to play a D, but an F natural might actually sound - as notation it is largely physical. The grip notation and Andy's cardboard cut-outs preserve hand shapes, not pieces of music; the music is a product of the process.

Nevertheless, *Seagulls* still preserves some characteristic Partridgeisms: the non-chord tones that don't resolve as expected (or at all) and the melodic shapes that avoid clichéd riffs and cadences. It seems, at least in this case, that even when Partridge was composing away from the guitar and using an unfamiliar process, he had a musical vocabulary inside his head that still manifested itself in the context of keyboard playing. This is especially interesting in light of his explanations of the gestation of *Seagulls*; he doesn't seem to have started with "OK, the first bit is basically in D minor with some non-chord alterations," but instead let his fingers discover places that, nevertheless, followed his fondness for the juxtaposition of unusual harmonies. In short, it still sounds like Andy. Did his fingers search until they found what his ears wanted, or was there a more experimental approach? If the cardboard cut-outs of Andy's hand shapes survived, they would form an appropriate musical companion to the photos of Pollock splashing his canvas; as artefacts of the creative process. It is precisely this exploratory type of approach that makes the next case so interesting.

SHARPENED MY GUITAR

The classical model of phantasia-followed-by-object sometimes became reversed in the world of rock'n'roll. Andy Partridge gives a curious example of this reversal in his account of composing *Senses Working Overtime* that appears in both *Complicated Game* and *This Is Pop*. Unusually in pop music, Partridge's songs for XTC are highly linear in concept - they depend more heavily on independent melodic lines than on vertical, chord-centred approaches. To follow many of his melodic ideas requires examination of where they came from and where they are going; much more so than by looking up and down (musically speaking) at the vertical harmony. Not only does Andy seem unfazed by what I might term "incidental dissonance" in vertical sonorities, he appears to revel in it - I suspect that some of these colours are the accidental by-product of his linear, melodic pursuits. Moreover, his "non functional" approach to harmony offers to the ear one of the most colourful palettes in the business; that is, the harmonic vocabulary of his songs, in addition to unconventional yet delightful melodic shapes, often features colour/timbre more than it features the traditional tension-resolution relationships (does he listen to Debussy?) The very nature of his compositional style permits any sound to follow any other sound.

The chorus for *Senses* is unusual for Partridge in that it is harmonically very sturdy and traditional. It is based primarily on three chords: I-IV-V. This is even more so in the melodic cadence that accompanies the words "one, two, three, four, five" based on scale tones 7-2-1, which clearly define the tonic of E major. This is not intended as a criticism, per se; Partridge tells us his goal was to write a hit single - result! He describes how he had already written the chorus for *Senses* in E major and then set about to write a verse in the same key, when he describes what happened next: "I threw my hands on the guitar..." but instead of the hoped-for E major, "threw them onto kind of an E flat place". Here we have both the gesture and the idea of a "place" for a chord. E flat major is, in this way of thinking, not a sound, but a place. Yet the result is not E flat at all, but G sharp minor - still within the key of E major, but at the rather less common third-relation from the tonic - C sharp minor would have been the more expected key area here.

The gesture of trying to do one thing (play E major) and missing the target, resulted in the accidental outcome of the (excellent) verse in the mediant minor. This mistake produced a set of intervals (I would say "intervals" or "sounds", rather than chords) that provided the seeds for the rest of the song: the "E flat accident": G#, B, D# and A#, B, C#. The G sharp minor sound is heard in alternation with an A sharp minor sound – definitely outside of E major – but for simple reasons of playing with hand shapes, Partridge retains the open B string. This jars against the A sharp minor sound, but in the longer term, serves as a common tone with E major and functions as a dominant pedal – a tactic that makes the arrival at E major for the chorus all the more worth the wait; and we get that chorus in E only once! In a reversal of the classical order, it was Andy's stumbling upon this group of sounds that seems to have enabled (or even compelled) him to compose the verse – one which, he tells us, resulted first in images from which he proceeded to create.

The relationships between the verse, chorus and bridge in this song are striking by their correspondence with the opening gesture – that "E flat accident". The A sharp that appears in the opening guitar part (the "medieval" evocation that Andy speaks of) finds a second musical home later in the song in an enharmonic function as B flat. The primary interval of the small-scale harmonic structures in this song (discussions of the melody will have to wait for another day) is a whole tone, but this is suddenly contracted to a semi-tone at the words "but to me they're very, very beautiful," by which time that same note now acts as a B flat, which, via the new dominant of C, takes the song into (mostly!) F major.

This longer-lens view highlights Andy's linear approach; he is thinking about where the music and images/narrative are going and less, if at all, about vertical considerations and conventions of form. For someone who was influenced by 60s music like the Beach Boys, for example, such internal modulations would not have seemed outrageous. Did they even register with him at all? Few pop-song writers since have managed a modulation so subtly as the one achieved in this song. It is fitting with the imagery of the song that we never return to Andy's hoped-for key of E major after the first chorus; our little medieval farmer sets out, never to return in quite the same way.

In the bulk of his songwriting, especially after *English Settlement*, Andy avoids harmonic and melodic clichés. His side-stepping of stereotypical forms of clear melodic closure may, in part, stem from his particular approach to songwriting. Not only is he typically careful to avoid the standard tropes and hooks of rock/pop music, but he has a fondness for angularity and juxtaposition of ideas (musical and otherwise) that help set the music of XTC in welcome relief from the majority of their contemporaries. Even when he appears to be tempted by more predictable melodic closure in harmonically stable and closed structures, in *Books Are Burning*, for example, he almost always appears to search for some other sound – any sound that denies cliché and predictability. Refreshingly, he almost always undermines clear resolutions. It is telling, if not also a little touching, that in XTC's final live appearance on BBC television in 1992 that as the band plays the final G major chord of *Books Are Burning*, Partridge sings the note G over the band's G major chord, but then holds that note long enough to drift down to F sharp, the leading-tone of the key of G major. That is, F sharp "should" have been the note that is resolved by the G. The result is not so much a far-out final chord (G major sharp 7) as a single note that acts to undermine or even deny the final cadence on G as he backs away from the microphone; the final chord remains unresolved.

Closure rarely comes easily.

> 'He had a musical vocabulary inside his head that still manifested itself in the context of keyboard playing'

WHAT DO YOU CALL THAT NOISE?

PHOTO © GARRY STUART

THE RHYTHM IN HIS HEAD

Terry Chambers feels the rhythm in rehearsals for English Settlement.

THE RHYTHM IN HIS HEAD

What was the UK music scene like at the time Terry Chambers pounded his way to attention? Kicking off a tribute to the XTC powerhouse by drummers from around the world, one fan surveys the post-punk landscape

BY MARCO ROSSI

Do readers' polls still actually exist anywhere? If you were a teenage doof in the 70s, the end-of-year *Melody Maker* readers' poll was a fantastic source of vindication or outrage, as your most beloved musical heroes were either garlanded or resolutely ignored. Some of us looked forward to the subsequent arguments as much as the polls themselves, as you and your mates locked horns over the relative merits of Keith Emerson and Rick Wakeman, or Eric Clapton and Steve Hackett, or Derek Longmuir and Sooty. How fondly one recalls the stubborn, maverick pride of lobbing Mike Ratledge into the mix, or Dave Stewart (the Egg/Hatfields one, obvs) – or, indeed, claiming with some justification that Jaki Liebezeit and Holger Czukay were in fact the most imaginative and distinctive rhythm section in the omniverse.

And then punk happened, and a certain adjustment of parameters was involved. In as much as arses were cheerfully bared at musos displaying anything more than the most rudimentary and confrontational technique, it nevertheless soon became apparent that there were some very serious players in the melee, all of whom brought a commendable and much-needed freshness to their craft.

Our favourite sport quickly became "who is the best drummer to have emerged from the punk/new-wave scene?" Our nominees were as follows. Billy Ficca of Television, busy, antsy and expressive; Stewart Copeland of the Police, whose dark prog past with Curved Air and use of orthodox grip didn't prevent him from developing a snappy concision; Rat Scabies, with the implacable momentum of an avalanche; Budgie of the Slits and Siouxsie and the Banshees, consistently unpredictable; and Terry Chambers of XTC.

In these discussions, Terry always emerged the winner. It was the sheer musicality of his playing that made all the difference. Redoubtably powerful, he could drive and regulate a track like a lion tamer with a whip in one hand and a metronome in the other; but by the same token he served the song with a diligent, unwavering focus. His signature style quickly established itself: a mathematically precise deployment of unusual, cyclical patterns and carefully considered recurrent fills that somehow combined a rod-straight chronometry with a subtly weighted sense of swing.

In Terry's hands, the hi-hat in particular emerged as a new weapon of expression and punctuation. The offbeat sequencing and elbow-nudging pushes in, say, *Making Plans for Nigel*, *Rocket from a Bottle* or *Scissor Man* add left-field detail and illustrative commentary to already vivid narratives. Besides which, no one else could jackhammer a set of tom-toms to such dramatic and emphatic effect. *Paper and Iron*, *Roads Girdle the Globe*, *Homo Safari* and *Travels in Nihilon* all feature colossal, air-pushing tom-tom figures that trigger something cabalistic and primordial at the base of your spine and cerebral cortex.

When he took himself off to Australia, his absence was keenly felt. XTC became something else, a cherishable ensemble of studio-based renaissance men with a limitless new box of paints; but Terry's pre-1983 importance to the band as an alchemical cornerstone, a pillar of structural strength and a source of fully functional decoration can never be underestimated. The fact that he's back in Swindon with a kit at his disposal is serious cause for celebration; his work on the TC&I *Great Aspirations* EP with his erstwhile XTC rhythm section partner Colin Moulding proves he's lost approximately none of his distinctively authoritative feel in the intervening years. More, please. Soon, please.

ALL ROADS LEAD TO BEATOWN

Andy, Dave and Barry remember playing live with Terry, while the drummers who took Terry's place reflect on his work with XTC

BY MARK FISHER AND YVONNE WOOTTON

What was it like to share a stage with Terry Chambers? Andy Partridge has one word for it: deafening. "It was like struggling with a steam train going at full pelt on a conveyor belt behind you," he says. "You know when they test cars and they run them at full whack on a circular not-going-anywhere track? That's what it was like, but with a huge steam train. He would also have his drums phenomenally loud in his own monitoring so that one beat of the snare was like a cannon going off next to your head. When you're on stage for an hour and three-quarters with thousands upon thousands of those snare drums going off... there is a reason why I developed mild tinnitus!"

But it wasn't all about noise. Turn down the volume and you'd hear a drummer who kept XTC on course for being one of the tightest live acts on the circuit. "Terry was a big part of the band when I joined," recalls Dave Gregory. "People used to come just to see him. He was the engine. He was very reliable. His tempo never wavered. He played the same part every night. He was dependable and played really well. By the time the band was at its performing peak, which I suppose was the last tour we did, he was a machine. He never let us down as a performer."

It's that tightness that Dave's predecessor, Barry Andrews, says marked Terry out. The drummers Barry has worked with the closest, Kevin Wilkinson and Martyn Barker, have what he calls a "loose fluidity" to their playing. "Terry's the opposite of that," he says. "Everything is as tight as anything. Kev Wilkinson used to be able to get horribly stoned, pissed and tripping and still wouldn't miss a beat, he'd just flow through this thing, whereas Terry - half a lager and he goes all over the place. As a machine, it's wound up."

Did someone say lager? Terry quickly learned that drink and drumming don't mix. "In the early days we were playing Manchester Electric Circus and the support band, the Drones, tried to sabotage us and got Terry really drunk," says Andy. "He never drinks before a show. After the show, get out of the way; if you've got a brewery, that's going to be desert in minutes. But before a gig, he never touched a drop. They got him: 'Come on, Terry, get this down your neck. What's the matter, you fairy?' Of course, he got rather drunk and was pretty much passing out on the drum kit."

That, though, was rare. Dave says he can only remember one show - in Staten Island in 1981 - where Terry's tiredness dragged the show down. "None of us was very good on that tour for some reason," he adds. For one disastrous gig in the USA, Terry had a good excuse for being less than machine-like. As Andy remembers: "He did a Keith Moon on us once and fell backwards over the drum kit and passed out. But I'll forgive him because he was very ill. He had some bug. 'Shit, it's gone quiet.' You turn round and it's just a pair of feet sticking up where the drum stool was."

Barry reckons the attitude to alcohol was as much philosophical as practical. "Terry looks on it like sport," he says. "You don't have a pint of lager before you play a game of football or do your gymnastics. It's a bit like that."

Like an athlete, Terry hit home with a formidable power. Barry remembers the toll he took on the drum sticks and snare heads: "There'd be a forest of bits of stick, because he hits so hard. I've never seen anything quite like it. It is music, but it's not approaching it terribly musically. It's his job. 'I just hits the bastards, in' I?'"

"He was not a musician," agrees Andy. "It was no good you saying to him, 'OK, we'll change it up when we get to the bridge.' 'What the fuckin' 'ell d'you mean, fuckin' bridge? I ain't buildin' no fuckin' bridge. Wave across.' It was no good being musical with him. He didn't do music. He was a sporting type. It was the visceral thrill of hitting things in repetitive patterns while touring."

Watching from the audience was Dave's brother Ian Gregory, aka EIEI Owen of the Dukes of Stratosphear. "If you ever saw the band live you will be aware of his incredibly energetic style and he would come off stage wringing wet," he says. "He is also very inventive - I was at the rehearsals when they worked up the intro to *Making Plans for Nigel* and thought what a great rhythm it was. That intro is one of the best in all rock music."

For all that, Terry was not a natural improviser. "You couldn't really jam with Terry," says Andy. "It was like working with a breathing machine. You started him off, you counted him in and he was going to go through his programming. I've never known any other drummer like that. It's not a musical thing, it's not even a drummer thing; he went into this Zen state where he could play the oddest things and you couldn't communicate with him while he was doing it. You'd be looking at him and thinking, 'Is he seeing me? I'm trying to indicate that we're going to end this section,' and he seemed to stare right through you. It was very thrilling, but it was not related to music. It was some sort of footballer mathematics. I've never known it in any other musician. It's like a naïve gift.'

Yet out of that raw mechanical power came something highly distinctive. He is a player who, according to *Nonsuch*'s Dave Mattacks, "put the song first". That's a sentiment echoed by *Wasp Star*'s Chuck Sabo. "Terry is a talented and creative musician," he says. "His drumming style is creative and musical. He seems aware of the song, and plays for the song. The kind of drumming I like!"

Oranges and Lemons drummer Pat Mastelotto is more enthusiastic still. "Love Terry!" he says. "Love, love, love Terry! That was one of the things I really dug about XTC, that Terry had really creative parts but they were not necessarily fast or syncopated and they weren't based on chops, always a bit off-kilter, they were just the right parts for the songs and they were played with precision, power and passion. And I absolutely love the drum sounds, big open barking British drum sounds. I think the Hugh Padgham/Steve Lillywhite records are still sonic yardsticks. I immediately related to Terry as a drummer and the way he was sort of a more modern and much louder, Ringo."

"He and Colin are a great rhythm section," says Barry. "And such a strange, stylised... I can see why Andy would like it... it's got a primary-colour quality. It seems modernist: big, bold, brutal lines, sharp and clear. The modern art equivalent is Miro. Here's a blob of yellow and a black thing that comes out of it. An exceptional rhythm section and they don't sound like anything else at all. There's a bit of a reggae thing in there, but not really. There's sort of a funk thing, but not quite either. Moulding really likes your man out of Free, that 70s thing where the bass drum and the bass are locked together; there's something of that in there but it's not as sloppy as that. It's tighter and harder."

Dave agrees: "He was pre-programmed, but he would always learn the parts and bring something else. He'd bring Terry Chambers to Andy's ideas. He needed Andy there to guide him, but once it was there, it was there and he did it better than anybody else. He's very modest and humble about his playing."

"I seemed to have a special relationship with him because I think he respected my rhythm playing," says Andy. "I would always find things for him in my songs and sometimes Colin's songs where you'd map out what he was going to do then I'd find holes in his playing for me to play. Or the other way around: I'd already decided what I was going to play for any given number and he would then stand there with me and we'd work out where he was going to hit in the holes. It was a bit like building a giant clock. This piece can't go round on its own, it has to turn another piece when it hits it and that piece turning has to click that little hand a bit more or else it's not going to work properly. It was all interlinked."

Once he'd mastered a pattern, Terry was almost unfailingly accurate, never one for speeding up or slowing down, nor for getting it wrong. "Nine hundred and ninety nine times out a thousand, it was really thrilling," says Andy. "I shouldn't say this because Terry's a wonderful drummer, but occasionally he would get his programming wrong. You could get him to play the most complex things, rolling sequenced patterns that a normal drummer would not be able to handle. He could handle it with ease. Then sometimes you'd ask him to play something quite simple and he would struggle with it or he would get on the wrong emphasis of the beat. A few times live, you'd think, 'Wow! What's he doing?' You'd turn round and he's sweating away, really into it, but where the 'one' of the beat is, he's putting it somewhere else. Those occasions were rare, but it was how he played."

Over a long lunch in London, a group of musicians join Rick Buckler, drummer of the Jam, to talk about the new-wave explosion of the late-70s and the rhythms that drove it

BY MARK FISHER

BEAT SURRENDER

Rick Buckler and Terry Chambers have much in common. They were born in 1955, five months and 64 miles apart. They took up the drums and joined their first bands in the early 70s. Then in 1977, they played on their debut singles: Buckler on the Jam's *In the City* released in April; Chambers on XTC's *3D EP* in October.

Where one band brought us *News of the World*, *"A" Bomb in Wardour Street* and *Down in the Tube Station at Midnight*, the other offered *Science Friction*, *This Is Pop* and *Statue of Liberty*.

For every *All Mod Cons* there was a *Go 2*; for every *Setting Sons*, a *Drums and Wires*. By the summer of 1980, they were checking each other out in adjacent studios, as XTC worked on *Black Sea* and the Jam laid down *Sound Affects*. The parallels continued all the way to 1982 when Terry said goodbye to XTC and Paul Weller disbanded the Jam.

All of that seemed good enough reason to invite Buckler along to a drummer's summit at a central London hotel to discuss the work of Terry Chambers. With him were a mixture of part-time drummers and professional musicians, gathered for a two-hour lunchtime conversation that ranged from musicianship to studio techniques, from session drummers to formative influences, from home-made kits to ride cymbals. See page 124 for a list of who was there.

Photography: Allison Burke
www.allisonburkephotography.com

Rick Buckler: I was always quite envious of XTC because they weren't put in the same pigeonhole as punk bands. They were regarded as a bit more arty than that. We always had to fight off this flag, being under the banner of punk, which we didn't really like because we felt we were a band in our own right. XTC never seemed to fall into that trap. They had that freedom.

Mark Thomas: I just thought of you as a mod band – only because of the look.

Rick Buckler: It was the press thing: everybody had to be pigeonholed. Even the punk thing was quite a minor part of what was going on. There was so much talent at the time. So many bands coming out. They just simplified it by calling it punk. Then it became new wave. We were striving ever so hard to create our own identity and what I'd say about XTC is that they stuck to their identity. They weren't swayed by commercialism. It was, "This is what we want to do."

Mark Thomas: I think in this period, a lot of bands were undervalued. It was cool to be not very good at playing their instruments.

Rick Buckler: I used to be annoyed by that.

Mark Thomas: And yet the list of people that came out of punk and became new-wave bands, they were all fantastic players. There were great drummers in all those bands.

Rick Buckler: You don't have a good band without a good drummer. It's building a house. You want decent foundations. It used to annoy me when people said the Pistols couldn't play. I saw the Pistols play and they were absolutely fabulous. The other thing, especially about XTC and Terry, was it was well produced. It had the support of a great producer. It wasn't just played strong, it really sounded strong. I was really envious of that because drums wasn't the big thing in Paul Weller's life. His thing was songwriting. If it wasn't for people who worked with us, sound engineer Vic Smith in particular, who really spent time over the drums, I'm sure we would have skipped over them and said, "Oh, yeah, let's just get this done quick." My memories are of a hell

of a lot of rushing around getting stuff recorded so we could get back on the road. It was 100 mile an hour. XTC were in Townhouse at the same time as us [XTC recording *Black Sea*, the Jam recording *Sound Affects* in the summer of 1980]. They had a great stone room, which was brilliant for drums.
Rohan Onraet: That was Phil Collins' "ba-bum, ba-bum, ba-bum, ba-bum" [*In the Air Tonight* pattern].
Rick Buckler: We did some recording there while Phil Collins was doing all of that stuff.
Mark Fisher: How early on were you aware of XTC?
Rick Buckler: I got into XTC with *Drums and Wires*. I had to retrace my paces to pick up on what was going on before that.
Mark Fisher: Because you will have been touring at the same time –
Rick Buckler: Yes and never got to see them play live. It was purely off records that I got into them. When you're touring yourself, you don't see other bands unless you're playing festivals. Every Saturday night, you're busy and when they're busy, you're busy somewhere else.
Mark Thomas: Was there a competitive thing going on?
Rick Buckler: No, no really. We used to get a lot of it through the press – "This lot have sold more records than that lot" – but you just don't believe any of that stuff.
Mark Thomas: When Andy told me you used to pop in when you were at the same studio, I thought, "That's so nice. Why isn't that reported?"
Rick Buckler: I was ear-wigging! I wanted to find out what they were doing. "Got any new ideas?" In the Jam, it was producer Vic Smith and that great stone room that made a difference but it was not an up-front thing like XTC had.
Mark Thomas: I remember going out and buying the single of *News of the World* and that's a great drum sound.
Rick Buckler: Do you think so? I really didn't like that. It all sounds too dumpy.
Mark Thomas: It's got some nice round-the-kit stuff on there.

Rick Buckler (left and above) recalls fighting off the banner of punk and looking enviously at XTC, in the company of (left to right) Mark Thomas, Andy Rankin, Sarah Palmer, Laurie Langan and Mark Fisher: "What I'd say about XTC is that they stuck to their identity. They weren't swayed by commercialism."

Andy Rankin: The drum sound was what grabbed me about *Sound Affects*. It was the first Jam album I really went, "Yes!" because the drums were really crisp and I loved the sound. It's where XTC comes in because the drum sound on *Drums and Wires* is awesome and he takes it to the next level on *Black Sea*. You can really hear what Terry's doing and it drives everything along on both those albums.

Laurie Langan: He's really muscular for a little guy. It's surprising.

Andy Rankin: He is. On *Towers of London*, he's the bloody navvy! He's digging that trench.

Laurie Langan: That fill on *Senses Working Overtime* – I replay that every single time. It's beautiful.

Rick Buckler: There's some lovely space around it, so you can actually hear what's going on. It's like something falling down the stairs. With Terry, it wasn't like someone just banging it out, there's a lot of thought behind what he was doing. That's what I liked about it because there was plenty to listen to and be inspired by.

Mark Thomas: Tell you what he didn't do: he didn't use the ride cymbal a lot. Was that a thing back then – that it was seen as too prog rocky?

Rick Buckler: I don't know. Being a three piece, you'd tend to try and fill it out. There were so few instruments live that's what you'd tend to do. But as soon as you go onto the hi-hat, it makes it so much tighter. If you want to make it splashy, the ride comes in – especially live. We based everything around the live sound and didn't think too much about the studio.

Mark Thomas: Did you go in and play live?

Rick Buckler: Yes.

Andy Rankin: Did you have the songs sorted out in your head, what you were going to play?

Rick Buckler: Yes, pretty much. I didn't like the idea of going into a studio and then trying to create something. By the time you've taken it out on the road you've got all the quirks ironed out. You'd think, "I wish we could go back and record it now we're so much better at it." You'd come up with a song and ten minutes later it's on tape. You'd think, "I'd much rather we worked this through a bit more, get rid of this rubbish and get some better fills in there." Oftentimes, Paul would suddenly decide he was going to stick in an accent on the guitar. It sounded great, but they'd already got the drum part done. I'd say, "Can I go and put an accent in?" And they'd go, "No."

Rohan Onraet: This is the beauty of a digital recorder these days – you can go back and fill in. With Fassine's drummer Jim, I generally get him to play the rehearsed version, then we'd do a couple of passes of him going wild, whatever he feels like doing, just getting adventurous and seeing what beautiful accidents occur.

Laurie Langan: Do you ever listen back and regret?

Rick Buckler: But only I would know this. Other people don't see it because it doesn't mean anything.

Laurie Langan: But I listen back to some songs and go, "I wish I had not done that or I'd done something else."

Sarah Palmer: I don't. I'm happy with what I did at that moment in time. I think if it's what we chose and it was right at that moment, you should never look back and go, "I wish I'd done it this way." But I like the stories of how you recorded with the Jam, because that doesn't exist any more. Firstly, you don't have bands that can play live any more. We can't even play what we create in the studio. It's so vast. But one day I'd love to be able to record like that, completely live.

Rick Buckler: That's the way we learnt and the way we approached everything. The studio came as a second skill. I read that Deep Purple used to go into the studio for a day, record something they'd been playing live, then go back out on the road, then go back into the studio. By the time we got in the studio, they'd say, "Right, you've got a month. Do the album." And you'd do everything in that month. Some songs were ready to go, some songs needed writing in the studio. I used to think, "Can we just stop recording, take it out on the road for a bit and try and think this through." When you listen to XTC songs – and this is probably just as an outsider – but it's lovely to listen to it in this way that you think,

BEAT SURRENDER

"They've got it right from the word go." You don't see all of the baggage that went along with putting it together.

Laurie Langan: Did the others feel the same as you about wishing you had more time?

Rick Buckler: I think everybody does when you record something, especially when you can look back 40 years. We did two live albums of any note. The first one was rubbish; it was put together in a rough-and-ready fashion. The second one had more thought put into it. But when you listen to the songs played live – and that was really our forte – they are so much better than the studio versions. It's got that life. There's nothing stripped out of it. It's not layered, overdubbed, cut up, joined or anything like that and it's just got that lovely feel to it. I feel it more than anybody because I know how it could have been, and it was sometimes, but it wasn't actually on the night we recorded it. I love the live albums because, for me, that's the big memory of it all. I was gutted to find out when XTC stopped playing live. I thought, "Well, now I've got a chance and I'm not doing quite so much, I'll go and see them..." Too late!

Sarah Palmer: But then you've got the wonderful studio albums so you've got the best of both.

Laurie Langan: Also there's a mystique. When it stopped, they protected a lot of that legacy of the stuff they'd done with Terry. It's just perfect. There's nothing bad. Every note is right.

Mark Fisher: I saw them twice live and Terry was astonishing to watch. People would go to XTC just to see him because he was this force of nature. It was like you could wind him up and he would just go.

Laurie Langan: He looked very angry all the time. There's no change of expression. He had very high sticks as well.

Mark Thomas: He'd have his hi-hat quite high because he'd have to get underneath it. On something like *Millions*, if you listen to the drumming, there's a pea-souping, reggae, skanking rhythm, but Terry wasn't happy just to do that. He would put hi-hat chokes in and accents on the toms. So he'd go underneath and he'd need that space.

As the conversation heats up, Louis Barfe (centre, bottom) joins the throng with word of Terry's latest kit: "He has gone vintage mad."

Rick Buckler: Yes, if you raise the hi-hat up, it gives you the hand-underneath space as well. You don't want to be encroaching down on the kit. If you're too close to it, it's not comfortable.

Laurie Langan: There's an amazing confidence if you look at the footage. The band don't need to check Terry. They can let him get on with it. They know he's going to do it. And Terry's just in his own little world.

Sarah Palmer: I think that's the same with all of them.

Laurie Langan: Yes, everyone's so confident and that fills you with confidence. You just know it's going to be brilliant.

Mark Thomas: Thinking about Dave, there's a lovely recording at Hammersmith - I think I might have been at the gig - and in *Burning with Optimism's Flames*, there's a lovely jazzy guitar solo. Dave threw in some extra notes and twiddly bits and you can hear Andy going, "Waay!" He loved it. So there was room to do things and startle each other.

Laurie Langan: When you're that good, there's so much more space. With a really good band, you can do things like that and you're always going to fall on your feet.

Rick Buckler: Some of it's to do with playing with the same people for a length of time. You tend to know. If somebody starts going off-piste, you can follow it, because you know what they're like musically. That's something that we had. We'd been together for so long and we musically evolved with each other. If Paul was going to go off on one, you'd just follow on. It was intuitive. We didn't have to worry about where he was going. It was really good. You build a musical relationship with people. I'm sure a lot of bands do this, you'd have an area in a song where you may extend it and there'd be little musical devices that come in that say, "Right, we've got to the end of the song now."

Without even thinking, that just happens. I think it only comes from the experience of playing with the same people for such a long time. You get the feeling that all the parts of XTC just locked together

> 'With Terry, it wasn't like someone just banging it out, there's a lot of thought behind what he was doing. There was plenty to be inspired by'

beautifully. I don't think there was anybody fighting anybody else.

Sarah Palmer: There's a gig that we watch all the time online: XTC live on VARA's Popkaravaan recorded at the Open Theatre, Berg en Bosch, Apeldoorn in the Netherlands in August 1980. It's a 20-minute set of unbelievable songs. You mentioned Terry not continuously filling – or anyone not continuously soloing – none of them are showing off what they can do, but they fit so well together and everyone gives space to everyone else. That's why you're never going to get Partridge on the front of *Guitar World* or Terry on the front of *Drum World* because no one looks at them as being a brilliant guitarist or a brilliant drummer – but they are. There are moments in that gig of brilliance from every single musician, but unless you're looking at it, you don't notice.

Rick Buckler: To me that's really important. A band is the sum of its parts. You start taking bits away from it, for some reason it doesn't work. I've seen it a lot with bands: Moonie died and I went and saw the Who play – it wasn't the same band, even though it was three-quarters there.

Mark Thomas: You can't imagine the Beatles without Ringo. He was castigated for being not a very good drummer, but I can't imagine anybody drumming with the Beatles. It would not sound the same.

Andy Rankin: With all those parts together, I think Terry played his parts beautifully.

Rick Buckler: And to give a bit of support for Ringo, he always made the song work. Whatever he put in made it work. He wasn't showing off. That's a skill.

Mark Thomas: Some of the minimal parts he played were so good, just little patterns on the hi-hat where he'd leave out something and you'd notice what he'd left out. It's such a clever thing.

Sarah Palmer: Laurie always says that people's limitations make them great. Because you don't know every single element of your instrument, you choose different things. As a drummer, he might be limited in some things, but that makes him perfect for that band.

Laurie Langan: Yes, Tom Waits is one of the best pianists and yet he's a terrible pianist. Just because you're the greatest at your instrument doesn't make you a great writer.

Andy Rankin: I played with an originals band in Sydney – a bit like REM – when their main drummer went overseas for a year, so I filled in. He was as sloppy as hell, but it fitted the band perfectly. We did some recordings and I went, "I sound like shit compared to him." I know I'm a better drummer technically, but he had the feel. Ringo was a leftie. I'm a leftie as well. He played leftie on a right kit and that gave a certain swing. It's actually a limitation, but he worked around it and he made that great Ringo sound.

Laurie Langan: Metronomic drummers do something to me that rubs me the wrong way. I can always hear a session guy. When you're in a cohesive family like a band, you need guys who do have a certain amount of limitations. Guys who've cobbled together a drum kit or who taught themselves are usually the best drummers.

Rick Buckler: I think you have to be a lot more inventive when you bump up against a wall. "I can't do that and I can't do this," but there is another way of doing it and you just find other avenues. That limitation guides you down a path that you probably wouldn't have thought of. You have to be more inventive about it. Nothing comes easy. You listen to people like Ian Paice of Deep Purple and how fabulous they are and you think, "I want to do that! But I can't!" But you find other ways of doing things. You think, "How can I get away with that? How can I make it sound like I'm doing this?"

Laurie Langan: Bowie's drummer, Sterling Campbell, has got the right elements of being a reliable session guy but also when you hear him kick that kick drum, it's like an earthquake. I love that. But for me that's not as desirable as Terry. I'd have a Terry any day over a Sterling Campbell. Imagine Sterling Campbell in XTC? It'd be weird. Terry just has this rawness.

Sarah Palmer: He's not loose in a timing sense, but he's not clinical.

Mark Thomas: I wonder if Terry listened to subsequent XTC albums, thinking, "I could have done that"? I'd love to know what he thinks about the session men that came in.

Andy Rankin: Interesting you say that because I think the only album that sounds like it could be Terry is the very last one, *Wasp Star*, with Chuck Sabo and Prairie Prince. That sounds a bit like Terry – *Playground* and *Stupidly Happy*.

Rick Buckler: Who were Terry's influences?

Mark Thomas: Andy told me Twink from the Pink Fairies.

Rick Buckler: Fabulous! I'd never have dreamt that one up.

Mark Thomas: He was into heavy metal. I tell you who else – who I liked as well – it was the drummer from Atomic Rooster.

Rick Buckler: Paul Hammond! I loved him. I thought he was great. The reason I bought a Hayman drum kit was because of him. He formed another band called Hard Stuff afterwards and I used to listen to that. It was full of these short drum fills and they were brilliant.

Mark Thomas: He was so good at that. He left bits out, didn't he?

Rick Buckler: They were in an era when Yes were beginning to get themselves together and the early prog rock bands.

Mark Thomas: Him and Simon Kirke of Free.

Andy Rankin: I can hear that because he's someone who digs in with the hi-hat.

Mark Thomas: And Terry was a bit of an Ian Paice fan as well.

Rick Buckler: How can you not like him? He was just absolutely fabulous. He could make it sound like he was gaining pace and intensity, yet he never changed speed. He would make something sound like, "We're really going to get going," then he'd strip it back and all of a sudden he'd be relaxed.

Mark Thomas: He could be really jazzy as well. He was an all rounder. Did you get bought a drum kit? Did you make one?

Rick Buckler: The first one, I made at school. I made all the shells then bought all the hardware. That lasted quite a while until I saved up enough money and went and bought the Hayman. It was a sturdy kit to take on the road. You knew it wasn't going to fall to bits on you.

Louis Barfe: The Premier kit that Terry used on the early stuff was in Swindon at the XTC Convention in September 2017. I went over and looked at it: the first tom was a 15", there was a 16" floor tom on the bass drum and an 18". It still has the stickers on it saying bought from Kempster. When I met him at the convention, I asked him what kit he had now. He said, "Oh, I've gone vintage mad." Colin was sitting next to him, saying, "Yeah, he's never off eBay." He said he was using a Beverley and he'd just got a John Grey Autocrat snare drum coming through and a couple of Olympics as well. He's really gone back, I suppose because he's not touring, so he hasn't got to have to have something that holds up fantastically well. Also the old drums, some of those Beverleys and Olympics, are so light, it makes such a difference.

Rohan Onraet: There are so many factors that can culminate in the perfect drum sound. I've recorded loads of kits and there is no set rule to a great sounding drum. There are so many variables.

Louis Barfe: What I think is amazing about Terry Chambers is his consistency. He had absolutely perfect time, absolutely perfect tone, but also he wasn't averse to doing things unconventionally, so you've got the *Making Plans for Nigel* drum part which is backwards to how you'd expect it to be. In some ways he was very conventional, in some ways he wasn't.

Rick Buckler: Everything he did must have been perfectly natural for him. That's what came out of his mind. He's not being put upon to do it. He's contributing his part to the band which is what gives it that signature. That's true of the whole of XTC. There's something there whether you're into guitar playing or even singing – some of the singing parts were off the wall – none of it is conventional and that's what's lovely about it. I like the idea that what he does is totally original.

Mark Thomas: Stu Rowe made a comment about each of the band and said that drumming was Terry's form of sport. He'd get behind the drums and it was exercise for him. He was a really good footballer and nearly signed up for Swindon Town.

Rick Buckler: Lucky escape there then!

WHAT DO YOU CALL THAT NOISE?

Pace setter: Terry Chambers rehearsing in Swindon for English Settlement.

DO YOU KNOW WHAT NOISE AWAKES YOU?

Drummers from around the world pick their favourite Terry Chambers moments, batting their opinions back and forth in a virtual conversation

WHITE MUSIC

CROSS WIRES

Sebastian Rüger: This is the song that stands out for me the most from the first album, not only drumming-wise, but because, all at the same time, it is the fastest, most frenzied, jazziest and punkiest song of the entire XTC-catalogue... a 2/4 that fast with a hint of swing? Outstanding! Interesting is how Terry, although being a straight rock drummer, manages to create a jazz feel here. I hadn't heard it in a long time and remembered a swing cymbal going through it, so much that the up-beat jazz frenzy had made a big impression on me. Playing it again, I was astonished to find it lasts for only eight notes during the chorus. The whole swing feel comes from the toms and the ghost notes with the kick. A slight delay may work for him too here, yet this isn't so easy to accomplish. It is even like he's mocking that swing thing, yet he pulls it off quite accurately.

Mikey Erg: That's a great one. I loved Colin's songs on that first record because they were so weird. He was like the hardcore punk of the band. My brother-in-law got me into XTC and, knowing I was a punk rocker, he gave me *Go 2* and *White Music* because he knew they'd be the things that got me in. They're so different from the average; they weren't Sex Pistols records. That's why those records stand out.

ALL ALONG THE THE WATCHTOWER

Terry Arnett: This track shows what a pocket player Terry can be. Once in the groove, he can funk it up with the best. It also showcases how Terry can keep the same rhythm and hold it in a repetitive loop. There's a real taste of unwavering tempo. Terry is all bone and muscle (meat and potatoes) and plays what the song needs – even with this rework of a Dylan/Hendrix classic. It's not overplayed. He is a human drum machine. The marriage of his drum patterns to Colin's bass phrasing works so well with this. I rate Terry and Colin as one of *the* best rhythm sections ever.

Sebastian Rüger: Yes, he is funky on this one and yet heavy. He rolls like a machine and yet has the nerve and the taste to have these micro-retarding moments within the ever-recurring breaks that give that swing feel.

NEON SHUFFLE

Todd Bernhardt: The first word that comes to mind when it comes to Terry is "generosity". By that I mean he is willing to leave space for other musicians to do their jobs – which, unfortunately, is not a common thing in drummers, especially those coming up. A lot of drummers have the tendency to do the whole "look at me" thing – "look at these fast chops and these fast fills" – but from the beginning, Terry is all bone and muscle, and almost no fat. Just like Ringo, he plays exactly what is right for the song. He doesn't overplay, he is rock solid in placing the beat and staying with the tempo (to my knowledge they never worked with a click track when he was in the band) and he makes such good choices. He was also willing to listen to other members of the band and take instructions from them. And he sometimes plays really unusual things. Terry has chops. It can be hard to play along with them – first of all from a stamina point of view. When I started playing drums, I would play along to the first couple of albums and they are fast. At the end of *White Music* and *Go 2* you are tired. And they would do that night after night. *Neon Shuffle* is a really hard song to play – it's eighth notes on the hi-hat, but he's playing them so fast, they might as well be sixteenths. After a while, I had these big Popeye forearms because I was an aficionado of Mr Terry Chambers.

Mikey Erg: Yes, it's so fast and also Andy's giving him all these stops, all these spaces in the music to do fills. Listening to a live version of it, it's double the speed of the album and is pretty amazing to hear.

Todd Bernhardt: In the early albums, Andy and Barry are always battling. Terry gives them room – staying out of the way while remaining married to what Colin is doing. The two of them together are such a good pair: his right foot on the kick drum is so well matched to what Colin is doing on the bass. What I love most about the early albums is the sheer joy of keeping up at breakneck speed with this hot-shit band that's having a lot of fun. You can just imagine people pogoing on the dance floor as you play along.

Mikey Erg: Once I started seeing video of them playing, it's funny to see how, on top of everything else, he's hitting the drums so hard. He's putting everything into playing. It's great to watch the footage of them during the *White Music* era and he's just bashing away. I went to Europe with a hardcore band. We had a 45-minute set and there were no ballads in it. Getting through it was pretty tough. I was winded after sets and would have to lie down. I remember coming back from that tour, completely changing my diet and running five miles a day. XTC's sets were about 90 minutes and just the fact he was bashing for that long is incredible.

Sebastian Rüger: Mikey is right. XTC were playing live a lot faster than on the records those days. It is fast on the record already - is it possible for this Speedy Gonzales to be even faster? Damn! And then these counter hits against the beat on the hi-hat - man, this stuff is exhausting to play, especially in a heavy manner.

GO 2

MECCANIK DANCING

Mikey Erg: *Go 2* in general is very interesting. *White Music* is a pop-punk album. There are definitely similarities between the two, but they really start getting into the more dancey stuff on *Go 2* - with the pea-soup beat [playing the off-beats on the hi-hat while opening and closing it on the beat in a disco style]. *Meccanik Dancing* is one of those. Not unlike *Neon Shuffle*, with the verses they're doing this dance beat, then they're going into straight-up poppy chorus.

Terry Arnett: I was exposed to *Meccanik Dancing* at school by an old schoolmate, John Hemsley. The offbeat hi-hat complementing Andy's riffs, and the bass drum following Colin's lines - it's a complete interplay exercise in how a good song will sound and flow better when all the parts are working together.

Sebastian Rüger: ... and that long snare roll in the middle. It is only simple 16ths but hard to do over eight long bars. I admire that; you can mess this up veeeery easily - the longer it goes on for, the more it takes stamina and yet control to make it sound good.

LIFE IS GOOD IN THE GREENHOUSE

Mikey Erg: It's a different drumbeat from anything else on that record and it's a completely different type of song, one of the more plodding songs. The drums are very spatial, serving the song as he needed to.

Sebastian Rüger: It is masterfully composed. Just when you get into the groove and learn how the chords and vocal lines correspond with this unusual rhythm, the feel changes in the chorus and so does one's feeling about the rhythm. It's a song that messes with our feeling of where "one" is and, as such, is like a little exercise for *Millions* on *Drums and Wires* later on.

Maurice "mOe" Watson: This song has always fascinated me. Growing up in an urban environment, and spending a decent amount of time playing and touring in metal/hardcore bands, I have never been a stranger to the half-time groove. This is when the snare drum is placed solely on the third quarter note, as opposed to the second and fourth, and gives the song a slow/sluggish sound. This makes things sound "heavier" and more groovy. So, imagine my surprise the first time I heard *Life Is Good in the Greenhouse*. I was listening to a song that saw 30 years into the future. Modern rap music is in the midst of a trend known as trap music where songs depend on half-time drum beats and menacing minor chord changes that are at times almost operatic. *Life Is Good in the Greenhouse* doesn't stop there, as the lyrical content also ventures into the hip hop vernacular with lines like "Do you wonder why I look so fresh?", *years* before the term "fresh" became slang for cool or hip. The laughing in the choruses is also reminiscent of the modern trap sound, which is often trademarked by silly sayings or sounds repeated ad nauseam for effect. How could one band be so damn creative? It's musical time travel!

SUPER-TUFF

Terry Arnett: I know my Fossil Fools chums are not overly enamoured of this one – but I love playing it! It's a catchy dub-reggae rhythm, caked in reverb, giving the track an air of space, with the angst of the hi-hat, just those eighths. His use of the bass drum and hi-hat accent is again complementing Colin's riffs. This track is so open, but Terry doesn't play anything that isn't necessary, allowing all the other instruments to shine through, along with Barry's vocals.

Sebastian Rüger: Ah, and to have these super-tasteful triplets appear in the break only. That's how you do it!

DRUMS AND WIRES

MAKING PLANS FOR NIGEL

Terry Arnett: After I'd heard *Meccanik Dancing* at school, it was the Devo-like deconstructed-and-reformed drum pattern of *Making Plans for Nigel* that initially grabbed my attention. This was 1979 when I was 14 and hadn't even played on a drum kit.

Mikey Erg: *White Music* and *Go 2* are great punk-rock records and Terry was a great punk-rock drummer, but he really gets more inventive starting with *Making Plans for Nigel*.

Rick Buckler: It was *Making Plans for Nigel* that got me started. It grabs your attention straight away. Drums! I like it! It just rolls on with that song.

Mikey Erg: If you listen to the albums in order, this is the first one you hear that's not your typical drumming. There's interesting and inventive stuff on *Go 2* and *White Music*, but it's not, "Oh, wow! I never would have thought to do that beat for this." But it feels like with *Making Plans for Nigel*, they wanted something different.

Laurie Langan: It feels like the track starts half-way through, like you've missed part of the song. You keep going, "I'm not sure where I am."

Mikey Erg: Absolutely. I bought an LP of it and I thought it was skipping the first couple of times I played it. I thought I'd have to get a digital copy so I could hear what it was supposed to sound like – and, lo and behold, that was actually it.

Andy Rankin: You feel the hi-hats – tss, tss – are just thrown in.

Rick Buckler: Yeah, he's got to be throwing it in.

Terry Arnett: The pattern of *Nigel* is not that difficult once you put your mind to it. It's just the reassignment of drum sounds. Instead of the constant eighth note on the hi-hat, this is now on the floor tom. The grace notes, normally played on the snare drum, are now played on the first rack tom. The bass drum is playing the first and second beat of each bar, while the hi-hat is played on the "and" of the third beat and the "and" of the first beat. The common mistake is to accent the hi-hat notes by opening the hi-hat as you play the note, physically lifting the hi-hat foot at the same time as you lift the bass drum foot. But, on investigation, Terry never did this – he hit those hi-hats when they were just softly closed. You can think of it as almost a reggae beat, much like Stewart Copeland's style on many of the early Police hits, as the backbeat is on the "three". Unique at the time – and still a fun pattern to play.

MILLIONS

Sebastian Rüger: What immediately strikes me is how accurate and analytical Terry's drumming is. For example, *Drums and Wires*, drumming-wise is really simple, there's nothing special in it, except

Making Plans for Nigel where you recognise the song just from the drumming riff. It's a famous drumming intro. Here are the first bars and, bam, that's it. But the other song that really got me and made me think, "OK, this is a guy who knows what he's doing and is capable of a lot more," is *Millions*. It stands out like the most complicated prog drumming I know because of the syncopation. The rhythm underneath is going so much against what the guitar does and the melody does. If you are a more emotional drummer like me, you link yourself to the melodies of the guitars or the vocals, and you are lost with a track like this because it is so austere. I always thought, "Where's the goddam 'one'?"

Todd Bernhardt: Sebastian brings up a really good point. There are songs where they turn the beat on its head and you are left wondering where the "one" is. *Millions* is a fantastic example of that. Once you figure it out, you can play it, but at the same time, there are things I have still not technically mastered. In the chorus, for example, what he's doing with his kick drum and his hands is really hard to play. The syncopation, coordination and the independence of limbs that are required is very tough.

Mark Thomas: *Millions* is a really good example. He puts a little Chinese splash cymbal in and you think, "Has he got another arm? Because where's he fitting that in?" I asked Andy if he'd put it in afterwards and he said, no, he played it live.

Mikey Erg: It's fascinating to listen to in the instrumental mix because there's so much going on. I'm not sure if he ever plays a snare drum on it - I feel like it's all tom work. It's an incredible pattern. It was that awesome period where Dave and Andy were playing these weird counter guitar parts that feel like they shouldn't work together but they do, and then Terry behind them doing his own thing. He's never playing your standard pattern. There's always something in there, like he's throwing in a counter off-beat.

Sebastian Rüger: It's a really complicated song. I wonder how the discussions were in composing this thing. We all know that Andy Partridge, if he is demoing songs, often has drum tracks in his mind. I'd really like to know how much Terry Chambers is in a track like this and how much is Andy influencing it and saying, "I want a syncopated off-splash cymbal there." His drumming is really mathematical. Very powerful, a sort of mixture of Jaki Liebezeit from Can, carrying through in a very sturdy, even manic, way, and at the same time very powerful like the later Phil Collins or Tony Thompson. It's a combination of Jaki Liebezeit and power drumming.

Todd Bernhardt: And again, being generous, leaving space for other people to do what they're doing and to serve the song.

Sebastian Rüger: In rock drumming, you mostly care about fourths, eighths and sixteenths. Mostly, that's it. He has this rock drumming thing, but also, in *Millions*, for example, he makes me think of the early Phil Collins when he played for Brand X - these short drum kicks in the off beat. It's almost jazz. Where does that come from?

Todd Bernhardt: Terry makes some innovative choices. There are a lot of songs where it would be easy to fall into a standard, clichéd rhythm, but Terry doesn't do that. He was always looking to do something a little different, just like the rest of the guys in the band. That's one of the things that makes XTC a musician's band. It helps the songs be deeper and more textured and stand the test of time.

Sebastian Rüger: On *Drums and Wires* there's not too much room in the sound for the drumming, just a little bit of reverb and stuff. How he managed to get from *Drums and Wires* to *Black Sea* and to incorporate this new drum sound is masterful. If a producer says they've got this huge drum sound, you have to get accustomed to it. It's like he invented this sound - but he didn't, that was the producer - so this guy really knows what he's doing. On the later albums, he gets used to this big-room drumming and it's so well played melodically. He knows where to put things when.

For example on *Tissue Tigers* he has to keep that

hammering eigth-feel with kick and toms, all is very low-end, just putting these accents on a high tom and hi-hat repetitively against the downbeat here and there, leaving a lot of space in between. The rhythm cries out for a heavy backbeat with a snare all the way through from the beginning, but he won't let it happen until a certain point.

When the song comes to the middle eight, a crash cymbal is heard for the first time. We feel something is changing. As the chords change, we hear high frequencies with cymbals in the drumming: "(Crash)! We argue (Crash!) *all... life... (Crash!) long*."

And so it goes on – all very heavy, down on the "one", thus turning our longing for the up-beat even more, as if he wants to tease the crap out of us... and then as the middle eight creates a crescendo on the last line with "I've trapped you ...*in my so-oong*," we finally get the backbeat on the "two" and the "four", the pumping rock'n'roll backbeat comes in with the snare we have all been waiting for and this thing goes AC/DC... but only for eight bars. Ha ha! Just to get back to the former rhythm afterwards with the chorus. It is so simple, but so effective. Right now I can't even sit still just thinking about it. It really is a rock drummer's orgasm without chops! Like as if the whole song was written around this moment. So tasteful and witty. Again I'd like to ask Andy, "Was that your idea or Terry's?"

BLACK SEA

ROCKET FROM A BOTTLE

Debbi Peterson: I remember when I first heard *Making Plans for Nigel* on the radio. It was probably very early 80s as songs didn't make it across the pond to America as quick in those days. I absolutely loved the song, especially the drum part. Boy, I wish I could've seen them live... Terry's drumming was so rhythmic; I was in Rhythmic Heaven! His use of the toms went so well with the bass lines, you could hardly tell where one ended and the other began.

One of my fave drum parts is *Rocket from a Bottle*. I love the use of the toms with the bass and that hi-hat that sneaks in once in a while. I was very much influenced by him. In fact, in the 80s/90s (and still today, I'll admit), I would drum along to XTC songs to warm up. It was very inspiring to me!

Louis Barfe: *Rocket from a Bottle* has got that slightly backwards feel like *Nigel*, hasn't it?

Mark Thomas: It sounds like the fizz of a rocket taking off with the hi-hat chokes. It's very clever. Illustrative drumming.

Rick Buckler: Things like that are interesting – especially from drums because it's a lot more difficult. If you hear a lyric and you think, "How can I illustrate the lyric with drums?" It's easy if you're talking about a train because you can make drums sound like a train, but a rocket is a different problem altogether. The sound conjures up a vision of what the lyrics are trying to say. That's clever – especially if it works and you can see something.

Mikey Erg: I've stolen from that beat a few times. You keep the rhythm on the floor tom, hit that snare almost like a surf beat and then go to the hi-hat with your left hand every once in a while just to keep it interesting.

Todd Bernhardt: *Rocket from a Bottle* is a great example. Terry is very good at riding on the toms. Usually you want to keep a steady beat with the right hand on the hi-hat or the ride cymbal, but Terry is very good at doing that ride on his floor tom, then he syncopates against that. In *Rocket from a Bottle* he keeps it driving the whole time not only by riding on the floor tom, but playing accents on the snare and other toms. Throwing in that hi-hat on the "four-and" is such a great accent – one that you wouldn't necessarily expect. And when he gets that pattern going, everything is able to work around it. That's probably the approach they would take: they were looking for that foundation and once they'd found it, they could build the house on top of it. Terry really was the foundation of the band and provided that solid footing so everyone could explore from there.

In *Rocket from a Bottle*, Colin's bass is not a particularly technically difficult part but it's perfect for the song, Dave's going chug-chug-chug on piano, Andy's got his little hook, then the vocals are another part still. Terry's playing eighths, everything's on the beat, and Andy's going, "I – I – I – oh-ho-hoo-hoo," so that's all triplets against the beat. Andy was lucky to have such a generous drummer who didn't want to step on his shit and Terry was lucky to work with a songwriter who was also intensely rhythmic in his approach, just as Colin was very rhythmic. Andy sings triplets a lot and, just as he likes to be dissonant and push notes against each other, he likes to push beats against each other.

All of a Sudden is like *Rocket from a Bottle*, but way softer. Terry does this little thing with the hi-hat that's so subtle and so perfect. He does a little chick with his foot on the hi-hat on the "three". It's all part of the pattern, but slipped in in the background. It's fitting for the acoustic approach and the lyrics. That's another thing I like about Terry: you can tell he's the type of drummer who cares about the subject of the lyrics and what approach the song is taking. He's way more thoughtful than even he would give himself credit for. He cares about this stuff.

NO LANGUAGE IN OUR LUNGS

Todd Bernhardt: I love *No Language in Our Lungs*. Technically, it's not a difficult rhythm to play, but the emotion that he brings to it, the feeling, the way he lays it down, the choices he makes – so good. The same thing is true for *Towers of London*. There are very few songs where he plays ride cymbal. He's a hi-hat guy. But on *No Language*, during the transitions from chorus to verse, and during the coda, he pulls it back and plays eight notes on the ride cymbal - which gives you a warm wash of sound – while playing these "tish, tish, tish-tish" accents on the hi-hat. That's not something you would normally think of. It's a great way of backing off, using the higher end – which is the sonic space the cymbals fill up – but a very different type of high end, because you get the sharp attack and quick decay of the hi-hat against the sustain of the ride cymbal. The effect is to keep things tight and focused.

Plus, I think he was trying to serve notice to the old-school people that this was a new type of music, more punk/new wave. Ride cymbals are especially popular in blues, jazz or swing, which is probably what his parents were playing. There are a couple of songs on *Go 2*, such as *Beatown*, where he's playing ride cymbal – but it's pretty unusual when he makes that choice. By *Black Sea*, he hardly ever plays it, except when he made that specific choice to back away and use those particular colours in his drumming paint box. And the overall drum sound on *No Language in Our Lungs* is just magnificent.

Sebastian Rüger: I am a big Mike Keneally Fan and, because The Universe Will Provide (Keneally insider reference), I had the joy to get to know him personally through a very good friend here in Cologne. When I turned 50 last year, I gave myself a treat by booking him for my birthday party. He played with his trio and then let me play about ten songs with him... Preparing for that got me back into listening to music analytically and counting it again. I listened to the music with a new ear.

I had played *No Language in Our Lungs* with Mike at an occasion a year before (you can find it on YouTube) because he once told me it was his favourite song. I didn't try to channel that Chambers-like style and took it to a more playful place... But that ride cymbal and the hi-hat just had to be respected in the outro at least.

LIVING THROUGH ANOTHER CUBA

Mark Cobb: Having played XTC songs covering their entire catalogue, I will say *Black Sea* is my favourite album. Much of this is a result of the power of Terry's drumming. His playing is muscular and streamlined in a way few other drummers have captured in the studio. While I have many favourites, the song that stands out is *Living Through Another Cuba*.

Despite the use of some electronic supplement (Terry utilised the Tama Snyper drum synthesiser also made popular by drummers such as Stewart Copeland and Billy Cobham), the slinky offbeat groove gives the song its frenetic urgency.

Terry Arnett: You can also hear the effect of the Tama Snyper on the snare drum on *Love at First Sight*, giving that disco down-pitching sound on the verses and middle eight. It's not played in the chorus! On *Living Through Another Cuba*, the effect is higher in pitch but still down-pitching – triggered from one of the rack toms, to replicate a falling bomb.

Mark Cobb: Having covered *Black Sea* in its entirety with a group I perform with in Atlanta called Nigels With Attitude, *Living Through Another Cuba* was the biggest challenge for me to pull off accurately. My favourite passage starts around the three-minute mark and weaves in and out of a guitar solo that complements the ska-driven sound that was popular in England around that time. The high-pitched Rototom backbeat also stands out in contrast to the typical snare drum used on most rock records. Terry's playing is timeless and defined XTC's sound more than any other single drummer.

Todd Bernhardt: I would agree with all of that. Even though *Living Through Another Cuba* is kind of a pea-soup rhythm, it's more than that: he actually plays a little double hit on his hi-hat every time. That's really hard to do consistently well and authoritatively over a long period of time. I've heard stories of Stewart Copeland standing backstage watching XTC play when they were on a double-bill together. If you asked a group of drummers who was a better drummer, Copeland or Chambers, they would say, "Oh, Stewart Copeland is just amazing." But Copeland knew how good Terry was. He would sit there and watch him because Terry had a feeling, attitude and approach he wanted to learn from. So, yes, *Cuba* is a really fun and hard song to do.

Terry Arnett: I love Terry's hi-hat work on *Cuba*, played on the "and" and the "a".

Mikey Erg: The thing I always love is he's playing a ska beat and then, probably because Andy says "-ba" where he does, he does this awesome pick up. I wish I was in the room with them when they were working the song out, but I assume he came up with that because he was listening to what Andy was doing.

BURNING WITH OPTIMISM'S FLAMES

Mikey Erg: One of my favourite drumbeats/grooves has always been *Burning with Optimism's Flames*. Having a straight drum beat and what he's doing with the hi-hat in that song always impressed me. It's fascinating to hear the instrumental mixes that have come out on the Blu-rays. There's so much you miss when the vocals are on. The first thing I listened to was the instrumental mix of *Burning with Optimism's Flames*, which is something I've always wanted to have.

Andy Rankin: He wrote parts. In the verses on *Burning with Optimism's Flames*, for example, he does these little 16ths on the hi-hat and he plays the snare on "three", then goes into a regular rock beat on the bridge and the chorus. Part for the chorus, part for the bridge, part for the verse.

Mikey Erg: Any other drummer would have done a straight tch-tch-tch-tch and he for some reason decided to do the roll on the hi-hat, which just made it that little bit more interesting. The only time I play my drums is at band rehearsals or at shows because, living in New York, the apartments are so small, there's no place to set up, but I've air-drummed to all that stuff. It's a challenge. *Burning with Optimism's Flames* is my song if I'm ever jamming at a soundcheck while everyone is getting their gear together. I just start playing that beat because it's so fascinating. I think I get it right – I'm sure it's not nearly as proficient as Terry played it, but it's a good approximation. He's right in there with Colin, they're perfectly in sync and Colin's doing a hard thing too. It's a groove that makes that album for me. It's one of those things you never forget were you where when you first heard it.

SGT ROCK (IS GOING TO HELP ME)

Maurice "mOe" Watson: Although I was completely immersed in XTC's work as a whole, it was one of the few bands that drum-wise, I wasn't super interested in. But about ten years after I'd gone to college, I was a part of a failed venture to have an XTC tribute show comprised of musicians from New York City and New Jersey. This led to me playing through XTC songs for the first time on the drum kit. The later-era stuff which made use of some awesome session drummers was fun and relatively easy to play through. The Chambers-era stuff? Different story...

Sgt Rock (Is Going to Help Me) is a fantastic example of how crucial the drums were to XTC's sound while Chambers was in the band. If you strip away the drum kit on Sgt Rock, you're left with a basic 4/4 shuffle feel. But, to play a basic shuffle drum beat to Sgt Rock is simply a "drum-solo-in-the-middle-of-Imagine" away from complete and utter sacrilege. The drum beat spans almost the entire kit left to right every single measure. Terry Chambers played with so much power and consistency, he rivals drummers of today, me included, who make heavy use of technology to even-out drum note volume and placement. By the time I made it to the end of practising this tune, I was *spent*!

Todd Bernhardt: Who plays like that? When people started posting YouTube clips of XTC playing live I realised I'd been making it much harder for myself when I tried to play the parts. They seem to be much more complicated than they are. Andy always says that about his guitar playing too. Sgt Rock is a really messed-up beat, but it's perfect for the song. There are a lot of other ways you could approach that song but none of them would make sense in the way it does, given the choices Terry made. Even though it's bouncy, bright and danceable, it's very offbeat.

Terry Arnett: It's a clever shuffle pattern, played with a sticking you would not normally think of, but Terry did. The hi-hat is played on the third note of each triplet beat with the right hand, and the main backbeat on "two" and "four" played with the right only. Then the first backbeat of each bar is complemented by an additional backbeat on the third triplet of that beat, played with the right hand. It's one groovy mother of a beat.

Mikey Erg: The rhythm just moves that song along so well. I feel like Terry always took what a normal drummer would have done and made it just a bit more interesting. "Here's what you would have done – this is what I'm doing."

Todd Bernhardt: One of the things that kill me are the accents he does on the toms – he's plugged right in to what the other guys are doing. It's not easy, it's very syncopated and it's not the kind of choice that most drummers would make.

Sebastian Rüger: Absolutely, yes! And the feel of that groove is hard to get flowing because it has to be "down", in the sense of "heavy", to make it danceable, but at the same time, the hi-hats and toms are "up", creating that offbeat, that swing. So you have to keep up two feels in your body at the same time plus the challenge of playing it hard! I watched some clips and even on *Top of the Pops* playback performances you can sense how much concentration Terry is keeping up. His whole body language, his arms and shoulders, tell you about the task of mastering this inner down-against-up struggle.

Maurice "mOe" Watson: To play one note out of place strips the song of its identity. It's difficult to name many songs like that. The drum parts on this song, and many others played by Chambers, are the choruses in the way they provide the identity and atmosphere of the entire song. Ringo was also quite guilty of this, despite being universally clowned among musos as a "bad drummer". In my opinion, creating music that would never be the same without you, makes you the best kind of musician – one that will always be remembered. I know, I'll never forget those amazing drum parts from tunes like *Knuckle Down, Burning with Optimism's Flames, Makin Plans for Nigel* and so many more.

Mikey Erg: I'm a huge Ringo fan too. He gets a lot

of flack for not being a virtuoso, but the stuff he played was what the song needed.

Sebastian Rüger: Maurice is so right on this: one mistake and the whole thing falls apart. To be so musical to listen to the song, to "get" the song in the first place (which is the biggest challenge making music in bands: to play the same song in terms of understanding what the composer has in mind or where the song and the sound should be going) and yet be tight enough to nail it down and not get carried away by what the others are doing... This is crucial for creating a good song, let alone a unique sound.

Andy Rankin: One common thing on *Black Sea* is he plays the hi-hat on the offbeat a lot – on the "and". It's almost like he's matching the melody. It's disco-reggae and it fits the song. The hi-hats on *Generals and Majors* remind me of *Heart of Glass* by Blondie where there's a repetitive pattern. Terry does that a bit more stretched out on *Generals and Majors* and I love the fact that he's taken what could be a disco beat and turned it into a new wave beat with more aggro to it.

Rick Buckler: I took it to an extreme on *Scrape Away* on *Sound Affects*. It was: how far can you push this thing? I'm going to leave everything out so nobody's going to know what's going on, but I've got this metronome going in my head, so you just keep it going. It's great when you can't hear what the drummer's hearing. He knows where he's putting stuff, but it's all the stuff that he's keeping secret that makes it sound really odd. You feel like you're going to fall over.

TRAVELS IN NIHILON

Sebastian Rüger: In acting school, we built a short theatre piece around an XTC song. It was my idea. I was always fascinated by *Travels in Nihilon* and I was fond of music having a visual or theatrical setting. *West Side Story* and the Beatles movies were big things for me. This song always triggered something visual inside my head, so I suggested to another guy in my class that we perform it live. He liked the song too and he suggested we should take some extracts from this long poem by Hans Magnus Enzensberger about the Titanic being an injury to modern society, and do it as a preface to the song. We created this short theatre piece that culminated with me standing at the drum kit in jeans and no shirt – my rock-star moment – with a guitarist and a bass player. I was playing and singing at the same time. What I remember is that within this song, it's all the same throughout, with two hits on the snare, but there are little alterations in the last repeating choruses where you would play four on the snare. Terry has a Phil Collins mind-set.

Louis Barfe: Andy Partridge has said that once the information had gone through and Terry had processed it, it was like programming a human drum machine. The one drum track that for me stands out is *Travels in Nihilon*. It's not a loop, he's playing it all the way through. Anyone else would have gone, "I'll just loop that." And I bet if you put a metronome up against it, it would not waver.

Todd Bernhardt: Throughout the bulk of *Travels in Nihilon* he's a human drum machine. No click track. It was one of those instances where they were just like, "Terry, go!" And he was like, "I'm going to play this pattern for ten minutes." You can tell because the drums fade in and fade out. That takes a hell of a lot of discipline.

Terry Arnett: This track was done, by Andy Partridge's account, in one take... *one take*! It's hypnotic. Eighth notes on the floor tom and bass drum, and the rack-tom notes played on the first beat and then playing a more rolling pattern over each two bars. There's a backbeat played on beat four on every second bar, with an accompanying snare beat on the "and" of beat three on every fourth bar. This swaps round to every second bar of four in the middle, then builds towards the end. Rock solid and so tight. Having played this live myself, it's a difficult one to keep a rein on.

Mikey Erg: If I was in an XTC covers band, I'd say, "Let's not do that one."

Andy Rankin: There's a covers band in Australia

called Scarecrow People. They played the *Black Sea* album from start to finish. They finished with *Travels in Nihilon*, but they had three people playing drums. In fact, four. They had the drummer, who's fantastic - he plays in a Frank Zappa cover band as well - and then two or three other drums set around the place to get the sound. It sounded amazing - but three people against one!

Mikey Erg: That's your article right there!

Todd Bernhardt: I remember Stewart Copeland at a drum clinic in front of a bunch of wide-eyed fans. He said, "Now, I'm going to play for you the hardest thing I can think of." Everyone thought, "Oh my God, we're going to see some flash from Stew." He gets up on his kit and he plays a standard rock 4/4 beat for about two minutes, just with feeling and consistency. Of course, everyone was surprised and he explained that if you don't have this - if you can't make it feel good and be simple at the same time - none of the other stuff matters. Terry is the personification of that. The music always felt good with him.

ENGLISH SETTLEMENT

RUNAWAYS/BALL AND CHAIN

Sebastian Rüger: In a song like *Runaways*, drumming-wise there's nothing happening, but where you would play the snare, he plays a stand tom. Very often he's playing a loud upbeat where you would put a snare. He does it differently. I would like to ask him if it was his idea or, let's say, Colin's to say, "No, it shouldn't get too rocky." It's a sad song about kids running away and it has a melancholic influence to it, so he chooses this pattern. You have to have a musical ear to choose something like that, to know, "This is what the song needs and I won't do anything else."

Todd Bernhardt: I would agree with that. Some of that is as a result of them all trying to be a bit different and not like every other band out there.

Mikey Erg: It's what I always think about if something feels a little too samey - all you have to do is hit another drum instead of the snare drum.

Terry Arnett: On *Runaways* and *Yacht Dance*, there's the use of the Tama Snyper drum synth, but this time on the bass drum, to give a real low end, down-pitching, thud. I do believe (though I may be wrong) that this may have influenced Stewart Copeland to use it in the studio and in live situations for *Ghost in the Machine* and *Synchronicity* to give definition to his bass drum sound. From seeing shots of Stewart live, there was a trigger attached to his bass drum batter head.

Sebastian Rüger: In *English Settlement* Terry discovered this Rototom that he puts everywhere. In *Ball and Chain*, for example, you have these repetitions. Listen to the "save us from the Ball and Chain" parts and sometimes he would do a sixteenth for the next bar, but other times ("The diggers and the tower cranes") nothing is in between. He knows exactly how to leave room and to leave the emphasis on "chain". This is the Jaki Liebezeit approach. He was a master of that also. Terry knows where to put things when, to carry the song and at the same time not to interfere with the vocals. He really has a great ear.

Speaking of his love for toms, it is funny to mention a song where he would use them in the album version but later changed it: *This Is Pop*. The album version has this tom rhythm underneath but was replaced by that more usual snare/kick/hi-hat-4/4 beat for the single version... and rightly so! The single version really kicks ass. The album version is definitely weaker and somehow undecided. So, here we see he also knew when to come back to something more usual if that fits the song. But again I'd like to know if this was brought up by him or Andy or maybe even the producer: "Play it straighter, boy! The song's name is *This Is Pop* not *This Is Experimental New Wave*!

Mikey Erg: *Ball and Chain* could have easily been a shuffle, but where a normal shuffle beat would be on the hi-hat, he's doing it on the toms instead. He figured out a way to do something different with it.

Todd Bernhardt: *Ball and Chain* is very unusual. The way he goes through the kit, using a combination of toms, the Rototom against the four-on-the-floor approach of the kick drum – that's a hard song to play consistently. It's athletic, musical and melodic because he's using the tuned toms with the rest of the instruments. Terry doesn't get enough credit for being a melodic drummer. He wouldn't go for a particular note, but he would make sure the drums sounded good and the tom choice he would make would be in the right sonic range for the part of the song. He had the musical taste to make the right choices in the right places.

Terry Arnett: I agree with Todd. It's unusual. But his flowing movements around the kit just make this track such fun to play. Not many people use the whole drum kit to play the main rhythm. Timekeeping is normally held by the hi-hat... the fact of a distinct lack of it in the verses proves Terry can make a rhythm groove, the anchor of the four-on-the-floor bass drum cementing every other note played – the foundation – only going to a more conventional pattern for the chorus and middle eight.

Maurice "mOe" Watson: The best part about *English Settlement* is the guitar playing, in my opinion. The drums provide a very basic canvas to really let the guitars fill out the songs ever-so. My favourite drum feel on the whole album is *Knuckle Down*. As repetitive as the drum pattern is (it literally doesn't change throughout the whole song), I can't get enough. Making use of a half-time shuffle feel, the song bounces all the way to the end. *Ball and Chain* is an awesome display of the raw power of Terry Chambers, which *English Settlement* lacks in comparison to *Drums and Wires*. The drum recording made beautiful use of the room mikes of the studio, propelling the tom-toms to massive heights in the verses by making them sound as big as can be. Throughout the entire tune, Chambers sounds ten feet tall, literally!

ENGLISH ROUNDABOUT

Terry Arnett: The great TC groove can be found on tracks such as *Super-Tuff*, *Millions*, *Generals and Majors* and *Ball and Chain*. And I'd give an exceptional mention to *English Roundabout*, a rock-solid groove of a 5/4 pattern, played over two bars (therefore making it an even time signature of 10/8). It never waivers and is just so in the pocket. He takes a less-is-more approach, as it is only bass drum, hi-hat and rim click – no other drums. Sublime!

Mikey Erg: *English Roundabout* is a ska song in 5/4! He's doing a snare rim-shot typical of most ska songs but I can't figure out where he's putting them because the song is in such an odd time. And yet it was only when reading Neville Farmer's book *Song Stories* that I even noticed it was in 5/4. I thought I had it all figured out, but I didn't at all.

Terry Arnett: "Terry never plays odd time signatures..." Pah! This is a fine example of him doing just that, but in his own way, playing an unwavering reggae pattern in 5/4, over a two-bar phrase, making it even! Again, this is another track that shows Terry's ability to play a very repetitive riff, with no deviation, solidly for the length of the track. It's just bass drum (four on the floor again), hi-hat and rim click. Only the introductory five bars are different, with a nice riff using the snare and, what I believe to be the two rack toms, then a flam on the snare... nice touch!

NO THUGS IN OUR HOUSE

Terry Arnett: This is Terry in full powerhouse mode. It's a driving, thunderous solid snare on every beat of the bar, a clever placement of the bass drum and an accenting of his hi-hat to lift the rhythm. Then in the middle eight, there's the juxtaposition: four-on-the-floor bass drum, eighth notes and the three-over-four feel of the hi-hat, building up the tension! A very well crafted track from Terry in my honest and humble opinion.

Mikey Erg: I read him say somewhere that he always just wanted to suit the song. On *No Thugs* *in Our House* he follows Andy's vocal line on the "woh-oh-oh-oh-oh-oh-oh" in the chorus. He plays exactly what Andy is singing, following whatever they're doing. The band I pretty much started out playing in was my own band, the Ergs, and I sang the songs and played drums, so I was always playing to my own vocal line. It was easy for me to do that because I knew what I was singing, but it's cool to hear a band when the drummer is following what the vocals are doing - that's not normal.

INDEX OF CONTRIBUTORS

TERRY ARNETT The drummer and backing vocalist with XTC tribute band Fossil Fools (see 143), Terry was also a member of the Fuzzy Warblers. Based in London where he works as a security analyst, he has played original music in Mellotronanism and Oil City Kings, and covers in the Dandy Highwaymen, 20th Century Boys and the Thrillers.

LOUIS BARFE A freelance writer, editor and broadcaster, Louis is the author of *Turned Out Nice Again: The Story of British Light Entertainment*, *Where Have all the Good Times Gone?: The Rise and Fall of the Record Industry*, *The Trials and Triumphs of Les Dawson* and *Britain's Greatest TV Comedy Moments*. He is also the assistant editor of *Vintage Drums Legendary Sounds* magazine, and a regular gigging drummer around Bristol and Gloucestershire, most notably with the Bristol Community Big Band. www.cheeseford.net

TODD BERNHARDT Co-author with Andy Partridge of *Complicated Game: Inside the Songs of XTC*, Todd has played drums with several bands in the Washington DC area. Working by day (and sometimes nights!) in corporate communications and marketing, he also freelances, having contributed chapters to several music-related books and articles for *Modern Drummer* magazine and other publications.

RICK BUCKLER With Paul Weller and Bruce Foxton, Rick played a pivotal role in the Jam, drumming with the band from its foundation in 1974 until its split in 1982. Since then, he has played with Time UK, the Gift and From the Jam, and worked as a producer and management consultant, while developing a sideline in furniture restoration. He is the author of *That's Entertainment: My Life in the Jam* and the graphic novel *Start to 77*. www.thejamfan.net

MARK COBB Atlanta studio drummer and Grammy member, Mark is the powerhouse behind Yacht Rock Revue, a hard-gigging 70s cover band, as well as a busy session musician and percussion instructor. He has also played with XTC covers band Nigels with Attitude. www.markcobb.net

MIKEY ERG (real name Mike Yannich) Starting with his own punk band, the Ergs, Mikey has played as a drummer, singer and guitarist with a variety of bands in his native New Jersey and beyond. As well as being part of the house band on *The Chris Gethard Show* ("My job is to play music and laugh"), he has worked with Star Fucking Hipsters, the Dopamines, the Unlovables, Dirtbike Annie, Parasites and Worriers. He released his first solo album, *Tentative Decisions*, in 2016 and there's another on the way.
mikeyerg.bandcamp.com

MARK FISHER A freelance writer and theatre critic, Mark was the founder editor of *Limelight*, the XTC fanzine, and is the author of *The Edinburgh Fringe Survival Guide* and *How to Write About Theatre*, as well as the editor of *The XTC Bumper Book of Fun for Boys and Girls: A Limelight Anthology* and *What Do You Call That Noise? An XTC Discovery Book*. He can't play drums.
www.xtclimelight.com

LAURIE LANGAN Surrounded by jazz from an early age thanks to his saxophone-playing father, he taught himself piano when he found a Liberace record lying around the house. After joining many bands, he decided to create his own project, Default Collective, with friend and drummer, James Hayward, after the two met in the same band. Later on, the two met Sarah Palmer and went on to form Fassine. www.fassine.com

ROHAN ONRAET A digital engineer, arranger, songwriter and producer, Rohan has worked with acts including Moloko, Gary Barlow, Mark Ronson, the White Stripes and Fassine.
www.rohanonraet.com

SARAH PALMER Some of Sarah's earliest memories are of attending her father's gigs and being enthralled by the electricity. She started singing in his band from eight years old and, at age eleven, was lucky to get her longed-for drum kit. She performed at any opportunity, be it her father's gigs or school assemblies. Throughout her teens and early 20s she played drums, sung and composed in a number of projects until Fassine was born. www.fassine.com

DEBBI PETERSON Drummer and singer with the Bangles, Debbi formed the band in 1980 with her sister Vicki together with Susanna Hoffs. After a mid-90s split, they reformed and play live to this day. Hits include *Manic Monday, Walk Like an Egyptian, Eternal Flame, Going Down to Liverpool* and *Hazy Shade of Winter*. www.thebangles.com

ANDY RANKIN A school principal from Sydney, Australia, Andy grew up in the UK where he worked as a professional drummer in covers bands, playing summer seasons and holiday camps. Trying to make it with original material, he gigged and auditioned his way around London and the southern UK before emigrating to Australia. There, he worked in several originals bands and with Weld, better known as the Australian Neil Young Show, before going part-time playing and teaching music.

SEBASTIAN RÜGER An actor and comedian, Sebastian is one half of German comedy duo Ulan & Bator who create their own absurdist mix of theatre, comedy, Dada, a cappella and German Kabarett (the German version of political satire). He has shown up on TV, film and radio here and there. He started drumming at the age of nine when he spent his first DM50 on a toy drum kit. Initially influenced by Ringo, Moonie, Gene Krupa and Animal from the Muppets, he got into all kinds of styles with a profound love of prog, Zappa, jazz and good pop. He instantly fell in love with XTC and Terry's drumming when hearing them the first time at age of 17. He became an actor but never stopped drumming. "Actor by profession, but drummer by heart," as he says.
www.ulanundbator.de

MARK THOMAS An illustrator by profession, Mark has drummed with friends since the age of 16 and once even had a drunken jam with Andy Partridge. His illustrations in the style of Tamara De Lempicka were used in adverts in *NME* and *Melody Maker* promoting the Jam's *Sound Affects* and a small detail (a skyscraper) ended up on the album sleeve itself. Other work includes covers for the *Guardian, Daily Mail* and the *Radio Times*. He designed the front covers of *The XTC Bumper Book of Fun for Boys and Girls* and *What Do You Call That Noise?*
www.markthomasillustration.co.uk

MAURICE "MOE" WATSON As well as being a session player, mOe has drummed with Vagus Nerve, Shai Hulud, and John Ginty Band. Raised in New Jersey, he discovered XTC after hearing *Drums and Wires* in 2002 and has been a passionate fan ever since.
soundcloud.com/m0ebocop

WHO'S PULSING?

Taking turns on the drum stool after Terry's departure were Pete Phipps, Ian Gregory, Prairie Prince, Pat Mastelotto, Dave Mattacks and Chuck Sabo. What was it like to grab the sticks, pick up the rhythm and set the XTC pulse?

BY YVONNE WOOTTON

"Phippsy, Prairie, Pat, Mattacks and Chuck (and others) all did fantastic jobs. All different, all great. Terry would have just been different." - Andy Partridge, Twitter, October 2018

Terry Chambers' departure from XTC in 1982 left a vacancy that was never permanently filled. Many of the fans were bereft; after all, Terry's drumming was integral to the music of XTC - its heart-pumping, pulsing-pulsing rhythms complemented the guitars and keyboards and drove the inimitable shifting melodies and mood with a distinctive style. Pity poor Pete Phipps coming in to sit on that still-warm drum stool as Terry's departing words - "Well, I'll be off then" - reverberated around the walls during the recording of *Mummer* (released 1983). As one *Limelight* reader anxiously wrote: "I mean, it's like Lennon without McCartney or Morecambe without Wise... Andy, Dave and Colin - yes, but not with Pete Phipps... I'll probably take an immediate dislike to Pete (whatever his drumming is like)." Even more ominously, another letter said: "The Pete Phipps person sounds threatening..."

"Glad I didn't know about that at the time," laughs Phipps today. Fortunately, the band were rather more welcoming. "Pete's a very amiable kind of fellow," said Andy Partridge in *Limelight* issue three. "He's not averse to trying out strange suggestions like rattling bits of chain or playing along with a drum box."

His big break into the charts was with glam rockers the Glitter Band in the early 70s; his path crossed with XTC later that decade. "I knew them because I was on tour with them as a member of Random Hold, who were the support band in 79," says Phipps. "They were great live - I loved the band when I saw them. Then in 1982 Andy was desperate because Terry had decided to leave."

One of Terry's reasons for going was his lack of enthusiasm for the songs, *Mummer* being a more pastoral and progressive album than what had gone before. It's one reason they contacted Phipps. "I think they thought I was a bit more jazzy," he says. "We did *Mummer* at the Manor, the drum sound there was really dead. I played a Sonor Phonic kit and the sound we went for was mellow and tuneful to suit the more folky elements of the majority of the songs on the album."

Despite Terry's reservations, there are many high-profile fans of *Mummer*, among them Todd Bernhardt and Steven Wilson. "That's great!" says Phipps. "A lot of my contemporaries say, 'Oh, I love those two XTC albums you did!' And yet they just didn't do anything. *Love on a Farmboy's Wages* is an amazing song. I love those parts I came up with. Andy was really stretching out on *Great Fire*, and *Ladybird* – I just wish I'd played it more different now. We didn't do loads of takes as we rehearsed it really well over three weeks before we went into the studio. So if they really liked a take, that was it. It wasn't my decision, it was theirs."

Phipps went on to record *The Big Express* (released 1984) which had a much more industrial and upfront sound. Despite what a lot of people think, it wasn't all LinnDrum. "We had a live drum room at the Crescent," he says. "It was a stone room in the cellar. You had to go down a spiral staircase and I only had monitor contact with the band and producer David Lord, so it was quite lonely. I did do some tracks upstairs but we got that big powerful sound from the ambience of the stone room downstairs."

Its conceptual songs inspired by Swindon are propulsive and compelling; what tracks does Phipps specifically remember? "I had to do a lot of takes on *Wake Up* – I did over six," he says. "Every time I did it, Andy said, 'Oh, can you do another one?' And then they decided which one was the best. I was exhausted after that. That was the only time when I felt, 'I'm not going to be able to do this!' It was intense, I was trying to better it every time. I enjoyed the first three takes and by the last three I was just losing it. I've got no idea which take they kept, I wasn't at the mixing."

Phipps agrees it's a shame *Mummer* and *The Big Express* are often overlooked because the sales were low, but he has no regrets. "It's sad but I'm still proud to have been on them and we had so much fun," he says. "I was always choking on my food the things Andy was coming out with. We had a lovely working relationship. I really enjoyed going into the studio every day. Andy had asked me if I wanted to be a permanent member, and I said. 'Yes!' It's a shame because I would have loved to have joined the band. We even had photos taken together with that intention. I guess it didn't come about because there was no touring to do: Andy wasn't going to tour again, that was pretty clear after *Mummer* was made. We got on really well; it was one of the best periods of my playing career. I loved every minute of it. If they rang me up and said, 'Do you want to do an album?' I'd say, 'Yes!' just for the fun of it and choking on my food again."

Despite many fans' love of *Mummer* and *The Big Express*, their low sales were overshadowed by the unexpected success of *25 O'Clock*, the psychedelic homage EP to the 60s created by XTC's alter egos the Dukes of Stratosphear. Perhaps the most unsung of all the guest drummers is Ian Gregory. As EIEI Owen, he comfortably slipped into the groove of flower-power pop pastiche on both *25 O'Clock* (released 1985) and its follow-up *Psonic Psunspot* (1987), thanks in part to his shared love of the era and as a regular player with various covers bands. Ian was also the go-to drummer for many of XTC's TV and video appearances, fitting them around his day job.

"I knew the boys pretty well having gone to many XTC gigs going right back to the days when Barry was in the group," says Gregory. "Dave and I shared a house – actually it was his house and I was the lodger – so once Dave had joined XTC they were frequent visitors. The decision to make the first Dukes record was made in a very short space of time, Andy having withdrawn from a project he was due to produce. So with a studio booked, the decision was made to use the time to make a psychedelic record. Terry had long pushed off to Australia, so a drummer was needed – somebody who had an awareness of 60s drumming, had studio experience, was playing regularly and - significantly - owned genuine 60s gear. I was asked to do it and naturally leapt at the opportunity - I do recall it being incredibly short notice."

True to the authentic nature of the project, Gregory played live in the studio for most of the tracks. "The drums were the first thing to be done, and it was tricky because I had no prior knowledge of the songs, so it was intuitive," he says. "Andy and Colin both had their own ideas for the rhythmic style and we got our heads together and got it done. In those days, the full length of the drum track would be recorded - I don't recall too many drop-ins - so you had to concentrate hard as we had very little studio time booked. Nowadays, there is incredibly sophisticated studio software, such as Pro Tools, that can make even the sloppiest of drum tracks sound great and in perfect time. Nothing like that was available to us - it had to be played in real time."

Getting that authentic 60s sound required a vintage kit. Gregory played a 1964 Ludwig Super Classic kit and some very old Zildjian cymbals. "I bought those drums when I was 19 - they were a genuine 'barn find' and in shocking condition. I restored them and used them exclusively back then. They were black when we did *25 O'Clock*, but at the time of *Psonic Psunspot* I had them professionally veneered in mahogany after I saw BJ Wilson's drums and thought they looked cool. Funnily enough, I got those drums out recently for a few gigs and they sound great. I alternate my stuff and tend to use smaller drums for live work, but for the immediate future I will be using those old Ludwigs."

He adds: "Again, the guitars used were all period 60s examples - Dave could tell you the make and no doubt serial numbers of those involved. Many 'errors' just added to the overall effect - if it worked, it was left in. *25 O'Clock* was recorded in a small studio near Hereford and we were able to borrow a Hammond organ from Mott the Hoople's keyboard player Verden Allen, who lived nearby. I believe this is the organ you can hear on *All the Young Dudes* to such great effect. Dave played this on several tracks, usually with some weird effect added."

Gregory's stand-out tracks are *Mole from the Ministry* and *Little Lighthouse*, not least because of the contribution of producer John Leckie. "He's a lovely man who had incredible patience - remember, as a top producer, he was used to working with the very best musicians in the business but he was always very encouraging. A great producer who knew exactly what was needed to make those records sound so good. Colin's *Vanishing Girl* is also good but in my opinion is too fast - I played the original version much slower but I was over-ruled and it ended up at that tempo."

How did the recording experiences differ between the two albums? Leckie produced both and although there was more time for the second one, was there a bit more pressure to follow up the success of the first? Gregory thinks not. "To be honest, I don't think any of us felt any pressure whatsoever, which is why it was so enjoyable," he says. "I think it was two weeks for the first one, maybe four max for the second. We all stayed in accommodation at the studios and worked during the day, had a meal together then carried on into the night. I don't recall any late-night sessions - it was all very civilised. We were at Sawmill Studios in Cornwall which is an idyllic location that can only be reached by boat. We even took time out to go sight-seeing and still got the record done within our limited time scale."

After the recording came the video and TV appearances, both with XTC and as the Dukes, including shoots in Europe. Gregory loved the experience. "The Portmeirion episode of *The Tube* was one of the greatest experiences of my life," he says. "Although it may not appear so from the TV footage, it was January and incredibly cold and our accommodation in 'The Village' was pretty spartan with no heating. We were there for a few days and had a great laugh – meeting Professor Stanley Unwin was brilliant and he was happy to talk to us about his work with the Small Faces on *Ogden's Nut Gone Flake*. The Mole from the Ministry video was filmed by the BBC at Clevedon and took about four hours. I was featured because the others would have been recognised as XTC!"

Playing regular gigs to this day, Gregory has found he's never far from an XTC connection. "The *éminence grise* of the band I am currently in is Pete Cousins, who was the bass player and singer in the Stadium Dogs, another Swindon band on the same circuit as XTC. They were on Magnet records and had moderate success. The keyboard player in the Stadium Dogs was Jonathan Perkins, who as die-hard fans will know was once in XTC. Wheels within wheels…"

The two Dukes of Stratosphear albums bookended *Skylarking* (released 1986), so it's no wonder some of the Dukes sound seeped into this album. It's one of XTC's most critically acclaimed records and one that also raised the band's prominence in the States, partly owing to its hands-on production by legendary American producer Todd Rundgren. As XTC were over the pond away from home, Todd recommended Prairie Prince, drummer from the Tubes. The drum tracks were recorded in the band's studio, the Sound Hole, in San Francisco surrounded by Prairie's paintings and murals.

"He looks incredibly like Robert Mitchum," said Andy Partridge in *Limelight* issue six about Prairie Prince. "He's his double. Very disturbing to look up and see Robert Mitchum sat at the drum kit sweating!"

"That's right!" laughs Prince. "There's a portrait of me in the double vinyl edition. We had that conversation about the Robert Mitchum thing throughout the recording session. And my whole life, ever since I was a teenager, people always told me I look like Robert Mitchum!"

Although it was Rundgren who brought them together, it wasn't the first time Prince and the band had met. "The Tubes actually performed with XTC on *Top of the Pops* in 1979," he says. "They were promoting *Making Plans for Nigel* and the Tubes were playing *Prime Time*, which was produced by Todd. So we actually got to meet them on the set of *TOTP*. That was when I got to tell Andy I was a such big fan. I did see them play in San Francisco about 1980 and I was blown away. The next thing I knew they had given up touring so I never got to see them again until six years later."

XTC started *Skylarking* at Rundgren's studio ranch in Woodstock, New York State before moving west. The producer was familiar with the studio and realised they could pick up a drummer at the same time. "I was part of the package!" says Prince. "He said, 'Would you like to do it?' and I said, 'Absolutely!' Actually, there was something illegal about that because I never got a proper drum credit. My credit was 'Prairie Prince plays the part of the time bomb.' Nobody knew what that meant!"

The tensions during the recording of *Skylarking* have been well documented. What does Prince remember of the atmosphere in San Francisco? "I so enjoyed it," he says. "I had worked with Todd previously on two records so I knew his demeanour. He has this odd demeanour and it was jibing with Andy's excited manner. Andy was asking him a million questions like, 'Why don't we try it this way?' and, 'Why don't we try it another way?' and Todd was trying to be accommodating…. It was too much, he kept saying, 'I was hired to produce this, and I have to be able to do the things that I think are the best.' I didn't witness a lot of that; it started in Woodstock and they'd felt a bit isolated there too, but when they came up they were refreshed, they were excited about playing with the drummer. When they got here we all got in the room together and started playing on a few tracks. We first did *Extrovert* and it was fun and beautiful. I was wishing we could have done more of that but they had already done preproduction work in Woodstock and had a lot of the tracks set up so I ended up just overdubbing most of the time."

As well as music, Prince and Partridge bonded over their shared love of art. "We were very similar," he says. "We like to work on music and art at the same time and when they coincide and relate to each other that's even better. Him doing designs for album covers and posters, I've done that my whole career as well: set designs, costume designs, music is integrated in the art. We had a lot in common with art and music, it was great. I loved his sensibilities and his sense of humour. I loved Andy - I wish I could work with the guy again. Some day, who knows?"

A lot of people cite *Skylarking* as their favourite XTC album, with its diverse arrangements and cyclical themes. What, then, stands out for Prince? "It's like a *Sgt Peppers* sort of thing," he says. "The tracks are so interesting; there is a whole world of textures and sound ideas in one composition. *Dear God* is one of my favourites. I love the way the drums sound on that - Todd did a really good job recording the drums, they have an open feel. I played an old Ludwig brass snare drum from 1929 and I used it on most of the songs on the record. *Earn Enough for Us* has got this incredible ring to it. It's just such a beautiful open sound so when people come up to me and say, 'I love that record *Skylarking*, particularly *Earn Enough for Us*, I tell them about that snare drum."

He adds: "I endorse Yamaha drums and I used my 22" bass, 13" rack tom, 16" floor tom plus the brass snare for most of the record. For *Sacrificial Bonfire*, I had two larger bass drums and played them like timpani drums for that mediaeval sound. One of my other favourite songs is *The Man Who Sailed Around His Soul* and I was directed by Andy to "play like an old jazz drummer on junk!" I feel I created that loud drum track without too much interference from anybody."

Following up such an acclaimed album meant XTC could take more time recording what became the double album *Oranges and Lemons* on the cusp of a new decade (released in 1989). To build on their stateside success, it was again recorded in the US, this time with a different American producer, Paul Fox, a talented keyboard player whose friend Pat Mastelotto, the drummer from Mr Mister was about to find out that a dream of his had come true. "We were so impressed," said Dave Gregory in *Limelight* issue eight. "We'd turn up to the studio at 11 in the morning and Pat would have been there two hours working things out."

"Do you know that saying, 'Sometimes God smiles?'" asks Mastelotto. "I used to do a lot of gigs as a side man with Paul Fox with a variety of singer-songwriters. Over time, Paul started doing more and more remixes and that led to him doing more production work. Since we're buddies, he could trust me to follow his direction and still converse and throw ideas back at him. So it worked out that I helped him on a lot of things he produced, mixed or remixed. Then one day I got the freakiest of all phone calls Paul says he's got another gig for me... XTC!"

He continues: "Paul knew that XTC (and King Crimson, the Beatles and Todd Rundgren) had consistently been my favourites. I'd been spouting off about XTC all over Los Angeles for years - in fact, I arranged for Mike Chapman to end a recording session early so I could take Mike and the entire Shandi band to the XTC show at the Whisky around 1979... honestly, I just loved them. And I'd got to see them live a couple other times as well. But still, you can imagine my reaction to Paul Fox's call. 'You're bullshitting me! This can't be real!' But he said, 'Yes, it's truly happening,' and told me to go out to my mailbox because there should be three cassettes filled with demos and I better get my ass in gear and start learning the stuff because they're going to come to America in a few weeks... He was also clear the band didn't know me and had other drummers they might be interested in using, so I might not keep the gig. I might just do some rehearsals and get let go. No hard feelings if it went down like that."

Knowing XTC were no longer a touring band and wouldn't be playing the music live had the advantage of opening up more creativity for him. "My attitude towards almost all the music I was involved in was the ends justify the means," he says. "I don't care if there's overdubbing or studio trickery as long as it sounds good on the radio – and dammit, I wanted XTC on the radio. They were superior to most everything else that was happening and it bugged me that their audience was limited. So if Paul and I had any agenda in making the record, it was to let them have a good experience (it was well known the agonising experience they'd gone through with Todd) and get them on the radio."

Mastelotto brought to the studio his battleship-grey Yamaha Recording series kit with its 8", 10", 12", 14" and 16" tom-toms over a 22" kick drum. "Those recording series Yamaha drums are birch and, as I learned later, birch does not have as much low end," he says. "I wish I'd been hip to it when we did the XTC record and I would've used one of my other kick drums. Engineer Ed Thacker meticulously miked those toms with 421s over and under; Ed is one of the only guys I've ever worked with that did that. It did give them a unique sound. I used a variety of snare drums and that big parade drum my ex-wife just brought home from the Rose Bowl swap meet. Also, Paul Fox used to play drums and he brought his old single-headed Gretsch drums down and we used those on something. My Simmons SDS5 was used quite a bit... In fact, *Oranges and Lemons* had several drum machines: my LinnDrum, the LM1, Paul's Linn 9000, a small Korg and a cheap little Yamaha beatbox. We also used some samples I played mostly out of my Casio FZ1 and also out of the Akai S900."

When it came to the cymbals, XTC weren't happy with the sounds they were getting at Ocean Way and kept asking Mastelotto to try something else. "Eventually I hit up on my Paiste crash and they loved them. At the time I was endorsing a new company called Sabian, so I got on the phone and called Rich Mangicaro, the artist rep for Paiste, and asked if I could be lent a box of Paistes for a few weeks to cut this record. He immediately drove up to Hollywood to bring me an assortment. When the session was over I returned the cymbals then went to do the next record for someone else and immediately missed them! I called Sabian to diplomatically depart and then called Rich Mangicaro and made the switch and I've been with Paiste ever since."

Oranges and Lemons is an accessible pop-gem encrusted album with international grooves and rhythms at its heart, so which tracks stand out for Mastelotto? "All of 'em," he says. "Despite the album title, there are no lemons on this record. In fact, we had worked up more material that wasn't used and some of those were awesome songs: *Gangway Electric Guitar Is Coming Through, The End*, etc."

He brought out his old 20" Rogers bass drum for *Scarecrow People* after Andy had demonstrated the sound that he heard in his head by wrapping his knuckles on a solid wooden wall in the rehearsal room. Then there were "all those pots-and-pans wood blocks" and lots and lots of tambourines. "Andy and Colin were nuts for tambourines, he says. 'During mixing, Ed mentioned he had no idea where to place all those tambourines in the mix and Andy replied, 'Oh, it's easy. They should be the second loudest thing – vocals/tambourine/track just like Motown records.' Sometimes Dave and I played tambourines together to get twice the jingles. And on one tune – *Cynical Days*, I think – it was Dave, me and songwriter Parthenon Huxley (he had dropped by to visit) all playing the tambos in unison, but like humans slightly out of sync, so the jingles were even wider... For the rest of the day they referred to us as 'tres amigos' or the 'three tambourines' or something like that."

This was the second time XTC had recorded in the US and Mastelotto tried to make them comfortable away from home. "I'd say we bonded over music and Indian food, unlike most of my other musical blood brothers bonding over music and drugs," he says. "I knew these were country boys so knew they were not comfortable away from home in a big city; Colin was especially nervous about the freaks of Hollywood he ran into at their apartments, Andy slowly deteriorated physically after his family went home and Dave was probably the most enamoured of Hollywood.

"Since I recently had number-one records, I had cash flow and was happy to take the guys out for meals or have them over to my north Hollywood house just a few blocks from Leeds rehearsal rooms. We'd make big Indian meals and we had a nice pool they could get their pasty white British bods privately chilled. Marianne and baby Harry spent afternoons at our place while we rehearsed."

XTC followed up *Oranges and Lemons* with another double album, *Nonsuch* (released in 1992). Produced by Gus Dudgeon, it was recorded on home territory back in the UK at Chipping Norton Studios. Dave Mattacks was still living in England at the time (he's since been in Massachusetts for 18 years). Chances are you own an album he has played on as his credit list is truly impressive, covering folk, rock and jazz. Already having drummed with some of the best in the business, he expressed a desire to work with XTC. "DM has THE BEST sounding kit I ever heard, tuned to perfection," said Andy Partridge in a tweet, October 2014.

Mattacks takes up the story: "I was on a UK tour with Fairport Convention and arrived at an afternoon soundcheck in Swindon to a note on my drum throne which read: 'Call Andy Partridge on xxx.' I thought it was one of our crew winding me up so I rang the number and said, with words to the effect of, 'This is Dave Mattacks - is that *the* Andy Partridge?' The reply was something like, 'Yes - Is that *the* Dave Mattacks?' Apparently, Dave Gregory's brother Ian, who is a Fairport Convention fan, had read in a recent FC programme that playing with XTC was on my bucket list. He'd conveyed this to the band..."

So had he heard all of their albums up to that point? "No... Only a few, but those had made quite an impression. *Oranges and Lemons* was the one that initially grabbed me. I went back to their earlier work after getting the call to record with them - I realised how good their songwriting was."

Although there was some tension between Andy and Gus Dudgeon, the drummer enjoyed being in the studio. Dudgeon's home recording of Andy lifting the mood with daft antics and voices gives people an idea of his sense of humour in the studio. "The Scottish tribute to Sir Andrew Lloyd Webber is still my favourite," laughs Mattacks, who played his Yamaha 9000 kit supplemented by snare drums and a variety of Zildjian cymbals. "I had a fantastic time with them. Although it was a rather big jump stylistically for them to work with Gus, the tracking sessions were really enjoyable. My understanding that the fallout happened towards the end of the project because of differing views on mixing. They're all wonderful songs. On *Omnibus*, Andy had an idea for the groove that at first I couldn't quite grasp; once I understood his concept, it came together. I especially love *Rook* and I'm not on it!"

Prairie Prince became the most recorded guest drummer for XTC when he was invited back to work on the much-anticipated albums *Apple Venus* (released 1999) and *Wasp Star* (2000). After the long strike and subsequent departure from Virgin, things did not run smoothly - a faulty studio in Sussex meant wasted time and money and the ensuing wrangle meant the master tapes were confiscated. The recording process had to be begun again in the Cotswolds.

The problems didn't end there, as Prince explains: "It took them a long time to get that record out after we recorded it, they did a lot of changes and Dave Gregory left in the middle of recording. And they fired Haydn Bendall - I actually had to talk him into coming back during *Apple Venus* at one point... I recorded every day for one month both those albums - and all I did was drums! We were at Chipping Norton Studios from ten in the morning till ten at night. It was quite a challenge for me to do that. There was a lot of drama and shit going on..."

He continues: "I thought it was going to be a double album but the record company just wanted to put out one album at a time. Maybe in between, Andy and Colin had too much time on their hands as they ended up getting Chuck Sabo to re-record my drum parts on a few of the songs. That was disappointing to me as I thought my playing on the original recordings was pretty good, I don't know."

After the friction of *Skylarking*, it makes Prince a veteran of XTC's most troubled recording sessions. "Yes, I'm the one drummer who's worked with them during the most difficult times but then I've not really spoken to any of the other guys," he says. "Except Dave Mattacks, he said it was difficult too – he also had to go backwards and forwards with Andy on so many of the drum tracks. So we can relate!"

Some see *Apple Venus* with its expansive, sweeping orchestral arrangements as XTC's apogee, while *Wasp Star* returned to a rockier, stripped-back sound. Does Prince have any favourites? "Everything about it!" he says. "One of the things was the slapping on my thighs for *I'd Like That* – they were very amused by that. I loved *The Wheel and the Maypole* – that was an amazing piece of music. And then with *Stupidly Happy*, Andy wanted me to play the same part: he said don't do any fills, don't do anything but this simple groove and I want you to play it until you can't play it any more! So basically played just a simple loop, although he said, 'No, I don't want to loop it, I want to play this part and make it sound like you're a robot and you don't change but everything else around you builds around it.' I thought that was a unique way, the drummer just has no passion at all, but then the music builds up all around him into this incredible sounding song. I love it."

Looking back, he's not surprised it was their final album. He says it felt that way at the time. "I was living with them and I had to daily deal with the arguments the three of them were going through, not just with the music but with everything in their lives: the record company, the management, the producer, just Andy being... Andy. I was witness first-hand to that and I thought it doesn't sound like it's going to be good place for this to continue. After I left, they got a different drummer and I thought it sounds like they're indecisive about what they want to do. They looked like they were going in different directions, then I heard Dave left. It was disappointing – when *Apple Venus* came out it was just Andy and Colin's picture on the cover..."

He continues: "And you know we did have conversations when we first got together and I was all excited and I said, 'Do you think we can have a band and I can be your drummer and we can do some gig somewhere?' And Colin said, 'No, I don't want to play live,' and Dave said, 'Certainly, I'd like to,' and Andy said, 'I can consider it, maybe we can have a live concert, not tell many people about it and just have a selective audience and then we could have a live feed on a radio station.' I thought that's a positive note, maybe it would happen... but then you know what happened."

Finally, then, Chuck Sabo was brought in to rework some of the tracks on *Wasp Star*. An established player on many hit singles, his drumming impressed the remaining XTC duo. "His playing was just really lovely," Andy said in a *Chalkhills* interview with Todd Bernhardt in 2000. "Colin and I were grinning at each other in the control room, thinking, 'Yes, we've really found a great player here.'"

"The tracks Prairie played on had already been recorded when I was called," says Sabo. "Programmer/producer Matthew Vaughan and I, worked on *The Lion King* album with Elton John, Marcella Detroit's album, and OMD's *Universal*, among others. So when Nick Davis asked Matt about drummers I was put forward, and Nick gave me a call. When he said it was for the XTC album, I very happily accepted, and looked forward to the session."

Knowing that XTC were no longer a touring band

made little impact on Sabo's approach. "I never think about what's going to happen on stage when I'm recording a song," he says. "I think about adding to the song, and making the best recording. Once the album is made, then you think about how you would like to perform it live."

He primarily used his Yamaha Maple Custom kit with a 10" and 12" snare drum, as well as his 14". "I usually had two or three different size snare drums on my kit," he says. "But I'll also use the Yamaha Beech Custom and Birch Custom kits. I've been endorsed by Yamaha for many years."

From a percussive point of view, *We're All Light* is a thrill ride of a pop song, and *You and the Clouds Will Still Be Beautiful* has a lilting swirling rhythm. Which tracks is Sabo proud of? "You mentioned two of my favourites," he says. "*You and the Clouds Will Still Be Beautiful* was already recorded with drums. But they asked me to just have a go at it and I'm so glad they did - and I believe they were too. I'm really happy with them all. It's one of the rare records that I've recorded and still listen to for pleasure. It has a lot to do with the way they write and record, and the freedom I had to express myself."

....

Some might say that Andy's determination to craft his songs to perfection can make for a testing time when recording drum tracks. Our guest drummers all survived the exacting experience... so how much did Andy specify what he wanted with the drumming?

Prairie Prince: Every detail! Pretty much every beat was scrutinised over. Andy wanted it done a million times. It didn't feel like I added much other than my personality. He was definitely directing musically.

How did you work with Colin Moulding by comparison?

Prairie Prince: Colin was less invasive to me. He would just say, "Play something that sounds good." With *Sacrificial Bonfire*, he had an idea - he said, "Make it sound very primitive, like something from the middle ages." He gave me a few ideas like that, but he wasn't a stickler like Andy was, like, "Just change that one groove on that one section backwards and turn it around here..." but that guy had really great instinct and I didn't want to argue with him. Everything he told me was necessary for the song and it sounds great. I would never had thought of some of the parts he had orchestrated for the drums.

Pat Mastelotto: Both Andy and Colin were very specific. They knew what they wanted and those demo cassettes that were in my mailbox already had drum machine parts on most of the material so things were well mapped out. Lots of things developed and changed in the rehearsals and, likewise, once in the studio, arrangements crystallised. It's not like they were dogmatic about it being exactly like the demo. Like all the best songwriters I've worked with, they also recognise those demos are just starting points.

Dave Mattacks: Andy was very specific on some songs, although he was more open to ideas and collaborations on others.

Pete Phipps: I had lots of input at the rehearsal. I listened to the demos and I played what was needed for it. We were a band, it wasn't like Andy was telling me this and Colin was telling me that. It all went swimmingly well.

Chuck Sabo: They were both expressive about what they were looking for from me. But they would usually express it with a mood, or feeling or colour. Then just let me do what felt right. They made me feel very at home. I really enjoyed it!

Ian Gregory: Andy was great with me, although I know he has a reputation for being a hard task master. I remember being at Chipping Norton when XTC were recording *Nonsuch* and I think David Mattacks must have done 20 takes of *That Wave* before Andy was satisfied. Needless to say, take one with Dave playing sounded fantastic to me. I have no idea what Andy was searching for.

Andy let me do pretty much anything I wanted – some tracks may have taken longer to sort out than others. Colin was on message as well – there seemed to be some very good vibes and the ideas were coming thick and fast.

What do you think of the band's musicianship?
Pete Phipps: They're fantastic players. I've got nothing but admiration for their musicianship. It worked instantly with the guys. There were never any places where we were clashing, no arguments. Andy is such a creative musician, he's got a lot of emotional qualities as well. I don't think he's one of these people who does 9-5. He writes when he's inspired and that's why his music is so diverse – he's not writing to a formula.

Chuck Sabo: It's top notch! They're great musicians and very creative and individual with their approach. I love the musical way they treat their lyrics, and how the song builds from that.

Prairie Prince: Excellent! Colin is one of my favourite bass players. I just love his style. I love his songwriting as well. Dave Gregory is an amazing keyboard player and major guitar player. Andy is just an incredible guitar player. I loved their musicianship from *White Music* onwards.

Dave Mattacks: They are all great musicians and Dave Gregory is among the best I've worked with.

Pat Mastelotto: All great. XTC knew far better than most how to use the studio as a compositional tool. They were meticulous without sucking the life or fun out of the process. A few songs had first takes where the vibe outweighed the meaningless errors. Other times we recut a song a few days later, when after living with it for a few days the satisfaction lessened. So they weren't afraid to re-assess their own feelings.

Ian Gregory: The XTC lads are great musicians. Dave's input to both those Dukes albums was immeasurable. He has an innate knowledge of British 60s psychedelia and came up with numerous reference points – how many can you spot? Because they are such great players, the tracks were done pretty quickly with not too many re-takes, thus keeping the "soul" of the project.

What do you think of the scope of XTC's music over the years?
Prairie Prince: Being in the Tubes, I can relate to all those different variations and developments of style. There's such a huge variety of music from jazz to punk to orchestrated music and psychedelia. I was introduced to them during the punk period and watched them develop over the next 20 years or so where their music took them, that was cool.

Dave Mattacks: Impressive, to say the least!

Ian Gregory: All musicians should strive to improve, and this is abundantly true with XTC. You can see the progression with every album, from the raw energy of *White Music*, through to the sophistication of my particular favourite, *Nonsuch*, a brilliant record. Dave frequently said it was like being with Lennon and McCartney as new compositions were offered up and he was able to get stuck in, adding his musicality and arranging skills. I always thought he was like the George Martin of the group, bringing out the best from those compositions. It's a great shame they went their separate ways but I guess that was inevitable. XTC have used many great drummers – I may not have been the best but I bet I had the most fun!

Pat Mastelotto: Spectacular, the body of work they assembled was, to my ears, consistently the best intellectual pop. Dukes is brilliant and combining that with XTC was something Paul and I talked about before starting the record, which fell right in line with Andy wanting to make the biggest dragster with *all* the chrome.

Chuck Sabo: This is one of those questions I could spend far too much time and space answering. But, I'll just have to say... they've become one of my favourite bands. They have, and will stand the test of time. They haven't made a bad record and our children's, children's, children will be fans!

WHERE DID THE ORDINARY PEOPLE GO?

Like the poetry of John Betjeman, the songs of Colin Moulding turn the everyday into the extraordinary. A cultural studies lecturer argues that the genius is in the detail

BY PETER MILLS

"People rarely mention a sense of place in music today. I think it is a good thing to talk about." – Colin Moulding, interviewed by *Dancing About Architecture*, 2018

Over the four decades since the *3D EP* was issued, Colin Moulding's music has changed, developed and grown, from the berserk sci-fi skiffling of the early-XTC sound right through to his 2017 return to writing and performing. This piece looks at some of those songs and how they reflect and connect with the work of some unlikely bedfellows, chiefly the late poet laureate Sir John Betjeman. Moulding and Betjeman started out from very different rungs on the social ladder, of course; Betjeman had a privileged childhood, attending Marlborough College and, later, Magdalen College, Oxford – he recalled much of this period in his famous "epic poem of ordinariness" *Summoned By Bells* (1960). A generation later, Colin Moulding's childhood was rather different and his memory map was there for all to see as part of the artwork for 1978's *Go 2* that gives us a portrait of the artist as a younger man. However it's my view that their work shares a surprising amount of common ground – notably an attentiveness to the fine detail of "ordinary" life not only in relationships but also in the environments where we live and work.

Red Brick Rash: Betjeman and Swindon

There is an unexpectedly strong connection between Swindon and John Betjeman. Marlborough College, where he was taught by TS Eliot, is only a dozen miles down the A346 from the town, and he lived in Uffington, within walking distance of the famous XTC-related white horse. An architectural autodidact, he was passionate about the built environment throughout his life; he was also charming and wildly ambitious and this combination saw him quickly getting published and on the air for the new BBC in the 1930s. An early snobbishness about buildings and the people who dwelt in them (exemplified by the title of his 1934 book *Ghastly Good Taste*) gave way to a more open and egalitarian view, and Swindon played a big part in this. Betjeman's first public encounter with the town was a 1937 radio broadcast in which he was so vituperative about the town and its "red-brick rash" that the council demanded an apology – he was carpeted at the BBC, a partial recantation was issued at the time and, in the years that followed, he never quite stopped apologising:

> "Swindon, so ugly to look at to the eyes of the architectural student, glows golden as the New Jerusalem to eyes that look beyond the brick and stone." (1948)

And

> "I know the people of Swindon first taught me not to be so la-di-da and architectural, not to judge people by the houses they live in, nor churches only by their architecture." (1949)

Yet even in the midst of his initial shudder at the "new" Swindon, he was very clear as to the virtues of the "old" and lamented the lack of thought that had gone into the town's expansion: "Town planning has come too late for Swindon, as it has for many other towns," he proclaimed. By 1950, the town had forgiven Betjeman sufficiently for him to be asked to contribute to the town's series of books on its own history. He also returned in the TV era to make documentaries, one of which he introduced standing in front of the North Star steam engine at the Swindon Railway Museum: the reference will not be lost on XTC fans (a punning allusion is slipped into *Red Brick Dream*) nor on Swindonians, this engine being commemorated in the town's North Star Roundabout and Avenue, close to the Southbrook Inn, site of the 2017 XTC Convention. For Betjeman, discussing the lives of the people of the town and the buildings of the town were effectively two ways of talking about the same thing: the sense and spirit of place.

Save Us from the Ball and Chain

Moulding's own most direct shout at the reckless wreckage of his town is *Ball and Chain*, a song of which Betjeman would have heartily approved – indeed, given he passed away in 1984, he may even have heard it. I wonder! Not only is it unambiguous in its mode of addressing the subject, it meets Pete Seeger's criteria for a protest song – make it clear, useful and easy to learn. Moulding has expressed mixed feelings about the song in the intervening years but it certainly works as a memorable, chantable act of resistance. This took an unexpected turn in late 2018 as the resident of the last house on Westcott Street in Swindon, which was pictured on the sleeve of the single version of the song, passed on and chose to have *Ball and Chain* played at his funeral at the town's new crematorium. Now that's a protest song!

> *Don't want demolition,*
> *Don't want your compensation,*
> *It's not just bricks and mortar,*
> *We are lambs to slaughter*

Betjeman had written in 1948 that there was something "beyond the brick and stone" of the places people lived in, and that sentiment is echoed here. The self-definition of both town and townsfolk is under attack ("It's not.../We are...") and the directness of the lyric added to the great percussive crunch of the song – its mechanical riff, its thundering drums – conveys the physicality of the assault; we're shot by both sides, as "the diggers" cut the ground from under our feet while "the tower cranes" loom above, river deep, mountain high.

Ball and Chain is perhaps his most Betjemanesque song in that the late poet laureate's great passion – which the poetry often seemed to serve – was preservation as a progressive idea rather than mere conservatism. I've never been sure if Ray Davies's use of the term (apropos the "village green" or the two Kinks albums aspiring to be a stage play) was sincere or satirical or some cunning combination of both but there's no ambiguity about Moulding's or Betjeman's views: save us from the ball and chain! Both men reserved the right to treasure the "ordinary" and call out the guilty; they articulate protest against forces of conservatism rather than argue for them. Betjeman infamously wished ruin upon certain places even as he advocated the preservation of others – "Come friendly bombs and fall on Slough" – but his *j'accuse* was targeted at town planners and councils, not the towns or townspeople, writing of "These small West Country towns where year by year/Newly elected mayors oppose reforms" in his 1954 poem *From the Great Western*.

Colin reflected on similar matters in relation to *Ball and Chain*:

> "When aldermen in council chambers were getting outrageously fatter on inner-city clearances, I offered up this little chant from the terraces. Perhaps a little overstated, I don't think it was ever going to save the 1980s equivalent of the Euston Arch, but it seemed quite relevant to the times. About the destruction of Swindon town centre, but it wasn't much of a song. I think I'd gone off the boil."

His mention of the Euston Arch is pure Betjeman. In 1960, the poet wrote about the planned destruction of Philip Hardwick's 1837 public monument outside Euston station in London. Moulding referenced the infamous 1961 demolition to illuminate the apparently more parochial "destruction of Swindon town centre". In both men's eyes the small detail connects to the wider picture. Moulding speaks somewhat dismissively of the tune here – "I think I was going off the boil" – and in some ways *Ball and Chain* is (perhaps appropriately) something of a blunt instrument, but for those same reasons it is a proper protest song with its chanted, "you can all join in" chorus.

It is also explicitly about Swindon – the first time he had written such a song.

The theme has cropped up in the later work too: *Wasp Star*'s *Boarded Up* imagines with dark humour the aftermath of the destruction. The blame is laid at a familiar door: "some town planner didn't know when to stop". In *Where Did the Ordinary People Go?* he laments the way new housing separates rather than connects people: "This street has changed so much/A line of fortresses, look but don't touch." Indeed, in his very latest recordings, he has returned to the topic; *Kenny* from TC&I's *Great Aspirations* EP is a wing-heeled salvo directed at the disappearance of playing fields from schools and public places, sell-offs sanctioned by the "rotten council" but now not just on his doorstep but "all over England, going, going". The motorways and office blocks are standing on the spot where footballing prodigy Kenny – perhaps based on local Swindon footballing hero Kenny Stroud – had played. This isn't so far from the howl of the Sex Pistols that shook the nation in 1976: "Your future dream is a shopping scheme." He even nods in the direction of his own immaculately poignant sketch of unrealised dreams: "Now bungalows will settle the score."

Colin noted in a 2018 interview with music blog *Dancing About Architecture* that:

> "Kenny is this footballer who did rather well for himself but it's more about the modern desire to build on every available scrap of land and these are the places where imaginations get nurtured."

More redolent of a Betjeman piece or perhaps even a Ken Loach movie than a conventional or overstated protest song, *Kenny* picks up where *Ball and Chain* left off, tracking the same processes of loss and damage to community that he'd noted in 1981. Tellingly, TC&I played *Ball and Chain* and *Kenny* cheek by jowl in the autumn 2018 sets in Swindon, inviting us to make the connection.

In this life, or in another life: Bungalow

"Are you getting on in life and anxious for a little sea air but not too much? Do you like what the guidebooks call a 'salubrious climate' and a 'respectable residential neighbourhood'? Do you like to hear a little good music on wet days? Then you want Bournemouth, Weymouth, Paignton, Weston-Super-Mare... they are inland life, settled down beside the sea." - John Betjeman, *Seaview*, BBC West of England, programme broadcast 11/5/38

"My parents' dream was to retire to a bungalow by the sea. Although hard-working people, it did not materialise and the best they got by the sea was the annual visit to the caravan site at Bowleaze Cove. I wanted to create the atmosphere of an English seaside caravan-site clubhouse. Cheesy Hammond organ, Come Dancing *saxophones and sombre Acker Bilk clarinets. But most importantly, a sense of total longing."* - Colin Moulding on *Bungalow*, *Coat Of Many Cupboards* booklet

John Betjeman's ability to locate the extraordinary in the everyday finds an echo in Moulding's "late XTC style". Here he moved from the issue-based writing that surveys history, culture and society, seeing patterns across the decades, even millennia (*King for a Day, War Dance, The Smartest Monkeys*) to smaller and highly specific sketches of human behaviour. They may be less obviously dramatic but are no less affecting - it's just that the focus has switched from the widescreen to the close focus, the kind of adroit and amused observation, tempered with empathy, that characterises much of Betjeman's work.

I am cheating slightly - I include *Bungalow* in this late style even though seven years separate its parent album *Nonsuch* (1992) from the debut of this approach to songwriting on *Apple Venus Volume 1* on the cusp of the 21st century. The song marks a sea change in his writing; this bungalow stood at a crossroads, the fork in the road at which his songwriting took a different path in terms of its feel, its subject matter, sound and depth of personal meaning. Introducing the song in its world premiere performances at the Swindon Arts Centre in autumn 2018 he picked up the thread of his *COMC* notes by making reference to his parents' dream of moving to the seaside upon retirement. Very movingly (to me, at any rate) he added that they never did "because they didn't quite understand what kind of people they were". I don't know what kind of people they were, but their son clearly did; it's right there in the song. The performances of *Bungalow* were among the highpoints of these shows, adding tear-pricking poignancy to an already very emotional occasion; indeed the piano chords that rock in uneasy see-saw throughout *Bungalow* provided the intro music for the shows, showing the importance Moulding attaches to the song.

So where does the emotional power of this little song come from? The poised stillness of those paired chords, permanently ready to change but never quite making the transition into the choruses, falling back into the pastel-coloured dream sequence of the verses? (The chords were supposedly inspired by the childhood favourite *Sparky's Magic Piano* - a link much clearer on the *Nonsuch* Blu-ray worktape). The familiar yet unsettling sound of the sampled male-voice choir - celestial or sirens? Colin's pronunciation of "gorse"? There is also the sound of the ensemble of the track - acoustic piano, bass, the promised Hammond-with-cheese and the shuffled end-of-the-pier drums recorded to suggest life slowing down. All of these, and more.

Two lines of the lyric read like text from a sales brochure - "Luxury accommodation traps the sun" and "Stand in prime position for the town", both examples of estate agent's speak, selling the dream, yet the rest of the lyric is so spare (echoing those paired chords on which the song balances) that it reveals the essence of the longing Moulding mentions; the word "bungalow" repeated until it is like a mantra, like the name of a loved one passing one's lips without conscious effort. The waiting, the planning, the getting through the working day in order to make the dream real: "So we're working every hour that God made/Working for a vision through this life/So we can fly away" and the music strives to reach up at the line's end, straining to take flight but falls back to the repetition of "bungalow". In this little moment, we feel all that sense of longing melding with stoical persistence: the reaching up, the falling back, the retention of hope. It is the move between the first pair and the second pair of chords that gives this tiny little musical hinge its emotional heft – gently opening and closing like the wings they could fly away on. The two pairs of chords function as images of the couple in the song; the first pair being their "ordinary" selves, the second pair, their transposed, transformed selves made new "in another life".

Colin mentioned Noël Coward as a "great aspiration" for the very first time in referring to *Bungalow* – "I also hammed-up the voice to sound a bit Noël Coward" (*XTC: Song Stories*) – but the song Farmer credits to Coward, *Let's Fly Away*, is actually by another of Colin's favourites, Cole Porter. The fey, did-it-in-a-minute feel of *Let's Fly Away* is something of a disappointment after *Bungalow* but has a light, tea-sipping charm to commend it: written in 1940, the first verse tells us what we need to know – it is a song of its time, as much as one for the ages:

> Let's fly away
> And find a land that's warm and tropic,
> Where Roosevelt is not the topic
> All the live long day!
> – Cole Porter, *Let's Fly Away*

Yet its dream is the same – escape from the humdrum repetitions of the daily round ("day in, day out") to a place where all is as it could and should be, an Arcadia by the sea. Colin has inferred that the dreamed-of move could have been from their landlocked home town to "Swindon-on-Sea", Weymouth, adjacent to the site of his childhood caravan-site holidays in Bowleaze Cove, where the Italianate high drama of the Riviera Hotel makes for a striking contrast with the rest of the resort. Betjeman mentioned Weymouth in his *Seaview* broadcast as a place where we find "inland life settled down by the sea", a description that suits the dream of *Bungalow* perfectly. Indeed, the bracing breezes of the English seaside resort in winter blow straight through this song, alongside warmer, climbing-rose tinted glimpses of a kind of golden autumn to a life lived settled down by the sea. Yet the location of the bungalow could be Narnia; it hardly matters to the song. What is key is the connection between the dream and the longing in the promise that is given, if not delivered upon, in the song's last line: "you wait and see." That's what we do "in this life": we wait and see.

Watching society scampering past – the "late style"

Moulding's post-*Nonsuch* material for XTC foregrounds the importance of the song in the most writerly sense – the words and the music. Not in the Brill Building tradition – which is often where investigations into the discipline of songwriting lead us – but his gaze is higher up.

As he has mentioned in interviews, he likes to have goals, great aspirations – the song *Greatness* on the TC&I EP lists a few, mixing up music and film – Hitchcock, Spielberg, Gershwin and McCartney with Winston Churchill thrown in for good measure. Legendary names certainly and the bar is set high if that's where you want to be. In the light of this and Colin's lifelong interest in stargazing of the astronomical kind, it's intriguing that the gaze of his songs falls most readily on the world around him rather than the firmament. That may well be the means via which he reveals the wondrous in the everyday, as he does in his "late style". The wilful eccentricity of the *Fruit Nut*, remaking Nick Drake's idea of the *Man in a Shed*, the daydreams of *In Another Life*, very different from those in *Bungalow*, the suburban indiscretions of *Standing in for Joe* (a kind of prequel to *Didn't Hurt a Bit*) and in *Frivolous Tonight* the profundity of glittering whimsy.

> "It's very provincial and small and that's what I like. As the evening wears on it just gets worse. It's what people like to do, talk about the stupidest things. But its not a venomous lyric. It's celebratory... it's probably the best thing I've ever written. It's more lyrically and musically complete... it's in the mood of Noel Coward's I've Been to a Marvellous Party [sic]. You can't fault him and Cole Porter lyrically." (Farmer p.291)

So, are the people in this song tenants of *Respectable Street*, the party being what's going on behind those twitched curtains?

> Let's pour ourselves a glass of stout
> And let our Rael Brook shirts hang out...

The reference to Rael Brook shirts is indicative of Moulding's eye for the telling detail – Rael Brook shirts were mass-produced garments very popular in the 60s and 70s, must-haves for the man-about-town and definitely marketed as advantageous to one's social life – "If Casanova were around today, he'd be wearing this Rael Brook shirt" ran one 1972 ad campaign. The go-getting young man in Betjeman's 1974 poem *Executive* would almost certainly be wearing one:

> I am a young executive.
> No cuffs than mine are cleaner;
> I have a Slimline brief-case and
> I use the firm's Cortina.

So far, so retro. Yet for those attuned to Swindon and its industrial past there seems to be a pun here – the Rael Brook shirt has replaced (or simply concealed) a Rail Work one, the gear change symbolic of the changes in the town. The lyric also contains that most Betjemanian item of clothing from a young lady's wardrobe, a pair of slacks – as worn by the girl at the meeting place in *The Licorice Fields of Pontefract* (whose legs were "flannel slack'd") while the "girls in slacks remember Dad" at "Christmas", appropriate as the party that "goes with a swing" when they "talk about the trivial things" feels like a Christmas one.

While Colin's nod to Noël Coward's recitation *I Went to a Marvellous Party* remains a great aspiration, *Frivolous Tonight* does capture some of the same sense of excited abandon, of the shackles coming off and people letting loose. Coward declaims excitedly about the outrageous yet ridiculous goings-on at parties closing each verse (or are they stanzas?) with a cry ecstatic yet also touched with desperation, "I couldn't have liked it more!"

> People's behaviour
> Away from Belgravia
> Would make you aghast
> So much variety
> Watching society
> Scampering past
> – Noël Coward, *I Went to a Marvellous Party*

Coward's reserved right of standing just a little aside and observing it all allows him to both enjoy and shudder, to wonder and despair at the same time. For *Frivolous Tonight* we are in suburbia (so beloved of Betjeman that he coined a name for it, Metroland) rather than Belgravia, in a semi-detached, not in Cap Ferrat, but the scene is the same – people escaping themselves. Moulding's song celebrates the silliness of its subject with equal verve and revels in it, choosing to describe the proceedings as all frivolous, nonsense, and – with that distance Coward allows himself – ridiculous.

> Let's reveal our childlike nature and leave our stocks and invoices to rot – let's go to pot!
>
> There's always one who wants to talk shop – we'll drive him through the door with a broom or a mop.

The cartoonish, 70s sitcom domesticity of this image - the broom, the mop, the weapons of the disgruntled housewife serving judgement on the idle, drunk, late-arriving husband - is also the slamming of the door on the world of "sensible" behaviour. The *Homegrown* demo is even more scandalous: "who did what at the office do/they say she was covered in paper and glue" as well as the reference to "the chap who put it on display". What it is is never specified but then it hardly needs to be. To me it feels like that most universal affair, the work or Christmas party. In Coward's world, darling, such events no doubt happened every night of the year but for most working people, be they rail workers or accountants, it was and remains Christmas when we are, for a while at least, free - free to "wallow in a bit of nonsense", what Betjeman called "the sweet and silly Christmas things", and that's the mood of *Frivolous Tonight* - sweet and silly. Tomorrow can look after itself.

Comrades of Pop

Vaudevillian touches abound on Moulding's late 90s songs - listen to the music-hall trills and uke-strum of *Fruit Nut* or the tight circles of notes as we hear on *Standing in for Joe* and *In Another Life* not so much riffs as little enclosures inside which the scenes play out - like the four walls of the suburban house or the confined space of the shed. The sound is not unlike the music Jim Parker (later famed for his theremin-flaunting theme for the *Midsomer Murders* TV show) provided for John Betjeman's quartet of albums for Charisma - a bit of Bonzos, a bit of Temperance Seven, a bit of razzle-dazzle silliness - they are light, but leave room for the dark. Colin clearly knows these albums, as he explained to *Dancing About Architecture*:

> "I don't think anybody had done this kind of talk-over thing, at least not in the pop idiom, John Betjeman did it with his poems and they were set to music but nobody has done that in a pop way and about the pop industry and taken a slightly wry look at its workings."

Although *Comrades of Pop* doesn't use the musical styles of these Betjeman albums, he invokes their spirit here. While an autobiographical take on lyrics like "The bassist and the drummer... never seem to get a lot" is hard to resist, we should resist overplaying it - while it is a truth universally acknowledged that the rhythm section of a band may be left behind financially, Moulding was in fact "the guy who writes the hits" for XTC. His nod to classic songwriting here is the nightingale in Berkeley Square, whose song is replaced by the trill of the lawyer's doorbell. That's the way the money goes - pop goes the weasel. What seems to hurt even more is the loss of friendship and "allegiance for all time" - the line is repeated twice for emphasis. A characteristic of Betjeman was a late "curveball" that changes our view of what has gone before and *Comrades of Pop* delivers one of those :

> Comrades of pop turn away
> In love and war all is fair
> A far worse fate awaits you
> On carpets made from human hair.
> Good night.

The swerve into the surreal at the close ("carpets made from human hair") is a poet's trick, and one tempered here by the droll sign-off, "Good night", as if he were closing a broadcast on the Home Service.

This mix of the serious, the silly and the surreal is a potent one - Andrew Motion (another former poet laureate) wrote of John Betjeman that he "cultivated comedy for serious ends" and showed a "reliance on familiar things to express unusually intense feeling". Much the same can be said about the work of Colin Moulding.

NOW THESE SHOES FIT ALL TOO WELL

How difficult is it for an XTC tribute act to match both the energy of the early years and the sophistication of the later albums? From Vancouver to Tokyo, cover bands talk about standing in for Swindon's finest

BY DAVID WHITE

It's nearly two decades since XTC's last release, yet interest in the band's songs has palpably increased. Driven by books, social media, fan conventions and continued radio play, the band's stock is high. Another way of keeping the flames of optimism burning has been by interpretation and recital – performing XTC's songs live as a tribute band. The term became familiar in the early 1990s as bands such as the Bootleg Beatles and the ABBA-saluting Bjorn Again faithfully reproduced the sounds of the original artists. Fans were keen to enjoy authentic-sounding live reproductions of much-loved songs in exchange for the inauthenticity of someone else performing them. Where do XTC tributes sit in this picture? Does a long-extinct group, not especially known for looks – and with only a handful of early-1980s hits – make promising material for a tribute?

It would appear so. I investigated some of the many bands and solo acts who have performed as XTC tributes and was surprised by the diversity of their backgrounds. By no means are all of them from the UK, nor even from the western hemisphere; by no means are they all male, nor are they old enough to have heard the music first time round. Unsurprisingly, very few have actually seen XTC perform live. Bear in mind, of course, you don't have to perform in front of anybody to enjoy recreating the wonder – the songs are a study in themselves and it's a striking thought that they continue to be poured-over, rehearsed and performed worldwide over 30 years after the band ceased to play them themselves. Did you know there is an annual XTC tribute in Minneapolis? A regular XTC-alike band in Los Angeles? And in Sydney, Australia? Swindon has more than one tribute, and you can find performances of Japanese and German versions of XTC online.

So, taking a sample of good people who kindly responded to me after my initial introductions, here is a snapshot of the tribute-band landscape – including a flashback to my own brief stint in Balloon:

"Play to the four people in your town who like XTC"

That's the advice of Zak Schaffer, who plays regular gigs as the Los Angeles XTC Appreciation Society, which he formed in 2017. Being LA, there is no shortage of top-quality players, and Zak is as much convener as musician, setting himself the challenge of coaxing as many players as possible to find time to rehearse and perform an evening full of XTC material, garnered from every period of the band's evolution. This is where the appeal of the band can prove uniquely persuasive. "XTC is a band that deserves to be celebrated," says Zak. "They are under-appreciated and really amazing."

Most compelling for Zak, however, is the social and political significance of musical gatherings such as this: "These are challenging times in this country," he says. "Taking time out of my life to do something good for other people (all the money raised goes to charity) is something I think we should all be doing at a time when our administration is operating with bad intentions and riling up their base to do the same. We're pushing back a little bit."

The collective works on the basis of one person handling three or four songs. Dave Gregory has been a source of advice and assistance relating to complicated chords and arrangements, and Andy Partridge even sent a short song on video, singing, "You don't have to get the chords all right, just play it on the wing." Accordingly, the musicians use their own instinct and knowledge to work out the

> 'Hugh launched a few more dawns of time, I added a wild guitar riff and it sounded far more exciting than the faithful reading we had planned'

songs' structures. Having a large number of well-connected musicians on stage helps guarantee a good-size audience, XTC hardly being a household name, but Zak does acknowledge that the enormous administrative challenge is hard work.

Asked how his band measures up to the almighty Swindonians, he claims that sometimes they turn out to be more faithful to the original recordings than some of Mr Partridge's occasionally wayward singing excursions he has found on YouTube: "What I'm trying to say in a roundabout and humble way is, 'Yeah. Sometimes we sound better than they did!'"

Doing it for a blast

A long-standing fan of XTC, Krispian Emert from Vancouver, Canada saw a post that featured a Japanese-based XTC tribute act. As a musician already playing in various cover bands, Krispian was inspired to form an XTC tribute band of her own. She placed a musician-wanted ad on Craigslist, listing her requirements: "Bass player seeking guitar, keys and drums for XTC cover band." XTC not being well-known in Vancouver, she received no responses, but persevered and renewed the ad each week. "After a few weeks, I finally got a response from a guy named Zac: 'We're guitar and keys! My girlfriend and I are nut-bars for this style of music (1978-79 and on).' I arranged to meet Zac and his girlfriend Elizabeth. Upon meeting them, I saw they were 20 years younger than me (I was 46 at the time), but the age difference wasn't an issue – we immediately hit it off. It turned out they thought the ad was a joke made by one of their friends because this project was so perfect for them!"

She adds: "We then set about trying to find a drummer, by placing a drummer-wanted ad, and entertained answers from a hilarious assortment of oddballs, including people who didn't even know XTC, finally meeting Mike, a huge fan of new-wave music and a fabulous drummer, to complete the line-up. We called ourselves The XTC Files and rehearsed regularly. Unfortunately, Elizabeth had to leave to go to China for her final year of university, so we disbanded before we got an actual gig."

Convening for the convention

Beginning in the late 1980s, XTC enthusiast Paul Wilde put together an annual series of XTC conventions in Manchester. In 1992, with a little time to go before that year's event, musician Hugh Nankivell asked me and multi-instrumentalist Kieran Cheung if we would like to perform as a one-off tribute. Based in Gateshead, Tyneside, the three of us were part of jazz-fusion band Fossil. Calling ourselves Balloon (after one of two mooted titles for *Nonsuch* – the other being *Milk*), we rehearsed just the one day, getting our teeth around five songs. Hugh wrote a day or so later to suggest we try *Pulsing Pulsing* and left us to work out our parts on our own. With Kieran on drums and Hugh on vocals as well as bass or keys, I was to play guitar and guitar-synthesiser, and share vocals. Maybe unsurprisingly, we found some of the guitar parts harmonically complex and difficult to replicate. Bearing in mind XTC had two guitarists and used various unconventional tunings, we would have to approximate the constituent parts, somehow…

We travelled to Manchester in Kieran's Rascal van, mulling over our songs, parts and song order. The convention, in a crowded upstairs room in

Above: Krispian Emert and XTC Files bandmate Elizabeth Arnold. Previous page: Tokyo's ETC featuring Takashi Nishii, Satoshi Yonaha(Yonafy) and Masaki Kitayama.

the Southern pub, featured an interview with band biographer Chris Twomey, a pre-recorded interview with Dave Gregory and a few tribute acts, comprising solo guitarists, vocalists and one or two bands such as ours. I feared on stage we would prove the most under-prepared.

Once Paul had introduced us, we kicked off with *Runaways*, Hugh and me sharing vocals and vocalising the lead keyboard figures. After the outro-fade, I struck up the opening chords of *Ball and Chain*, which we cleverly diverted into *Seagulls Screaming*... I remember the crowd appearing to enjoy this lurch, with vocalised percussion shushes and tocks, my guitar-synth handling the euphonium part. With Hugh having sung this one, it was my turn to sing on *Great Fire*, and I was aware of the crowd singing along heartily, despite our departure from the original's string-quartet arrangement.

Hugh regaled the crowd with a reminiscence about sneaking into the *Top of the Pops* studios in 1981 and meeting Colin and Andy. He remembered the conversation turning to jazz, which Colin professed not to like, but prompted Andy to play Ornette Coleman's *Ornithology*. Things having settled-in satisfactorily, we joked with the audience about the oddness of improvising a Wiltshire accent, which I did on the next song, *Respectable Street* - a relatively straightforward one, which again received warm appreciation.

"We've not rehearsed this one, except by post," Hugh explained, as we kicked off the decidedly odd *Pulsing Pulsing*. While musically satisfactory, it started to eat into the credit we'd hitherto amassed, with Hugh improvising the words he'd forgotten – was that "a beat in his heart" or "a bee in his arm"?

Though I felt rather embarrassed about openly rehearsing a song in front of an audience, the momentum so far built-up hadn't been lost, and next I opened the vocals for *Across This Antheap*, which I'd tried to memorise in an Edinburgh café - tested by my girlfriend - just the day before. I was mindful this might be the first time the song had been performed on stage, XTC having abandoned playing live years before. All went well until the solo section, intended to make use of the "Muted Trumpet" pre-set on Hugh's keyboard. That's when Hugh accidentally selected instead "Dawn of Time" - an abstract, gong-like "boo-wooosh!" which launched things in an altogether different direction. Improvising somewhat desperately, Hugh launched a few more "dawns of time" and I added a wild guitar riff and, of course, it sounded far more exciting than the faithful reading we had planned.

Having been given a life-lesson in "quit while you're ahead", the three of us acknowledged the generous applause and Paul announced, "Thank you, Balloon! Well done, you went up, lads!" Hugh announced that, given we were in northern England, he would like to hear from anyone interested in putting together brass-band versions of XTC songs, to which Paul responded, "All right, give over – it's me who does the funnies..."

Wanting more than cheese

Les Rankin, based in Sydney, Australia had the notion of forming an XTC tribute when he found himself dissatisfied with his peers' adoration of the sweet harmonies of the Beach Boys. Realising he was looking for inspiration from quirkier quarters than the cheesy music the gig circuit tended to favour, he found he had a shared perspective with friends Jess, John and Rob – all musicians. Forming a band, they decided to "have an XTC play" one day, which prompted Jess to book a gig, giving them two months to concentrate their minds, and decide on a name - Scarecrow People.

Already gigging a large Zappa tribute band, Les decided to expand his new XTC tribute to afford the complexities of later songs' arrangements. He found it easy to persuade keyboardists and trumpeters alike to join in, even if they weren't familiar with the Swindonians.

"So that's seven of us," Les explains. "We play infrequently, partly due to Jess being the busiest guy in Sydney (as a drummer/percussionist/singer with about a hundred bands, plus the Sydney

Symphony Orchestra), but mainly because the scene for this type of gig is so limited here. An Australian 'tour' realistically means a gig in Sydney, then travel 1,000km to Melbourne for one, then it's 2,000km back up the coast for a speculative Brisbane gig. Still, we've managed to do about ten sold-out gigs, all at the same venue (the 160-capacity Camelot Lounge), apart from three poorly-attended out-of-towners."

The gig circuit is, however, something of an uphill climb: "Increasingly, people aren't leaving their homes to see bands. Colin, in one of his most morose moments, knows what I'm talking about..."

Meanwhile, in Wiltshire, England

"The UK's Top XTC Tribute" is how gig-posters describe Fossil Fools, the band Terry Arnett formed in 2007 with friend Ed Percival, its name prompted by XTC's double-CD compilation album *Fossil Fuel*. He and Ed had previously been in XTC tribute band Fuzzy Warblers and were keen to experiment with their own version. Ed had also been in X-sTatiC, which disbanded in 2005 (see below). Performing several gigs over a year in Swindon, Royal Wootton Bassett and London, they resurrected Fossil Fools in 2017 and played that year's memorable XTC Convention in Swindon. While he focuses on drums and backing vocals, Terry's bandmates Ed, Dan and Matt handle guitar/vocals, keyboards/guitar/vocals and bass/backing vocals. In common with many other XTC tributes, Terry performs original music, in neo-prog-rock outfit Mellotronanism, and he has performed in covers bands the Dandy Highwaymen and 20th Century Boys, along with Ed and Matt.

Ask Terry for a typical set-list for Fossil Fools and you'll need a pen: upwards of 23 songs (all of them among XTC's best) culled from the length of the band's career. Early boppers such as *This Is Pop* and *Are You Receiving Me?* rub shoulders with mid-period perennials such as *Making Plans for Nigel* and *Senses Working Overtime*, and later gems such as *That Wave*, through to *We're All Light*, some penned by Partridge, some by Moulding.

'It's fantastic to play such weird and wonderful patterns'

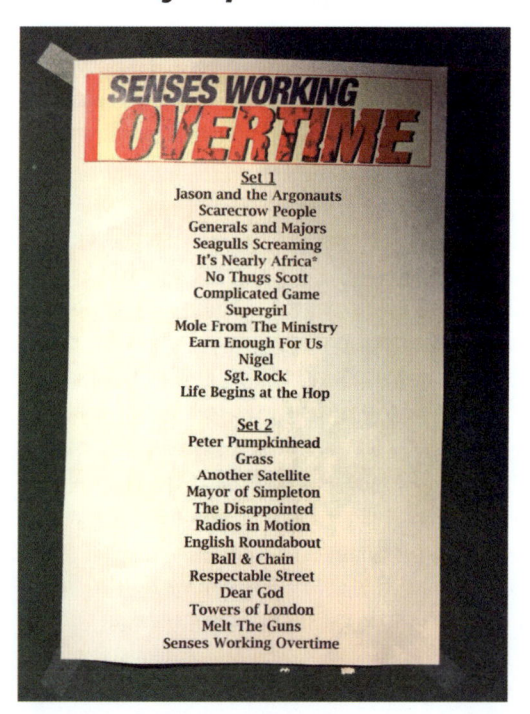

Set list from XTC: An All-Star Tribute at the Turf Club, St Paul's, Minnesota, 2018.

Clearly this is quite an undertaking. Why do they do it? "Personally, I do it for the love of the music and that we can never see them play live again," says Terry. "From a drumming angle, it's fantastic to play such weird and wonderful patterns." The enjoyment from being in a tribute band, he says, depends on the audience: "When the audience is on your side and know the stuff, it's a trip down memory lane for them. To others, it's a voyage of discovery. For me, it's been a lifelong dream to play the stuff live."

The disadvantages again depend on the audience: "We have played to no one before – it depends on the venue, promotion etc. Fossil Fools performed frequently throughout 2010 and 2011, but when things began to fizzle out, that was disheartening, considering the amount of effort involved in rehearsing all the material. I also found the London gigs difficult to get the support for at the time."

Despite such erstwhile frustrations, Terry and bandmates still enjoy exploring the songs and learning as musicians: "We find what we can do and how we can do it. We have purposely restricted ourselves to a four-piece band to keep the essence of the live stuff, but when it comes to post-*English Settlement* material, with all the extra orchestration, it becomes increasingly difficult, though not impossible. That's where Ed's MIDI guitar set-up comes into play, and we could (but haven't thus far) use any sequenced backing for that extra orchestration. We try not to circumvent issues – wanting to perform the music to the best of our abilities – but, for example, we have changed the key of *Ball and Chain* to suit Dan's vocals better. In the past, we performed all the songs in the original key... but age is getting the better of us all, I guess!"

For a drummer, the first four Chambers-era albums hold a particular appeal for Terry A. The others sound percussively different, he says, which in turn appeals in a different way: "I can't really say there's a bad apple in the bunch of XTC material that I don't like to perform." If the band are having trouble working out the tricky bits, they can turn to tools on the internet such as the Chalkhills website and to

'Fellow fans have a personal stake in what happens tonight – just as we do'

people such as Jeff Truzzi (aka Darrell Harvey) who has transcribed a large portion of material. "There's plenty of information if you look for it," he says.

He would encourage other potential XTC tribute bands: "Go for it, but be prepared for some rough seas on your voyage! We saw a few bands at the XTC Convention in Swindon last year who played some amazing stuff. My personal favourites were the Fiddly Bits from the USA – their drummer Todd Bernhardt is also the co-writer of *Complicated Game* (see below). We try to be as authentic as we can."

As a footnote, Terry adds the following nugget: "In 2010 when we supported Tin Spirits, Dave Gregory called us "The Official XTC Tribute", and it was our first gig! – which was a lovely acknowledgement."

"Less like a gig, more like being among friends"
Guitarist and drummer Ed Percival, Terry Arnett's Fossil Fools bandmate, has a lengthy and honourable record of XTC tribute-paying, having joined X-StaTiC, the band put together by Dan

Barrow and name-checked by comedian Stewart Lee in *The XTC Bumper Book of Fun for Boys and Girls*. As Dan describes on their website, x-static.org, driving back to London after a gig in Swansea, it struck him what a fitting idea an XTC tribute would be, for him and for the world at large, starved of the genuine article since 1982: "A combination of tiredness, apocalyptic blues, and finding a copy of *Nonsuch* in the glove compartment and driving past Swindon, planted the seed. By the time I reached London, it was a concrete tree of an idea: a tribute to my favourite band – a band that no one seems to know about, except for a legion of fans joined at the un-hip across the internet."

After posting a message on the *Chalkhills* website, Dan set about putting together his band: regrets included the fact that most responses came from America – well-meaning but impracticable – and that so many respondents were guitarists, the talented Dan initially having to reconcile himself to playing drums.

However, after a more-stop-than-start gestation, with much reconsideration, the band finally took to the tiny stage at London's Hope & Anchor in June 2002 with a new drummer, Adrian Ogden, and Mick Casey on guitar. As Adrian writes, it was a complete thrill: "It's amazing how many people take the time to congratulate us on the performance. 'Terry [Chambers] would have been proud,' someone tells me. Still breathless, I can barely manage more than brief words of thanks. It's just too overwhelming."

He continues, "Tonight I'm tributing a band who are not well known on the tribute circuit. Or indeed at all. If people come and see us tonight it's because they very specifically came to see us. To hear songs played live which they will not hear anywhere else. To see if we can do justice to the band that gave us those songs. Tonight we are playing to fans. Fellow fans. They actually have a personal stake in what happens tonight. Just as we do."

The band's career highlights are, for the XTC fan, almost dizzying. Their third gig was in a small pub, Riffs, in Swindon. Having sent a press release

Matt Bell, Ed Percival, Dan Farmer and Terry Arnett in Fossil Fools: "The UK's top XTC tribute."

to the local paper, the band were surprised to find themselves featured prominently that day. The piece might have had an effect, as Colin Moulding's wife Carol and son Lee turned up to enjoy the gig, dropping off a bag of well-wishing goodies from Colin, and expressing gratitude for keeping the songs of XTC alive. Dan then got a call from Andy Partridge's mum and dad, passing on best wishes for the gig from their son.

As if that weren't enough to perplex the most seasoned XTC tribute, during the interval the band were introduced to Andy Partridge's daughter Holly. She had been tipped-off about the gig by her flattered (and embarrassed) father. When the astonished band re-convened and launched into *Playground*, Ed explains, "Holly is leaping up and down in the crowd and shouting the backing vocals for all she is worth. She is beaming. Everyone is beaming." Holly, who sang backing vocals on the recording of that song, went on to render the band "open-mouthed" as she told them how proud she was to be hearing her dad's songs live for the first time. "She seems genuinely thrilled," says Ed.

If that were impossible to match, on the band's return to Swindon for two gigs, Lee Moulding joined them afterwards to play drums – on the eve of his wedding! Lee joined them again for their last gig, at Swindon's Furnace, in October 2005. By that time the band's set list had grown to around 30 songs.

Writing on the band's website, Ed Percival rounds the story off fittingly: "When we started up X-sTatiC, our aim was to bring XTC's songs back to a live audience. Along the journey we've tackled many, won some, lost some, but always pushed ourselves to do better. X-sTatiC's remit was never to be a touring, boring tribute act. It was a one-off experiment to see if it could be done and a celebration, because there should be one. The band came together for just eight gigs, spread over three years, culminating in their final gig in XTC's home town of Swindon, to fans who had congregated from every corner of the planet for two days to meet, greet, sing, dance and share their love of this music."

Hair-raising Hallowe'en Fund-raising

A recent addition to the pantheon of one-off XTC cover bands is Metropolitan Farms, who appeared at a 2018 Hallowe'en event in Portland, Oregon, raising funds for an anti-sexual violence charity. Sharing the bill with tributes to the B-52s, the BeeGees, the Go-Go's and others, they put together a short set for the evening, comprising *No Thugs in Our House*, *King for a Day* and a medley of *My Bird Performs*, *Then She Appeared* and *Vanishing Girl*.

"We've all played in other tribute bands before, and some material can be so simple that playing it gets tiresome pretty quickly," says the band's Josh Mayer. "That's never true of XTC tunes; they're always smart or odd enough to hold our interest, even before considering how catchy they are."

Familiarity with the material is essential in learning the songs, as is a general musical knowledge. For Josh, this is part of the fun of it: "I think anyone who would want to cover XTC probably has at least some small amount of music theory under the belt, even if it's self-taught. You have to know reflexively that modulating from G Major to A Major is going to provide an unmistakable sense of lift, or that following G Major with a C Minor is going to provide a sweet sadness that desperately wants to be reunited with the tonic." Beyond that, Josh says, it's a case of "listening and recreating carefully note-by-note to identify the constituent notes and how they're voiced".

Did his band do justice to the originals? "The material is so good that we're elevated just by drifting in their wake," says Josh. "I was genuinely surprised by how many people approached me after the set, raving about being big XTC fans, and feeling so happy to hear these songs performed live."

Silly or Fiddly?

Todd Bernhardt's name will be known to readers of *Complicated Game*, the fascinating book he co-wrote with Andy Partridge. His band, from Washington DC, got together casually to play XTC material among themselves rather than in front of people, and earned the moniker "Silly Sods" from Andy, after Todd played him their punkish re-working of *Life Is Good in the Greenhouse*.

Todd takes up the story: "A sub-set of the band travelled across the Atlantic to play at the XTC Convention in Swindon in September 2017, becoming known as the Fiddly Bits in tribute to Dave Gregory, who was assigned such parts by Mr Partridge. We were (and remain) John Relph [of *Chalkhills*], guitar, bass, backing vocals; Jefferson Ogata, bass, keyboards, backing vocals and electronic wizardry; Keith 'Mr Fiddly' Dowling, six and 12-string guitars; and Todd, drums and lead vocals." The song list for the band's set that night was an eclectic mix of demoed songs and album tracks by both Colin and Andy – no singles.

Todd acknowledges the challenge in the songs: "It's fun. Keeps us sharp. And helps us respect the band even more, because we realise these songs are not as easy as they might sound to some. It's a challenge to try to live up to the high standards set by the band. And it deserves to be played and heard more widely. It ain't easy pulling this off, but when you play at a fan convention, and do a good job, you can't ask for a better audience and reception."

Among the limitations of performing this material, Todd says, is people's unfamiliarity with XTC, but he sees it as part of the challenge: "Just got to keep at it. It's like being in any band – you've got to win the audience over. If you've done your work, and play well, it's not that hard."

He continues: "It's certainly easier to play the pre-*Mummer* stuff. Everything after that requires more instruments/instrumentation. But it's all great. I enjoy playing and singing *I'd Like That* as much as *No Thugs in our House*."

Echoing other musicians, he says the band relies on coordination and motivation on the part of its members. Their keyboardist Keith was a special problem-solver, finding videos of XTC playing, and picking-apart the new 5.1 mixes to isolate parts and work them out. To other XTC tribute bands, or someone thinking of starting one, Todd would say,

"Go for it! You'll earn the admiration of literally tens of people!"

His respect for XTC seems beyond earthly, or practical: the words "gods," "great," "wonderful," "boots" and "lick" come up a lot. He says his own band compares poorly: "Our feeble attempts at imitating XTC sound wretchedly and pathetically inadequate... we would rather be sealed in a pit of our own filth than dare tread on the same stage with them."

An exaggeration, maybe, but goes to show...

Gentlemen, Gleam Your Engines...
Sharing the same home-town with XTC, Steve Cox re-purposed his band Mr Love & Justice to become Red Brick Dreamers for the September 2017 XTC Convention in Swindon. Steve, on vocals and guitar, was joined by regular members Rob Beckinsale (guitar and keys), Chris Kerslake (bass) and Trevor Smith (percussion). Normally performing their own material, this time they played *Grass, Red Brick Dream, Life Begins at the Hop, Dear God, Rook* and *You Bring the Summer*.

Steve says he has been a huge XTC fan since 1978 and was motivated by some local pride: "I am Swindon born and bred and very pleased and proud to play a couple of XTC covers whether at the convention or with my band... We drank the same Swindon tap water growing up, I guess, but I think they must have drank from a bigger and better musical cup than the rest of us."

His approach was maybe looser than other tributes, in that "we were not attempting to be a facsimile and were not bound to being 100% faithful to the original. Truth be told, I fumbled towards chords I felt comfortable playing in the style of our originals band, so sometimes I may have accidentally got it right, most times it was at best an approximation that I felt was a hybrid that tried to do justice to those great songs but in a style that felt I was being true to my own. Best you can do with a cover of any band I think but perhaps even more so with a band as idiosyncratic as XTC."

The Craftsman Spirit

Visitors to the 2017 XTC Convention in Swindon and Colin and Terry's TC&I gigs in 2018, will have been struck by the presence of fans from Japan who had loyally ventured halfway round the globe. Visitors to YouTube pages featuring Japanese XTC cover bands will also have been struck by the wonder of *Yacht Dance*, for example, being sung by Japanese-speakers who are delightfully taking the notion of song-fandom to new heights.

Among the more recent gatherings mounted by Japanese XTC fans was one in Osaka in 2016, where a one-off "XTC Osaka Band" played, and in Tokyo in May the following year, where three bands performed, among them Shima E Iku Boat, whose versions of *Happy Families*, *Wake Up* and *Love on a Farmboy's Wages* are on YouTube [https://is.gd/Fwsubj]. Among the guests was Saeko Suzuki - whose 1987 album *Studio Romantic* involved Andy Partridge and Dave Gregory - and some tribute bands. Steve Warren, XTC's former roadie, was there as a guest for a Q&A session and has been literally instrumental in keeping Anglo-Japanese XTC relations buoyant.

"Buoyant," again literally, as an "XTC Boat Party" took place on a chartered vessel on a Tokyo river in June 2018! Hisashi Ishikawa, playing guitar and singing, was joined by Kukkuru, who records and performs under the moniker Lo-Fi Club, and bass player Kazuyuki Tsurumi, a big prog-rock fan whose wife educated him on XTC. Maybe not altogether unexpected on a river boat, there were some difficulties with the acoustics and sound-monitoring, but the video, shot by Steve Warren, is wonderful. [https://is.gd/Lh7uCT]

An interesting aspect of this is, of course, XTC lyrics being in English, not Japanese. "Some Japanese people say they have learned a lot of English language from XTC songs," says Luna Lure, who used to co-run the Japanese XTC fan club with Akiko Kogure. "Other Japanese people who are not keen on learning English or don't understand much of the language say they love XTC because their songs are so nice, catchy and complicated."

It's a sentiment echoed by fan Yashida who says the Japanese tend to listen to western music for its melody rather than lyrics. Plus, as evidenced on YouTube, some XTC songs have been translated into Japanese in order to be performed.

So, why such a strong following in Japan? "It's simply because they love the music, and if they play musical instruments, they probably cannot resist playing it themselves," says Shigemasa Fujimoto, who compiled the diary-cum-discography *XTC Chronology 1966-1999* [https://is.gd/xB8km0]. "Perhaps they have a strong desire to take bits of XTC into their system so they can feel close to the band. I also imagine it must be technically

Left: Kukkuru, Hisashi Ishikawa and Kazuyuki Tsurumi take to the water.
Above: Osaka XTC Tribute Band starring Tohori Ishitobi, Yudai Kurita, Yamato Kawada, Akira Murakami, Hisashi Ishikawa and Kukkuru.

challenging to play and sing XTC songs, and that's appealing to musicians. Japanese people generally appreciate the 'craftsman spirit,' and those words often come up when they talk about XTC."

Rewind and press play

Studio musicians and home recorders also like to get in on the tribute act. Releases include *Testimonial Dinner*, the professional 1995 compilation on which XTC themselves made a secret appearance as Terry and the Lovemen, and a compilation due out in 2019 on Futureman Records. The role taken by early cassette compilations such as *Obscene Collection*, *Atmosphere to Ocean*, *Beasts I've Seen*, and *Skylacking* has been taken over by sites such as Soundcloud and YouTube, where you'll find the prolific output of Erich Sellheim (see next page).

In the pre-digital era, the man who did more than most to keep the tapes rolling was Richard Pedretti-Allen. He produced three cassettes – © (1996), *Don't Ring Us* (1997) and *Modern Time Neros* (1998) – and one CD, *King for a Day* (2003), featuring the three previous releases plus additional material, totalling more than 140 tracks.

Fittingly, the series emerged from the online XTC community at *Chalkhills*, then an email digest run by John Relph, where someone suggested that the musicians in the group should each cover a song. "Being a recording producer, I offered to compile a tribute, putting up my own money for the cassette replication and selling them at cost," says Pedretti-Allen. "I didn't play judge or jury on what was acceptable, I just reserved myself a spot and offered up the rest until the tape was full. It was great and horrible and interesting and fun."

The results were varied. "It ran the gamut," he says. "Studio-quality recordings to one-take jams (complete with cigarette coughs) to 'I stopped at a friend's studio on the way home from work and recorded an a capella version of *Rook* for you' – that is stunning!"

And the best part of it? "Establishing a more personal connection with members of *Chalkhills* (many are still friends 20-plus years later) and a friendship with Andy, Colin, and Dave. They even invited me to the *Apple Venus* orchestral sessions at Abbey Road Studios."

I'm very grateful to Shigemasa Fujimoto and Steve Warren, whose *XTC Taken From Behind*, a book of photos from his time touring with XTC, sold especially well in Japan, leading to his close association with the Japanese XTC community.

A DISCO TROT FROM GERMANY

Working his way through the XTC catalogue with German-language YouTube covers, one fan holds up a European mirror to England's most English band

BY ERICH SELLHEIM

In the life of any fan there comes a point when you wonder what to do with all your passion. How many autographed football jerseys will fit into your wardrobe? How many international pressings of one and the same album do you need? It was questions like these that I started asking myself about ten years ago. I've been an avid XTC fan since 1990, and I'd done it all: collecting absurd quantities of records and memorabilia, travelling abroad to fan conventions, writing letters to the band members.

And somewhere along the line, it must have struck me: I don't want to sleep in XTC bedclothes and I don't even want to meet or be friends with Andy, Colin and Dave. What I want - and what I've always wanted - is to be in that band, playing and recording that music, writing those lyrics. But let's face it - being invited into one of Britain's most respected pop bands was never going to happen to an obscure German musician; especially considering the band doesn't exist any more.

So what could I do? Oh wait, I could try and recreate the songs in my mini-studio. And to make it more interesting, I could write German lyrics, thus creating the rarest of beasts: really great German pop music (you wouldn't believe the blandness and mediocrity of this country's musical output).

As with most band recordings, I generally start with the drums; and as I can't play them myself, I asked my friend and bandmate Andreas Jäger, who always does a fabulous job mimicking the style and sound of Terry et al, to play along to the original tracks over headphones in order to get the tempo, feel and sequence of parts just right. And then I come in, adding bass, guitars, keyboards, percussion plus lead and backing vocals. Which is pretty much all that is needed for the earlier songs - I work chronologically, and now that I'm getting to the more heavily orchestrated tracks (*Mummer* at the time of writing), I'm hiring local brass and string players, sometimes patching up the real instruments with synth ones to get a fuller sound.

Being primarily a guitar and bass player, many of Colin and Andy's parts come relatively easy to me -

sure, XTC's music has been living in my musical mind for nearly three decades, and still it's amazing how much of their rhythmic and melodic versatility and originality has crept into my own playing over the years. Replicating some of Dave's parts, however, is a constant challenge which I meet with diligence and unabashed trickery. For example, I recorded his solo in *Real by Reel* bar by bar and at half speed (later speeding it up again), and even then, I could hardly play it. When I uploaded the song (all of my covers are available on YouTube), I promptly got applause for my "perfect" solo, and I hung my head in shame. Keyboard-wise, I'm a big fan of Barry's madcap style, so re-playing his random noodlings note by note was a silly but fun experience.

One of the fascinating things about trying to do carbon copies of your favourite songs is the kind of detail you find listening with headphones – when recordings you've loved and lived with for more than half your life suddenly reveal new and surprising little touches and nuances. Before starting this project, I had never noticed the unplugged, closely miked electric guitar in *Pulsing Pulsing*, the whispered singing that backs up the lead vocals in *Making Plans for Nigel* and *Me and the Wind*, and (seconded by drummer Andreas) the percussive complexity of so many XTC songs, like *Millions* and *Living Through Another Cuba*. And there are still things I miss, buried in the mix and completely baffling me when I listen to the instrumental mixes on the current 5.1 re-release series.

As for the vocals: obviously I've always been a fan of XTC's songwriting, but I'd never really appreciated how spot-on and effortless much of Andy and Colin's singing is. In particular, Colin's songs, like *Wonderland*, are in a punishingly high register, and my feeble attempts at getting near his vocal range should be treated sympathetically. I don't use Auto-Tune, but maybe I should. I'm more at ease aping harmony, and again, I'm always astonished to find how much of XTC's vocal arrangements shines through when I play and sing with other musicians.

English-German song translations are a tricky matter, because the English language uses a lot of one-syllable words, so you generally need more syllables to say something in German than to say it in English. So if you want metre, accentuation, content and diction to stay true to the original, you have to find new and more concise ways of expressing something that has already been expressed so beautifully in English. "Gen'rals and majors" for example, takes up three syllables less than the German equivalent "Generäle und Majore", so I changed my song title to the five-syllabic *Kriegsgeneräle* (*War Generals*). Likewise, *Marienkäfer* doesn't match the original *Ladybird*, so I used the shorter and punning *Frau Marie* (*Miss Marie*).

And then, of course, there's the rhyming scheme, which I always try to stick to in order to maintain as much of the original's flow and elegance as possible. This isn't much of a problem with Colin's songs (he's a rather laissez-faire rhymer); more so with Andy's lyrics, which tend to be more complex constructions, using elaborate and even internal rhymes, as in *Burning with Optimism's Flames*.

Juggling all these components is never easy, and quite often it's a struggle involving logic, heart, humour and a fair amount of crossword puzzlery – in other words, all the things I love about XTC.

As you might say, I'm stupidly happy the words got in the way.

So what I intuitively felt ten years ago has proven true: collecting the records was just the start for something different, and browsing through the internet I realise I'm not alone in that. So many of us aren't content merely consuming XTC's music; we need to talk, write, sing, even dance about it. Creative fandom – what a beautiful, paradoxical feather to stick in the collective hat of Andy, Barry, Colin, Dave and Terry.

Danke, Jungs.

Watch and listen to Erich Sellheim's covers on his YouTube page: https://is.gd/6Va5N9

ME AND MY MATE CAN SING

Patient to the last, the editor of Limelight waited 37 years to get his first interview with Barry Andrews. Finally meeting in Swindon, they enjoy a free-flowing conversation that ranges from leaving XTC to finding a musical voice

BY MARK FISHER

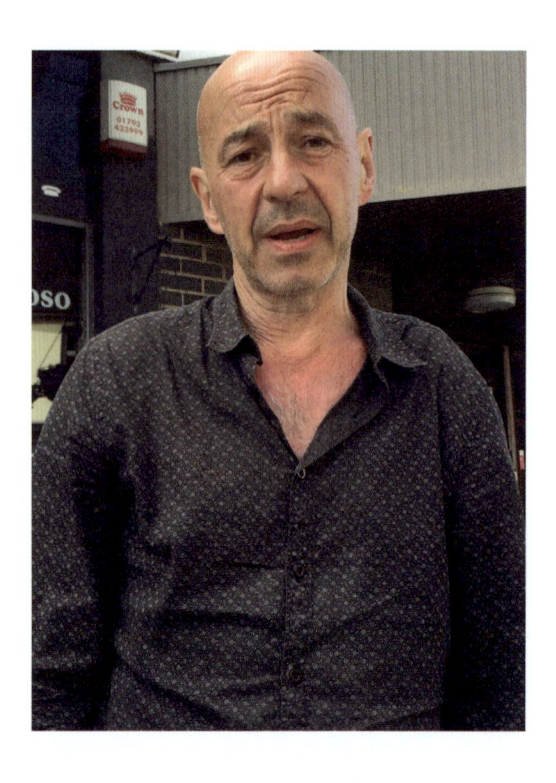

When it comes to talking about XTC, Barry Andrews has a reputation for being standoffish. He chose not to contribute to the Charlie Thomas documentary *This Is Pop*, for example, and although he went to the trouble of sending me a three-page letter in 1981 after I'd requested an interview for the first issue of *Limelight*, he wasn't exactly keen. "I don't know if I can get very excited about discussing XTC's early career," he wrote, arguing it was a subject that had been well covered elsewhere. They had, it seemed, "sucked all the juice out of this particular segment of history". He did say he'd be happy to talk about his post-XTC work, but musically he'd moved on.

And, to be fair, why wouldn't he have done? Although his keyboards helped define the sound of *White Music* and *Go 2*, Barry was a member of XTC for only two years. Even by the time he wrote to me, he'd spent as long out of the band as in it. Today, he's approaching 40 years with Shriekback, the band he formed with Dave Allen, Carl Marsh and, later, Martyn Baker, and that's in addition to solo releases and stints in Restaurant for Dogs,

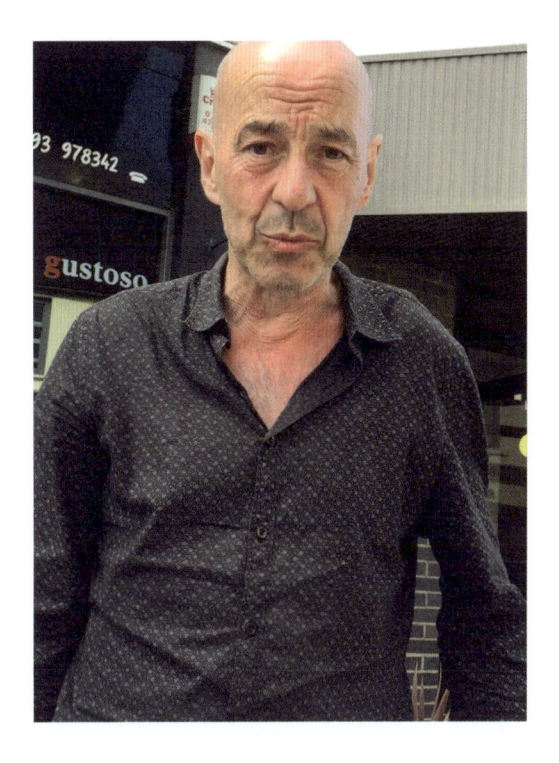

Illuminati and others, not to mention his 2007 reunion with Andy Partridge on the improvised *Monstrance*. By comparison, his stint with XTC is a historical blip. He's got better – and fresher – things to talk about.

With that in mind, and with a spot of matchmaking by Stu Rowe, I approached Barry all these years later, suggesting we talk about his post-XTC work. It seemed fitting that in a book featuring so many musicians talking about music that Barry should get the chance to discuss his own approach, be that to melody, rhythm, vocals, songwriting, keyboards, recording or playing live.

He replied to me quickly, saying again he was "not too bothered about sinking down into the depths of time to bang on about my days in XTC" (some of which he'd done, in any case, on his extensive Shriekback Tumblr blog), but that he'd be happy to be involved. As it turned out, in our lengthy and lively chat sitting outside a café one sunny Swindon afternoon, he was, if anything, more reluctant to talk about the album he'd just finished with Shriekback than he was about XTC. Nothing was off limits and the conversation flowed.

DONE PLENTY BUM GIGS IN MY TIME
Live chaos, studio control and improvisation

Mark Fisher: In 1981 when I was setting up *Limelight* you wrote me a letter that said, "If music criticism has any value then it is to prod people like us out of complacency about our work and make us examine our ideas for their value now."

Barry Andrews: I do apologise for my younger self for being so up himself: "If criticism…"

Mark: Can I prod you out of your complacency?

Barry: Prod away, man

Mark: You're looking very complacent. I have a related question about the word "now", always looking forward and not looking backwards. You were not looking backwards in 1981 and you're not looking backwards now. Where do you sit on the spectrum between your legacy - all the recorded albums - and the sense of always wanting to create more and do the next thing?

Barry: I do like the collections. I like that there's a load of physical stuff lying around that I did. If anything, I've been in a position of arguing against doing live stuff. It always seemed like a bit too much trouble, but then when you actually do it (Shriekback went back on the road in 2017) it's hugely enjoyable. There's something about getting out of bed to do it I don't like.

Mark: Depending on the nature of the live event, it could be very repetitive.

Barry: I remember Andy saying to me one time when he was getting fucked off with the road, if you paint a picture no one asks you, "Can we have *Guernica* again, please, Picasso? And another 500 times all round the world."

Mark: There were all those years when you didn't play live as Shriekback - 25 years was it?

Barry: First couple of years we didn't play live. Then we did. Then we stopped at the end of the 80s. Mid 90s we started with the acoustic band, we were playing all over the show, playing like world-music stuff in Europe, then Shriekback just went on hiatus from 1995. It's a messy thing, live. It has lots of uncontrollable variables which are a bit of a pain. I like it in the studio where you're in control of everything. It's just nice and safe.

Mark: But the variables can also be exciting.

Barry: They can. I'm talking against myself in a way. Going on stage at Shepherd's Bush Empire and after that, Paradiso, it was, "Oh fuck, that was such good fun, I just love this." It's like childbirth or something - you can't quite remember what it was like afterwards.

Mark: Within the scope of a live gig how much improvisation and leeway do you allow yourselves in Shriekback?

Barry: Not a lot. We started off going, "Yeah, man, leave it to the vibe on the night. Just jam it. We'll just stop when it feels right." But actually, most of the time, if you do that, you hit the skids. People can't always hear each other properly on stage and it starts to become disparate and sometimes really messy and unpleasant. So we decided there's a virtue in drilling the shit out of it. Do it again and again and, when you think you've got it, do it again. "I'm really sick of it." Do it again. Finally, when the panic hits you on stage you'll remember it. Your training will kick in.

Mark: And with the control you were talking about in the studio, you don't need to be doing it again and again.

Barry: That's the real beauty, especially now - you can just improvise. We can take that little thing that came into your head and we can put it there. You can capture things that you couldn't before. In the early days of Shrieks we'd just be jamming over 24 tracks over a drum rhythm. When the verse finally starts to exist and there's a little two-bar gap, you'd have to hope you did something good in those two bars. "No, there isn't anything. Damn!" But now you can just take something from over there and drop it in.

Mark: Do you have any interest in the jazz idea of musicians who know their instruments going up on stage and, knowing the chord structure, just seeing what happens?

Barry: Yes. *Monstrance* was in that area. A little bit before *Monstrance* me and drummer Martyn Baker had been playing with Clare Hirst, sax player, in an outfit called the Fire Judges which was put together by David Somerville, a filmmaker. The idea was to do a handful of gigs at which this film was projected and we'd respond to it and improvise our way through. It was great. It was completely different every night. Then there was a band in Swindon called Trip Dress that Pete Cousins formed with me, Stuart Rowe, Mark "The Harp" Gowland and Brendan Hamley. Our raison d'être was to go on stage and jam for the whole evening. The last one we did was a couple of years ago. With *Monstrance* and with Trip Dress, the first thing you do is almost always the best, the second thing is not quite as good and then there's a steep falling off because you've found the tricks. You just do that same thing and it becomes like boring old sex. "I'll react in this way because that seemed quite effective last time." You've lost your innocence.

Mark: It sounds as if you're saying you're not particularly mad about living in the moment and always doing the next thing.

Barry: There's a place for it but the main reason I do any of this is to construct new things, to make new things happen. Unfortunately, you can't do that with just pure improvisation. The planned things bolt together and are predictable. You can't use all that craft if it's pure improvisation.

THINGS FALL TO BITS
Song, sculpture and meaning

Mark: As you were talking, you were making gestures of physicality and movement. You are a sculptor and furniture maker as well…

Barry: I was for a while. I did it for about six years. But yes, I very much see songs as sculptures. People ask what a song is about, but are less inclined to ask what that big piece of bronze with some glass sticking out is about. "I don't know. It could be about lots of things." I see a song as being an assemblage of bits that go together. The noises and words make something happen in your head. It's not necessarily addressing anything in the real world.

I did a book which is a collection of blogs with some extra stuff and there's one I wrote called *Jewels and Binoculars Hang from the Head of the Mule – or Do They?* It's about songs meaning things and lyrics being decipherable. If they're not decipherable, what are they? What are they meant to do? I make a comparison with a vitrine of Joseph Beuys where he had two little bowls of lard connected by a piece of copper and a dead hare nailed to a blackboard. That was the first time I saw sculpture as, "Oh fuck, that's brilliant." It's about death, it's about power, it's about corrosion and decay, recycling, energies… all of these things, like a little poem of stuff that makes something go off in your head. That's what I try to do with a song.

Mark: For you as a spectator in a gallery, that meaning is your meaning, which may or may not coincide with Joseph Beuys's meaning.

Barry: Sure, yes. That's art generally.

Mark: Conversely, if you've sculpted a song, is it important that it means something to you, that you have an emotional connection to it or a literal meaning?

Barry: No. Again, I go back to sculpture. You put emotion into something and there's a certain energy behind it that comes from life, but I always find that if it really is about, you know, a girl in summer, it's too on the nose for me. I like music to do more than that, to make something that's "I've never seen one of those before," rather than, "Yes, of course, it's one of those."

Mark: When somebody writes a song that is nonsense verse or abstract, I always think, "Well, how do you even remember the words?" Because if it's completely abstract, it could be improvised.

Barry: There's an album called *The Elated World*, which was a bunch of commissioned music. Shriekback said, "Give us £200 and we'll write you a two-minute tune. You can suggest the title but nothing else." We ended up doing about 20 of them. It was really good fun because you didn't have the worry of "this is the way we do things in Shriekback Land". You could pretty much go anywhere you liked and try out new things. On one of the tunes, I got really stoned and improvised the lyric, which I've never done before. It has its moments. I haven't done it again, so it has its limitations.

AND IF NOT YOUR BAND…
The right song for the right group

Mark: You just said the rules of the group could impose a sort of order about the way a Shriekback song is supposed to sound.

Barry: Yes, they do. Over the years, there's a way we do things. In fact, me and Carl had a contretemps on the last album because he'd written three songs that I felt were more like his other unit, Men with Ven, which is a cheeky-chappie, ironic, postmodern Chas-and-Dave type thing. It's very good fun. But I was like, "No, no, no, these are wrong." He was like, "Surely if we do it, that's us doing it. How can it be wrong?" "But there's an aesthetic!" I didn't feel very comfortable being the guy who was saying, "Take your children," because that's what happened to me in XTC. I had a lot more sympathy with Partridge for that time. I would have done exactly the same thing. There was an aesthetic that XTC had and I wasn't part of it. I wasn't there to be part of it. I was there to make some good keyboard noises. That's all I was required to do. But, of course, with the megalomania of a 21 year old...

Mark: And the megalomania in the group...

Barry: There was quite a lot of megalomania in the group... more than its share.

Mark: When you were coming up with those songs, did the thought not cross your mind that you hadn't written songs for XTC before and now you were? Did that seem controversial to you?

Barry: It's hard to remember what the feeling was. I suppose it was, "I'm in a band. Everything's up for grabs. I'm going to do my thing. I'm me! You're lucky to have me."

Mark: On Twitter the other day, Andy was talking about country music for some reason and he said something like, "I have problems with genre." I don't think he or you are people who say, "Right, I'm going to write a country song now." Related to the question of whether Shriekback has to sound a certain way is the quesion of whether, in your head, every song is different or whether it's actually following a "western white pop with funk influences" template.

Barry: That's what it is and I don't think you can depart too much from that. And I have tried.

In the *Big Night Music* period, we said, "No to sequencers and drum machines. We're going to play this." We had a really good band around us. It was lovely. We were stretching out. "We've got these chops, man." I was the only writer in the band at the time, because Carl wasn't there, and there was this feeling that we go over here, over there. I wrote stuff that sounded cabaret-ish and one that was very country. I got a grip in time: "Actually, no, you're just excited because you're doing something you don't usually do and it doesn't mean it's something you *should* be doing." It was loads of ersatz shit. The building up of a voice as a musician is a long task. It takes a while. It comes from the experience of going down the path of life, finding out things and people that you've worked with. Bit by bit you build up your self-expression. You don't just throw that away and depart from it in a casual way. It should be taken quite seriously because it takes a lot to get it.

Mark: Are there voices, plural, that you've built up?

Barry: A little bit but not that much.

Mark: I'm thinking about the piano album you did, *Haunted Box of Switches*, which was revisiting Shriekback material. It was you but it's not what you'd heard before.

Barry: No, exactly. The next thing I'm going to do is a solo album and that has been preoccupying me. There are certain songs that are really not Shriekback. In the piano world, it's easier because of the instrumentation. It's such a generic thing. "This is a piano song." Whereas if you took one of those songs, how do you score it? Orchestra? Rock band? Are there going to be lots of guitars? Any one of those decisions is going to influence how it will be received.

If I do a solo album and it's a ragbag of styles, songs where the only thing in common is that they're not Shriekback, then it wouldn't be a very satisfying project. Yes, there are different voices, but none of them I have worked as hard on as the Shriekback voice, which is why it's the most developed.

Mark: I'm thinking now of your XTC voice, then your *Win a Night Out with a Well Known Paranoiac* voice...

Barry: You have done your homework! I've never done anything like it since. I sometimes listen to it late night on YouTube. I don't know where that came from.

Mark: Does it feel like it's not your voice?

Barry: It's part of the Baz solo thing. Quite a lot of that is parodic. Like anything, you have to sit down and do it for a while, make a lot of mistakes, throw a lot of stuff away and perhaps there will be distilled at the end of it something worthwhile.

Mark: But it's curious. Although you're saying Shriekback is your band - and other people's, but the thing you've worked hardest at - it's still, I don't know, like putting on a set of clothes, a uniform. "This is how I'm going to behave today."

Barry: The grubby rubber clown suit of Shriekback! Slightly soiled. Yes, it's exactly like that. The latex cat suit of Shriekback.

Mark: But is it a comfortable clown suit?

Barry: Yes, it's very comfortable. It's got boundaries though and the thing with boundaries is you bang into them. It can be frustrating. You find stuff you'd like to do that that format won't let you. I'm sure Carl feels the same. "I can't use those songs because it's not part of our collective consciousness."

JAM SCIENCE
Finding the Shriekback groove

Mark: Which is presumably why you're talking about a solo album.

Barry: Yes. I'm at the stage with *Why Anything? Why This?* that I really can't bear to listen to it. I've just listened to it again and again in such a way that any enjoyment has been rinsed out of it. My deformed drooling child! "I will ignore you on the street."

Mark: You will have to talk to me about it though! Is it exploring new territory or is it rehashing the same old Shriekback...

Barry: The same old bullshit, yeah. Throw another one out. It's all this money coming in. It just corrupts us. But, yes, it's a few feet in that direction. A lot more of Martyn playing the drums. Live drums on all but one track, so Martyn's stretching out more than he has on any other record, which is beautiful. The sheer loveliness of the drumming. I like to watch. It's like a great animal running across a field. It gives you joy. This is the first album since *Oil & Gold* in the mid 80s where me and Carl have split the writing 50/50, so that's made a big difference.

Mark: How does it work? Do you come in with your 50% of songs and he comes in with his and you meet in the middle or do you create together?

Barry: It tends to be I write the grooves or me and Martyn come up with the groove, then Carl will go, "I like that one." We'll pick them out of the tank like lobsters and go off with them and do our stuff, then bring them back.

Mark: The expression you just used was that the two of you will come up with a groove. If you were on your own, you'd come up with something looking like a song, but what you're coming up with is, what, a rhythm?

Barry: Yes, back in the day it was a LinnDrum going round in a two-bar loop, then Dave Allen would do a two or four-bar bass line and I'd add bits and pieces. We haven't really improved on that process even though we go off to our studios and fuck about in Cubase [music software]. For the lyrics, Carl and I go to our corners - there's never any collaboration on that. In some songs, he won't do anything else apart from the lyric and I'll put all the instrumentation in. Some, he puts guitars on. Mostly it's me fleshing it out.

Carl comes with this skeletal, honed thing that fits in the middle and I add colour if I think it's necessary.

Mark: At the end of that process, does it feel like a Barry Andrews song or a Shriekback song? Can you remember where it started and where it developed? To take the example of the Beatles, you can tell that's a Paul McCartney song and that's a John Lennon song because they didn't collaborate apart from the early days.

Barry: No, we use the Beatles model (apart from singing on the same mic). It is collaborative, but it's definitely, "That's a Carl song and that's a Barry song." You know which of us it was.

Mark: There must be millions of musicians who don't have the good fortune to bump into someone who they can collaborate with. Did it take a long time to realise you all liked wearing that same suit?

Barry: With Martyn not so much because I head-hunted him after I saw him at a gig. But I was kind of lumbered with Carl because Dave Allen had hired him. If you wanted to be in a band with Dave Allen, you had to have Carl! He was originally a guitarist, so it wasn't apparent for a while that he was going to be a songwriter. Very slowly and over a good few years, he started writing and I started writing and this thing developed. After he left the band after *Oil & Gold*, I carried on and did quite a few albums and touring without him. When he came back in and wrote his first song on *Life in the Loading Bay*, it was something incredibly familiar, something you know you've influenced and has influenced you because it's been so much part of your life. This weird bit of your head where your aesthetic lives, Carl Marsh is in there. Even after 20 years, it's still there. It's really strange to have that relationship with somebody. It's quite unlike anything else. I don't know another way in which you can have that thing with another human being. It isn't so much about how much you hang out with each other or even if you like each other very much. There's this thing that you do that you've put quite a lot of your self-respect, energy and your essence into and that somebody else is in there as well. You float about together in that crucible.

SACRED CITY
Swindon, London, Stroud...

Mark: How important is place to you? It's central to XTC's music.

Barry: It does matter to me where I am. I was in London for 25 years and in 2004 my dad died so I came back to Swindon to look after mum. I was here then for another ten years. Fucking Swindon! Pulled me back in! As soon as I got to London in 1979, I felt like I was at home. The whole parochial, everybody knows everybody, everybody's bitching about everybody... XTC weren't treated all that well by people in Swindon. "Oi, you're in that fucking band, aren't you, mate?" "Yeah. Sorry!" I get a lot of inspiration from the things around me. I'm obsessed with cities. I did a whole album about city. I live in Stroud and there are loads of Londoners there. It's like a Londoner's version of the countryside. The good thing about Stroud is I'm getting out of Swindon. It's a lot nicer. If my son wasn't ensconced in my flat, I think I'd move back to London.

Mark: He's a musician, isn't he?

Barry: Yes, the Veils. The apple don't fall far from the tree.

Mark: Is it a competitive relationship? Do you have to mark out your territory?

Barry: Yes, we definitely have to do that. We get on extremely well, but I do think with Finn, doing anything – I was decorating the flat once and pretty much anything I liked he didn't. There's a project I'm working on called *Vile Homunculus* which has a lot of outside voices and Finn is one of them. Because that's completely my thing and he's just a performer in it, he's fine. He takes direction really well and puts everything he can into it to get it to work for me. That works. What wouldn't work is if we were like, "What do you think?"

Mark: As he was growing up did you ever play musically with him?

Barry: What we mainly did when he was smaller was films, acting, animations, drawings. We made a series of movies: *Merlin and the Goblins*. We converted the living room into the set. Finn was Merlin and I was one of the goblins. It was great.

Mark: That seems to me like another expression of creativity. You made a comment on your blog about realising you were a creative person and that is the definition of you. It doesn't matter whether it's a Merlin film or…

Barry: I don't think it does, no. Jordan Peterson has a personality test with five criteria with things like conscientiousness, industriousness, agreeability and openness. Openness is the big indicator of creativity. I did one of his tests and scored extremely highly for openness - in the 90s - and very low for agreeableness and conscientiousness! He says if you've got such a high degree of openness, it's not necessarily a good thing, but it is going to define your personality and what you can do with your life. There's no point fighting it. If you don't do something creative you will be miserable. So you have to do it. On the other hand, it's very difficult to monetise it, you have to jump through hoops, it's going to be as much a curse as a blessing. But if you've got that sort of personality, you've got no option. I can see Finn's got it, Andy's got it, I've got it. After I did the personality test, I was inspired to go back and look at the blog I wrote about XTC [*Keyboard Playing Part 2: '75-79 (or: "I'd been to XTC but I'd never been to me…")* https://is.gd/8QbOC5]. I thought, "Yes, that was madness. You can't have one of them doing that, a polo pony doing something that polo ponies obviously can't do."

Mark: It was a very interesting analysis. Did you figure it out for yourself or had you been through therapy?

Barry: I've been through all sorts of things, but the creative thing wasn't the result of doing any kind of "work" on myself. It was living it, just the realisation that that's what it feels like when you're doing that and that's what it feels like when you're doing this.

Mark: Most people don't know themselves very well. It's always somebody else's fault. The rest of the world is to blame.

Barry: I've got a few things to say about the rest of the world!

Mark: But then to say, "Well, actually that was my contributing factor to the reason that wasn't working"…

Barry: Well, you're a bit fucked if you blame everybody else. There's nothing you can do about them. But you can do something about yourself.

ALL HUMMING NOW
From Classics for Pleasure to Roast Fish and Cornbread

Mark: I was going to ask about melody. The piano seems to me to be a melodic instrument - it plays tunes. But if I think about your music, rhythm and abrasiveness and language are prominent. You're not writing *Yesterday*.

Barry: It's rhythm and language. A lot of it is working with substandard voices. Carl and I can't carry a tune. That's what you've got so you've got to work around it. I really like melody and I think I'm quite good at writing them and in the *Vile Homunculus* project it has been nice to write more lavish lines and getting somebody else to sing them. I would like to do more of that. The great thing about the piano is you don't have to make the notes. With a guitar you've got to make the actual note. With a piano, it's, "Bonk. There you are. It's an A."

Mark: I haven't quite worked out your musical education. At which point did your grandad stop teaching you the piano and when did you start teaching yourself? Did you ever have lessons?

Barry: My parents wouldn't get me piano lessons. They really did me a favour there. When you hear my piano playing, I play too hard. It's not very lyrical. As soon as synthesisers came along, your left hand is spent doing this *[twiddles an imaginary knob]* so that atrophies and you're doing one-finger things up here.

Mark: Did you just have enough musical curiosity to use those building blocks to go further?

Barry: Yes. I really, really wanted it. As I say in my blog [see *Inside the Haunted Box of Switches,* over page], I finally got to the school piano. It was sexual in its intensity. "Oh, God, imagine getting in there." And then a nice teacher, Mr Keen, came along and said, "Why don't you come in the evening after school and stay for a couple of hours?" I can't say how great that was. Grandad got me started, then there was a working-men's club down the bottom of town that my dad used to go to and I carried on playing there, then the school piano and then I got an organ in the mid 70s.

I was listening to classical music. I was passionate about that. I saw the piano as my route. I'd get this manuscript paper from school and Sellotape it together so you could score about 50 instruments. It was always the first page I liked. The actual notation got a bit arsey after a bit. But it was, "Yeah, I've got a double brass band on this one. How many trombones? Six! And harps." I loved the idea of building this sound. It's amazing how you can do it with a computer.

Mark: At the age you were, piano is deeply uncool and classical music is deeply uncool. Were you able to see beyond that?

Barry: I don't know if the piano was deeply uncool because it did stop you getting beaten up at school. "You're that clever kid. Play that." If you could play pop songs by ear, the hard-nuts liked that and it bought you a bit of peace and quiet.

Mark: You talk about music being in your family going back generations. It does strike me that you've just got an ear for it. How hard did you have to work?

Barry: That really did come pretty naturally. Coming back to classical music, I started off listening to your *Classics for Pleasure*. There was a cigarette brand where you could send off and get these albums – it was *The Planets, Romeo and Juliet,* bits of Beethoven. As I got more into it, more of the 20th-century stuff, Sibelius, Britten and Stravinsky. "You're really never going to get a girlfriend, Barry."

Mark: So you joined a punk group!

Barry: Makes sense!

Mark: I was watching a compilation of clips of bands making their first appearance on TV, people like Ian Dury and the Blockheads, Elvis Costello, the Beat and Madness. It was interesting watching one after another, from 1978 or whatever the year was, and thinking, "These people can really play their instruments." It wasn't the myth of punk being a load of people who couldn't play their instruments.

Barry: Yes, but that was the second wave, the people who were trying not to let on that they'd learned to play really well, because it was pretty bad news at the time. I remember some gig in London and somebody watching the support band – and I knew they were going to say the same thing about us – and saying, "They're just a fucking rock band that's had their arse kicked by the new wave."

Mark: Both things were true: you could reject the pomposity of prog rock and accept the energy of new wave, but also have a musical skill.

Barry: The equation in my head was that sophisticated long-form music – there's *The Rite of Spring,* there's Beethoven's *Ninth* – is really complicated, so don't tell me something by Yes is the same: "Yeah, we're really great musicians, man." It's just horrible and it doesn't sound as nice. It sounds like you're trying to use these tropes of classical music but the actual sounds aren't as nice as an orchestra. It's jumped-up and pretending to have more depth and sophistication than it actually has. It's plastic and horrible, whereas the Pistols, the Drones and Chelsea is very simple. It's not pretending to be anything it's not. It's got this energy, obviously, but it's got this nimbus around it of politics, rebellion and youth. It seemed exciting in a way that classical music had lost its nimbus – or the nimbus it had was that it's straight music for posh people.

Mark: When you joined XTC did you feel kindred spirits musically?

Barry: No, never. We got on like a house on fire – much more than any group I've been in (and I've been in a few). Everyone was really funny.

Mark: You got in without them hearing you, didn't you?

Barry: That's right. We just went to the pub. Andy threw up in the toilet. We just had a great time. I loved them. I thought they were the funniest people. But I wasn't really into the music. It was slightly on the poncy side and pointlessly stylised, it seemed to me. But, hey, we're all in the same town, they all seem to know what they're doing, they seem really ambitious, it's not going to get much better than this. That's why I joined.

Mark: Do you listen to your old stuff?

Barry: Yes. I didn't think I did anything that was any good until *Rossmore Road* and *Win a Night Out with a Well-Known Paranoiac*. That's when I feel like, "That's me." The other stuff is faffing about, including the *Go 2* tunes. They're sort of all right, but I didn't know what I wanted to say. It sounds like juvenilia to me. *Town and Country* as well. They have some merits but I don't hear an artist in there yet.

Mark: Are your influences unexpected? We've talked about playing pub songs in a working-men's club and classical music, but the rhythmic stuff that Shriekback is known for seems to be more influenced by black music, soul and so on.

Barry: Yes, I had an epiphany when I heard James Brown. There was a Bristol diaspora in London – people from the Pop Group and the like. The painter Dexter Dalwood who I was squatting with at the time, and all of that crew were really into old-school 70s funk. It seemed sexy and dangerous. I guess that and reggae. There was an XTC gig in the Electric Circus in Manchester, a real bomb site, a shitty old cinema, a wasteland, and our roadie who used to go to school with Partridge, Jeff Fitches, was a big dub reggae guy. It was quite strange; he did Latin at Oxford, so quite why... He had all these white labels and tutored me in reggae. It was a hot day outside and all the doors were closed, so it was cold inside. They had the big speakers up. It was one of the first tours we ever did with the big PA. It was playing Lee Perry's *Roast Fish and Cornbread* dub. I'd never heard anything like it. It filled the space and hit you in the solar plexus. There is a tiny woodblock that just ticks – how is a woodblock that loud? "Clip clop, clappity clappity clappity clap, aye..." What is this? It was as close to an epiphany as I've ever had, enough that I just listened to all the dub records I could, Lee Perry especially. A lot of the Shriekback mix perspective comes from that. There is funk but it's mostly to do with reggae.

Mark: As a keyboard player, did it mean reinventing what you did, because you're not a bass player or a drummer?

Barry: Yes. Who's your role model going to be as a keyboard player? You had the tasteful rock'n'roll guys, Nicky Hopkins, Billy Preston, but you don't hear them very much, they're not heroes in the way that Keith Emerson is. I was thinking, "I'm not sure this is the path I know how to pursue – or could if I wanted to." So the reggae idea when you hear Bob Marley's keyboard player with these little tasteful things in there... You can't even hear one person in it; it's a collage of stuff.

Then there was the really stoned reggae thing where you're off your tits and what even is it? That inspired me a lot.

Interview conducted in Swindon 8 May 2018.

INSIDE THE HAUNTED BOX OF SWITCHES

The keyboardist's lot is a far from simple one, writes the Shriekback noisemaker as he traces his musical history from schoolboy pianist to XTC organ player and beyond

BY BARRY ANDREWS

Leaving to one side – only for the moment – the densely textured and fibrillating tale of Shriekback, I want to talk about the vexed topic of keyboard-playing in rock bands, which was what I started out doing, before the demon of Self-Expression possessed my ass: XTC, of course, Fripp's League of Gents and the troubled Iggy Pop album, *Soldier*. After that, apart from the odd session, I played keyboards only on things I had some aesthetic control over. Which meant I almost stopped playing keyboards altogether. By the early 80s (*My Spine*, *Lined Up*, etc), I didn't even own a keyboard any more (had to borrow Ian Caple's £30 Casio).

Interesting, eh? You bet. But you need some background.

Many keyboard players start out as piano players, as I did. The transition is an awkward one, I think, since you necessarily have to metamorphose from a classical music creature to a rock'n'roll one.

Jerry Lee Lewis didn't - oh, and Garth Hudson. They went from gospel to rock'n'roll, which is not such a leap but is rare in my experience (in the UK anyway).

Usually, your young pianist (who knows their way round the *Moonlight Sonata et al*, maybe had lessons) decides they want to be cool (uncoincidentally when the shagging hormones start kicking in) and tries to work out how to join a band. It's tricky, or it used to be: keyboards and their amplification are more expensive than drum kits and way more expensive than guitars and amps. So there is, straight away, a class/privilege scenario that colours things.

Q: Are the sort of bands led by the keyboards always going to be a bit poncy, lacking in that hungry, streetwise edge, because only kids from comfy backgrounds can afford keyboards? Discuss, mentioning prog rock and concluding with acid house.

And there's the question of motivation. Guitarists typically have to save up for (or steal) their first axe - they have to really want it. Piano players tend to slide into the role because - ever the big, intractable, heavy lump of furniture - the piano is just there. Once you've hidden inside it, slammed the lid down dangerously a few times and made the cat walk over the keys, you might as well learn to play the fucker. As you will see, my story was a bit of a hybrid of these tropes but is, I think, far from unusual.

In the spirit of gaining, then, a deeper understanding that will, I hope, transcend the (admittedly absorbing) personal psychodramas of Barry Andrews and ripple out to immerse some Universal Themes, here is an abridged preamble to my piano album of a few years ago, *Haunted Box of Switches*, which sets the terribly awkward scene...

Haunted Box of Switches

This is an album of piano pieces - songs and improvisations - that represents, for me, some kind of summation of nearly a lifetime's relationship with that instrument. My, there's portentous, but there it is. I feel towards the piano the kind of uncomfortable emotional ambivalence that characterises most people's relationships with their families, and, in some ways, the piano feels like just that: a family member.

You could say this record is like going on holiday, after a long absence, with a relative I knew well as a child. The feelings are deep ones but there's no way of knowing what we will mean to each other now. It will probably be a holiday fraught with Mike Leigh-style grisliness; snapshots that tell more than you want to know; maybe some tough home truths will emerge that only those who know you best can impart. Perhaps there will be wonderful things too. It will definitely be intense.

I use this comparison advisedly, since, as I will explain, the piano and my family have always been inextricably linked, and - families reliably being sources of both comfort and pain - it's not surprising that my personal pianistic voyage has covered similar territory.

It was, initially, not even an instrument I wanted to play. First of all, in my I-want-to-be-a-classical-composer days (six-seven years old, yeah I know, I am Lisa Simpson), I thought a violin would be the way to help me write those vast orchestral panoramas I saw as my destiny. Parents weren't keen. *So* unfair.

And when it was time to rock - well, you want to be the killer axe-man, don't you? With mighty power chords blazing from your electric pseudo-phallus as you prowl the stage, not some nerdy, site-tenacious furniture stroker. That wasn't going to happen either. It was too late: I could already play piano and I was in a hurry.

An aside: I remember reading somewhere Tom Waits talking about the piano "taking things indoors". Very true.

In a Simple Minds video in the 80s, the chaps were standing on a cliff, presumably in the Scottish Highlands, emphasising – rather too literally I feel – their affinity with things unspoilt and windswept and Mick MacNeil has his electric piano up there. Game over as far as I was concerned.

True, it would have been worse had it been a concert grand but, even so, pianos aren't wild – they don't live on cliffs – they're about bars, concert halls, drawing rooms – about civilisation with all its codes and constructs. It's fucking furniture, man - it's got history – and not very cool history either, born of the cerebral, Imperialist West with all its precocious technology (and with all its unforeseen consequences). Synchronous with, and dependent upon, the rise of organised capital. Exploitation, class and racial hierarchies intrinsic in its construction and its cultural deployment ("ebony and ivory," already!) That's a whole other story and well worth telling, though probably not by me.

Let's keep this personal. On my mum's side, everybody seemed to play piano. It seemed to be like driving is today, something you just did – no big deal. Grandad – who showed me – both mums' brothers, my cousin, even my mum (albeit covertly). They were the "We had to make our own entertainment *Roll out the Barrel* Spirit of the Blitz" generation. People "got round the piano" had "a good old sing-song". It seemed to be a sort of campfire substitute. The comforting sound of those sentimental 40s pop songs bashed out on the old Joanna was the necessary counterpoint to the air-raid siren and the eerie whine and eerier silence of the doodlebug.

I heard all this as bed-time stories and saw the vestige of this culture growing up in the early 60s, but the piano was now exiled into the "front room" (the shrine-room/museum of working-class English culture) and the songs now emanated from the radiogram: often Max Bygraves (*Singalongamax*, numbers 1 through 1,712) – same songs but with a smooth orchestral arrangement and Max's consoling, relaxed voice which even then I found insufferably bland but then I hadn't just survived the bloodiest conflict in the History of the World. I guess a bit of blandness sounded pretty good to them.

The other shift that this mass-media post-war moment seemed to produce was that the piano turned from a friendly convivial anyone-can-do-it machine to a High-ish Cultural Endeavour. By the time I was at school it had become "clever" to play the piano in my family like it would become "clever" to go to university or to quote things from books and that was the time when I first ran into it – in the front room at my nan and grandad's in West Norwood, South London. The fusty damp of that mausoleum; the big scary Victorian sculptures of cherubs killing dragons (payment in kind from old ladies grandad had done decorating work for) and the WH Barnes upright painted by grandad in shitty black stain inexplicably covering up the high-quality polish visible under the lid.

Grandad was perverse in many ways, as it goes. Despite my protestations, he always called me Bill, as, indeed, he also called my cousin Brian and my cousin Malcolm. I never found out why. He was a big grizzly old geezer who was a sergeant major during the first world war, inveterate card-cheat, slack carpenter, smoker of tarry and unstable roll-ups, German-hater even up to the 60s – he gave me (aged six) a good talking-to for my traitorous pleasure in a Fokker Triplane Airfix model – and, of course, old-skool pub pianist. He passed on his wisdom to the kids in a fine patriarchal way. Brian got snooker and I got the piano. *Oh Can You Wash Your Father's Shirt* (just the black notes) and *Old Man River* (one finger two octaves below middle C – mmm, growly).

That was it – all downhill from there on in. We moved to Swindon and I played whenever I could – in the backrooms of dad's working-man's club and, transgressively, on the out-of-bounds school piano, which taught me two things:

1) some pianos are much better than others
2) The Man doesn't like you getting your hands on the really good stuff.

I need hardly add that this prohibition made the school piano a subject of almost sexual longing.

I would have to wait a few years until Mr "Beaky" (enormous nose) Keen who, with genuine magnanimity, allowed me in the music room after school to play their fine instrument. I would sit there every night until the caretaker threw me out. Mr Keen also taught me as much as he could about orchestration which was the beginning of me thinking properly about the sound of things in the abstract (Mr Keen and Lee Scratch Perry – I wonder how they'd get on?) It's great when you get a Mr Keen, I always think, and heartening that almost everyone seems to have one.

But I digress. When I was 11, grandad died of a heart attack and left me the old WH Barnes Mean Machine. Ma and pa had it schlepped down to Swindon and it became my Place to Go (as well as a place to hide Special Things where my mum's unilateral cleaning programme could not legitimately disturb them). When I'd had a bad time at school; when I wanted to make up stories in my head and drift off with them; when I wanted to score my Meisterworks for unlimited orchestral forces or the humbler school orchestra, there I would be, bashing away, self-taught, unbridled Piano-Boy free at last.

But then came *rock* and it just wasn't loud enough. Dave Marx and his Gibson saw to that. I yearned for an instrument that would compete in the Rock Arena and eventually I got my first electric organ, the Crumar Group 49, and new realms opened to me. The world of the shrieking sustained note and the bowel-affecting drone were now accessible.

Where this all led, of course, is tangential to the present story, suffice to say that the piano – when I wasn't kicking it, breaking its keys, pushing it brutally around the stage and spray-painting it with vile slogans – was, in my recorded work, relegated to the role of self-parodic bit-player: little tasteful sprangs, fragments of highly stylised adornment and solos in heavy inverted commas were its contribution in the studio. It was like being ashamed of this remnant of childhood (of myself) in front of cool, new, multi-timbral friends. Organs and eventually poly-synths were about drugs, sex and rockist weirdness: awash with exotic possibilities; free of associations; up for anything. The piano was the past, my unexceptional roots: one boring sound that everybody knows and which is lumbered with the embarrassing emotions that have no place in a gifted, over-stimulated young maniac on his way to Unprecedented Things.

The songs on *Haunted Box...* are in four categories: Old Ones – if only to see what's left when you take all that production away; New Ones, because they're my favourites at the moment; Ones with No Other Homes to Go To – some of which I have never played to anyone before; and Made-up-on-the-Spot-Ones. The improvs are the sort of thing I do for myself usually, and particularly in those I found myself drifting back to that space of 38 years ago: using the piano as trance-machine, atmosphere producer, therapy. I include them as little sketches of moments – records of what my brain and hands did right then and there. Which is I guess what all of these tunes are – holiday snapshots left on the dunes till winter. It was a good holiday, actually. I'm smiling in this one...

To the memory of John (Jack) Langan 18 June 1888-22 November 1966

This article was first published at shriekbackmusic.tumblr.com

WHAT DO YOU CALL THAT NOISE?

Dave shows off the Fool, as played by Eric Clapton on Sunshine of Your Love.

TUNES OF GOOD

TUNES OF GOOD

Spending a day in the company of Dave Gregory for the most in-depth interview he has ever done gets two fans thinking about his contribution to the sound of XTC, from the high-energy solos of Drums and Wires to the magisterial arrangements of the orchestral years

BY MARK FISHER

Hugh Nankivell and I are sitting in a Swindon curry house trying to make sense of our day. It's heading for 9pm and we've been in the company of Dave Gregory since early afternoon. Having left his house, we've got something like six hours of conversation to digest. Neither of us is sure where to start.

We order our food.

"Did the experience of interviewing Dave change your perspective on his contribution or confirm your suspicions?" I say to Hugh.

"I think it does both," he replies. "It's clearer: the fact that he really takes care over everything he contributes – and that he thinks about both music and words. It was illuminating to see that care and attention he gave, how he hears a new song then works out what that song is and what it needs."

As well as his guitar parts, our conversation had focused on Dave's keyboard and orchestral arrangements, something he has scarcely been interviewed about despite their pivotal role in the XTC sound in everything from *Rocket from a Bottle* to *Washaway* and beyond. When a man has a collection of 80 guitars, it's easy to forget his musical interests go beyond one instrument. Yet where would recordings such as *I Remember the Sun*, *The Smartest Monkeys* and *Ballet for a Rainy Day* be without his input as an arranger?

In the studio years, it was a facility that allowed the group to expand its musical palette without having to bring in outside help. How many other guitarists could have risen to the challenge so capably? Hugh was particularly impressed by the musical notation Dave showed us – not only his neat hand but his distinct scoring for different instruments. His string quartet arrangement for *1000 Umbrellas* does not look like the tentative work of a beginner, but an assured debut, brimming with confidence.

"He's clearly paying attention to what the words are doing and finding parts that fit that and work with the chords to do interesting things," says Hugh, laughing at Dave's story about playing cello in the school orchestra and being thrown into the deep end with Peter Warlock's *Capriol Suite*. "The conductor was completely mad to think they could play it, but actually it was a good experience for Dave. It had a big impact upon him."

Big enough, perhaps, to have the confidence many years later to write scores for professional players – something he continues to do to this day.

As a working musician himself, Hugh was interested in Dave's role as a musical intermediary, neither the songwriter nor the producer and yet someone who contributed immeasurably to how the recordings turned out. In a culture that likes its auteurs, do we have an adequate way of acknowledging that contribution? You only have to witness the list of iconic names reeled off in TC&I's *Greatness* to see how much we like the idea of the solitary creative genius. But in our rush to acclaim the Spielbergs, the Gershwins and the McCartneys, do we neglect those who have helped fulfil their artistic quest? Couldn't you argue that a recording is "composed" by everyone who works on it? "Having talked to Dave, I'm more sympathetic," says Hugh. "Especially to think how much time he spent, for example on getting the solo right on *That Wave*, which he's clearly very proud of. That role in-between the initial songwriting invention and the final production mix is where Dave lives."

When I speak to Andy Partridge later in the year, he agrees: "Huge respect to him," says Andy. "He may not be able to write songs, but his solos and the way he constructs parts within a song are as creative as anything. They just come from a different angle. I'm coming from the west pole and he's coming from the east pole. Dave is very different but equally creative. People say to me, 'You're the creative one behind the band,' but no, Dave is coming up with creative ideas in the detail and the execution."

He adds: "I've come to really respect Dave's contributions over the years. When you're in the eye of the hurricane you don't think about what anyone in the band does. They're just one of the lads and that's their thing. When you get some distance from it, you think, 'God, he was really good, the way he invented those phrases and that arrangement.' Dave just likes music. It's his *raison d'être*. He's got the right *d'être* covered in raisins - and chocolate as well."

This chimes with comments Colin Moulding made in issue seven of *Limelight* about Dave's contribution to the songs he and Andy presented him. "Gregsy spends hours painstakingly deciding which chord to play at a certain place, which is really good," said Colin. "If he's got to polish a turd as far as me and Partridge's songs go, it gets us out of a tight spot. I'm just glad that he's competent and that conscientious to do that after all these years."

In an email, no less a figure than Peter Gabriel adds his praise. "I have been a fan of XTC and their songwriting in particular, and it was Steve Lillywhite who suggested that Dave Gregory would have something to add to the third album," he says. "Dave was a great musician and easy to work with so I have good memories of the experience."

I also talk to Daniel Steinhardt, Dave's colleague in Tin Spirits for ten years until the band's amicable split in the autumn of 2018. He confirms Hugh's analysis. "Dave Gregory is such a creative soul, but he is a facilitator," says the guitarist. "When he gets a whiff of an idea, he takes it and does amazing things with it. I've been playing with him for ten years, at least once a week, and I still couldn't tell you how he does what he does. I love the way Andy recognised in Dave someone who would add to the process. He wasn't just after a painter of sounds, which so many people who are purely creative might have been drawn to; he recognised in Dave someone who could expand on these ideas and take them to a new place."

Dave's combination of inventiveness and technical dexterity continues to astound Steinhardt. "It's amazing, spending as long as I have with Dave and watching so closely to try and work out where his bent is for certain harmonies and I'm still clueless," he says. "In a middle of a chord change he'll just pull out something. I think it comes from spending years round Andy and Andy not wanting Dave to play anything obvious, Dave always having to search and reach quite deep, and always managing to pull out the goods. As great a guitar player as Dave is, it can be no bad thing being in a band with one of the greatest songwriters ever."

François Ribac is another collaborator with Dave. He brought him in to play three live dates in 2013 and work on *Into the Green*, his 2017 album with Eva Schwabe. He is in awe of Dave's musical precision. Ribac discovered that whatever guitar sound he had in mind - say, a track from a King Crimson album - Dave would have an opinion about it. "He is always working with the background of the sounds of pop music," says Ribac. "I asked him to look at this song with a very saturated guitar. I had in mind the sound of Robert Fripp at the end of *Islands* when he does this very fuzzy solo. When we started to rehearse, he played something for me with very sophisticated plans to put this pedal before that one, the distortion before the wah-wah, and so on. He was completely OK to go to the Robert Fripp sound and try to sound exactly the same. What is fascinating is the sound he made when we went into the studio was absolutely not the same as Robert

Fripp, because it was just a place to start. I love that. Many musicians would say, 'I am not here to imitate somebody,' but the bigger they are, they don't care. They say, 'It's good to listen to that.' At the end, it sounds completely Dave. It doesn't sound like an imitation of King Crimson."

When they played live, they covered George Harrison's *All Things Must Pass*, attempting to emulate the Phil Spector sound. "Dave was perfect for that because he came with his pop dictionary about the sound of the guitars, recent sounds and how to put all those things together," says Ribac. "I was impressed by Dave's discipline. He says music is everything for him. It means he's always at the rehearsal on time, the guitar is tuned and his concentration is always at the top. He always listens to what you ask and has an incredible modesty. What's most important to him is to get the sound to be precise. When he doesn't play well, when one note in one chord is flat or when there is a little feedback... for him everything has to be perfect. This perfection is always dynamic, smiley, very intense. I have rarely worked with somebody who can be so professional and creative."

You can learn a lot about Dave just from sitting in the living room of his modest suburban house. He's a man whose cultural interests go from near to far, from music to comedy, from art to industry. Look around and you'll detect something of the open-minded globalism of *Jason and the Argonauts*, the home-grown railway imagery of *Train Running Low on Soul Coal* and the silly humour of the Dukes of Stratosphear. And his love of music is everywhere. On the walls are prints of steam engines, a historical map of the world and a framed poster of 30-odd electric and acoustic guitars. There's a piece of African art covering the fireplace (just beneath a signed card from Japan wishing "*arigato*" – or "thank you" – to the Tin Spirits) and a stuffed *South Park* figure on top of a bookcase. On the shelves, you'll see titles such as *Rolling Stones Gear, Mellotron, Hendrix Experience, The Beatles* (by Hunter Davies), *Glyn Johns Sound Man* and *The Black Strat*. There's also an Italian dictionary and a stack of magazines that he can't quite bring himself to throw away ("It has to stay in the house for a certain amount of time to get my value for money!")

Not far from the two amps – one a recent acquisition from a local auction house – is a towering pile of DVDs, among them releases by the Rutles and Dave's band Big Big Train, and one about Swindon. Although his six shelves of vinyl in the adjacent room are meticulously ordered, alphabetically by artist and then chronologically by release date, he admits the papers on his desk are usually a chaotic mess. In a sign of the times, there are five remote controls balanced on the arm of his couch.

Dave himself is looking younger than his 64 years, with his full head of hair and trim figure. Wearing moccasins, jeans and a green jumper, he switches swiftly into storytelling mode, with his keen memory, sharp eye and wry sense of humour. Because of his diabetes, he stops once to check his blood-sugar levels, but remains relaxed and attentive throughout. He seems to enjoy it as much as we do. For our chat today, he's dug out his old XTC manuscripts to refresh his memory. Some are simple chord progressions, others four-part arrangements, all hand written. "It's ancient history now," he says. "Being a Virgo, I'm an inveterate list maker. I love making lists. Maybe I should have been a librarian and honed my filing skills."

The conversation ranges from melody to dissonance, from musical notation to taking instruments apart, from improvisation to the Dukes of Stratosphear. Later Dave says it's the "best - and longest! - interview" he's ever done.

GANGWAY, ELECTRIC GUITAR IS COMING THROUGH
Instruments, influence and analysis

Hugh Nankivell: I work with kids and in care homes, helping other people to make music. I met a boy recently who was four. If you gave him any instrument, for instance a drum, he would get a stethoscope and listen to it. You gave him a ukulele and he would take all the strings off. You gave him a xylophone, he would take all the bars off and see if he could fit them all inside. In one of the XTC books, you say that when you get a guitar, the first thing you do is take it to pieces. I wondered how similar you were to this lad. When you get something new – a new song from Andy or Colin, just as much as a new guitar or a Mellotron – to what extent do you need to understand it before you can do anything with it?

Dave Gregory: That is a very insightful question and one that hadn't even occurred to me. But now you come to mention it, that probably does apply. I do like to immerse myself in whatever it is I'm involved with. If it's something I'm passionate about, I have to be totally immersed in it in order to understand what its function is, what its purpose is. If it's a song, where it's going, what the intention is. If it's vintage guitars, they have to be dismantled to clean them. Most of the ones I buy second hand are in dreadful shape and have to be restored. If it's a new guitar and it's set up properly, I usually just leave it alone – and smell it from time to time! I do like to smell things. The Mellotron was a curious piece of electro-mechanical hardware.

Hugh: When you got it, did you want to look inside?

Dave: Yes – and did, because there were problems with it. It's always needed a new motor; I used to have to set it up and let it run for an hour before we could use it. Most of the heads are wearing out and it needs a thorough overhaul. But I did sample every one of the tapes and keys into this Emulator 20 years ago; that worked great and stayed in tune. The problem with the Mellotron was that with a big, five-finger chord, the flywheel would slow down and the pitch would drop. It was fine with single notes and two-note chords – and a two-note chord on a Mellotron is a big sound. Often, there's just enough magic there. The R&D costs and the transport costs make me wonder how they ever made it a business. It would have been laughed out of *Dragons' Den*! You've got 36 repro heads – 36 of the bloody things! They all have to be individually soldered and wired to the amplifier. Then this series of wooden keys with a rubber roller on physically press the tape onto the repro head as this flywheel is going round dragging the tape across only to be retrieved by a giant spring after eight seconds. I think, "Well, if that's what it takes," because it's a really emotional sound. It's a good job I never had a Hammond organ because, again, I would have had to dismantle it. I still don't know where that big old sound comes from.

Hugh: Was that interest in how sounds are made from a very early age with you?

Dave: Yes, I think it probably was. I remember when I was very small hearing somebody like Edmundo Ros on the radio. There was a guy playing guitar and I didn't know what it was. It was some kind of jazzy, plummy sound. I asked my dad, "What instrument is that?" He scowled. "Sounds like an electric guitar."

Ah! Electric! Guitar! Those two words. I just thought, "Wow! Is it dangerous? What could it possibly be?" There was always a curiosity about where sounds came from.

One of the scariest sounds I remember hearing that I couldn't figure out – and it always used to freak me out when it came on the radio but I loved it – was on *Johnny Remember Me* by John Leyton, a Joe Meek production. It's the girl's voice singing, "Johnny Remember Me," in this echo chamber. That was something else I asked my dad about. "Sounds like an echo chamber."

"Echo... chamber! Where can you get one? That's really spooky."

Music was just... I couldn't imagine life without it. It's always there. Fortunately, my parents loved music. There was always music in the house. I had my dad hammering away at the piano. He had a collection of shellac 78s, all classical with a little bit of opera. There was also the *Oklahoma!* soundtrack on three 78s. I loved those songs and they probably introduced me to the importance of melody. Every single song on that collection is a gem. It's like an aural tonic.

In the 1950s, there wasn't very much to listen to on the radio. The BBC was still a stuffy, post-war organisation that didn't like pop music, not that there was much of it. Rock'n'roll was still in its early stages, skiffle was a joke. I don't think I would have embraced skiffle, but I know that if I'd heard Little Richard and Chuck Berry at the age of seven or eight, it would have turned my head a lot sooner than it eventually did. Up to that point I was listening mainly to classical music, then my mum and dad sent me off to piano lessons - I was eight or nine - which I enjoyed to a point. About ten or eleven, I started being aware of pop music and electric guitars. Then eventually the Beatles came and the ball was over the wall.

STRINGS FOR A DAY
Scoring for keyboards and orchestra

Hugh: For you, were music and manuscripts interlinked from an early age?

Dave: Absolutely, because I learned to read music virtually as I was learning to read and write. I still find writing out charts laborious, which is why I tend to shy away from it now. If people ask me, I'll say, "I'll do you a string arrangement, but it's going to cost money." That usually scares them off. But after XTC had done a couple of drum and guitar-based albums, we all felt we needed to progress. I started to get back into playing the piano because the studios we were working in had wonderful state-of-the-art grand pianos, way better than anything I'd ever played. To sit at the keyboard, play some simple chords and hear this big, rich sound reignited my interest. Around the time of *English Settlement* or even by the time we'd finished *Black Sea*, I was thinking it was time we thought about more keyboards. We had a little synthesiser we used to carry on the road for sound effects, but I wanted to work more with the piano. On the *English Settlement* sessions, we went to the Manor and had a lot more time to muck about. We had things like *Blame the Weather* and a lot of piano on the album itself, enough to broaden our palette. Once I'd got the idea of sitting behind the piano, I started scratching out charts so I wouldn't forget what I'd decided to play.

Hugh: What did Andy and Colin say?

Dave: They just took it on board and said, "Yeah, that's great, Gregs." It was usually Colin who was more amenable to my input because his demos weren't as finished as Andy's. Even in the days before Andy had a studio, he had a four-track cassette Portastudio and that would mean he'd pretty much have the whole thing scratched out, although in the days when we still rehearsed as a band, lots of stuff got changed and I was able to contribute a lot more. But because Colin's songs weren't as fully developed, it gave me a lot more scope.

Mark Fisher: I'm remembering back to the first time I heard *Blame the Weather* and thinking it doesn't sound very like XTC - in a good, creative way because it sounded like a whole new palette. Did it feel like an experiment?

Dave: Yes, it was and it was also a test of my ability. Did I have sufficient skills at the keyboard to cut a record? I hadn't factored in the fact that you can drop in and out in the studio and, as long as the engineer knows where the in-and-out points are, it makes life a lot easier. You don't have to learn an entire piece and perform it perfectly from start to finish.

Hugh: Did you play all the piano on *English Settlement*?

Dave: Yes, but there isn't very much on *English Settlement*. *Mummer* has a lot more keyboards generally.

Hugh: So that tiny bit of piano on *Runaways*?

Dave: Oh yes, that's not me, actually, that's Colin. I think that's the only time he played piano. My one big contribution on *English Settlement* was the pretend marimba on *It's Nearly Africa*. Andy had this highlife scrubby guitar and was singing this song with this odd devil's interval in the melody. I thought, "It's nearly Africa, so let's get a sound that's nearly African." I sat down and worked out this jolly little melody on the Prophet synthesiser marimba.

The other big change was the 12-string Rickenbacker. It's a big part of the sound of that record. That was one of those new toys that you couldn't stop playing with. It's such a lovely sound. I'd been looking for one since before we did *Black Sea*. On the first American tour I did, I went shopping for a Rickenbacker but was distracted by a Gibson Firebird and that was all my spending money gone, so the Rickenbacker had to wait for another year. It'd be interesting to know what *Black Sea* might have sounded like with a 12-string. It's very much a rock record, though, so it's probably just as well I held off.

Hugh: Back to the question of you taking something apart. Because you read and write music and the others didn't, when you heard a new song by Andy or Colin, do you think your mental processes were quite different from theirs? Were you analysing it in terms of chord relationships and melodies?

Dave: Yes. They were fortunate in that they weren't schooled musicians. They didn't have a set of rules. They went on instinct. From a creative point of view, that's liberating. I would always think, "I don't know about that chord change. That's not going to work. How can we make that work?" There weren't very many instances like that, but occasionally I'd think, "Oh, that harmony's wrong there." But, of course, that's part of the essence of XTC for a lot of people – the dissonance. It took me a while to accept it, because I did feel that, rightly or wrongly, part of my role was to straighten things out. I liked the spikiness of Andy's approach and his deliberately off-the-straight-and-narrow approach. He'd make a point of being eccentric. I'd always be thinking, "This is a great song, if only I could smooth those hard edges off and round some of those nasty spikes," which I think I probably did.

Hugh: Can you think of examples where you did that?

Dave: We didn't actually come to blows. There was never any serious falling out about how we arranged the songs. We all fell in with each other. It's something that's overlooked: the guys who wrote the songs would always get the credit in parenthesis under the song title on the record. So everyone would think, "This is a good song. Who wrote this? Oh, it's an Andy song or a Colin song." In order to get that song on the record the way it is requires performance from more than just one person. The idea – yeah, that's great. But the record – that's the band. The performances of the individuals are often overlooked.

It sounds like I'm blowing my own trumpet, but in some cases there were performances that defined how the song sounded in its finished state. Without wishing to take any credit away from anyone (because without the initial spark of creativity, there'd be nothing), to get it in a finished state requires not just me, but the drummer, the producer and engineer... They have to hear what's going on and blend it like a chef would with sauces to make the finished product palatable. For example, with *Yacht Dance*, I decided to play the nylon-strung guitar part that I wrote from scratch. Hugh Padgham got it straight away and I think we got it down in a couple of passes. That guitar almost defines the song. I often felt Andy could have offered me a co-write on that.

Hugh: That's the key question about this conversation because there are other moments where you've done string arrangements on *1000 Umbrellas* and *Rook* that crucially add significantly to the song.

Dave: *Rook*, to be fair, was Andy's. I just scored out what he'd demoed. I can't take credit for that, but certainly I did most of the work on *Wrapped in Grey*

> *'Electric! Guitar! Those two words. Wow! Is it dangerous? What could it possibly be?'*

and *Dear God*, which was never credited because, of course, it wasn't on the original pressing of *Skylarking*. But I think everyone knows those are my string arrangements on *1000 Umbrellas* and I've actually got a lot of work as a result of that. I've had a couple of well-paid gigs, although people might feel short-changed because in most cases I haven't had a song as good as *1000 Umbrellas* with which to work. There's a couple of exceptions: Pugwash did a song called *A Rose in a Garden of Weeds* and I was very happy with that. We did that at Abbey Road and it was one of my favourite string sessions. Thomas Walsh is a really good songwriter and the song was a joy to work on - and, God bless him, he paid me.

But, yes, it's a shame it's always the singer-songwriter who gets all the attention. For example, David Bowie: a great artist, the way he developed from the shy fellow I remember in the 60s, who wasn't very good, and eventually blossomed into this amazing artist. But then again, look at the help he had. There was a guitar player called Carlos Alomar who was brilliant. I just thought, "Well, why doesn't this guy get any credit at all?" His name's on all the records, he worked with Bowie for years, but nobody has ever said what a fantastic job he did. That's just one example. Richard Tandy in the Electric Light Orchestra must have done most of the arranging for Jeff Lynne, I would think, during his time. My girlfriend is a big ELO fan and I said, "Do you know who Richard Tandy is?" She said, "Richard Tandy? Hmm. Go on."

DEAR TODD
Playing Clapton on That's Really Super, Supergirl

Hugh: I've been reading Brian Eno's *A Year with Swollen Appendices* (the appendices are little essays) and he talks about his role when working on a record: is he a producer or a co-composer? Talking Heads is a good example. He became the fifth composer in *Remain in Light* and was credited on the sleeve. But he said the role of producer will involve composition, social melding, being an engineer, a whole range of things, and if he's being commissioned to be a producer and in advance that's very clear, he won't then ask for a composing credit. He says the important thing is the conversation in advance.

But in a band it's very different, isn't it, because in your case, Andy and Colin write the songs and for most of your career, there was only you as the extra person. When you then compose an extraordinary guitar solo in the middle of *That's Really Super, Supergirl*, you think, "Well, surely that is as much of the sound world of that piece as the lyrics and the harmonies and the melodies."

Dave: And it's interesting you chose that song because all the keyboard work was done by Todd Rundgren. That whole arrangement is Todd's. But, thank you for the compliment. I always liked that little solo. It was written specifically for that song. But to claim a co-write for a 20-second solo? I don't know.

Hugh: Andy is up-front about saying you went and squirrelled yourself away in your lodge over quite a long time. Didn't you have a special guitar you were playing on?

Dave: Todd Rundgren had Eric Clapton's old Gibson SG - the psychedelic painted one, the Fool, which Todd used to refer to as Sunny because Clapton played it on *Sunshine of Your Love*. It had been an iconic thing for me. When I started playing guitar, I'd see Eric Clapton with his perm, his kaftan and this psychedelic guitar just pouring out this liquid honey, beautiful solos. It was such an inspirational instrument. So I walked into Todd's studio and there it was, sitting on a stand, neglected in the control room. It actually had acoustic guitar bronze-wound strings. I said to Todd, "Do you mind if I change the strings before I play this solo?" And he was like, "Why do you want to do that?"

He reluctantly allowed me to change them but, of course, once I had the strings off, I was able to look inside. A lot of stuff had been changed on it over the years. It was damaged; there was a big split in the body, because those SGs are quite thin. There's a common fault in all of them, over time, where if you hammer the jacket socket with any force, it'll cause a split where the cavity is at the back for the controls. That had happened. You could have snapped it off if you were determined enough, so I had to treat it with extreme care.

I took some photographs and I just sort of smelt it and thought, "This guitar – the stories it could tell! This is just a 20-second solo; I'm going to make the most of every note." That's one of the highlights of that entire trip.

Hugh: Which I gather was quite fraught...

Dave: It was for Andy and it was for Todd, but for me it was the best adventure. I was such a huge fan of Todd Rundgren. Listening to him, listening to Stevie Wonder, listening to Donald Fagen... the way they arranged chords, the shapes, those wonderful major ninths, all of those keyboard chords, those glorious, uplifting harmonies... that saw me through the miserable 80s. I thought the 80s were a disgrace for pop music. I've been watching the *Top of the Pops* re-reruns from 1984/85 and it's like, "For God's sake, did the Beatles never happen? What is going on? And what did we look like?"

Hugh: Back briefly to *That's Really Super, Supergirl*, as you were saying, Todd is the producer and therefore he was being paid and, presumably gets royalties, whereas you wrote that solo – you're "writing" that and yet the song is "written" by Andy Partridge.

Dave: He's credited as the writer, yes. Well, I know that bands have fallen out and split up because of stuff like this. I didn't feel it was fair on the writers to be muscling in on their work. That's how I saw it. Without the songs, there'd be nothing. They were providing me with the most ideal scenario in which to work as a guitarist or even as a keyboard player. What a luxury to have these songs to work on, because they were really original. We didn't have a big hit to have to follow up. There was never any of that, "Oh, you've got to make it sound more like *Senses Working Overtime*," or whatever it might be.

There was nothing that was sufficiently massive enough to define what the XTC sound was. We were free to be as imaginative as we could be.

Hugh: That's very generous of you. You're right about bands splitting up. The Smiths went to war with each other over the role the bass and drums played. Then U2 is the famous one where they divide all their royalties five ways – the four members and the manager – for everything. In one way it makes complete sense and in another people go, "But he's the manager!" But Bono said something like, "Yes, but we wouldn't exist if it wasn't for what he has done."

Dave: This is the difference: he's a good manager. We had one guy who deserved the job description of manager and that was Tarquin Gotch. In the short time he was with us, he got us out of this horrible shithole of a law suit we were going through. That whole business could have finished us, not just as a band but as individuals. We could have all been put into bankruptcy. He had great connections here and in the United States, he was well liked and he knew how to get the records onto playlists legitimately. He was a good motivator and, basically, a nice guy.

Tarquin was convinced he could convince Andy to put the band back on the road and tour. He very nearly did succeed. He did, at least, get Andy over to the States to do the Letterman show. In fact, had it been one of Andy's songs, I think he would have refused to have gone. Because it was Colin's song, *King for a Day*, Colin said, "What Letterman? Bloody hell, yeah!" And I said, "I'm happy to do that as well."

We said, "Look, they've got the studio band. All we've got to do is show up and play our parts and sing. Couldn't be easier, could it? No stage fright there."

That probably helped sell *Oranges and Lemons* because the album did really well. It bailed us out of this awful financial misery we were mired in.

Hugh: It's been really interesting to talk to you because of what your role is. What percentage has your contribution been?

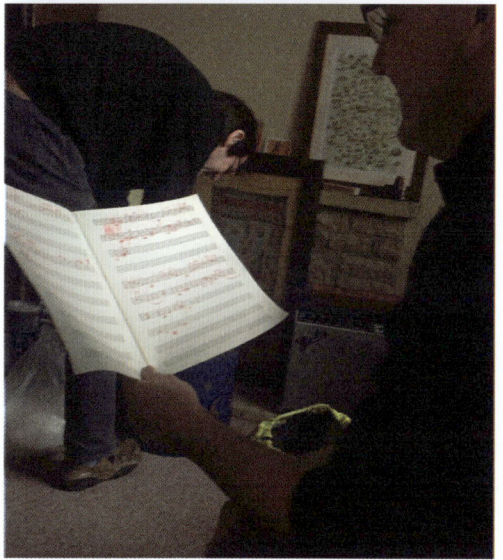

Hugh studies Dave's scores: "It's a compositional way of thinking."

Dave: It would vary from song to song. Going back to Todd Rundgren, *Skylarking* is as much his album as it is ours. He had such a hands-on approach to the point that he constructed it from Andy's demos. It was his concept. It works as an album and I would say it was 50% him and 50% the rest of us. But it does vary from project to project. And some producers had more input than others.

REHEARSING FOR THE BIG SQUARE WORLD
Demos, sessions, and collective creation

Hugh: What leeway did you have? Did you ever suggest to Colin or Andy changing a lyric?

Dave: No. Should have done!

Hugh: Would either of them have responded if you had?

Dave: Actually, I didn't generally have a problem with Andy's lyrics. Andy was a very intelligent lyric writer. I was quite astounded at some of the things – he is a brilliant poet. But, then again, he came up with this song called *Obscene Procession*. Good melody but the picture it painted was unpalatable to me. I just thought, "Why would you want to sing this awful, horrible... Why would you want to paint this picture?"

Hugh: As a fan of XTC, I've always wondered why Andy and Colin didn't write together. You think about Lennon/McCartney. A good chunk of their writing was separate but they always credited each other. They would share them with each other first and even if one of them only changed one word, it was usually a very good one, or supporting someone when they were feeling unsure. That would have been an interesting thing for Andy and Colin, but they clearly never did. All three of you had different roles in arranging material, but if you didn't feel you could comment on the words, could you have commented on the harmonies or the chords or the melody?

Dave: When we rehearsed as a band, this would occur quite naturally. There might be a chord movement, you might hear the implication of a

G major 7 chord and I would play a G major 9, so that would give it a more jazzy feel. As long as no one said, "I don't like that," it stayed in. We'd play together until it sounded comfortable to all of us. Very rarely did anyone say, "I don't like what you're doing. Can you change it?" It did happen once or twice. We used to have this shorthand. We'd say, "Are you happy with your part?" And then you'd have to think, "Oh my God, what will I do now?"

Of course, as time went on, Andy's demos became more and more fleshed out and finished, the opportunities for events like that diminished. There was less and less for me to do. Colin never really had a home studio and anything more than basic recording equipment. He wouldn't go into the same detail that Andy did.

Hugh: Would you say that's his nature?

Dave: You have to remember he's the bass player. He was a great bass player and that's what he did best. He could strum an acoustic guitar and he could sing, but he wasn't a keyboard player and he wasn't a guitarist and, without wishing to be patronising, he knew his place. He was happy to say, "Here's the latest thing I've written and it goes like this," and off we'd go. We'd sit around and play along with it until we all had our parts down.

I remember with *Sacrificial Bonfire*, he wrote that diddle-diddle-ding bom-bom part and I played it on the record. He did have sufficient knowledge of the guitar to be able to write specific parts. It took a while, but it came eventually. Also the odd voicings of *Dying* – those two acoustic guitars playing a slightly dissonant harmony (if that's not a contradiction in terms) – he figured that out with an odd tuning. So he did get more adventurous as time went by. In terms of getting it on the record, he was quite happy for me to play the parts and more willing to share than Andy was.

On the *Apple Venus* sessions his songs sound a little separated from the general feeling of that album. Although I wasn't there for all of it, I did a lot of the basics. Andy did very little to the songs that Colin had written, to the extent that I think on *Fruit Nut* and certainly *Frivolous Tonight*, I played everything apart from the bass, drums and singing. All the instrumental parts are mine. Andy was wrapped up in his own stuff.

Hugh: Did you determine your own parts in the sense that you wrote them?

Dave: Yes, certainly the piano on *Frivolous Tonight*. Colin had written it on acoustic guitar and I said, "This is like a pub song. Why don't we try it with a jangle-box piano, like an old upright, nothing too posh?" He liked the feel of it, so it stemmed from there. That became the flavour of the song.

I WOULD HAVE MADE THIS INSTRUMENTAL
Solos, tuning and improvisation

Hugh: So you felt your role with the group was that you could affect the flavour, at times considerably, at other times less so.

Dave: Yes. In fact, if you think about it, Andy's guitar sound didn't change from *White Music* pretty much until the *Nonsuch* period. It's always this spiky, scratchy... it doesn't have a lot of tone or body to it.

He did become very good at playing acoustic guitar and he's just a brilliant rhythm player. He has an amazing sense of rhythm, very tight and absolutely in the pocket.

As time went on, he began to appreciate more and more the power of perfect tuning. If any instrument is only slightly out of tune, the impact would be lessened – monumentally in some cases. There's nothing more pleasing to the ear than a perfectly tuned instrument playing a loud chord. It's part of the learning process. If you listen to the original mix of *Drums and Wires*, the guitars are all over the show tuning-wise. It has a certain charm.

But Andy didn't have this love of guitars that I have. He still has the same three or four instruments. I think he's added a couple more since I quit.

Hugh: He talks about using his daughter's first guitar for *Church of Women*.

Dave: Yes, and he wrote the entire *Big Express* album, I think, on that little guitar by tuning the guitar to a chord, though it wasn't used on the record. As time went by, I gathered more and more instruments, so I'd bring them into the studio because I couldn't wait to get them on record. I got my first proper Gibson Les Paul when we were recording *Skylarking*, but right at the end of the sessions when there wasn't much more left to play. I used it on *Dear God* and *Extrovert*. But after *Skylarking*, and certainly during the Dukes of Stratosphear period when it was like, "Bring all your toys in, we're going to have some fun now," that wouldn't have happened without the plethora of instruments and effects pedals that I had at my disposal.

Having said that, Andy has a guitar style. He's a great guitarist. He just works with the instruments he's always had, in some cases since before the band was signed. I'm thinking now of *Burning with Optimism's Flames* where there was a little break in the middle that became a guitar solo. It was just this odd rhythm clomping along and he dropped in this gorgeous highlife-meets-jazz picked solo. You can almost hear his brain working as he's going through it. I don't think he had anything written. It was just, "Can you play some guitar to connect this chorus to the next verse, Andy?" I know it's one of Andy's favourite songs and a lot of it has to do with the guitars, how they work together.

Hugh: In *That's Really Super, Supergirl*, you went away, wrote the solo, brought it back in. And I know you weren't playing that stuff live, but presumably if you had been, you would have played that solo because you composed it. Did Andy do almost the opposite – was the solo on *Optimism's Flames* improvised in the studio?

Dave: It was improvised in the studio, but it became such an integral part of the song that when we played it live, I would play it. His part was basically the chops that sit with the drums and is the rhythm track. Obviously, if he took a solo that would vanish, so it was given to me to play live. When we were compiling the *Black Sea* liner notes, I went back to my diaries and noticed that he used my amplifier to play the solo in the studio. It must have been set up and he just plugged his guitar into it. That's how it used to be. It was the line of least resistance with Andy and guitars. He didn't spend a fraction of the time on his guitar playing as he did on his vocals. He'd just look for the nearest amp. It probably was done on the spur of the moment with the closest thing to hand. Once he's switched on, just take advantage of the fact that he's in create-mode. Record everything because there's going to be some magic moments.

It was the same on stage when he'd take a guitar solo. On YouTube there's a thing we did in Paris when we were promoting *Drums and Wires*. In an encore we played *This Is Pop*. Again, there's a little guitar break between the end of the first chorus and the second verse. Every time, it was slightly different. I'd forgotten all about this performance but it's a little piece of genius that I doubt he could play again. He couldn't learn to play it. He just happened to be in that mood at that moment.

Mark: Yet I don't think of XTC being an improvisatory band. Andy talked about the live sound being tightly connected to the records.

Dave: Yes, I preferred it that way. I get too flustered on stage to be relied upon to do something brilliant. It might happen, but more often than not, it won't, so why not stick to what you know, don't take any risks? We used to do *Battery Brides* live and that was always a big tour-de-force rally as a guitarist. Sometimes it worked, sometimes it didn't. I reckon it was a 60/40 failure rate, but the 40% could be transcendent. A lot of that would depend on me rattling away at this arpeggiated thing through a Roland JC-120 amp with a fast vibrato setting so it sounded like a synthesiser. My job was to play these fifths and octaves in G while Andy did his thing. Sometimes it would go on for weeks and my hand would be, "Finish this now!"

Mark: On the Steven Wilson *Black Sea* remix there are two songs you recorded in Swindon Town Hall – *Travels in Nihilon* and *Living Through Another Cuba* – where it sounds like the songs emerged through jamming. I don't know if that's true, but that doesn't seem to be typical of the way the band worked.

Dave: No, it wasn't, because then it would be starting to get closer to "ra-wk", bands that spent all their time on stage wailing their guitars which is not what we were about. *Travels in Nihilon* was one guitar riff and this dissonant melody over the top. I loved it. Andy did actually write most of it himself.

Mark: The other one that seemed to have been even more exciting live was *All Along the Watchtower*.

Dave: We did play it on the very last tour. I don't know why we decided to do that. I was playing Prophet synthesiser and trying to duplicate what Barry Andrews was playing.

Hugh: When you took over from Barry did you feel you needed to be like him?

Dave: This is so typical of XTC: they didn't do anything that people expected them to do. They'd replace a quirky, eccentric keyboard player with an R&B guitarist. When they asked me to audition I crammed my head with the first two albums. All I had at the time was a Stratocaster and a Gibson 335. I took those in and a little 20W Fender Tremolux amplifier - no reverb, just a vibrato channel. I guess they thought, "We know how he plays. He's not going to sound like Barry. Besides, any keyboard player is going to be compared with Barry, so why don't we just struggle on with the old stuff and redesign the band?" Very brave of them.

I wasn't sure, even after they offered me the job, how long it was going to last. I thought they'd have to either replace me with a keyboard player or get a keyboard player in. I wasn't even sure how long the band was going to last because at that point they hadn't had any hits. They'd made two albums and I knew the record company was desperate for the band to succeed. It was like the *Drums and Wires* period and my joining was a last-ditch attempt to get the band a hit record. It was never said in so many words, but that was the impression I got.

We did *Life Begins at the Hop* and met Steve Lilywhite and Hugh Padgham. They were brilliant. The pair of them really helped us. We jumped two or three rungs of the ladder as a result of working with

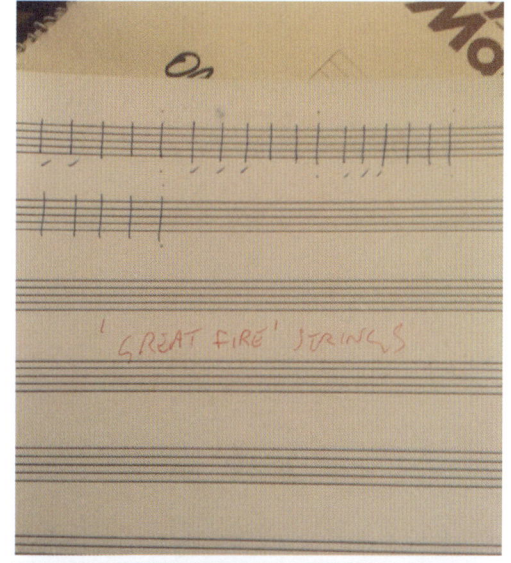

Bring water: string parts for Great Fire and the arrangement for The Man Who Sailed Around His Soul.

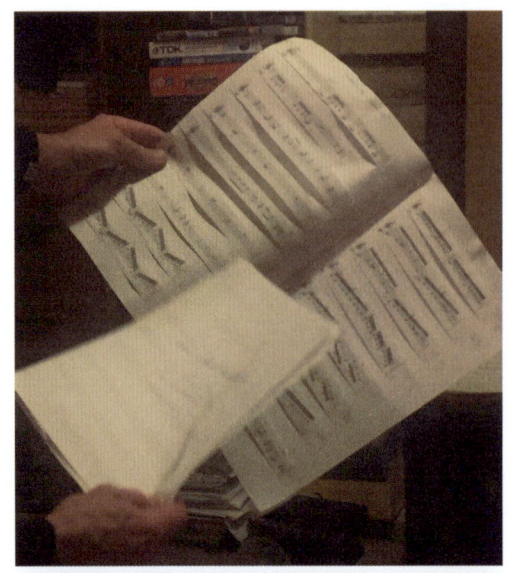

"He's clearly finding parts that work with the chords to do interesting things."

those guys because they had the contemporary sound in their ears. They knew what was going on and could hear the potential of the songs and what we could do. The fact we did *Drums and Wires* in a little over a fortnight and it was mixed in four days is quite an achievement. But I didn't feel threatened by Barry because they never said to me, "You must play like this," or, "He's played this here, can you do something that's as close as you can get to it." There were a few disgruntled fans but not enough to make a huge difference.

PERMANENT MORGASM
That Wave and the pleasure of playing

Hugh: In *Complicated Game*, Andy describes working out the bass part for *Mayor of Simpleton*, which he says he very rarely did. For you, how different did you feel being told what to play as opposed to making it up yourself – a creative role as opposed to a re-creative role?

Dave: He didn't instruct me that much. We fell into a pattern of me reacting to what he would throw at me and, as long as he didn't object, then it would stick. There were a few times when he definitely didn't like what I did. One was the original solo I played on *That Wave*. I skimmed through my diary last night and apparently I'd done two improvised solos. I was trying to improvise around these odd chord movements (it's a G minor 6 thing, then a B flat thing). I got something down on tape that we were OK with, then on the last day, Andy took me to one side and said, "I don't like these solos you've played. Can't you do something I'd like?" I said, "No. I've already struggled with this over the last couple of weeks. I've had enough of it. I don't want to even think about it." He said: "Oh, well, we're going to mix next week. I'd really rather have something else in there." So I thought, "Well, if I'm not going to be on the record, I'd better do something. If you're going to take my guitar off me in my big showcase..."

That's when I got this rather inspired idea. I had a Fostex R8 eight-track tape recorder on which I was doing a lot of demos and the *Remoulds* things. He sent me away with the basic track with no guitars on it. I put it on two tracks of the Fostex and started improvising on the other six tracks. As I was playing it back, I thought, "Oh, I like this little section here. Let's see what's on the other tracks." Eventually, I was able to hear a pattern – a proper solo. It didn't last very long, it's only 30/40 seconds, but because there's so much movement in the chords and it's an unusual movement, it was essential to get something that would work. To be honest, I wasn't 100% happy with what I'd originally done. I just didn't want to go through the same pain of finding something a second time.

Hugh: There's something about doing it in semi-public, whereas if you come back here to your home studio…

Dave: Yes, you can work within your own headspace, no one's listening. Don't let anyone hear it until it's ready. That's how I wrote that solo.

Hugh: So you did six versions of it?

Dave: Well, maybe four or five. I ended up writing it down because I had to practise it. It wasn't something I could scoot around. It's a difficult thing to play. I decided, "Yeah, this has a form and a shape that fits the chords, and it sounds like it's surfing on a wave. If he doesn't like this, he can go fuck himself because I think this is pretty good." But I had to learn to play it and I had three or four days. I got to the studio. Nick Davis was behind the desk and was doing a great job. This was at Rockfield. I actually had two Fender amplifiers. One was a brand new thing called the Twin – it was a twin reverb with these big Electrovoice speakers, 100W each. I was able to hook up those speakers to a little Fender 40W Super Amp from 1963 and then we cranked everything to the max and stood well back. That's the sound with the Stratocaster, and Nick put a little bit of delay on it.

I said, "There's nothing wrong with that sound, Nick, let's go for it."

Andy said, "I'm going shopping now. I'll be back at 4pm."

By 12.30pm it was done. Andy came back and said, "Oh, that's brilliant! That's fantastic, Gregs… Just one thing. I just want to change one note."

One note!

We had to go back and drop in this one note.

Hugh: Was it better?

Dave: It was just different. It was OK. I was happy to do it. At least we got it down. It's one of the proudest moments of my guitar-playing career, even to this day.

Hugh: It is a really wonderful solo and going back to the composing credits, I don't know how long Andy took to write that song, but according to some reports, not very long. Some songs come very quickly. But the amount of time you spent on that section of the song, it would be interesting to ask, "How many hours did it take?" If you were being paid by the hour… Composing often means work; if you compose an essay, it means doing that work.

Dave: It's like Steven Wilson says, if you're doing something you're totally immersed in and love and is as vital to you as sleeping, eating and breathing, you can't call it work. It's a joy, a pure pleasure. But, of course, it's Andy's pure pleasure. He probably spent an afternoon writing that song, but for me to get into his world and to be compatible with what he was doing and to follow his brain pattern, that's work for me.

Mark: Your anecdote about *That Wave* is making me think about my own experience as a journalist when someone comes back and says, "That first paragraph is really not working." Your first reaction is always to defend yourself and say, "It's a brilliant first paragraph." Then later you realise, of course, they were right and they just had that perspective that you don't. So my question is do you think XTC, all the different members and the producers, were good at not accepting second best, at forcing you to do the solo for the third time? Was the bar set quite high?

Dave: Yes, it was set quite high. I didn't always undertake these instructions willingly. I would get upset and offended at times, because Andy could be very blunt. But my own set of standards meant

I wanted it to be as good as it could be. It was quite often laziness or bloody-mindedness that would prevent me from attempting a better job. Now today, as a result of what I did with *That Wave*, that's how I work out my solos with Big Big Train and Tin Spirits. As long as something is written, I know what I have to aim for, even though I might fuck up half way through and I'll have to improvise my way out of it, at least there's a pattern. And once it's on the record, that's part of the song and that's how it goes. It's very rare that I'll hear a piece of music and improvise a solo that's any good. It always feels like fun at the time, but if anyone's recording, you listen back and think, "What was I thinking?"

YOU CAN'T GET THE BUTTONS THESE DAYS
Creating the sound of the Dukes

Hugh: With the Dukes albums you were in a slightly different world. Was your role different?

Dave: Yes. I was given a lot more freedom. It was only meant to be a bit of a laugh. We didn't realise it was going to be embraced by so many people and sell so many. It did a lot for our career at the time. For example, if you listen to the title track of *25 O'Clock*, there's a Farfisa organ solo that I play after the second chorus. It goes into this early-Pink Floyd Richard Wright keyboard solo. That was improvised because the rule was we'd get one take, just like they did in the old days when they had three hours to make a record. There'll be no dropping in, no repairs and we want first takes of everything, so make sure you know what you're doing. It was fairly elementary. Even fumbling had the same feeling you got from those psychedelic records where they were just noodling round creating patterns of sound rather than brilliant solo pieces. There's a key change after the Farfisa organ and the 12-string electric fuzzy guitar drops in. There was no physical way I could get from the Farfisa to the guitar, even though I'm playing both solos. I got to do both because it was my fuzz box and I had the keyboard facility.

Hugh: So you were given more leeway. Is that because Colin and Andy were less precious about the material?

Dave: I think so. Certainly, Colin was, because he wasn't completely on board with what we were doing. He's that bit younger and he became aware of rock music later than Andy and me and didn't have the same affection for that freak-beat period. He came more from the early 70s, Mott the Hoople, Black Sabbath and those kind of bands. He came to the 60s stuff a lot later. But he came up with this song called *What in the World??*... which is one of my favourite things we ever did. It's just daft enough to be authentic and it's a really good song. Andy plays bass on that, Colin played rhythm guitar and I played Hammond organ and there's a Manfred Mann Mellotron in there. All the keyboard lines were mine.

All of the songs on *25 O'Clock* should have been band compositions – even my brother's drumming, which has never been mentioned by anybody apart from a few drummers. He took a week off work to come and play with us after one rehearsal and John Leckie said he was one of the best prepared drummers he ever worked with – and John's worked with everybody. Ian loved it. So, yes, I had a lot more to do on the Dukes albums. It was a lot of fun. But the production details, all the sound effects, were all John and Andy. John knew exactly which tape machines gave the best echo and feedback. And we finally got to live out our schoolboy dreams.

EMOTION AT THE DROP OF A HAT
Big expression on I Remember the Sun

Hugh: I was really glad you suggested we talk about *I Remember the Sun*. Do you remember what Colin brought originally and what your role was?

Dave: I was determined to use the piano. I'm not sure whether it was Colin's idea to use the piano but I know he didn't demo it like that; I'm not sure if there's even a demo for it. We rehearsed that album in a shop at the bottom of Victoria Road and

Pete Phipps used to come to Swindon. Because it's tucked away in the middle of side two of *The Big Express*, it's overlooked, which is a shame because it's one of his best songs. My only criticism is it runs a little bit fast. For the part I'd figured out for it, I would have preferred it to be maybe one or two beats per minute slower.

Donald Fagen is always in my thoughts. Whenever I sit at a piano keyboard, I think, "What chords would Donald be finding at this point?" There's a strong Steely Dan influence in the piano playing. As a young fellow in my 20s, my dream band was Steely Dan. They were the most brilliant pop masterminds. They had the intelligence of jazz musicians applied to pop and rock music. They did it so brilliantly, with amazing lyrics. They were always intriguing and enigmatic. The piano playing is just perfect. The chords he finds and the way he applies them to these melodies is just perfect. So this was a homage, in my feeble and clumsy way, to pay tribute to his influence on my musical thinking.

Hugh: Did Andy play the quirky guitar line?

Dave: Yes he did and I never liked it. He picked up a guitar and it was almost like, "Here you are. Have that." I've got used to it over time, as with everything we did. I had slight misgivings about a lot of things. [We play *I Remember the Sun*.] What a shame! It's such a great song and it's a mess. It needs a remix. This album and *Mummer* are the ones most desperately in need of Steven Wilson's re-think.

Hugh: It's so interesting listening to it, sitting with you, because I've never thought it was a mess, but I can completely see what you mean now. In a glorious way! You've got Andy's very wonderful, quirky part and you're definitely channelling Donald Fagen and, at times, when you hear them together, you think, "They are different worlds, aren't they?"

Dave: They are. I'd forgotten about the key change at the end. That was very nice. It would have been David Lord's suggestion.

Hugh: The piano lines are really wonderful, especially in the chorus, they're quite fast little runs.

Dave: That's right. The chorus is where I feel it's falling over itself tempo-wise. But it should have been a dreamy summer's day of a song and it sounds like a clattering racket. I couldn't see why those guitar lines were appropriate to the feel of the lyric. I don't think he listened closely enough to what Colin was singing about. It's too abrasive for my ears. And it should have been a nice long rallentando at the end, which there isn't - it seems to implode on itself.

Hugh: If you were in another band, what would you have said to the lead guitarist to do?

Dave: I would have said, "I like what you're doing in the choruses: big chords, that takes it up another level, that's great. But don't play that horrible clattery thing you're doing there. That's not setting up the verse at all. It's just a nuisance." But production decisions were often a source of conflict, particularly between me and Andy.

Hugh: When you hear a song for the first time, particularly an Andy or Colin demo, do you listen to the music or the words first?

Dave: They both had that gift of being able to match lyrics with the melodies they were writing. The song was neither one nor the other, it was both things: it was the lyric, it was the melody. They would never throw songs my way until they were finished as written pieces, so there was never a question of, "Oh, I was thinking of writing about a coal mine in this one." It would always be a complete idea, so the lyric was as important to me as the music. To this day, if someone sends me a track to work on, I always say, "Do you have any lyrics or a guide vocal

> *'This is a great song – if only I could smooth those hard edges off and round some of those nasty spikes'*

Taking notes: "OK, I'm going to have to learn how to write in the alto clef."

or can you tell me what the song's about?" That will define what instrument I'm going to play and the style I'm going to play it in.

Sometimes, I see people on social media being flattering about my work and one of the things that often comes up is I never do anything that detracts from the song. I thought everybody would have thought like that. If they were a guitar player in the band, surely the whole point of what you play has to relate to what's being expressed lyrically. Maybe it isn't with most bands.

Mark: I can't imagine *I Remember the Sun* without the keyboards. Was it a very elementary structure that you were given?

Dave: I've got a complete mental block. I would have sat at my old, out-of-tune upright piano and worked out every note, because that is not something that I could have sat down and come up with on the spur of the moment. The verse, chorus and middle eight are all separate pieces.

Hugh: It's a good song to analyse the differences in Dave Gregory's and Andy Partridge's playing! I have a friend who loves Andy's guitar-playing.

Dave: Ha-ha! It's a humorous thing as well. I think Andy was being slightly tongue in cheek when he played that.

ANIMAL AND PANICKING
Holly Up on Poppy and
The Smartest Monkeys

Hugh: *Holly Up on Poppy* is a song we could talk about.

Dave: That was just an acoustic guitar from Andy. It was a demo he hadn't done much with. I knew the song was about his daughter and her new rocking horse. I thought, "Maybe the rocking horse could be one of the horses on the stripy poles on a fairground carousel. Let's find a patch on the Proteus that sounds like a calliope and work on a jaunty arpeggiated thing."

There's some really nice bass playing I discovered recently when I was listening to Steven's remix of *Nonsuch*. Moulding plays some very interesting stuff I hadn't noticed before. I worked long and hard on the keyboards to *Holly Up on Poppy*. Likewise on Colin's song, *Smartest Monkeys* – I had a lot to do with the music on that. People have suddenly noticed the little keyboard solo that I knocked up in the studio.

Hugh: Is that a keyboard? I wondered if it was a guitar with a wah-wah.

Dave: It's a keyboard with a 1967 Vox Wah-Wah. And the string lines are all my work. The synth strings were overdubbed with real players.

Hugh: [Looking at Dave's sheet music] Here are the string parts for *Smartest Monkeys*. "First violin, second violin, viola" – still not in the alto clef, Dave? [Violins are written in the treble clef; cello in the bass clef and, traditionally, violas in the alto clef.]

Dave: No, it wasn't until I did a string session for Gary Clark at the Strongroom in London that I took a score to the viola player and he was not chuffed. "Why've you written this in the treble clef?" I did wonder about those ledger lines! He took it away and transcribed it but he wasn't a happy bunny. I thought, "OK, I'm going to have to learn how to write in the alto clef."

Hugh: Do you remember your discussions with Colin about *Smartest Monkeys*?

Dave: It wasn't discussed. We rehearsed it in his living room. We used to drive over to his cottage and I remember it well because it was the start of the first of the Gulf wars and the news was full of this stuff while we were working on these songs. We would have sat there and I would have played the string part and nobody objected so I carried on.

GIVE THE STARS A STIR
You and the Clouds Will Still Be Beautiful and the lost solo

Hugh: [Looking through scores] Oh, *You and the Clouds Will Still Be Beautiful* was around in those days... and *Rip Van Ruben*.

Dave: There are a couple of great songs that we never got round to doing. I'd have loved to have done *Ship Trapped in the Ice* – what a great song.

You and the Clouds Will Still Be Beautiful was a heartbreaker because I'd worked out a guitar solo. I'm a big fan of Albert Lee, the country player, who had this thing called *Country Boy*. He used to use this delay and if you played in a certain rhythm, you'd get a single repeat of each note and double your speed as long as you didn't stray from the strict tempo.

I figured out a solo for *You and the Clouds Will Still Be Beautiful* that crossed over this weird rhythm that Andy had constructed, a very funny groove. It was in triple time and then my solo was in strict 4/4 time, using this repeat feature, that went over the chords. It sounded very clever, as though I was some kind of guitar playing genius!

We got a version down at Chipping Norton and I was so happy with it. Then Andy came in and said, "The trouble is, though, it's in mono." I said, "Yeah. It's just on one track." He said, "I think it'd be better if we separated it into stereo and put it in an auto-panner."

I said, "If you put the repeat note in a separate track, that's just shedding way too much daylight on the magic. That's not going to work. Why don't we leave it in mono and then you can spin it around in your auto-panner and put whatever repeat effects you want on it? As far as I'm concerned, that's the solo I've written and it's intentionally on one track."

He said, "No, it's got to be in stereo. That's how I'm hearing it."

He liked what I'd done but couldn't resist fiddling around with it. It sounded like little drops of rain. I used a Vox Phantom guitar, the skinniest sound you could ever hear. It sprinkled itself beautifully over these chord changes and this odd groove.

That was one of the many disagreements we had during the course of *Apple Venus*, that painful record. Before the record could be mixed, I quit so I didn't care any more. I haven't heard what he did with it because to this day I have never heard *Wasp Star*. Don't want to hear it. It could be the greatest album since *Sgt Pepper* and I would not like it. "There are none so deaf as those who will not hear."

I regret not getting to work on *We're All Light* and *The Wheel and the Maypole* because I thought they were just brilliant.

Hugh: When you hear XTC influences in contemporary bands how does that make you feel?

Dave: I always think, "Andy would be interested to hear this band." I don't personally hear any of my work in the bands that are supposedly influenced. Whenever I hear a band that uses 12-string Rickenbacker, I think, "I wonder if they got that idea from *English Settlement* or *Mayor of Simpleton*." But no, it would be very vain to assume these bands were out copying your work. Franz Ferdinand is one of the bands that is often mentioned, but I don't really think that. And Blur have always professed to have been influenced by XTC, but I don't really... maybe in some of the guitar sounds.

People in the past have sent me things, saying, "We're big fans of XTC, we thought you might like this."

"Well, what gave you that impression? It sounds like a band I used to be in a long time ago."

It's flattering and it's nice that people have been listening and I know for a fact that we've inspired a lot of groups - how successful they've been at cashing in on that inspiration, I wouldn't like to say.

BLACK VALLEY OF THE VINYL
Mixing and remixing from Drums and Wires to Skylarking

Hugh: What role did you have on *Wake Up* because the beginning is fantastic?

Dave: That's all Colin. He came up with that chip-chop guitar idea. Andy and I played a couple of different inversions of G7 - that's all it is. Slightly different from Colin's demo, but the same basic feel. That was the hook of the song, then we brought in the CP70 for the big choruses at the end. I wasn't crazy about how it ended because they were a fairly predictable three chords: F, G and A minor, but he had to do it, he had to finish the song.

Hugh: Another friend asked me to ask you whether you did the solo on *Train Running Low on Soul Coal*.

Dave: No. That really dissonant thing - you can tell that's Andy, can't you? He tuned his daughter's guitar to open E and wrote the entire album in that style. So he showed me how to play this riff, then in the middle section it goes into half time and the 12-string Rickenbacker comes in with this big jangly blang-blang-blang-blang... Great, great lyric in the middle-eight section. It was one of my favourite things Andy ever wrote. Then I played this nutty banjo-style part which I couldn't play today - it's way too fast - right at the end of the middle-eight section with a contrapuntal tune played with a flat pick. I don't know how I did it. I must have had a very strong right-hand technique in those days.

Hugh: Was there ever any discussion that he would be doing the solo in that song?

Dave: That's the funny thing. We never had any rivalry as guitarists. So, no. "You wrote the song, you want to play the solo, go ahead." It absolutely works in that context. That's probably my favourite. The entire album needs a proper remix because it sounds so horribly brittle and cold, but there's some great work on it.

Hugh: Is that to do with the LinnDrums?

Dave: Yeah, that's part of the problem. Pete Phipps did a lot of work on real drums, but it was split 50/50. It was new-toy syndrome. "We've got a machine that keeps perfect time and doesn't get drunk!" Not that Pete would get drunk! It was very rudimentary compared with what you can buy today. I think the album was mixed to DAT. That's where a big part of the problem lies. So, assuming we can still locate the original multi-tracks, it should be possible to do a nice analogue remix.

Hugh: Did you ever have much of a role in mixing?

> *'If it's a new guitar and it's set up properly, I smell it from time to time. I do like to smell things'*

Dave: Not as much as I'd have liked. We all sat in the control room. We all threw our opinions in. The only album we hands-on mixed as a band was *Drums and Wires*, because we didn't have much time. We'd sit at the desk and we'd all be given two or three faders and we'd run it through, you'd have Chinagraph pencil marks for your cues on the desk and you'd push your fader up and pull it back as appropriate. There was something about that. It was a musical way of creating. It wasn't programmed. You were using these analogue faders and it was all going to analogue tape. When you moved a fader you could really hear the difference.

With the dub section at the end of *Scissor Man*, I remember George Chambers, the assistant engineer, on his hands and knees because there was a Drawmer gate or something that was right at the bottom on the effects console and he had to throw a switch at a certain point to get these dub effects going. It could be frustrating after seven or eight passes and it still wasn't right, but it was fun.

As time went by, flying faders, digital automation and all the rest of it took all the fun away.

Hugh: I was reading that you were the one giving instructions to Todd Rundgren about remixes of *Skylarking*.

Dave: No, he called me. Someone had called him, probably from the record company – I dare say it was Jeremy Lascelles – saying, "We want the record remixed." I'd gone to bed, it was three o'clock in the morning and the phone rang. It was Mary Lou Arnold, his assistant. She said, "Dave, I'm so sorry to wake you but we can't get hold of Andy. Could you talk to Todd about this album remix because he's about to start doing it?"

Where they were it was ten o'clock at night, so he was going to knock this mix off before he went to bed – the entire album!

He was like: "Whaddaya want me to do with this record?" I said, "Oh, Todd, I'm sorry, but there were some digital glitches."

He'd mastered it to this new digital-analogue tape. It was a reel-to-reel system that Mitsubishi had just brought out and it was in its experimental R&D stages. They'd given him this machine and he'd decided this would be the perfect opportunity to mix the album to a digital master. Anyway, there were faults, there were drop-outs here and there, very minor things, but we could hear them and each time we played the album they got worse and worse. Little ticks and things get louder as time goes by.

I said, "The other thing is we can't hear any bass guitar. It seems really lightweight and flimsy."

He said, "Man, you got me doing what I love to do: remixing!" He really hated it. He just didn't want to do it. "I'm going to do this remix and I don't want to hear any more about it."

So off he went.

The new mix came in and it wasn't very much better, although the digital glitches had been removed. It was a case of: "Todd's refused to do any more work, so let's take it to Metropolis. Andy, you go and work with them and see what you can do with them until you're happy with it."

Out it came and within weeks *Dear God* had been picked up by this radio station in LA and suddenly it was a turntable hit and it wasn't on the album. Geffen freaked out. "Recall the album! Repress it! We've got to rethread it into the running order somehow." *Mermaid Smiled* was tossed out and *Dear God* put in in its place. It meant we had to effectively re-release the album.

Then 30 years later, there was a remix on vinyl and the late John Dent, who was in charge of mastering, discovered there was a phasing issue. It was a polarity problem where the two sides of the stereo where fighting each other. Everyone blamed Todd, but I think it was done after it left Todd's studio. He mastered albums with Greg Calbi in Sterling Sound – he's been doing it his whole life. That was his career. I think that fault occurred either in Metropolis or when it was reassembled. Nobody picked it up then, did they, and yet Todd has been blamed for it.

THE TREASURE HE'D BEEN SEEKING
Time changes in The Man Who Sailed Around His Soul

Hugh: Do you remember what *The Man Who Sailed Around His Soul* was like before Todd made it into a spy movie?

Dave: Yes, it was just acoustic guitar and not much else. It was in 4/4. I'm pretty certain it was Todd that changed it to 7/8. I had a guitar part that I had to slightly adjust to play in the seven time. I was trying to sound like Vic Flick *[known for using a Fender Stratocaster]* with a Gibson Les Paul. Todd found the sound with his extreme use of EQ and turned a jazz guitar into this twangy Stratocaster thing. And then that amazing brass section which Todd pretty much knocked up over night. Recording with Todd was an experience I wouldn't have missed for the world.

It was one of the highlights of my life – not just my recording career.

Hugh: When you came back from that did you have a sense of confidence as an external arranger, because before that you'd only arranged for yourself?

Dave: Yes, I think I did. But I never got any real feedback from Colin or Andy about it. It was, "That job's done, onto the next one." But it did mean they could trust me if they needed strings arranged. But eventually it was Mike Batt they used and what a marvellous job he did. I could not even have imagined the job he did on *I Can't Own Her*. It's gorgeous and I would never have got close to that. Before I left, I did arrange strings for all those songs on *Apple Venus*. We brought in a string quartet, but they were a bit unprepared, the studio wasn't working properly and the sessions were trashed after a day which I was very embarrassed about. They ended up somehow finding the money to hire Abbey Road and bring in Mike Batt.

Mark: Had your arrangements been used would it have improved the songs?

Dave: Not necessarily. I heard what Mike Batt had done and thought, "Oh, right, fair enough."

SHILLING FOR THE CELLO
Scoring the 1000 Umbrellas quartet

Dave: During 1985, there were a number of distractions in Andy's life. Holly, his daughter, was born. He hit a dry spell creatively. He called me up one day and said, "You know, Gregs, I don't think I've got any more songs left inside me. I can't seem to get the creative juices going at all."

I said, "Have you got anything at all? It'll surely come back. It's just a question of waiting until the time is right." He picked up his acoustic guitar and said, "I just came up with this earlier." And he played *1000 Umbrellas*, this rather miserable chromatic thing going down.

Hugh: Which is on *Fuzzy Warbles*, isn't it?

Dave: Yes – and it doesn't last very long. I thought, "I've just bought this sequencer. I'm anxious to do an experiment with this thing." When we were working on *The Big Express*, David Lord had this Roland JX-3P synthesiser. I bought one and it had its own built-in sequencer. I thought, "This is great. You programme 16 notes and the machine will play it for you at any speed. You don't even have to practise!" I started researching these things called sequencers and how you could hook them up to MIDI with these samples. I thought it should be possible to assign a channel to first violin, second violin, viola and cello and you've got an instant string quartet. I bought a Roland MSQ-100 which had 16 MIDI channels. I wanted to do an *Eleanor Rigby* type thing.

Hugh: Had you done any string arranging before?

Dave: No, not at all. But this made it easy. Rather than sitting at the piano with a pencil between my teeth imagining how this was going to sound, I could hear it back in 3D and run it as many times as necessary until it sounded right. After a couple of weeks, I said, "I've done this string arrangement, Andy. Do you think it'd be possible to bring some string players in and do it like this?"

He liked that idea. Meanwhile, he'd found his muse and started writing again. He said, "I really like this idea, but a couple of things: can you change this, can you do this, can you make it a bit more florid here and there." This went on for a couple of weeks and it went through about 11 drafts.

Months had passed and Todd Rundgren had agreed to do the record. I thought, "This is great. Perhaps Todd can factor some string players into the budget and I'll take this over." When Todd sent his proposed running order to Andy, *1000 Umbrellas* wasn't in the mix because Andy hadn't sent him my demo, only his acoustic guitar demo. The running order had been decided so I thought we'd just have to set it aside for another album.

We got to Woodstock and we were discussing the running order because Andy wanted a few things changed and Todd was talking about doing some edits. There was a lot of editing in *Dear God*. At some point, I asked Todd if he'd heard my string arrangement for *1000 Umbrellas*. He hadn't. As soon as he heard it, he agreed to adjust his running order. I remember sitting at his piano with my sequencer and a pair of headphones, writing it out as the other sessions were going on.

Hugh: So on that album, you did quite a bit of getting on with stuff on your own, didn't you?

Dave: Yes. With *The Man Who Sailed Around His Soul*, we didn't know what Todd had in mind until we got to his studio and he wanted to do this spy movie theme. That meant putting my John Barry hat on, thinking, "How would he have done the piano for this?" That's me playing piano and it was not pre-planned. I must have come up with that in the studio.

Hugh: Staying on *1000 Umbrellas*, that was your first string arrangement, you spent ages and *Eleanor Rigby* was your model. Where there any other models? Did you think, "Well, I'll go and listen to some Ravel string quartets?"

Dave: No, because I like pop strings. But I do like Peter Warlock's *Capriol Suite*. It still is one of my favourite pieces of music. There's a certain sort of magic, a very British magical quality to the strings in that piece, similar to some of Elgar's stuff, but more modern. It's something I was always conscious of.

Hugh: The only reason I mentioned Ravel was the *Second* string quartet is quite poppy and jazzy. So there were things in your head like Peter Warlock – and you'd heard that as a child?

Dave: I heard it at school. I'd been given cello lessons. In the last two years I was at grammar school, they were trying to get recruits for the Swindon Schools Orchestra, so they were anxious to give tuition out of school hours. Because I'd been such a big Beatles fan and had heard *Eleanor Rigby* and *Strawberry Fields Forever*, I thought that cello sound is the sound to die for.

I thought, "If I could learn to play that, it would be a great thing to have in my repertoire. I could be a cellist as well as a guitarist."

They provided a cello and brought in this teacher, a nice old boy, Reg Bennett, who was a fine cellist. He was very pleased with me because I was top of the form.

I hadn't played the cello before but I'd played a stringed instrument. So he encouraged me.

After I'd been playing for about a year, he said he'd put me up for the Swindon Schools Orchestra which would meet every Monday evening. Geoff Stanley, who was music master at Commonweal School where I was, was the conductor. He was a forward-thinking, modern musician. As well as teaching, he had various side projects and was a very progressive thinker and a bit of a beatnik.

I got to my first encounter with the orchestra and I'd never heard this piece of music before – it was the first movement of the *Capriol Suite* and that's what we were playing, sight unseen. "Right, let's see how far we can get with this." There was this cacophonous noise, as these little kids tried to find their way around this very odd piece of modern [1926] British music. I'd never heard it, so my first experience was trying to follow this score, which I wasn't in any way prepared for. But there was something magical about it. I wanted to hear it again. It was so off the scale. And yet it's melodic and it's got these lovely harmonies.

I left school in 1969 and had to return the cello. Mr Bennett was upset because he said, "You can't just give it up. You've got to keep on with this. You could go far with the cello. I had you down as a star pupil."

I said, "Well, I really want to play guitar in a rock band." He was horrified! But I still love the cello. It's one of my favourite instruments.

Hugh: I'm interested that *1000 Umbrellas*, which is a really wonderful arrangement, was your first encounter. You'd listened to stuff and you've clearly got a good ear – and I know now you'd had two years of cello playing under your belt – but it's interesting that Andy, Colin and Todd thought what you'd done is fine.

Dave: It was a feather in my cap. All the strings on that album were recorded in an afternoon. The arrangement Todd did for *Sacrificial Bonfire* had really demanding parts for those players. Rather than book an orchestra, he booked a string quartet and kept tracking them up until it sounded big enough. They had their work cut out. Even though listening to it now it's not the most perfect performances you'll ever hear...

Hugh: ...You can hear that chorus effect of doubling up. I often think of it as an XTC string sound. The doubled-up strings is different from the right number of strings.

Dave: Exactly. That was illustrated to me last week when I went to Abbey Road Studios for Big Big Train. We had the opportunity to work with an 18-piece ensemble, all strings, in studio two. I sat there and I virtually wept.

It was so beautiful and everything that I'd imagined when I first set up to record strings for this piece, *East Coast Racer*. If only XTC had had the budget to hire a full orchestra and go to, say, Abbey Road – in my dreams.

Hugh: So you left school at 16, didn't do any more formal music education and all this is self-taught or remembered? You didn't go to the library and get a book about string quartet writing or orchestrations?

Dave: No, it was all done from the sequencer, which had a little window to show you rhythmically where the notes were, so it was a question of converting that code to that one.

Hugh: When people compose for sequencer, it often doesn't work because they're not thinking of the real instrument, whereas this is clearly string quartet writing. So it must have been in your head...

Dave: I'm always aware of what is physically possible with all of the players. I think I have in the past written in bowing suggestions.

BLUE OVERALL
The rhapsody of Dear God

Dave: We rehearsed *Dear God* in my living room in Stanier Street round my piano. Next to the piano was the Mellotron. Andy said, "I really like those bluesy sounding strings that George Gershwin was so fond of in *Rhapsody in Blue*." String sections playing bluesy chords and sliding around.

I said, "We haven't got any strings but I'll work up something on the Mellotron that has something in the style you're describing. I'm not George Gershwin, so it's not going to be quite as luxurious."

We recorded a demo on my TEAC four-track. It was much longer. Todd said he wanted to edit it first. We sat in his control room and had a big pow-wow about which bits were going to be chopped out to make it more edible. Once that was decided, it was down to me to score for the string players what I'd written on the Mellotron but with cuts.

Hugh: What I love about what you've just said is that you just had a little conversation about Gershwin, you knew what Andy was referring to and I like the way you said, "I'm not Gershwin, but I'll have a go," and for me that sounds like an incredible confidence. A lot of people who are musically articulate like you are would have said, "Oh God, I don't know how to do that," whereas you said, "I'll get on with it."

Dave: It was, "Let's do something with the same feeling," because there's no way we're going to duplicate that style of orchestration. I don't have that facility.

Hugh: But did you feel confident and comfortable to be able to say, "I'll get on with it"?

Dave: Yeah. I just felt, "This is my gig. I'll do that. It's not a keyboard part. I'll just write a keyboard part and give it to the strings." Actually, another thing that inspired my thinking for the Mellotron part was the Four Seasons' song, *Beggin'*. There's a Chamberlin line in the verses that was tugging at my ear.

Hugh: [Looking at the score] Dave has clearly given the instruments different roles. You might think they would be all be playing the same kind of thing, whereas no, the second violin is playing the melody here, then they come together here and the cello is playing a counter melody. They're doing contrapuntal parts. It's a compositional way of thinking. I'm surprised at your confidence, Dave. People who have come out of three years of composition at university of conservatoire level often don't have that confidence.

Dave: I'm flattered. I'm sure a lot comes from being brought up in a house that was full of classical music playing for a good part of my upbringing. It was just in the air.

Hugh: What did your parents think of your musical career?

Dave: They had no interest in it whatsoever. I forsook the piano for the electric guitar in 1967 – I was sacked by my piano teacher for not practising – and that upset my mother greatly. She had high hopes for me as a concert pianist and I was never going to be that. I struggled with the piano. I was working to take a Grade 5 exam and I couldn't really cope with it. My head was so full... if you remember what was going on in 1967 in music, you couldn't ignore it.

Hugh: Weren't they excited when you took up the cello?

Dave: It ameliorated the situation slightly. They were happy to pick me up from school and take me to orchestra practice.

Hugh: Was there nothing in your musical life you could share with them, like *1000 Umbrellas*?

Dave: You'd think so, but I would take an LP round to their house and say, "Here's our new LP," and it was, "Put it on the table, we'll listen to it later." I do remember my dad asking me if I'd played piano on such-and-such a song – it might have been *Great Fire*. That was the only note of recognition I ever had from either of my parents.

Hugh: You say you got to Grade 5 and then couldn't cope. If you listen to your piano playing on things like *I Remember the Sun*, and I know it's not grade music, but you're clearly able to do distinct things with different hands.

Dave: Yes, but a lot of it had to do with what I was being given to learn for Grade 5, which was stuffy classical stuff that wasn't very inspiring, whereas *I Remember the Sun* was all my own work.

Mark: Did your keyboard skills continue to develop beyond the formal education? If you did the exams now would you get to Grade 8?

Dave: No, I don't think so, because it's getting more into the classical training. I still struggle. I went through a phase of learning Beatles songs on the piano because I liked McCartney's attitude, his approach to the piano. Something like *Martha My Dear* with that bouncing E flat thing, when you figure out what he's doing, it's very simple. He's just found the right black notes and created a tune. What a brilliant facility to have for a bass player in his 20s! When you crack the code of what he's done on *Lady Madonna*, it's really quite simple but sounds amazing. McCartney has been so maligned by people who should know better. He's one of the few people you could adequately describe as a genius.

Interview conducted Swindon, 14 March 2018.

> '*Recording with Todd was an experience I wouldn't have missed for the world – one of the highlights of my life*'

WHAT DO YOU CALL THAT NOISE?

Andy Partridge playing in sea major.

A CHORD IN MY HAND

He can't tell you what key he's in, but Andy Partridge knows his way around Logic Pro X. How did he learn more about plug-ins than musical theory?

BY MARK FISHER

In a delightful exchange on Twitter, somebody going by the name of Grant @bluetshirt asked Andy about *You're the Wish You Are I Had*. Partridge had come across a cover of the song by the Dukes of Simpleton on YouTube [https://is.gd/Ml8pSo] and had been impressed: "Not often a tribute band impresses me. This bunch did a great job," he wrote. "The vocals alone are excellent. Not an easy tune to work out."

Grant had a pertinent question: "Does the verse have any.... chords? I mean, in the traditional sense?" Andy's answer was revealing: "From the bottom up... 8.7.0.0.8.8 is the first chord (don't know its name), B is the 2nd. Chorus is in E."

Knowing the name of chords is not of interest to Andy. That was always Dave's department. Taking the bait, Grant keyed in the notes and came up with seven possible names for it. They included Csus (b5, add9) and F#maj7 (b5, #5, no3)/C. As Grant went on to explain, it depends "which note you consider the root, which ones you consider fundamental parts of the chord, and which ones are embellishments or ornamental".

Andy's response was honest and characteristically funny: "Sorry, a lot of musical stuff is still Martian to me. Does that chord really have all those names, like an aristocrat?"

There are, of course, many aristocratic chords in the XTC canon and Andy, the humble songwriter, can do no more than doff his cap to them. "I just like the sounds and colours of them," he went on to say. It echoed the sentiments of the conversation I'd had with him a few weeks earlier when he had talked about the musical language of XTC, the art of collaboration and the brave new world of digital recording.

PAVEMENTS OF GOLD
The art and craft of song-building

Mark Fisher: When you're trying to sell a house, the idea is to decorate it very blandly so people can come in and imagine themselves in it, rather than thinking, "Oh, I don't like that couch he's got there." The musical equivalent of that, when you're writing songs for other people, is you could just do chords and keep it minimalist or you could do it as elaborately as possible. Which do you prefer?

Andy Partridge: It's whatever you're going for. Sometimes I'll do something quite bland. I'll do a couple of acoustic guitars strumming away, a simple drum-machine pattern and maybe a bass to root it. Or I'll go the other way and make an effort to give it a vibe, thinking they can pick up on the vibe as well as the structure, melody and lyrics. If I'm writing for somebody else, it's more along the lines of being the Dukes. You're play acting. You're being an impressionist. It's not a bad thing, some of my favourite people are impressionists, it's just a different discipline from putting your hands down into your stomach and pulling your guts out, saying, "Well, I don't want to look at it again but there you go, that's it."

Mark: Do you think of the composition of a song and the arrangement in the same breath? You've got the example with XTC when you'd have Dave coming in and doing his own guitar part. It's all creative but where does composition stop and arrangement start?

Andy: It's an incredibly mobile and moveable feast. In the early days of XTC, you would have in your head the idea of what you would like to sound like, but you had no way of capturing that. You would strum a guitar in a rehearsal room and say, "These are the chords," or, "This is the figure it's built on," and, "I sort of see it sounding a bit like this..." Then you had to describe it to the others. "I want it to sound a bit like Johnny and the Hurricanes and you're hearing something at a fairground out of a fuzzy PA system, but I'd like the drums to be an old rockabilly rhythm and the bass to be more dubby." You're smashing together descriptions. It's like Clough Williams-Ellis who collected the buildings and put the miniature versions of them in Portmeirion. You're smashing together these bits of architecture. "Yeah, I want a big dome like the Taj Mahal and if we can hang these nice verandas around the edge like that building in southern Italy, and at the top, can we put an old BBC broadcasting tower?" Because I had no way then of demoing stuff, I had to describe what was required.

Mark: In that sense, is it correct to call it your song, because it was the band creating the final thing?

Andy: It's them translating my requirements. Invariably, it would take on another character. They would interpret your descriptions and make a third thing. It wasn't what you started out with and it would get pretty close to what was in your head, but it would be a fresh third thing, interpreting and misinterpreting what you were after. When Dave joined, he is a good, natural arranger. If I was playing in one octave, Dave would inevitably pick a higher or a lower octave. With Terry, I would usually play stuff between what he was playing. It's no good me playing on the snare beat because he's going to cover it up with his cannon explosion. So I've got to play skank which is good for the funk, for the rhythmic aspect of it. Each member of the band would bring in their influences and their own way of playing.

Take *Life Begins at the Hop*, for example. Colin's brought this idea up and he wanted it to be about going round to the St Peter's Church Hall hop, which we both used to go to as kids. You couldn't drink there, so it was just Coca-Cola and lemonade. A lot of the records played there would be Tamla Motown. So we said, "Can we put an essence of Tamla Motown into this?" I suggested to Terry that he do that popular Tamla rhythm, a constant one-two-three-four on the snare with the bass drum interjecting. Dave put the tremolo on his amplifier and came up with this repeated pattern which is like one of those repetitive Tamla bass runs that bubble along underneath [*sings something very like the bass part to* I Can't Help Myself *by the Four Tops.*] We're trying to interpret it like a memory of a Tamla Motown thing that hasn't existed and getting it all a bit wrong. I liked the idea of doing these minimal stabs over the top of it and catching them in an echo, like spears sticking through the music. It made it rather dream-like. Nothing like a Tamla record but that's where it came from.

It did change over the years. In 82/83, Colin and I were hearing about a portastudio. "What, you can record four tracks on a cassette? Wow!" We got these ludicrously expensive machines, one each. With some cheapo drum box or banging kitchen implements yourself, you could almost make a drum track. I went round the junk shop and got a bass guitar. From then onwards, we were handing over cassettes of recordings that gave you more of an idea and, to some extent, it started to kill off their interpretation.

Dave, especially, got pissed off with me giving him very formed demos. By the time I went up to eight-track recording, I was playing his parts, the bass parts and what the drummer was going to be doing.

Mark: In the case of *A Whiter Shade of Pale* there was a court case where Matthew Fisher, Procol Harum's organ player, said something like, "My keyboard was so distinctive, I should be getting a royalty." Yes, you're the person who's come together with the chords and the words, but then Dave is the person who's bringing up the guitar solo or whatever. In certain cases, it can define the song. The same with Barry on keyboards.

Andy: That touches on another area – and bands

> *'We're trying to interpret it like a memory of a Tamla Motown thing that hasn't existed and getting it all a bit wrong'*

get into terrible fights about this – which is the publishing. It's who is due what on any given song. Sometimes, the song will be 100% the creation of one person. Another time, it will be the kind of jamming that certain bands like U2 do where they all end up with an equal credit. We worked the Beatles way where one or the other would bring a tune up and the other two or three would contribute to it. Our publishing deal when we started was 60/40, with the band getting 60%. I got Colin to agree that out of that 60%, the writer would get half, ie 30%, and would give 10% to each other member of the band. So the writer gave away half of his money (if there was any) to the rest of the band, whether they contributed anything or not. Somebody might come up with an interesting riff and they'd earn their 10%. The writer who's invented the song in the first place gets 30% and somebody who may or may not have contributed to the recording or the very landscape of the song will still get their 10%. We felt that was pretty good for band cohesion. For us, it wasn't an awful lot of money, but we gave it to whoever else was in the band (if they left the band, the good-will stopped).

TIN TOY CLOCKWORK TRAIN
Making a song tick

Mark: When I hear cover versions of XTC songs, and this is also true of covers of Beatles songs, it's quite rare to hear something that is completely off the wall. Normally, people keep not just to the words and the chords, but the arrangements as well. It's as if you've built-in the setting of the songs.

Andy: Yes, it's because the song is a little machine. If you take apart the machine, it's not a clock any more and you can't tell the time by it. Mind you, I think Lennon and McCartney's songs are much more friendly to interpretation. People who have covered their songs have had hits. Nobody has had hits with covers of ours. They've done great versions like *The Man Who Sailed Around His Soul* by Ruben Blades and Manhattan Transfer. I like both of them, but it's an odd song to start with, so I don't think you can have a hit with it.

Mark: In both cases, although they're good versions, they're not complete revisions. They're following the template you laid down.

Andy: It's a song that's in the lyrics, in the chords, in the melody. You can't really get away from that. It's the same with any band that's got a distinctive architectural style. You could hear it if somebody covered a Small Faces song or a Kinks song or anybody with a set thumbprint.

Mark: What's come into my mind is the Nouvelle Vague version of *Making Plans for Nigel* which is a reinvention.

Andy: But it's a reinvention where you're supposed to go, "Ho, ho! That's funny!" There's a measure of comedy involved. It's the concept of making cheesy easy-listening versions of things that were a little more edgy. If they were worth their salt they'd pick up a few Captain Beefheart numbers and Vague them. I challenge you!

Mark: I have a question about you being untaught and unable to read music…

Andy: Funnily enough, Erica threw in the basket in the toilet a book she bought for herself called *Music Theory for Dummies*. I've tried several days to make sense of this book. I am such a dummy. I cannot make head nor tail of what this book about understanding music is telling me.

Mark: You're a complete charlatan.

Andy: I am a complete Charlotte Hatherley. I don't know what the hell I'm doing. But McCartney can't read music and it hasn't stopped him. I don't think Captain Beefheart even understood about bar lengths. He certainly never understood recording technology: "You've got to wear headphones if you want to sing and be in tune and in time with the music." "Oh really? Well, I prefer not to wear headphones." So you get those great moments on *Trout Mask Replica* where he's still singing a line and the song has finished. "Oh shit, I don't know how I'm ever going to get that ending." But I get by. I don't understand music notation in the slightest. Yeah, "Every Good Boy Deserves Fruit," but I don't know what that really means.

Mark: Dave, as a trained musician, is in awe of what you can do, precisely because you're not trained and you can go places where, as far as he's concerned, you're breaking the rules. That's very exciting because he then realises those rules are there to be broken.

Andy: It's good to know rules before you break them, but I don't, so I don't have that inbuilt criminal guilt feeling that you're busting something. Dave is very different from me in how he thinks about music. I'd say, "Oh, Dave, can you do the solo in this song? Can you come up with something that's a little bit hillbilly or very twangy or minimal and buzzy?" He'd go away and he'd work diligently for days, writing out what his part is going to be. He would sit and learn it from sheet music. Whereas I don't know what I'm going to be playing on any given song usually until the last second. It's not always the thing you're supposed to be thinking about. I might be thinking about the rhythm of it more than what the correct chords are going to be.

Mark: When you've done those things where it's spontaneous are you aware of being in the right mood or the right zone and sometimes it works and sometimes it doesn't?

Andy: Oh yes. There's a lot of rejecting. If I've got a solo to play, I'll have a go, not knowing what I'm going to play. Dave used to say, "Parts is having fun again." I would grab something and sometimes it would just work first go or second go. But if I didn't get it four, five, six, seven, twenty, thirty, fifty takes, I'd get really despondent. I'd have to clear my head and try to get back to first-take mentality. I'm really crap at learning, whereas Dave is very good. He maps his guitar solos out and I couldn't do that.

PROCESSION TOWARDS LEARNING LAND
When practice becomes theory

Mark: But at the same time, you can't be as naive as you were when you were 16. There must have been stuff you picked up along the way.

Andy: I've picked up quite a lot. I still don't totally understand when people say, "Write out a tab of it." I'm thinking, "Well, if I sit and think, I can maybe unpick it." Anything that slows down the creative process is not good for me. I have to get it out quick, because it goes very quick. I've got a goldfish brain. Erica says my racy-brain syndrome is very difficult to keep up with. It must be, for people living with me or dealing with me because I can't stay on the same subject for more than a few seconds. In my brain, I'm zipping and zapping around.

Mark: Pushing this idea about learning and musical theory: you record *Life Begins at the Hop*, you now know what it's like to have a Tamla beat. Maybe you could do a Tamla beat again. You've learned what it sounds like. Is it possible ever to unlearn that? You learn that a D goes with an E. You've obviously learned a lot of stuff as you've progressed which is like musical theory, it's just not written down.

Andy: Yes, totally. I still haven't learned the musical theory and how to properly go from this bit to that bit, but I've picked up a few hints over the years.

Mark: Talking about the Monkees and the Christmas single *Unwrap You at Christmas*, for example, you said you put a key change beneath the saxophone, so you know what a key change is.

Andy: Yes, that sort of cheesy music would have a key change. There's a few of them in XTC music, but not that many. *Rocket from a Bottle* has got one and it's disguised by Dave's solo. So, yes, you pick up things. But I watch Jacob Collier on YouTube and I'm thinking, "How is he doing that?" He can play anything in any key in any style. He knows what chords are inside out, what they're called and how they go together. I don't know any of that. I still don't know the names of a lot of the chords I use. I'd be so embarrassed, as I am sometimes if people come up to me in a pub: "Ah, I love that song! I play piano. I can never quite work out what key that starts in." Oh dear. I can't tell them. Change the subject because I don't know. It's not important to me. It's what gets that thing in your head, that weird blob of floating grey plasma, into the world and makes it solid. I usually never knew the chords to my songs, but I definitely never knew them to Colin's. Dave would be very conscientious: "That's just a C, G, D and an A minor 7, I've got those." So I was like, "OK, so Dave's got the chords covered, I better look for the motif or the curlicue." Dave would be getting the house built, so I could give myself the task of deciding what colour each room's going to be. My playing on Colin's songs tended to be more out-there than the playing on my songs.

Mark: What if you're writing for somebody else, because you said you were very good at imitation?

Andy: Yes, writing for other people is largely imitation or, if it's a specific job for Artist A, you think, "OK, I'm going to write stuff that I know Artist A sings or plays like, so I'm going to get inside that mind-set or that style of music."

Mark: And you just feel your way into it? Because there are some people who would be able to say, "He's clearly playing this in the key of F sharp."

Andy: No, I have to blunder my way in. It's like an acting role. You want a bit of Richard Burton? Right, I better try and do the body language, the accent and what he would wear for this part.

Mark: Acting is a good example, because there are a lot of actors who are instinctive not intellectual.

Andy: Which is why I'm embarrassed if I'm trapped and people ask me questions about structure or the key of a song. "What are the first five chords in *Easter Theatre*?" I don't know. My fingers can kind of remember the shapes. That's how I learned to play. There are an awful lot of triangles when you're learning the guitar. D is a triangle that sounds yellow. E is this greeny, khaki shade but the triangle has fallen over a bit. Trumpets are like orange eggs. In the last few years, A seems to me almost turquoise or sky blue (I may have said a different colour in the past).

It's part of that synaesthesia thing. I used to have the same fever dream over and over as a kid. I even tried writing a song about it but I couldn't capture it. It was lots of misshapen Perspex boxes with letters in them jiggling round. They would all be the same letter, so this Perspex box with the light shining underneath it would have lots of the letter R in there, all jiggling around. And the next misshapen Perspex box would have lots of letter Ts. Imagine a printer's tray with all these letters about 2in or 3in long being magnetically excited. That was a repeat fever dream and maybe something to do with being a slow reader and being intimidated by print.

> *'I don't know what I'm going to be playing until the last second – and I might be thinking about the rhythm of it, not the correct chords'*

WITH LOGIC AND LOVE
Mixing it up in the shed

Mark: Has songwriting always been easy for you?

Andy: Yeah. In fact, it's got a bit too facile. All day I'm making up songs, trying to make Erica laugh. Just stupid songs, like, "How many songs can I sing where the phrase 'poo-poo' is included?" I'm doing it constantly. I can't stop it.

It's like brain diarrhoea. Maybe it's a way of letting the overflow out.

Mark: But you've occasionally gone through periods of writer's block, have you?

Andy: Yes and it's very oppressive. I've always found that when the writer's block broke... *Rook* came at the end of quite a long writer's block, several months of nothing and I was desperate to find things. *Rook* scared the pants off me. A) I never knew where it had come from and B) it really frightened me – am I looking at a song about my own mortality? I cried my eyes out, but, it was like, "Thank you, I've broken the duck."

Mark: Does all of that stuff you've been saying about being untutored and not theory-based go out of the window when you turn on your Logic Pro X and you're dealing with delay panning and parallel compression?

Andy: Over the past few years I've got pretty good at mixing. A lot of it is to do with my friendship with Stuart Rowe who I first met on the *Monstrance* sessions. I was stood in the studio, saying, "I wish I had a wah-wah pedal for this piece," and in walks this jovial, bald-headed fellow and says, "My name's Stuart, I'm a teacher here. I've got a wah-wah pedal. Do you want me to run home and get it for you?" I thought, "I like this bloke!" I struck up an immediate friendship. He's a ludicrously positive individual. He was teaching Logic to kids at Swindon College and I found that by looking over his shoulder, I was learning how to work Logic. I was on Cubase at the time.

Mark: You will also have picked up the general principles just by being in professional recording studios.

Andy: Yes, absolutely. You forget how much of that goes in. There was a time when I'd go into Stuart's house every Thursday and Friday. He'd be recording local artists or working on his own music or some of our own stuff as the Clubmen, which still has to see the light of day. We'd be learning how to mix and trying out techniques we'd read about. We were into helping each other. Then we worked on *Gonwards* together and I'm rather happy with the way that came out in terms of recording and mixing. I did *Apples and Oranges* and *Humanoid Boogie* to convince myself that I can do finished-quality stuff that doesn't have to sound like a demo.

Mark: Is it a different part of your brain because it does seem contradictory to say the person who doesn't know what chord he's playing actually does know how to make a finished mix.

Andy: Yes, I guess it's because I need to know how to make a finished mix, how to make that bass guitar sound good and how to get that snare drum to sit properly against that piano. I need to know all that but I don't need to know how to write music. It's not useful to me, but recording and mixing is useful to me. It's chimp like; this typewriter is no use to this chimp, but how to open that banana is really useful. It's a necessary skill, but I still can't drive a car and I still haven't learned to swim. I never really needed to be a car driver. I don't need to read music or know the names of the chords; I can do that with my ear. It sounds like it ought to be the right chord at this point and if it's not, I'll thrash away until I find it. But I do need to make the computer work enough to run Logic and to know what to do with that compressor plug-in and the pre-delay of that reverb plug-in.

Mark: Not only are there millions of plug-ins, but even on a single plug-in there are a trillion settings. Do you just have to say, "Right, go for roughly that," because the level of precision is far greater than the human ear can ever hear?

Andy: Yes and a lot of it can bog you down. "OK,

> *'D is a triangle that sounds yellow. E is this greeny, khaki shade but the triangle has fallen over. Trumpets are like orange eggs'*

I've got this idea for a guitar figure and I want to capture this quickly. I think it needs a lot of reverb on it, but I'm going to bang it down real quick and forget the reverb for now."

Then you go back and refine it later rather than letting the precise technical nature of what's required stop the creativity. You mustn't stop the kid from creating. Don't stop the kid throwing the paints around, spraying the glue and slapping the Plasticine on every surface. You can clean it up later if you need to.

Mark: Presumably you can spend days and days getting more and more obsessed by your own home recordings.

Andy: And I do. I think, "I slapped down that bass so quickly, I can do it so much better and those are not quite the right notes." Before you know it, you've spent two or three days re-doing a bass, getting precisely the notes you want and it's infinite. If you're not careful, as you walk through the maze, you can see an awful lot of pathways in front of you that you mustn't be too tempted to follow. Don't take your hand off the left side of the wall or you'll get lost. Stay on the mission.

Mark: The technology that even a casual music creator might have now on their computer compared with what Elvis had or Chuck Berry had is infinitely better, but Elvis and Chuck Berry still sound fantastic.

Andy: They were unburdened by anything technical which, to some extent, I wish I was still. But, then again, because I can't afford £1000 a day to dick around in a studio for two or three weeks, I have to have my own studio to dick around in - and to dick around in it, I've got nobody to work it. I would like it if I could just walk into this lovely valve-equipped, pegboard-covered studio at the foot of the garden and ask the fellow in the Bri-Nylon shirt with the metal shirt-sleeve clips to stub out his cigarette for a moment and get the microphone working because I've got a whole load of soul. But, no, you've got to be your own engineer, your own sweeper-upper, your own builder sometimes.

Mark: If you went back to Elvis and Chuck Berry, could their recordings actually be improved by the technology that exists now?

Andy: Yes, but it would kill it. "Improved" would be the wrong word. It would be an alternate thing. They could be not what they were. Roughness is its own excitement. You can fake roughness but it's not as good as genuine roughness.

Mark: When you're in your shed do you try to create a bit of roughness?

Andy: Unfortunately, it does tend to be ironed out because you want to sound as professional as possible. You think, "People are just not going to buy too lo-fi a quality from me." Part of me wants to bang it down quickly and if it's a bit out of tune and a bit of wrong EQ, "Never mind, they'll swallow any old shit..."

No, my quality control now means I can only let stuff out if it's a certain technical standard. That does tend to smooth off the rough edges.

Mark: Because you're not in a band, you can't say, "Well, this is what the band sounds like."

Andy: No, you've got to plan everything out. I can leave a drum rhythm going and sketch out a whole song with one pattern, but then I'll go back: "Oh, I need a lovely little roll for that bit. And I need that roll to be a little more exciting. Can I edit something from some loops? If I get the microphone over the snare at the back of the room, can I drop in the rolls manually? Why don't I take the drums off and do it on tom-toms instead?" You're still searching for what's inside your head. You're still fumbling around, not totally in the dark but certainly in a poorly lit room - or a psychedelically lit room and it's a bit confusing. It would be nice to have Abbey Road or Sun Studios at the bottom of the garden.

Mark: But you also enjoy the whole mixing aspect of it.

Andy: Yes and it is my job, so thank Sod, I enjoy doing it. Can you think of a better way of living than that?

Interview conducted on 10 October 2018.

JUST FOR ME TO MIX IN SPACE

I have learned to mix rather well in the last five years, if I say so myself. For all the home recorders out there, here are my favourite tips which you'll find all over Gonwards and Apples and Oranges/Humanoid Boogie...

BY ANDY PARTRIDGE

PARALLEL COMPRESSION
- or New York compression. Set up heavy compression on a bus, send almost anything you like to it, instant record sound!

STEREO SPACE
- either mono reverbs panned away from sound or a copy of sound set back timewise and panned away. Makes width in mixes.

BASS
- always leave till last, like Macca and Colin. Find your space better and don't over-play like many people who track bass and drums first can be prone to do.

BEST BASS
- I struggled with bass sound for years until I did this. Split/copy bass to two tracks. Have nothing above 100k for deep bass track... Compress and limit hard. High bass track = nothing below 100k, sculpt with EQ and compress to fill in detail in track.

BEST AUDIO
- and it's free: Voxengo visual EQ picture meter: www.voxengo.com/product/span/. If your home studio isn't flat, which it won't be, download this to see rogue frequencies. Best thing that happened to my home recordings. Subtractive EQ also the only real way.

EQ REVERBS
- set EQ up before reverbs. Roll off bass (so easy to crowd) and roll off tops on longer reverbs. Reverbs will sit better and not add problems by doubling up frequencies that are a bit "active". Learn to make rhythm with your pre-delay also. Delay before reverb is good.

DARK DELAY
- roll tops and bottoms off delays, like tape would do. This makes delays easier to sit. Pan them away from source sound.

COMPARE YOUR FAVES
- every ten minutes or so, listen to your favourite recordings to see if you are in the ballpark. Are you as deep, bright, loud, etc?

MIX BUS
- experiment with mix-bus chain. I like EQ first, then a UA version of an SSL mix bus compressor, then a limiter and SPAN, while ready for mix (recently I have been adding a device that centres the low frequencies first in the chain). Always take off SPAN pre-mix.

COMPRESSOR
- always overdo the compressor like crazy to hear the rhythm of the attack/release of instrument, then back off until feels good/not false.

ACOUSTIC GUITARS
- mic away from hole, at neck join or bridge. Again overdo compressor to find best rhythm. Always roll out bass unless acoustic is solo.

SPACE FOR BASS
- sculpt off bass from keys, as bass and bass drum need the space. Let kick have the low floor, cut bass just above to sit it.

COMPARE COMPARE COMPARE
- listen to your favourites, I say it again...

THE LINE
- with SPAN you'll notice the best-sounding records are virtually a flat line, ie, all frequencies are taken care of and none are too under-done or stick out. It's a good thing to aim for. If you run your favourites through SPAN you'll see this.

BEND THAT ECHO
- if you have a delay that can modulate the sound, use it. Gives more life and movement to your delays. Pan delays away from source.

TOP WHACK
- if your computer will allow, always record at 96kHz or up. This is an eater of space but bass will sound richer and tops less distorted.

PILE UPS
- watch out. It's easier with visuals, like SPAN, to see where frequencies pile up. Two spots that crowd are 100Hz and 1kHz, most instruments have lots of these in them. You have to decide who will dominate. Roll out frequencies on those that are not so important.

ROLL IT OFF
- cutting frequencies is so important to allow space for others to come through. Guitars can be cut below 100Hz. High percussion things like hi-hat and tambourine can be cut below 200-300Hz, you won't need it. Vocals roll off gently below 100Hz. Backing vocals even higher

HOW FAR IS IT?
- remember, things you want farther from the mic have less bass and top. Nearer = more.

LIVE DRUMS
- kits mix themselves, so one mic usually does the trick. Try to get separate bass drum and overheads if you have limited space. You'll always need more kick in the mix than you think.

CYMBALS LATER
- if you have limited space and only a few mics, work on snare and toms sound primarily. Drop cymbals on later, synched to bass drum.

NO DRUM ROOM
- tiny room? Take drum mix that sounds balanced, feed to room reverb, then record. Then compress that reverb until it pumps in rhythm and feed to drum mix to make fake ambience.

GUITARS
- distorted guitars, run through de-esser, find "ouch" high frequencies, tame and then can add EQ later, without ear piercing.

PIANO (sampled)
- for more real pianos, once you have your part, drag to another track and add another piano sound. Blend/tune/pan both.

NUMBER ONE
- don't record/master too loud, allow for some dynamic range and let the music breathe.

YOUR BEST BUTTONS
- mono, to check how it all sits. Turn the volume down, mix quietly. Check the stereo picture in cans.

DEEP CENTRE
- keep your low sounds in the centre. Higher sounds can go to the sides of the stereo picture. Balance: tambourine one side, hi-hat on the other.

WHAT DO YOU CALL THAT NOISE?

LIFE BEGINS AT THE HOP

LIFE BEGINS AT THE HOP

PHOTO © LOU DONNETT YOUNG

They were the gigs nobody imagined possible. A full 36 years after the last ever XTC concert, Terry Chambers and Colin Moulding took to the stage once more. Fans from around the world congregated for the six TC&I shows at Swindon Arts Centre. There was jiggling in the seats and singing in the stalls. Adults were seen to weep

BY MARK FISHER

Andy Miller has a theory. The author, editor and original *Limelight* reader reckons the story of TC&I is structured like a Victorian novel. Think of a sprawling epic by Dickens or Hardy and there'll always be a character in the first chapter who gets banished to a faraway land. For the sake of argument, let's call him Terry and imagine he's been whisked off from Smalltown, Wiltshire to the other side of the world, never to be heard of again. Thirty chapters in, after heights have been scaled, arguments have erupted and conflicts resolved, it looks as if balance has been achieved in Smalltown. The protagonists – we'll call them Colin, Dave and Andy – have worked out a way to live in reasonable proximity, no longer the old gang of music-makers, but maintaining some kind of equilibrium.

A lesser author would finish the novel there on this bitter-sweet but underwhelming note. A master storyteller, however, would play the trump card. Suddenly, on a dark-and-stormy night, that enigmatic character from the first chapter, the one the protagonists thought they'd never see again and the readers had forgotten about, is discovered on the streets of Smalltown. After 30-odd years in Australia, Terry is back. And he has unfinished business.

Initially, his old chums are pleased to see him, but his presence changes everything. The uneasy truce that has been keeping Smalltown peaceful can hold only for as long as Terry shows no favouritism to Colin, Dave or Andy. Any coalition will require a redrawing of the boundaries. Terry's aim is to turn back the clocks and get the band together again, but failing that, he'll throw his hat in the ring with anyone who'll join him. By striking an alliance with Colin, he gives the novel a fresh dynamic. Matters, gentle reader, will never be quite the same again.

Hence the *Great Aspirations* EP and the gigs nobody, not even the most attentive reader, expected to happen. Way back in chapter one (or was it even the prologue?), Colin and Terry played Swindon Arts Centre for the first time. That was in March 1973 and it was their first post-Star Park gig. Whole books have been written about the intervening years, but now, at the end of July 2018, the bass player and drummer announce they are returning to the stage. The last time that happened was 36 years earlier. "It's exciting times," says Chambers. "Eighteen months ago I couldn't see this happening – I'm as excited about these gigs as I was in 1973 playing our first gig at the Swindon Arts Centre as a 17-year-old Helium Kid, and the first time to be playing with Colin together on stage since San Diego."

The long-standing rhythm section say they will be joined by Steve Tilling on guitar and Gary Bamford on keyboards and guitar. Multi-instrumentalist and session musician Tilling is the man behind CIRCU5, whose debut album *The Amazing Monstrous Grady* featured a guest appearance from Dave Gregory. Swindon musician Bamford has an extensive history of writing, orchestrating, teaching and collaborating. Tickets for the first four dates will go on sale at 10am on Monday 30 July. At least one American fan sets his alarm clock for 3.30am so he'll be online at the right time.

Talking to DJ Iain Lee on Talk Radio at the start of August, Colin and Terry sound in good spirits. Terry looks back on his split with XTC with the wisdom of age, realising that had they had better management, perhaps someone suggesting they take six months off, the band could have stayed together. As it was, he couldn't see his drumming style fitting in with the songs for *Mummer* and didn't reckon the material was up to par (he says Andy even suggested ditching them and writing a load more if he would stay). Heading to Australia with his new wife looked like a better option, but he can now see how things could have been different with more understanding.

At this stage, they're coy about the set list, despite Lee's efforts to get them to commit. What Colin does say is that the songs will be in a less polished state than the recorded versions. "We booked it all ourselves," he says. "We thought, 'Let's form a combo with two other guys, we'll have a little bit of rehearsal and let's just play the songs in their raw state – no back-screen projection, folks.'"

"We're still trying to sort the running order of these

songs out," says Terry. "We may tell you something now and it might not be the same in three months' time. We're still trying to get the material together with these other two guys, as well as ourselves. It's taking shape but we're still juggling where they're going."

Colin adds: "A lot of them have got very high production values, the XTC things. We're doing them on a completely different palette."

Later, Terry says they'll be playing "some songs from nearly all the albums," which means he'll be playing on material he paid little or no attention to when it was released. "The fact that they continued on was too close to my heart, thinking, 'What would I have done in those circumstances?' They had some great guys playing and I'm trying to tread in their shoes."

Colin calls it "Pete Best syndrome" in reference to the drummer who left the Beatles before their greatest triumphs. Terry adds: "I'm having to tread as close as I possibly can in the footsteps of great drummers. That's been challenging in itself, let alone trying to remember what I did myself."

The two of them are overwhelmed at the response for the gigs, having imagined just their friends would turn up and not fans taking transatlantic flights. "We've got an ordeal of the most grievous kind," laughs Colin, joking that it's been so long since he's been on stage he'll have to be shown where to stand. Even in the days of XTC, it was Andy who was the face of the band, flanked on stage by Colin and Dave. "Never having been a front man, I obviously have much to learn," Colin tells me later.

Terry tells Lee the Arts Centre was the first place they played when they were 17: "I'm probably as nervous now as I was then, despite over those years we played some pretty big places and it didn't bother me too much."

Lee seems surprised at their modesty and reminds them of the tremendous affection being expressed by fans on social media. He says they could read the phone book and fans would show up. "Someone said perhaps Colin will read some notes from a gardening book and Chambers will be just drunk in a corner, so perhaps that might be sufficient," laughs the drummer.

In early September, Colin tells Charlie Crane of the *Stereo Hysteria* podcast (www.podomatic.com) there's a big difference between XTC in the era of *Black Sea* at the height of their live power and the place he and Terry find themselves today. "The top of the touring machine we were then," he says. "We were pretty locked in. But you've got to remember that we'd been playing gigs since the mid 70s every week, so you do get pretty tight. We just put in the time gigging. Playing together now, God knows what it's going to be like. We're going to be the loosest we've been for ages because he hasn't played drums for half his life and I haven't played live either. It's going to be interesting but you can never be that tight again."

Asked about the difference between working in the studio and playing live, Colin says he prefers recording because of the creative opportunities it opens up, but having been focusing on the Arts Centre gigs for several months, that's where his head is currently at. They each require their own way of thinking, he says, and as the gigs approach, the idea of studio recording has faded into the background: "It wouldn't be as easy now to make that flit between one and the other, whereas we used to do it without a by your leave."

Rehearsals are in progress, he says, preparing to step up the work rate now they're operating as a four-piece with Tilling and Bamford. Crane wants to know if the muscle memory is still there for his old parts, but Colin's attitude is to approach the material anew. "We're deferring to the recording, but we're not slaves to it," he says, pleased to be renewing his acquaintance with songs that would otherwise have been confined to the past. "Those recordings were a moment in time that XTC did. It's better to be a first-class version of yourself than a second-class version of somebody else and this band should have a life all of its own. We don't want to copy what the other guys did. What the other guys did on the records was fantastic, but that was XTC. To try and copy a moment... you can never get four guys to sound like 15. I could have got more people on stage and we could have got things closer but I just didn't think it was the right thing to do."

With the gigs a month or so away, intrigue steps up as Colin tells *Broadway World Music* that "we will go for the more idiosyncratic songs that I wrote for the band, songs that were tucked away in corners. We seem to have gone where the tribute bands never go."

The social media chatter intensifies. What could those "idiosyncratic songs" be? *Find the Fox*? The *Good Things*? *Bungalow*? The conversation in the TC&I Facebook group speculates not just on the set list, but the set order. How prominent will the *Great Aspirations* songs be? Will they save *Generals and Majors* and *Making Plans for Nigel* till last? What would be the opener? Suggestions range from *Washaway* to *Deliver Us from the Elements*, from *Runaways* to *Wake Up*. Or might they work chronologically through the catalogue kicking off with *Cross Wires*? One fan, David Bandler, compiles a list of about 70 Moulding songs. Another, Peter Steckel, imagines a tantalising segue from the "slow outro of *Blame the Weather*... blended into *The Good Things*". A rumour goes round that there could be a cover version. Kieron Bowker, one of the page's administrators, scotches that idea but hints they might play one of Andy's songs. All anyone knows, as group member Chris Chennell predicts, is that "many songs will be played, there will be clapping and cheering. Much feasting in the aisles will be had."

Towards the end of September, Bowker announces on Facebook that the support act will be George Wilding, a 22-year-old singer-songwriter from Avebury, Wiltshire. Like just about everyone in the local music scene, Wilding has worked with Stu Rowe, who mixed TC&I's *Great Aspirations* as well as working closely with Andy Partridge.

At the start of October, Swindon's Gaz Barrett, one of the organisers of the 2017 fan convention, realises Steve Tilling is one of his neighbours. He takes the opportunity to quiz the guitarist about being in TC&I's band. They talk about Tilling's musical training, formative influences (Hawkwind's *Levitation*) and his circuitous route to releasing his CIRCU5 album in 2017. Meeting Colin and Terry, he says, took place through mutual friend Stu Rowe in a local pub: "I was a bit nervous as I've been an XTC fan for years, and not because they're local - I just love the music. But we got on really well. It's hard not to - they're great blokes."

Having signed up to join the band he went away for a month to learn the songs. "Then I had my first session in Colin's studio, where he showed me the proper chords, and I learned them again," he says, adding that the choice of material has primarily been down to Colin and Terry based on what they feel comfortable performing. He's seen the set-list speculation on Facebook, but has to accept they can't play everything. "Rest assured, we've considered them all," he says. "If we're playing them, it's because we think they can stand up to the originals. Be gentle, folks."

He tells Barrett he'll have five guitars on stage, mainly to cope with Colin's "exotic tunings": a Fender Telecaster Thinline 72, a Fender Strat, a "souped-up" Epiphone Les Paul, a Kremona classical and a Washburn Cumbernauld acoustic. He'll be putting them through a head-spinning array of compressors, overdrives and pedals, channelled to his Fender Hot Rod Deluxe IV amp with Cannabis Rex speakers and a Marshall AS100D acoustic amplifier. "Colin's songs are sonically lush, so needs must," he says.

Most importantly, he's loving being in a band with Colin, Terry and Gary, enjoying their musicianship as well as their sense of humour. For all the nervousness in the build-up to the gigs, he can't wait to get on stage. "Expectations are high and mistakes may happen," he says.

"But I think people are in for a treat. We're going to do the very best we can and enjoy ourselves - and hopefully the audiences will too."

To Ian Leak on Frome FM, Terry talks about his return to Swindon after so many years in Australia and hooking up with Colin again - initially just on a two-week visit and then permanently. "Why do you think you work so well together," asks Leak. "We grew with each other as regards our early playing," says Terry. "He was the only bass player I ever played with throughout that period and likewise as a drummer, he never really played with anybody else until I left the band. We developed quite an understanding. Thirty-four years sounds like a long time, and it is, but it didn't seem difficult to get back in with him. Prior to that we'd spent so much time together, it's like an old pair of shoes."

The opportunity to play four nights in a row in a venue as intimate as the 212-seater Swindon Arts Centre will also be an advantage for recording the gigs. They'll be able to leave the recording equipment in place and choose the best performances for a possible live album. "Over four nights, hopefully we can get some decent stuff," he says. "Then we'll mull over that."

Leak has been following the set-list conjecture among fans on Facebook and wonders if Terry can give any more clues. Terry sticks to the party line, but says: "We're touching every album apart from one. Don't ask me why that is, it just turned out that way. We're going to be playing a few songs from most of the albums. All the songs are Colin's songs apart from one that he didn't write, but is an XTC song - that's about as far as I can go! It's a bit like going to a movie and someone bleating out, 'It was the butler that did it.'"

Cue fevered speculation about which Partridge composition they will choose and which album will not be represented. "I can't give anything away," says Tilling on Facebook. "Terry would spank me!"

At around the same time on the *Life Elsewhere* podcast, Colin gives an overview of his career and his approach to songwriting before host Norman Batley (aka Norman B) picks a handful of questions from fans sent in on Twitter. Gaz Barrett is first up, wondering where Colin would most like to play live. It's an opportunity to plug the Swindon Arts Centre gigs as Colin admits the venue's intimacy and personal history makes it perfect for him. Could there be set-list clues in Colin's answer to another question about the ten XTC songs he would include in a Moulding-only XTC album? Norman B suggests he narrows it down to three. "I'd have to put *Nigel*, maybe *King for a Day* and a lot of people like *One of the Millions*," says Colin, who says if he could re-record any of his songs he'd return to *Cynical Days*, which was "a bit too loungy in places," as well as doing *Say It* "in a more professional manner". The gigs, he adds, are a way of "re-associating" himself with the songs he'd said goodbye to in the studio.

On his *Dancing About Architecture* blog, Dave Franklin quizzes Colin on how they're going about playing songs live that had previously been done only in the studio. Colin's approach has been to treat TC&I as a band in its own right and to fashion the songs accordingly, without the pressure of sounding like the recorded originals. "We can only play the songs in the way that this combo can do them," says Colin, adding that Bamford's jazz background is bringing a Dudley Moore quality to the mix. "Dudley Moore is playing *King for a Day*!" he jokes, inadvertently revealing a song from the set list.

A few more hints slip out as Colin talks to John Robb of the *Louder than War* website. They'll be playing "mainly idiosyncratic kind of stuff that perhaps tribute bands couldn't play the chords to because it's too convoluted," he says, more or less confirming that *Making Plans for Nigel* will also be in the mix. "I chose stuff slightly left of centre and peculiar to me as an individual."

He says they've had to change some of the keys, not only so he can still sing the songs, but also because the speed of the recordings was sometimes changed in the studio, causing them to "fall in-between two keys". "I also tried to make the stuff as exciting to play as possible and a little bit odd as well," he says, confirming the plan to play a Partridge song as a tribute. "It would have been churlish not to play any of his songs and it's so I can tip my hat to him and say hello." He sounds like he's in fine spirits, but asked if he's nervous, he doesn't hold back. "'Nervous? I'm terrified! Jesus! this is a bit different after all this time! Let's hope there is a lot of love in the room."

Standing in front of Terry's drum kit again has been exciting, Colin tells Dave Jennings, writing on the *Shadow of a Dream* blog: "I'd forgotten what a violent drummer he was, it's like an explosion in your eardrum. I've played with other people over the years, session guys etc, but getting back with Terry is quite refreshing, he has a certain energy with his playing and he's quite physical live which is all to the good, thinking about the upcoming gigs."

Close to a fortnight before the first gig, *Record Collector* hits the shelves with a three-page feature by Iain Lee based on his radio interview with Colin and Terry from August. Little more emerges from the TC&I camp even when Kieron Bowker secures an interview with Bamford for the band's Facebook page. The multi-instrumentalist, whose musical influences range from big-band jazz to prog and new wave, says lots about his musical education and mentions that he and Tilling were at New College in Swindon together in 1989 without knowing each other that well. He gives away next to nothing about rehearsals, however. "The music's superb, the playing's great and the guys are really fun to hang with," he says. "There are worse ways to spend one's time."

As the days tick down, seven, six, five..., fans check in on Facebook, sharing their headshots and describing their planned journeys. Jason Beck says he's coming from Winnipeg, still awestruck that the musician he thought had left the music business was no longer in "the past tense". Others are flying in from Washington, DC, Los Angeles, Italy and Israel. By sheer good fortune, New York drummer Mikey Erg has a TC&I-shaped gap in his touring schedule: being in Frankfurt on Sunday and Birmingham on Tuesday, he can race to Swindon in between.

Five days in advance, Charlie Thomas, director of the *This Is Pop* documentary teases us on Twitter: "Last time I saw XTC was at the Lyceum in 1980. Last night, 38 years on, I caught a sneak preview of Terry and Colin's show and it was a joy to see and hear one of the great rhythm sections back in action. Those of you with tickets to next week's shows are in for a treat." Turns out there have been two secret warm-up gigs at the Victoria pub in Swindon, booked as a private party with two sets each night. According to friends of Kieron Bowker, the music "sounds great and TC&I are in top, top form." Just to keep those in the know on tenterhooks, the Vic gigs skipped a couple of songs that will be at the Arts Centre.

The day before the first gig, fans are already arriving in town and posting pictures from the first drinking session in the Tuppenny, the pub across the road from the venue. Knowing how to please its market, the bar has refashioned its menu to include a *Dear God* burger accompanied by an XTC playlist on the house PA.

And so Monday 29 October arrives and the chatter on Facebook and Twitter becomes intense. "I am beyond excited," writes Nigel Waller, as he sets off from Yorkshire. "Remember that Christmas Eve feeling when you were young? That's how I feel and I'm 55! I cannot wait." He's not the only one whose inner teenager has awoken. "I've been waiting for this since I was turned away from a cancelled *English Settlement* gig 36 years ago," says David Nolan, signing off from Facebook to avoid spoilers before his Tuesday gig.

It's a clear, crisp day in Swindon, the first bite of winter chill in the air but bright and sunny with it. On Twitter, Andy sends good vibes to his old band mates: "Wishing Colin and Terry much fun and success with the forthcoming TC&I shows. Break a stick chaps." In return, they send him a message of thanks. Fans have started hooking up with each other over the afternoon, gravitating to the Arts

> *'This isn't the fiery XTC of old, all breakneck speed and thow-yourself-about aggression, but a band with a more nuanced selection of songs'*

Centre in good time for the 7.45pm kick off. The air is friendly and subdued, nobody quite believing this is actually happening. Manning the stall selling TC&I gig T-shirts and the vinyl edition of the *Great Aspirations* EP, Colin's wife Carol Moulding and Terry's girlfriend Lynn Farrar are in good spirits, pleased to see the fruits of their partners' summer of hard work finally paying off. Taking the stage promptly before the seated audience, support act George Wilding runs through an acoustic set or original material, enjoying the attention before the main attraction. "I've just been told I've got two more songs," he says. "Which means two more songs till TC&I."

Almost as soon as he has left the stage to warm applause, we hear the familiar chords of *Bungalow* and, without fanfare, the band take their places behind their instruments, Colin keeping his back to us before turning to acknowledge the applause. It's a restrained arrival, whether through nervousness, modesty or keeping expectations in check. It sends a message: this is going to be a gig about songs not showmanship, although Tilling, boldly melding the guitar parts once played by Andy Partridge and Dave Gregory, goes all-out to connect to the audience, showing no sign of the heavy cold he's suffering (later diagnosed as laryngitis). For the moment, Colin is focusing on the music and, after a brief *Bungalow*-based instrumental workout, provides the first surprise of the night as they segue into *Say It*. His last song for XTC becomes the first in TC&I's debut set and the crowd roars its approval.

While Bamford keeps his head down, stage left, alternating between keyboards and rhythm guitar, Colin's son Lee Moulding joins Tilling for backing vocals and extra percussion on the other side. At the back of the stage, Terry keeps out of the limelight. He's a powerhouse not a showman, concentrating on serving up a precise and powerful rhythm with only scant acknowledgement of the crowd – or even the band for that matter. His kit is a mixture of Premier, Royale, Ludwig and others, while Colin's basses include the custom-built instrument made for him by Dennis Fano and, for one song only, his Epiphone.

It's natural to expect Colin and Terry to delve into classic XTC-era repertoire because that's when they last worked together, yet who would have guessed their first track from *Drums and Wires* would have been *Day In Day Out* – a song they didn't play live the first time round? It sets the tone for the evening: this isn't the fiery XTC of old, all breakneck speed and throw-yourself-about aggression, but a band with a more nuanced selection of songs that befits not only the age of the musicians (and most of the audience), but also the nature of Colin's post-live material.

Colin is thrown – and a little agitated – by his monitors not working for the first couple of songs, but from the audience's point of view it's a full, well-balanced sound from the start.

As if to make a point, they stick with *Drums and Wires* for *That Is the Way*, another song that was never in the XTC set. That's after Colin has welcomed the 200-strong audience with a generous offer. "Don't go off into the night until we've met you," he says, a reminder this is a home-town gig in the best sense – they want everyone to feel at home here. Nor is Colin above acknowledging the strangeness of a night few people, including him, ever thought would happen. "This is another one from the Jurassic period," he jokes before launching into a crowd-pleasing *Ten Feet Tall*.

Time to remember how the gig came about in the first place with a double helping of *Great Aspirations*; first *Greatness*, then *Scatter Me*, with Susannah Bevington joining the band to reprise her heavenly soprano in the song's closing section. "Here's another throwback," says Colin, introducing *Wonderland*, one of the highlights of the night, ironically because they don't treat it as a throwback. With Terry playing jazzy triplets on the cymbals, Colin playing a funky bass line than seems to nod to Motown, and Tilling on slide guitar, it becomes a tougher proposition than on record, without sacrificing the dreaminess. I speak to at least one fan whose feelings about *Wonderland* go from dislike to like, thanks to this interpretation.

Proving this is a set that ploughs its own furrow, they turn to the collector's favourite *Where Did* the Ordinary People Go?, the download-only single recorded in Andy's shed in 2003. By the time we get to Grass, Terry has switched to mallets, in keeping with the softer nature of the material. He proves adept at taking on the parts played by his successor drummers while bringing his own muscularity to a glorious version of The Meeting Place before an unexpected interval – apparently a requirement of the venue. It feels like being woken in the middle of a dream, but having pinched ourselves in the bar and convinced each other this really is happening, we return all the more certain we're in for a good time.

It also gives the band a chance to surprise us again with a second-act opener that nobody expects. A didgeridoo-like throb initially throws us off the scent of Sacrificial Bonfire, a song too fragile to withstand normal rock-gig treatment but a powerfully atmospheric way to ease us into the second half. Things step up with a War Dance that does justice to the song's slinky rhythmic texture, underpinned by the stately drumming of Terry, who goes on to give real punch to Big Day.

Another highlight as Colin puts down his bass and Terry leaves the stage for a mesmerising Bungalow. Colin, in strong voice throughout the night (no legacy of years on the touring circuit for him), closes his eyes and counts time with Bamford's plaintive keyboard chords, tastefully supplemented by Tilling's nervy guitar. Later, Stu Rowe tells me he encouraged Colin to go for a stripped-back approach not only to bring out the song's yearning beauty but also to give tonal variety to the evening. His instinct was right – and, had the fate of TC&I been different, the song could have flourished even further.

For now, though, it's time to up the pace with The Smartest Monkeys followed by an odd reworking of Cynical Days. Colin's instinct to avoid the smooth edges of the record might be justified, but this arrangement, with its shuffling verses and rockier beat seems to flatten the song and rob it of its subtlety. Full marks for trying something different though (and other opinions are available: Paul Pledger on Flipside Reviews finds it "tellingly transformed"). A driving version of Kenny lets them "continue with the theme of demolition" as they go into Ball and Chain, showing Terry in all his thundering English Settlement glory. Like Wonderland, King for a Day has a new-found funky groove, enhanced by Terry's deft cymbal work. The mood stays buoyant with a bouncy Standing in for Joe – another revelation for many fans.

Entering into greatest-hits territory, Terry has us clapping along before we even know we're into Generals and Majors, given such a raucous roar of approval that Colin can only grin. "I guess I'm back then," he says with a mixture of modesty, bewilderment and pride. Making Plans for Nigel ends the main set – how could it not? – with the audience gleefully joining in on the backing vocals. The final surprise of the night comes with the first encore. It's time for the much speculated Partridge song, which turns out to be Statue of Liberty, Colin singing it like it was his own and delighting us all the more. Andy would have been proud. They go out with a thumping parallel-universe hit in the form of Life Begins at the Hop to a crowd who have well and truly loosened up (on later nights Colin slips in the bass line of Pretty Woman with a cheeky grin just as the song kicks off).

"You were incredible," says Tilling the next day to the TC&I fans on Facebook. "You couldn't have made Colin, Terry and the band feel more welcome. We were blown away." Among the fans, the reaction is a mixture of wonder and disbelief. The people I talk to are impressed by the extensiveness of the set – 24 songs in all – and the professionalism of the band. Nobody can believe they have gone to such effort to perform just six gigs in such a small venue. This could easily have been a cynical attempt to capture the 1980s nostalgia market, or a sad spectacle involving two men approaching pension age pretending to be teenagers. It is neither. What TC&I pull off is an artistically coherent revisiting of the Moulding songbook that places early observational classics such as Day In Day Out alongside later slice-of-life favourites from Skylarking et al and shows them to be on a single continuum. They make no pretence at being the high-voltage band that tirelessly toured the world in the late 70s, much as Terry's drumming combined with Colin's bass-playing remains a powerful force. Nor do they put undue emphasis on the hits – such as they were. This is not the set of a shallow tribute act but of a band called TC&I that just happens to have a 40-year catalogue to draw on, one that ventures thematically from workplace boredom to first romance, from death to militarism, from urban destruction to pagan ritual. They are what Paul Pledger's crit on *Flipside Reviews* calls "self-effacing and quintessentially down-to-earth songs that tug at the heartstrings as well as the brain".

"XTC fans are the warmest people in the world," says George Wilding at Tuesday's gig. Having broken the ice the night before, Colin is visibly more relaxed. It might just be me, but Terry seems louder, his rhythms ever more supple. Now diagnosed with laryngitis, Tilling leaves the backing vocals to Lee Moulding and Bamford, and the sound is less full as a result. Tilling, though, shows no less puppy-dog enthusiasm as he knocks out his guitar licks. On Twitter, Larry Stevens reports that "the lady at the reception says she's ... NEVER seen anything like this. People coming from all over the world, shivering in excitement; grown men crying for joy. She said I knew XTC were from here but I never knew they had such a devoted following."

The hard-core bunch of us who are in town for the first four shows agree that Wednesday's is the best yet. The set list is identical and Tilling's laryngitis is no better (mid afternoon he felt so bad he wondered if he'd make it at all), but the band are growing in confidence and starting to smile. Not only that but the audience are in raucous mood, much quicker to get on their feet and dancing at the foot of the stage by the end. Terry still slips behind the drums without fanfare, but Colin's entrance is now unapologetic; it's not exactly showbiz but he does manage a welcoming wave. Better still, all the musicians take a bow at the end, giving the crowd a chance to show their love.

They repeat the trick for gig four, having found their feet as a serious live band and giving themselves space to enjoy it. "At this rate we might get home in time for *Newsnight*," jokes Colin after charging through *The Smartest Monkeys*. At the end of *Scatter Me*, he presents Susannah Bevington with a bunch of flowers. "I didn't know that gigging could be that enriching," Colin says later on Facebook. "It's as if the crowd were willing us on. We seemed to levitate on a magic-carpet ride of love – quite extraordinary."

What strikes home is how thoughtfully put together the set is. Thematically and dynamically, it is an intelligent journey through the Moulding catalogue. The opening *Bungalow* work-out on electric guitar anticipates the elemental rendition later in the set. The choice of *Say It* as the first song readies us for unexpected turns. The gathering of songs roughly according to album gives textural coherence. The juxtaposition of *Ball and Chain* and *Kenny* highlights Colin's thematic consistency. Opening the second half with *Sacrificial Bonfire* lends dramatic variety. The closing run of hits pushes up excitement levels to the max. It's a pop gig for sure, but it's artfully done.

As fans exchange opinions on social media, Joe Turner captures it best: "My wife, on the train back to Reading, kept telling me, 'You look like a kid who just opened the best birthday present ever.'"

Jive around, make fools of ourselves, then stop

On 13 January 2019, Bowker breaks some news that makes the gigs feel even more like a dream. It's a letter from Colin. In our Victorian novel, it would be a poignant epilogue. Or could it be a cliffhanger?

> I'd just like to say that I am calling it a day with TC&I and have no plans to do any more. And music itself is on the back burner for now, as I wish to spend more time with my family. I hope people are not too disappointed in me, and I'd just like to thank everyone for the support they have shown Terry and I in these last two years. And to all who came to the gigs and gave us such a triumphant return – I thank you from the bottom of my heart.
> All the best
> Colin

WHAT DO YOU CALL THAT NOISE?

PHOTO © LOU DOMMETT YOUNG

"It's better to be a first-class version of yourself than a second-class version of somebody else," says Colin Moulding in the run-up to the gigs. Taking their curtain call at Swindon Arts Centre, left to right, are Steve Tilling, Terry Chambers, Lee Moulding, Colin Moulding and Gary Bamford.

INDEX OF TITLES

Title	Pages
Abbey Road	34
"A" Bomb in Wardour Street	103
Across this Antheap	48, 91, 146
Action Trax 1	46
Alice's Adventures in Wonderland	84
All Along the Watchtower	113, 185
All Mod Cons	103
All of a Sudden (It's Too Late)	27, 42, 43, 118
All the Young Dudes	128
All Things Must Pass	174
All You Pretty Girls	41–42
Altercations	93
The Amazing Monstrous Grady	210
American Flagg	93
And Your Bird Can Sing	38
Another Satellite	26, 27, 75
Apples and Oranges	204, 206
Apple Venus Volume 1	37, 49, 51, 81, 91, 92, 93, 132, 133, 139, 153, 183, 191, 194
Are You Receiving Me?	67, 147
Atmosphere to Ocean	153
The Avengers	62
Ball and Chain	45, 122–123, 137–138, 146, 148, 216, 217
The Ballad of Peter Pumpkinhead	25, 34, 35, 66, 83
Ballet for a Rainy Day	32, 33, 171
Banana Seat Summer	93
Battery Brides	67, 184
Beasts I've Seen	153
Beating of Hearts	58
The Beatles (book)	174
Beatown	118
Beggin'	197
Being There	57
Big Day	80, 88, 89, 216
The Big Express	30, 65, 71, 72, 75, 78–79, 90, 127, 183, 189, 194
Big Night Music	160
Black Sea	19, 25, 26, 28, 31, 44, 47, 53, 65, 73, 90, 92, 103, 105–106, 116, 117–122, 178–179, 184, 211
The Black Strat	175
Blame the Weather	73, 178, 212
Blue Overall	72, 79
Boarded Up	34, 138
Books Are Burning	34, 35, 49, 50, 55, 97
Brainiac's Daughter	40
The Breakfast Club	88
Bristol Community Big Band	124
Britain's Greatest TV Comedy Moments.	124
Bungalow	35, 56–57, 63, 139–140, 212, 215, 216, 217
Burning with Optimism's Flames	53, 62–63, 108, 119, 120, 155, 184
© (tribute tape)	153
Cambodia	46
Capriol Suite	171, 195
'Cause it's Love (Saint Parallelogram)	27
Chalkhills (website)	30, 133, 148, 149, 151, 153
Chalkhills and Children	12, 21, 69
The Chris Gethard Show	124
Church of Women	26, 183
Classics for Pleasure	163–164
A Clockwork Orange	74
Coat of Many Cupboards	43, 93, 139
Collideascope	38
Come Dancing	139
The Compact XTC	67, 80
Complicated Game	27, 48, 52, 58–59, 68, 69, 91
Complicated Game: Inside the Songs of XTC	11, 61, 95, 96, 124, 148, 150, 186
Comrades of Pop	142
Country Boy	191
Cross Wires	113, 212
Cynical Days	27, 131, 213, 216
Dark in the Spotlight	75
Day In Day Out	63–64, 140, 215, 216
A Day in the Life	40
The Day They Pulled the North Pole Down	43
Dear God	32, 35, 40, 41, 71, 76–77, 87, 88, 130, 151, 180, 184, 193, 195, 196, 214
Dear Madam Barnum	35, 64, 83, 89
Dear Prudence	47
Death by Chocolate: Redux	93
Deliver Us from the Elements	212
Didn't Hurt a Bit	23, 141
The Disappointed	77
(Don't Fear) The Reaper	61
Don't Lose Your Temper	27
Don't Ring Us	153
Down in the Tube Station at Midnight	103
Drums and Wires	19, 24, 27, 47, 52, 54, 57, 58, 59, 64, 65, 73, 80, 86, 90, 103, 105, 106, 114, 115–117, 123, 125, 71, 183–186, 192–193, 215
Dying	30, 32, 63, 91, 183
Earn Enough for Us	32, 39, 80, 82, 87, 88–89, 130
East Coast Racer	196
Easter Theatre	23, 49, 203
The Edinburgh Fringe Survival Guide	124
The Elated World	159
Eleanor Rigby	194
Eleven Different Animals	57
Ella Guru	62
ELO	50, 180
The End	92, 131
English Roundabout	12, 30, 90, 123
English Settlement	27, 42, 45, 47, 52, 53, 57, 65, 73, 86, 90, 92, 93, 97, 98, 112, 122–124, 148, 78, 192, 214, 216
Eternal Flame	125
The Everyday Story of Smalltown	30, 65, 93, 210
Executive	141
Extrovert	129, 184
Find the Fox	12
Fly on the Wall	27, 45
Fossil Fuel	147
Frère Jacques	40
Frivolous Tonight	141, 142, 183
Fruit Nut	140, 142, 183
Funk Pop a Roll	58
Fuzzy Warbles	93, 194
Gangway, Electric Guitar Is Coming Through	131
Garden of Earthly Delights	84–85
Generals and Majors	24, 31, 46, 47, 62, 67, 121, 123, 155, 212, 216
Ghastly Good Taste	137
Ghost in the Machine	122
Giant Steps	81
Glacier Girl	76
Glass Onion	93
Glyn Johns Sound Man	174
Go 2	25, 44, 55, 67, 81, 85, 89, 103, 113, 114–115, 118, 136, 156, 165
Going Down to Liverpool	125
Gonwards	204, 206
The Good Things	212
La Grange	73
Grass	26, 28, 32, 33, 63, 77, 80, 89, 151, 216
Great Aspirations	31, 99, 138, 140, 210, 212, 215
Great Fire	53, 57, 127, 146, 197
Greatness	140, 171, 215
Green Man	89
Guernica	158
Happy Families	152
Harvest Festival	86
Haunted Box of Switches	160, 164, 166–169
Hazy Shade of Winter	125
Heart of Glass	121
Heatwave	42–43
Heaven Is Paved with Broken Glass	47
Helicopter	24, 59, 60
Help!	35
Hendrix Experience (book)	174
The Henry Cow Legend	57
Hey Jude	50
Holly Up on Poppy	60, 83, 190–191, 194
Homegrown	142
Homo Safari	99
House of Fun	46
How to Write About Theatre	124
Humanoid Boogie	204, 206
(I Can't Get No) Satisfaction	74
I Can't Help Myself	200
I Can't Own Her	49, 194
I'd Like That	27, 133, 151
I'll Set Myself on Fire	53
I'm the Man who Murdered Love	33
I'm the Urban Spaceman	40
In Another Life	140, 142
In Loving Memory of a Name	26, 29, 30
In the Air Tonight	42, 105
In the City	103
I Remember the Sun	171, 188–190, 197
It's Nearly Africa	75, 90, 178
I Went to a Marvellous Party	141
Jason and the Argonauts	55–56, 90, 93, 174
Johnny Remember Me	177
Kenny	138, 216, 217
King for a Day	139, 150, 181, 213, 216
King for a Day (CD)	153
Knights in Shining Karma	47
Knuckle Down	44–45, 120, 123
Ladybird	30, 57–58, 127, 155
Lady Madonna	197
Late Show with David Letterman	181
Less Than Heroes	93
Let's Fly Away	140
Levitation	212
Liarbird	72
The Licorice Fields of Pontefract	141
Life Begins at the Hop	23, 31, 46, 151, 185, 200, 202, 216
Life in the Loading Bay	162
Life Is Good in the Greenhouse	114–115, 151
Limelight (fanzine)	11, 124, 126, 129, 130, 156, 157, 172, 210
Lined Up	166
The Lion King	133
The Little Express	92
Living through Another Cuba	26, 27, 118–119, 155, 184
Love at First Sight	63, 119
Love on a Farmboy's Wages	21, 22, 23, 31, 50–51, 127, 152
The Loving	71
Making Plans for Nigel	24, 27, 28, 30, 31, 49, 51, 54, 55, 58, 66, 67, 90, 99, 101, 111, 115, 116, 117, 120, 129, 147, 155, 201, 212, 213, 216
Magical Mystery Tour	49
Manic Monday	125
Man in a Shed	140

INDEX OF TITLES

The Man Who Sailed Around His Soul 32, 34, 80, 130, 194-195, 201
Martha My Dear 197
Mayor of Simpleton 22, 26, 27, 61-62, 83, 84, 186, 192
Meccanik Dancing 19, 30, 43, 45-46, 114, 115
The Meeting Place 32, 39, 80, 216
Mellotron (book) 174
Melt the Guns 52, 55, 73
Merlin and the Goblins 163
Mermaid Smiled 32, 193
Midsomer Murders 142
Milk 145
Millions 69, 72, 107, 114-116, 123, 155
Modern Life Is Rubbish 27
Modern Time Neros 153
The Mole from the Ministry 128, 129
Monstrance 68, 157, 158, 204
Moon Knight 93
Moonlight Sonata 167
Mummer 19, 31, 50, 51, 57, 58, 65, 75, 90, 126-127, 151, 154, 178, 189, 210
Music Theory for Dummies 201
My Bird Performs 150
My Love Explodes 43
My Spine Is the Bassline 166
Neon Shuffle 26, 113-114
News of the World 103, 105
19th Nervous Breakdown 43
Nonsuch 25, 32, 34-35, 44, 50, 60, 64, 66, 75, 77, 80, 83, 85, 89, 91, 101, 132, 134, 135, 139, 140, 145, 149, 183, 190
No Language in Our Lungs 38-39, 118
No Thugs in Our House 23, 74, 93, 123-124, 150, 151
Nowhere Man 35, 38
Obscene Collection 153
Obscene Procession 182
1000 Umbrellas 32, 33, 76, 80, 171, 179, 180, 194-197
Ogden's Nut Gone Flake 129
Oh, Can You Wash Your Father's Shirt 168
Oil & Gold 161, 162
Old Man River 168
Omnibus 64, 83, 132
One of the Millions 27, 213
Oranges and Lemons 37, 44, 69, 71, 77, 85, 91, 101, 130-132, 181
Ornithology 146
Pale and Precious 50
Paper and Iron (Notes and Coins) 44, 99
Paperback Writer 40, 43
Penny Lane 49
Peter Gabriel III 172
Pet Sounds 50, 58
Pink Thing 72
The Piper at the Gates of Dawn 38
The Planets 164
Playground 34, 110, 150

Jackson Pollock 95, 96
Poor Skeleton Steps Out 25, 37, 75
Pretty Woman 216
Prime Time 129
Prince of Orange 48
Psonic Psunspot 87, 127-129
Pulsing Pulsing 145, 146, 155
Punch and Judy 73
Radios in Motion 46
Ra Ra for Red Rocking Horse 72
Rag and Bone Buffet 73
Rain 44
Rattle and Hum 92
Real by Reel 64, 68, 72, 74, 155
Red Brick Dream 30, 137, 151
Reign of Blows 72, 79
Remain in Light 180
Respectable Street 12, 20, 21, 30, 62, 141, 146
Revolver 33, 35, 38
Rhapsody in Blue 196
Rip Van Ruben 191
The Rite of Spring 164
River of Orchids 26, 30, 71, 72
Roads Girdle the Globe 57, 99
Roast Fish and Cornbread 163, 165
Rock-a-bye Baby 74
Rocket from a Bottle 72-73, 99, 117-118, 171, 202
Rolling Stones Gear 174
Roll out the Barrel 168
Romeo and Juliet 164
Rook 34, 35, 70-71, 132, 151, 153, 179, 204
A Rose in a Garden of Weeds 180
Rossmore Road 165
Rubber Soul 33, 35
Runaways 122-123, 146, 178, 212
Sacrificial Bonfire 32, 130, 134, 183, 196, 216, 217
Say It 213, 215, 217
Scarecrow People 26, 53-54, 75, 122, 131
Science Friction 103
Scissor Man 54, 59, 68, 99, 193
Scrape Away 121
Seagulls Screaming (Kiss Her, Kiss Her) 95-96, 146
Season Cycle 27, 32, 87
Seaview 139, 140
Senses Working Overtime 24, 26, 45, 51-53, 57, 68, 93, 95-97, 106, 147, 181
Setting Sons 103
Sgt Pepper's Lonely Hearts Club Band 130, 191
Sgt Rock (Is Going to Help Me) 67, 90, 120-121
Shake You Donkey Up 26, 60-61
Shangri-La 57
Ship Trapped in the Ice 191
Singalongamax 168
Skylarking 25, 26, 27, 31-35, 39, 53, 60, 69, 76, 77, 80, 81-82, 85, 87, 88, 91, 129, 130, 133, 180, 182, 184, 192, 193, 216
Skyscraper Souls 76

The Smartest Monkeys 34, 35, 139, 171, 190-191, 216, 217
Snowman 42, 52
Soldier 166
Sound Affects 103, 105, 106, 121, 125
Sound and Vision 67
South Park 174
Sparky's Magic Piano 139
Special Beat Service 25, 26
Standing in for Joe 31, 33, 140, 142, 216
Standing on the Corner (Watching All the Girls Go By) 62
Start to 77 124
Statue of Liberty 103, 216
Stop Making Sense 59
Strawberry Fields Forever 195
Der Struwwelpeter 54
String Quartet II (Ravel) 195
Studio Romantic 152
Stupidly Happy 27, 34, 93, 110, 133
Summer's Cauldron 25, 26, 28, 29, 32, 33, 70, 87
Summoned By Bells 136
Sunshine of Your Love 170, 180
Super-Tuff 115, 123
Susan Revolving 38
Symphony No 9 (Beethoven) 164
Synchronicity 122
Take Away/The Lure of Salvage 43
Take This Town 73-74
Talking Drum 50
Taxman 43
Telephone 90
Ten Feet Tall 46, 215
Tentative Decisions 124
Terrorism 39-40
Testimonial Dinner 153
That Is the Way 27, 85-86, 215
That's Entertainment: My Life in the Jam 124
That's Really Super Supergirl 32, 80, 180-181, 184
That Wave 49-50, 134, 147, 171, 186-188
Then She Appeared 43-44, 60, 83, 150
This Is Pop 49, 62, 89, 103, 122, 147, 184
This World Over 27, 42, 79, 89
3D EP 67, 103, 136
Times Square 73
Tin Drum 50
Tissue Tigers 73, 116
Top of the Pops 120, 129, 146, 181
Towers of London 25, 38, 48-49, 66, 106, 118
Town and County 165
Toys 26, 27
Train Running Low on Soul Coal 21, 27, 42, 52, 69, 70, 71-72, 78, 174, 192
Transistor Blast 85-86, 93
Travels in Nihilon 52, 64, 67-69, 99, 121, 122, 184-185
The Trials and Triumphs of Les Dawson 124
Trout Mask Replica 57, 62, 202

The Tube 128
Turned Out Nice Again: The Story of British Light Entertainment 124
25 O'Clock 65, 127, 128, 188
The Ugly Underneath 75, 83
Universal 133
Unwrap You at Christmas 202
Uptight 74
Vanishing Girl 23, 87, 128, 150
Vile Homunculus 162, 163
Wake Up 39, 73, 75-76, 127, 152, 192, 212
Walk Like an Egyptian 125
War Dance 34, 139, 216
Washaway 171, 212
Wasp Star 31-35, 51, 92, 93, 101, 110, 132, 133, 138, 191
Waxworks 85
We're All Light 134, 147, 192
West Side Story 121
What in the World??... 65-66, 188
The Wheel and the Maypole 30, 34, 133, 192
When You're Near Me I Have Difficulty 23
Where Have all the Good Times Gone?: The Rise and Fall of the Record Industry 123
Where Did the Ordinary People Go? 138, 216
White Music 25, 26, 31, 36, 44, 49, 53, 55, 67, 80-81, 85, 89, 92, 113-115, 135, 156, 183
A Whiter Shade of Pale 200
Why Anything? Why This? 162
The Wicker Man 49
Win a Night Out with a Well Known Paranoiac 161, 165
The Wizard of Oz 84
Wonderland 27, 28, 29, 31, 155, 215, 216
Wounded Horse 33, 51, 52
Wrapped in Grey 23, 27, 50, 69, 83, 179
The XTC Bumper Book of Fun for Boys and Girls 11, 124, 125, 149
XTC Chronology 1966-1999 152
XTC Convention (2017) 111, 137, 147, 148, 151, 152, 212
XTC Music and Friends Convention 145
XTC: Play at Home 21
XTC: Song Stories 123, 140, 141
XTC: This Is Pop (documentary) 62, 82, 83, 95, 96, 156, 214
Yacht Dance 46, 122, 152, 179
A Year with Swollen Appendices 180
Yesterday 163
You and the Clouds Will Still Be Beautiful 51, 134, 191
You Bring the Summer 151
Young Cleopatra 93
The Young Ones 65
Your Dictionary 51, 71
You're the Wish You Are I Had 199
Zenyatta Mondatta 73

221

INDEX OF NAMES

ABBA	144
ABC	51
Alehouse	19
Dave Allen	156, 161, 162
Verden Allen	128
Carlos Alomar	180
Barry Andrews	11, 12, 19, 43, 49, 100-101, 113, 127, 155, 156-169, 185-186, 200
Finn Andrews	162, 163
Animal from the Muppets	125
Adam Ant	45
Terry Arnett	113-124, 147, 149
Mary Lou Arnold	193
Art of Noise	48
Atomic Rooster	110
Australian Neil Young Show	125
Balloon	144-146
Gary Bamford	210-219
David Bandler	212
The Bangles	11, 125
Anton Barbeau	51-53
Simon Barber	75-77
Louis Barfe	107-124
Barenaked Ladies	39
Martyn Barker	100, 156, 158, 161, 162
Gary Barlow	125
Gaz Barrett	212, 213
Syd Barrett	81
Dan Barrow	149
John Barry	195
Norman Batley (aka Norman B)	213
Mike Batt	194
Batteries	45
The Beach Boys	28, 69, 77, 84, 97, 146
The Beat (aka the English Beat)	25, 26, 164
The Beatles	28, 30, 32-35, 38, 40, 48, 49, 50, 52, 55-58, 61, 73, 74, 77, 84, 87, 92, 109, 121, 130, 144, 162, 178, 181, 195, 197, 201, 211
Imogen Bebb	22-23, 31
Jason Beck	214
Be Bop Deluxe	90
Rob Beckinsale	151
Captain Beefheart	57, 62, 201
The BeeGees	150
Ludwig van Beethoven	164
Matt Bell	149
Bellowhead	41
Haydn Bendall	132
Reg Bennett	195-196
Todd Bernhardt	11, 113-124, 127, 133, 148
Chuck Berry	178, 205
Pete Best	211
John Betjeman	11, 136-142
Joseph Beuys	159
Susannah Bevington	215, 217
Big Big Train	69, 175, 188, 196
Acker Bilk	139
bis	45
Bjorn Again	144
Black Sabbath	25, 188
Ruben Blades	201
Bloc Party	36
Blondie	121
Blue Rose Code	65
Blur	27, 28, 36, 65, 84, 192
Bono	92, 181
The Bonzo Dog Doo-Dah Band	40, 142
Boo Radleys	81
Bootleg Beatles	144
Blowzabella	71
David Bowie	28, 31, 64, 67, 110, 180
Kieron Bowker	212, 214, 217
Chris Braide	76-77
Brand X	116
Richard Branson	24
Benjamin Britten	49, 164
James Brown	165
Tracey Bryn	60
Rick Buckler	11, 102-124
Budgie	99
Allison Burke	103-111
Richard Burton	203
Tim Burton	55
Chris Butler	60-62
Buzzcocks	64
Max Bygraves	168
The Byrds	44
David Byrne	55
Greg Calbi	193
Sterling Campbell	110
Can	49, 116
Ian Caple	166
Tim Carney	61
Lewis Carroll	40
The Cars	25
Sam Carter	42
Eliza Carthy	42
Giacomo Casanova	141
Mick Casey	149
George Chambers	193
Terry Chambers	12-21, 69, 72, 74, 80, 98-127, 149, 152, 154, 155, 200, 209-219
Chance the Gardener	57
Mike Chapman	130
Chas and Dave	160
Howard Chaykin	93
Anton Chekhov	84-85
Chelsea	165
Chris Chennell	212
Kieran Cheung	145-146
The Church	27
Winston Churchill	140
CIRCU5	210, 212
Eric Clapton	99, 170
Gary Clark	191
Steven Clark	45-46
The Clash	22, 51
The Clubmen	204
Phil Collins	105, 116, 121
Mark Cobb	118-119
Billy Cobham	119
Ornette Coleman	146
Compagnie Ribac-Schwabe	55-57, 173-174
Concerto Caledonia	42
Steve Conte	73-75
Stewart Copeland	99, 119, 122
Cosmic Rough Riders	67
Elvis Costello	36-37, 51, 64, 164
Pete Cousins	129, 158
Tony Cousins	43
Henry Cow	57
Noël Coward	140, 141
Steve Cox	151
Charlie Crane	211
Crowded House	27
Curved Air	99
Andy Cutting	71-72
Holger Czukay	99
Dexter Dalwood	165
The Damned	64
Dandy Highwaymen	124, 147
Hunter Davies	174
Claude Debussy	96
Deep Purple	106, 110
Default Collective	125
Ray Davies	57, 75
Miles Davis	48
Nick Davis	66, 133, 187
Al Denholm	66
John Dent	193
Marcella Detroit	133
Devo	115
Charles Dickens	210
Chris Difford	36-37
Dirtbike Annie	124
Becki diGregorio	37
Dogs Die in Hot Cars	36
Dollar	51
Lou Dommett Young	208, 218
The Doors	28
The Dopamines	124
Keith Dowling	151
Downes Braide Association	76-77
Nick Drake	81, 140
Dr Hook	54-55
The Drones	100, 165
Gus Dudgeon	40, 66, 132
The Dukes of Stratosphear	38, 39, 40, 43, 44, 50, 62, 66, 87, 101, 127, 128, 129, 135, 174, 175, 184, 188, 199
Duran Duran	25, 31
Ian Dury	164
Dutch Uncles	36
Bob Dylan	56, 64, 113
Echo and the Bunnymen	25
Egg	99
Einstürzende Neubauten	48
Electric Prunes	30
TS Eliot	136
Keith Emerson	99, 165
Krispian Emert	145
Camille English	78-79
Brian Eno	67, 180
Hans Magnus Enzensberger	121
Mikey Erg	113-124, 214
Ludwig Erhard	56
Everything Everything	36
Donald Fagen	181, 189
Fairport Convention	132
Jason Falkner	64-65
Andrew Falkous	58-59
False Lights	42
Dennis Fano	74, 215
Dan Farmer	149
Neville Farmer	123, 140, 141
Lyn Farrar	215
Fassine	48-50, 75, 106, 125
Franz Ferdinand	36, 192
Billy Ficca	99
Field Music	36
John Fields	39
Jeff Fitches	165
Fiddly Bits	148, 151
Neil Finn	27
Fire Judges	158
Mark Fisher	11, 36-77, 100-111, 124, 156-165, 170-205, 208-219
Vic Flick	194
Foo Fighters	58
Fossil	145
Fossil Fools	115, 124, 147-148
The Four Seasons	197
The Four Tops	200
Paul Fox	130, 131
Quinn Fox	85-86
Bruce Foxton	124
Black Francis	59
Dr Frankenstein	63
Free	101, 111
Robert Fripp	173-174
From the Jam	124
Shigemasa Fujimoto	152-153
Futureheads	36
Future of the Left	58
Fuzzy Warblers	124, 147
Peter Gabriel	172
Gang of Four	51
Abel Ganz	65
Marvin Gaye	74
Gentle Hen	53
George Gershwin	140, 196
Billy Gibbons	73
The Gift	124
The Go-Go's	150
Gogmagog	16
Go Home Productions	44
Leslie Gooch	88
Tarquin Gotch	181
Mark Gowland	158
Dave Gregory	11, 12-21, 38, 41, 42, 45, 46, 54, 56, 66, 68-71, 74, 76, 90, 91, 100-102, 108, 116, 118, 126, 127, 128, 130-135, 144, 146, 148, 151-156, 170-197, 199, 200, 202, 203, 210, 211, 215
Ian Gregory	101, 126-135
Glitter Band	126
Steve Hackett	99
Brendan Hamley	158
Barry Hammond	66
Paul Hammond	110
Brian Hanrahan	90
Hard Stuff	110
Thomas Hardy	210
George Harrison	73, 84, 174
Mark Hart	27
Hatfield and the North	99
Charlotte Hatherley	201
Hawkwind	212
James Hayward	48, 125
The Helium Kidz	16, 21
John Hemsley	114
Jimi Hendrix	113, 174
Clare Hirst	158
Alfred Hitchcock	140
Robyn Hitchcock	27
Susanna Hoffs	80, 125
Hoodoo Gurus	29
Nicky Hopkins	165
Trevor Horn	51
Hot Hot Heat	36
Garth Hudson	167
Parthenon Huxley	131
Ice House	69
Illuminati	156
John Irvine	52, 64, 77
Hisashi Ishikawa	153
Tohori Ishitobi	153
Joe Jackson	51
Andreas Jäger	154-155
The Jam	11, 103, 105, 106, 124, 125
Japan	50
Jellyfish	64, 65
Dave Jennings	214
Elton John	133
John Ginty Band	125
Johnny and the Hurricanes	199
Phill Jupitus	11, 45
Kaiser Chiefs	36
Yamato Kawada	153
Mr Keen	164, 169
Mike Keneally	57-58, 118
Chris Kerslake	151
King Crimson	130, 173, 174
The Kinks	30, 48, 55, 65, 137, 201
Simon Kirke	111
Masaki Kitayama	143, 145
Akiko Kogure	152
Gene Krupa	125
Kukkuru	152, 153
Yudai Kurita	153
John Langan	169
Laurie Langan	75, 105-125
Mutt Lange	43
Jeremy Lascelles	193
Ian Leak	212-213
John Leckie	66, 67, 128, 138
Albert Lee	191
Sara Lee	51

INDEX OF NAMES

Iain Lee — 210, 214
Stewart Lee — 11, 149
Mike Leigh — 167
Joseph Lekkas — 47
Kyrsten Leland — 24-31
Tamara De Lempicka — 125
John Lennon — 40, 126, 135, 162, 182, 201
Jerry Lee Lewis — 167
Leveret — 71
John Leyton — 177
Liberace — 125
Jaki Liebezeit — 99, 116, 122
Steve Lillywhite — 28, 74, 101, 172
The Liquid Scene — 37, 38
Little Mix — 33
Little Richard — 178
Andrew Lloyd Webber — 132
Dennis Locorriere — 54-55
Frank Loesser — 62
Lo-Fi Club — 152
Eric Longmuir — 99
David Lord — 75, 127, 189, 194
Luna Lure — 152
Jeff Lynne — 50, 180
Michael John McCarthy — 45, 52, 77
Paul McCartney — 34, 39, 40, 44, 66, 126, 135, 140, 162, 171, 182, 197, 201
Anne McCue — 46-47
Malcolm McDowell — 74
Sean McGhee — 50-51
David McGuinness — 42-44
Mclusky — 58
Mick MacNeil — 168
Madness — 46, 164
Rich Mangicaro — 131
Manhattan Transfer — 201
Manfred Mann — 188
Danny Manners — 69-71
Charles Manson — 92
Bob Marley — 165
Carl Marsh — 156, 162
George Martin — 76, 135
Dave Marx — 169
Pat Mastelotto — 37, 69, 101, 126-135
Dave Mattacks — 66, 101, 126-135
Kevin Mathews — 85
Josh Mayer — 150
Joe Meek — 177
Mellotronanism — 124, 147
Men with Ven — 160
Freddie Mercury — 41
Metallica — 25
Metropolitan Farms — 150
Trevor Midgley — 90
Andy Miller — 210
Peter Mills — 136-142
Miro — 101
Moloko — 125
The Monkees — 44, 202
Keith Moon — 45, 100, 109, 125
Dudley Moore — 213
Kev Moore — 89-91
Jim Moray — 40-42
Eric Morecambe — 126
Alanis Morissette — 80
John Morrish — 12-21
Mott the Hoople — 128, 188
Carol Moulding — 150, 215

Colin Moulding — 11, 12-21, 26 31, 37, 39, 40, 43, 44, 46, 49, 50, 51, 56, 57, 58, 63, 64, 66, 67, 69, 72, 74, 75, 77, 90, 91, 92, 99, 101, 102, 111, 113-115, 118, 119, 122, 126, 128, 131-142, 146, 147, 150-155, 172, 176, 178-183, 188-192, 194, 196, 200, 201, 203, 206, 208-219
Lee Moulding — 150, 215, 208-219
Andrew Motion — 142
Mr Love & Justice — 151
Mr Mister — 130
Akira Murakami — 153
The Muppets — 125
Christopher Nadeau — 91-92
Hugh Nankivell — 11, 32-35, 45, 52, 64, 77, 145, 170-197
Bill Nelson — 90
Neu — 49
The News — 90
Nigels with Attitude — 119, 124
Takashi Nishii — 143, 145
Kevin Nixon — 198
David Nolan — 214
Craig Northey — 38-39
Nouvelle Vague — 201
Gary Numan — 52
Steve Nye — 50
Brian O'Connor — 75-76
Oasis — 49, 81
Odds — 38
Jefferson Ogata — 151
Adrian Ogden — 149
Henning Ohlenbusch — 53-54
Oil City Kings — 124
OMD — 31, 133
Rohan Onraet — 103-111
EIEI Owen (see Ian Gregory)
Hugh Padgham — 28, 42, 101, 179, 185
Steven Page — 39-40
Ian Paice — 110, 111
Sarah Palmer — 49-50, 103-111
Palmghosts — 47
Parasites — 124
Jim Parker — 142
Andy Partridge — 11, 12-21, 23, 25-28, 30, 32, 34, 36, 37, 38, 40-77, 78-93, 94-97, 100-102, 105, 108-111, 113, 114, 116, 118-122, 124-135, 144-147, 150-155, 157, 158, 160, 163, 165, 172, 173, 176, 178-197, 198-207, 210-217
Harry Partridge — 60, 132
Holly Partridge — 60, 83, 150, 190-191, 194
Richard Pedretti-Allen — 153
Ed Percival — 147-150
Pere Ubu — 55

Jonathan Perkins — 129
Lee Scratch Perry — 165, 169
Debbi Peterson — 11, 117, 125
Guy Peterson — 11, 125
Jordan Peterson — 163
Vicki Peterson — 125
Pete Phipps — 90, 126-135, 189, 192
Pablo Picasso — 158
Pink Fairies — 110
Pink Floyd — 28, 30, 38, 66, 188
Pink Warmth — 16
The Pixies — 59
Paul Pledger — 216, 217
The Police — 25, 73, 99, 115
Jackson Pollock — 95-96
The Pop Group — 165
Iggy Pop — 166
Cole Porter — 140, 141
Practical Dreamers — 90
Elvis Presley — 205
Billy Preston — 165
Prairie Prince — 80, 110, 126-135
Sergei Prokofiev — 49
Procol Harum — 200
Pugwash — 27, 28, 180
Al Quinn — 90
Radios in Motion (band) — 46, 47
The Ramones — 30
Random Hold — 126
Andy Rankin — 102-125
Les Rankin — 146
Mia Rankin — 24-31
Mike Ratledge — 99
Maurice Ravel — 195
Robert G Rawson — 94-97
Red Brick Dreamers — 151
James Reimer — 84-85
John Relph — 151, 153
REM — 29, 30, 110
Restaurant for Dogs — 156
François Ribac — 55-57, 173, 174
Keith Richards — 44
Righteous Brothers — 72
John Robb — 213
Rob Roberts — 83
Mark Ronson — 125
Edmundo Ros — 177
Marco Rossi — 98-99
Stu Rowe — 75, 111, 157, 158, 204, 212, 216
Roxy Music — 67
Sebastian Rüger — 112-124
Todd Rundgren — 76, 82, 87, 129, 130, 180-182, 193, 195
The Rutles — 40, 175
Chuck Sabo — 101, 110, 126-135
Michio Sakurai — 143
Jean-Paul Sartre — 55
Rat Scabies — 99
Scarecrow People — 122, 146
Eva Schwabe — 55-56, 173
Zak Schaffer — 144
Pete Seeger — 137
Erich Sellheim — 153-155
Sex Pistols — 104, 113, 138, 165
Shai Hulud — 125
Shandi — 130
Max Sharam — 69
Harry Shearer — 62
Shima E Iku Boat — 152
Shriekback — 156-169

Jean Sibelius — 164
Bill Sienkiewicz — 93
Guy Sigsworth — 48-49
Judee Sill — 56
Simple Minds — 168
Lisa Simpson — 167
Martin Simpson — 71
Silly Sods — 151
Siouxsie and the Banshees — 99
Slade — 89
Iain Sloan — 65-67
Small Faces — 129, 201
Patti Smith — 30
Trevor Smith — 151
Vic Smith — 104, 105
Chris Smylie — 62
Sodajerker — 75
David Somerville — 158
Gregory Spawton — 69
The Specials — 36, 37
Phil Spector — 174
Jim Spencer — 88-89
Steven Spielberg — 140, 171
Split Enz — 25, 30
Squeeze — 36
Chris Squire — 77
Stadium Dogs — 129
Star Fucking Hipsters — 124
Ringo Starr — 101, 109, 110, 113, 120, 125
Peter Steckel — 212
Steely Dan — 50, 189
Daniel Steinhardt — 67-69, 172, 173
Larry Stevens — 217
Dave Stewart — 99
Sly Stone — 74
Igor Stravinsky — 164
Kenny Stroud — 138
Joe Strummer — 23
Andy Summers — 73, 74
Super Furry Animals — 36
Saeko Suzuki — 152
The Sweet — 89
Swindon Schools Orchestra — 195
Sydney Symphony Orchestra — 147
Fox Talbot — 43
Talking Heads — 59, 180
Richard Tandy — 180
TC&I — 11, 31, 43, 99, 138, 140, 152, 171, 208-219
Television — 99
Temperance Seven — 142
Ed Thacker — 131
Charlie Thomas (see XTC: This Is Pop)
Cormac Thomas — 32-35
Mark Thomas — 103-125
Tony Thompson — 116
The Thrillers — 124
Steve Tilling — 208-219
Time UK — 124
Tin Huey — 60, 61
Tin Spirits — 67, 68, 148, 172, 174, 188
Peter Tork — 44
Toto — 72
T Rex — 89
Trip Dress — 158
Jeff Truzzi — 148

Kasayuki Tsurumi — 152-153
The Tubes — 129, 135
Joe Turner — 217
Twentieth Century Boys — 124
Twink — 110
Chris Twomey — 146
Ulan & Bator — 125
Ultravox — 52
The Unlovables — 124
Stanley Unwin — 129
U2 — 181, 201
Vagus Nerve — 125
Vincent Van Gogh — 46, 84
Matthew Vaughan — 133
The Veils — 162
Rosie Vela — 47-48
Mark Vidler — 44-45
Butch Vig — 59
Voice of the Beehive — 60
Tom Waits — 110, 168
The Waitresses — 60
Rick Wakeman — 99
Scott Walker — 81
Nigel Waller — 214
Thomas Walsh — 180
Peter Warlock — 171, 195
Steve Warren — 152-153
Maurice "mOe" Watson — 112-125
John Wedemeyer — 72-73
Paul Weller — 103, 104, 124
Erica Wexler — 201, 202, 203
Paul Wheeler — 69
David White — 45, 64, 77, 143-153
The White Stripes — 125
Kim Wilde — 46
Oscar Wilde — 62
Paul Wilde — 145
George Wilding — 212, 215, 217
Kevin Wilkinson — 100
Clough Williams-Ellis — 199
BJ Wilson — 128
Steven Wilson — 27, 61, 77, 184, 187
Marty Willson-Piper — 27
Eric Winick — 87
Ernie Wise — 126
Stevie Wonder — 74, 181
Yvonne Wootton — 12-21, 100-101, 126-135
World Party — 49
Worriers — 124
Richard Wright — 188
Daniel Wylie — 67
The Wynntown Marshals — 65
X-sTaTiC — 147-150
XTC Appreciation Society — 144
The XTC Files — 145
Yacht Rock Revue — 124
Mike Yannich (see Mikey Erg)
Yashida — 152
David Yazbek — 62-63
Yes — 164
Satoshi Yonaha (Yonafy) — 145
Neil Young — 30, 125
Steve Young — 41
David Yurkovich — 92-93
Frank Zappa — 57, 62, 122, 125, 146
ZZ Top — 73